THE NEW GERMAN LAW OF OBLIGATIONS

The New German Law of Obligations

Historical and Comparative Perspectives

REINHARD ZIMMERMANN

OXFORD
UNIVERSITY PRESS

*This book has been printed digitally and produced in a standard specification
in order to ensure its continuing availability*

OXFORD
UNIVERSITY PRESS

Great Clarendon Street, Oxford OX2 6DP

Oxford University Press is a department of the University of Oxford.
It furthers the University's objective of excellence in research, scholarship,
and education by publishing worldwide in

Oxford New York

Auckland Cape Town Dar es Salaam Hong Kong Karachi
Kuala Lumpur Madrid Melbourne Mexico City Nairobi
New Delhi Shanghai Taipei Toronto
With offices in
Argentina Austria Brazil Chile Czech Republic France Greece
Guatemala Hungary Italy Japan South Korea Poland Portugal
Singapore Switzerland Thailand Turkey Ukraine Vietnam

Oxford is a registered trade mark of Oxford University Press
in the UK and in certain other countries

Published in the United States
by Oxford University Press Inc., New York

ISBN 978-0-19-929137-3

Summary of Contents

Table of Contents

Abbreviations

ABGB	*Allgemeines Bürgerliches Gesetzbuch* (General Civil Code, Austria)
AbzG	*Abzahlungsgesetz* (Act concerning Instalment Sales, Germany)
AGBG	*Gesetz zur Regelung des Rechts der Allgemeinen Geschäftsbedingungen* (Standard Terms of Business Act, Germany)
Anh.	*Anhang* (Appendix)
Art(s).	Article(s)
Aufl.	*Auflage* (edition)
BGB	*Bürgerliches Gesetzbuch* (Civil Code, Germany)
BGH	*Bundesgerichtshof* (Federal Supreme Court, Germany)
BGHZ	*Entscheidungen des Bundesgerichtshofs in Zivilsachen* (Decisions of the Federal Supreme Court in private law matters, Germany)
BVerfG	*Bundesverfassungsgericht* (Federal Constitutional Court, Germany)
BVerfGE	*Entscheidungen des Bundesverfassungsgerichts* (Decisions of the Federal Constitutional Court, Germany)
BW	*Burgerlijk Wetboek* (Civil Code, Netherlands)
C.	*Codex*
Cap.	*Caput*
CISG	United Nations Convention on Contracts for the International Sale of Goods
COM	European Commission/Commission document
D.	*Digesta*
Disp.	*Disputatio*
ECR	European Court Reports
EC	European Community
ECJ	European Court of Justice
ed(s).	editor(s), edition(s)
edn.	edition
EEC	European Economic Community
EGBGB	*Einführungsgesetz zum Bürgerlichen Gesetzbuch* (Introductory Law to the Civil Code, Germany)
Einf.	Einführung is another German term for introduction
Einl.	*Einleitung* (introduction)
EU	European Union

FernUSG   *Fernunterrichtsschutzgesetz* (Distance Teaching Act, Germany)

Gai.   Gaius

GG   *Grundgesetz* (Basic Law, Germany)

HausTWG   *Gesetz über den Widerruf von Haustürgeschäften und ähnlichen Geschäften* (Doorstep Selling Act, Germany)

HGB   *Handelsgesetzbuch* (Commercial Code, Germany)

HKK   *Historisch-kritischer Kommentar zum BGB* (Historical Commentary to the BGB, Germany)

Iav.   Iavolenus

Lib.   *Liber* (book)

n(n).   note(s)

no(s).   number(s)

OJ   Official Journal of the European Communities

OLG   Oberlandesgericht (Regional Appeal Court, Germany)

OR   *Obligationenrecht* (Code on the Law of Obligations, Switzerland)

Pap.   Papinianus

Paul.   Paulus

PECL   Principles of European Contract Law

PICC   Unidroit Principles of International Commercial Contracts

pr.   *principium* (beginning)

PrALR   *Preußisches Allgemeines Landrecht* (Prussian Code)

RG   *Reichsgericht* (Imperial Supreme Court, Germany)

RGZ   *Entscheidungen des Reichsgerichts in Zivilsachen* (Decisions of the Imperial Supreme Court in private law matters, Germany)

Tit.   *Titulus*

transl.   translated

UCC   Uniform Commercial Code

UklaG   *Unterlassungsklagengesetz* (Injunctions Act, Germany)

ULIS   Uniform Law for the International Sale of Goods

Ulp.   Ulpianus

UN   United Nations

VerbrKrG   *Verbraucherkreditgesetz* (Consumer Credit Act, Germany)

vol(s).   volume(s)

Vorbem.   *Vorbemerkung* (preliminary remark)

Introduction

On 1 January 2000 the German Civil Code (BGB) became one hundred years old. It had been remarkably resilient throughout a century marked by catastrophic upheavals and a succession of fundamentally different political regimes. Two years later, however, on 1 January 2002, the most sweeping individual reform ever to have affected the Code entered into force. This was the Modernization of the Law of Obligations Act.[1] It had been triggered by the need to implement the European Consumer Sales Directive.[2] But it went far beyond what was required by the European Community. The then Minister of Justice had decided to use the tailwind from Brussels finally to implement an ambitious reform project dating back to the late 1970s.[3] It had led to the appointment of a Commission charged with the reform of the German law of obligations which had duly prepared a report as well as draft legislation.[4] That draft was used as a basis for a Discussion Draft of a Modernization of the German Law of Obligations Act which was published in September 2000.[5] Vehement criticism raised against the Discussion Draft led to substantial revision but came too late to abort the reform project, or to confine it to the amendments required by the Consumer Sales Directive. The most important aspect of the Act of 2002, from the point of view of legal practice, is the fundamental reform of the German law of (liberative) prescription. Doctrinally the most remarkable feature of the revised BGB is the new regime concerning liability for nonperformance in general, and for non-conformity in sales law in particular. More than by any other component of the reform process, however, the face of the BGB has been changed by the incorporation of a number of special statutes aimed at the protection of consumers. The draftsmen of the new law have thus made

---

[1] *Gesetz zur Modernisierung des Schuldrechts of 26 November 2001, Bundesgesetzblatt* 2001 I, 3138. As a result, the BGB was re-promulgated on 2 January 2002: *Bundesgesetzblatt* 2002 I, 42.

[2] Directive 1999/44 EC of the European Parliament and of the Council of 25 May 1999 on certain aspects of the sale of consumer goods and associated guarantees, OJ L 171/99, at 12, easily accessible in Oliver Radley-Gardner, Hugh Beale, Reinhard Zimmermann and Reiner Schulze (eds.), *Fundamental Texts on European Private Law* (2003), 107 ff.

[3] Hertha Däubler-Gmelin, 'Die Entscheidung für die so genannte Grosse Lösung bei der Schuldrechtsreform', [2001] *Neue Juristische Wochenschrift* 2281 ff.

[4] Bundesminister der Justiz (ed.), *Abschlussbericht der Kommission zur Überarbeitung des Schuldrechts* (1992).

[5] Easily accessible now in Claus-Wilhelm Canaris (ed.), *Schuldrechtsmodernisierung 2002* (2002), 3 ff.

an effort to streamline, or harmonize, general contract law and consumer contract law.

These, then, are the four topics covered in Chapters 2–5 of the present book: prescription (or, to use a term more familiar to English lawyers: limitation periods),[6] remedies for non-performance (or, to use the term chosen in German law: breach of duty),[7] liability for non-conformity, and consumer contract law. In all these cases either a historical or comparative perspective has been adopted in order to analyse, and assess, the new rules of German law. Other aspects of the reform (credit transactions, contracts for work to be done) will be referred to incidentally. The new set of rules dealing with the restitution of benefits after termination for breach of contract will be discussed elsewhere.[8] As is immediately obvious from this survey, the German reform legislation, though sailing under the title Modernization of the Law of *Obligations* Act, has very largely been confined to the law of *contract*. It is only in one respect that it significantly affects the other branches of the law of obligations: prescription. But even here the title of the reform legislation does not convey an accurate picture of its scope. Prescription is dealt with in the General Part of the BGB (as opposed to the General Part of the law of obligations), and it therefore also covers claims arising in the areas of property law, family law, and the law of succession.[9] While the wisdom of this decision may be questioned,[10] the wide scope of application accorded to the law of prescription still remains an established feature of German private law. Use of the phrase 'modernization of the law of obligations' can be explained only in the light of the earlier reform project which was indeed supposed to cover, apart from a much wider range of matters within contract law, the law of extracontractual liability, unjustified enrichment, and *negotiorum gestio*.

The essays collected in this volume are based on a number of lectures delivered over the past three years: the second CMS Cameron McKenna Lecture at the University of Aberdeen in July 2002 (remedies for non-performance);[11] the tenth John M. Kelly Memorial Lecture at University College, Dublin, in November 2003 (liability for non-conformity); a lecture at a congress on the third part of the Principles of European Contract Law in Lleida in May 2004 (prescription); and the J.A.C. Thomas Memorial Lecture at University

---

[6] On the terminology, see *infra* pp. 127 f.

[7] See *infra*, Chapter 2, text following n. 58 and n. 217.

[8] 'Restitution after Termination for Breach of Contract: German Law after the Reform of 2002', in Andrew Burrows and Alan Rodger (eds.), *Mapping the Law: Essays in Memory of Peter Birks*, forthcoming.   [9] §§ 194 ff. BGB.

[10] *Infra* pp. 131 ff.

[11] An earlier version of the lecture was presented at the University of Rome (*La Sapienza*) and has appeared in the series of *Saggi, conferenze e seminari* of the *Centro di studi e ricerche di diritto comparato e straniero*, edited by Michael Joachim Bonell.

College, London, in February 2005. These lectures have all originally been published elsewhere.[12] For the purpose of this volume they have been revised, updated and harmonized. They are preceded by a chapter entitled 'The German Civil Code and the Development of Private Law in Germany' which attempts to place the recent reform legislation in its historical context. Parts of that chapter are based on my contribution to the *Essays in Honour of Bernard Rudden* which was written in early 2001, at a time when the reform had not yet been enacted.[13] I am very grateful to Michael Joachim Bonell (Rome), Elspeth Reid (Edinburgh), Paul O'Connor (Dublin), Antoni Vaquer Aloy (Lleida), Jessica Hughes (London), and John Louth (Oxford) for their permission to use the earlier publications in order to prepare the present volume. I am equally grateful to Ben Steinbrück and Angelika Owen (both Hamburg) for editorial and typing assistance.

There is one aspect of the reform legislation that should be mentioned, even if it will not be discussed in the chapters that follow. This is the incorporation into the text of the BGB of a number of doctrines that had previously come to be recognized *praeter legem*; in particular: *culpa in contrahendo* (§ 311 II BGB), change of circumstances (*Störung der Geschäftsgrundlage*: § 313 BGB), the possibility of terminating, for good reason, contracts for the performance of a recurring obligation (§ 314 BGB), the duty to have regard to the other party's rights and interests which may result from the content of an obligation (§ 241 II BGB); and the existence, in some cases, of such duties on the part of third parties (§ 311 III BGB).[14] Little has changed in this respect but for the fact that a statutory home has been provided for these doctrines. The German Government wanted the living law to be reflected in the wording of the code.[15] Most commentaries on the BGB have, therefore, just moved the respective exposition from one place to another in their new editions: from § 242 to § 313 in the case of change of circumstances and from § 242 to § 241 in the case of the

[12] (2002) 6 *Edinburgh Law Review* 271 ff.; *John Kelly Memorial Lecture Series, No. 10* (2004); Antoni Vaquer Aloy (ed.), *La Tercera Parte de los Principios de Derecho Contractual Europeo* (2005), 451 ff.; [2005] *Current Legal Problems* 58.

[13] 'Modernizing the German Law of Obligations?', in Peter Birks and Arianna Pretto (eds.), *Themes in Comparative Law in Honour of Bernard Rudden* (2002), 265 ff. A German version of Chapter 1 of the present volume can be found in Mathias Schmoeckel, Joachim Rückert and Reinhard Zimmermann (eds.), *Historisch-kritischer Kommentar zum BGB*, vol. I (2003), 1 ff.

[14] § 311 III BGB implies the existence of such duties also *vis-à-vis* third parties; whether the provision can thus be regarded as a statutory legal basis for the contract with protective effect *vis-à-vis* third parties is disputed; see, for example, Peter Gottwald, in *Münchener Kommentar zum Bürgerlichen Gesetzbuch*, 4th edn., vol. IIa (2003), § 328, n. 101; Hans-Peter Haferkamp, 'Der Vertrag mit Schutzwirkung für Dritte nach der Schuldrechtsreform—ein Auslaufmodell?', in Barbara Dauner-Lieb, Horst Konzen and Karsten Schmidt (eds.), *Das neue Schuldrecht in der Praxis* (2003), 171 ff.

[15] For a critical assessment of this intention, see Barbara Dauner-Lieb, 'Kodifikation und Richterrecht', in Wolfgang Ernst and Reinhard Zimmermann (eds.), *Zivilrechtswissenschaft und Schuldrechtsreform* (2001), 305 ff.

duties to have regard to the other party's rights and interests,[16] or from § 276 to § 311 in the case of *culpa in contrahendo*. More than anything else this demonstrates that, just as the BGB in its original form, the reform legislation is intimately related to past and contemporary case law and legal scholarship. It is 'no more than a moment in the development, more tangible, certainly, than a ripple in the stream, but, none the less, merely a ripple in the stream'.[17] Also in its new form, the German Civil Code, therefore, continues to be a characteristic manifestation of German legal culture.[18] At the same time, the reform in general has moved German contract law considerably closer to European thinking patterns; the then Minister of Justice even regarded the 'modernization' of the BGB as 'a milestone on the path towards a European Civil Code'.[19] It thus appears to be appropriate, when analysing the reform, not only to adopt a historical perspective and emphasize the elements of change and continuity, but also to take texts such as the Principles of European Contract Law[20] as points of reference for a comparative assessment.

[16] This has resulted in a reduction of the size of commentary to § 242 in *Münchener Kommentar* by about 50 per cent: see Günter H. Roth, in *Münchener Kommentar zum Bürgerlichen Gesetzbuch*, 4th edn., vol. II (2001), § 242 (233 pages) as opposed to Günter H. Roth, in *Münchener Kommentar zum Bürgerlichen Gesetzbuch*, 4th edn., vol. IIa (2003), § 242 (116 pages). This observation confirms that a general provision such as § 242 BGB (good faith) is often needed only for a transitory phase until a rule is sufficiently well established to stand on its own legs; see Simon Whittaker and Reinhard Zimmermann, 'Good faith in European contract law: surveying the legal landscape', in Reinhard Zimmermann and Simon Whittaker (eds.), *Good Faith in European Contract Law* (2000), 30 ff.

[17] Bernhard Windscheid, 'Die geschichtliche Schule in der Rechtswissenschaft' (1878), in *idem, Gesammelte Reden und Abhandlungen*, ed. Paul Oertmann (1904), 75 ff.

[18] For an introduction to which, see my contribution to Mathias Reimann and Joachim Zekoll (eds.), *Introduction to German Law*, 2nd edn. (2005), 1ff. The appendix to that essay contains an introduction to the standard German legal literature in private law and to German citation conventions. Quotations from German books, articles, court decisions, and provisions of the Code are given, throughout the present book, in an English translation. The translation is my own, except where otherwise indicated. Concerning translations of the provisions introduced, or affected, by the reform of the German law of obligations I have used, as a starting point, the translation that can be found in the German Law Archive, www.iuscomp.org/gla.

[19] Hertha Däubler-Gmelin, as quoted by Heribert Prantl in *Süddeutsche Zeitung* of 20 September 1990. In the Parliamentary Debate of 11 October 2001, Volker Beck, MP for one of the two governing parties (*Bündnis 90/Die Grünen*) expressed the hope that the BGB would become a model for a European Civil Code (Stenographic Report, Plenary Proceedings 14/192, 18749). See also the statement of the Minister of Justice, in the same debate, at 18758 and Däubler-Gmelin, [2001] *Neue Juristische Wochenschrift* 2289 (by means of its new law of obligations, Germany will be able to make a contribution on an international level).

[20] Ole Lando and Hugh Beale (eds.), *Principles of European Contract Law*, Parts I and II (2000); Ole Lando, Eric Clive, André Prüm and Reinhard Zimmermann (eds.), *Principles of European Contract Law*, Part III (2003).

1

The German Civil Code and the Development of Private Law in Germany

I. The Codification Movement in Europe

The codification of private law from the late eighteenth century onwards is regarded, very widely, as a turning point in the development of private law in Europe.[1] Obviously, some of the more naïve expectations entertained by intellectuals of the Age of Enlightenment have not been fulfilled: the codifications have neither made the learned lawyer redundant, nor have they led to a lasting consolidation (or ossification) of private law. They have, however, significantly contributed to the national fragmentation of the European legal tradition: for codification constitutes a piece of legislation which is applicable only within the confines of the territory for which the body responsible for legislation is competent to legislate. There had been signs of such fragmentation at the time of the *usus modernus pandectarum* in the seventeenth and eighteenth centuries when the 'institutional' writers had no longer discussed Roman law as such but Roman-Dutch or Roman-Scots law, *ius romano-hispanicum* or *ius romano-saxonicum*.[2] But it had always been clear that these were merely regional or national variations of a common theme: different manifestations of one and the same legal tradition. With the enactment of the codifications this began to change. The awareness of a fundamental intellectual unity got lost and legal scholarship degenerated, in the much-quoted words of Rudolf von Jhering, to a national discipline the intellectual boundaries of which coincided with the political ones.[3]

At the same time, the codifications brought to an end the 'second life' of Roman law, i.e. the story of its practical application in Europe. Since the days

---

[1] See Reinhard Zimmermann, 'Codification: History and Present Significance of an Idea', (1995) 3 *European Review of Private Law* 95 ff. (with further references).

[2] Klaus Luig, 'The Institutes of National Law in the 17th and 18th Centuries', [1972] *Juridical Review* 193 ff.

[3] Rudolf von Jhering, *Geist des römischen Rechts auf den verschiedenen Stufen seiner Entwicklung*, vol. I, 6th edn. (1907), 15. Jhering regarded this state of affairs as 'humiliating and undignified'.

of the 'reception' Roman law had provided the basis for the administration of justice in western and central Europe and had become a *ius commune*, or common law.[4] In the process, it had been subject to considerable change; in particular, it had absorbed many elements of canon law, indigenous customary law, mercantile custom, and natural law theory. The *usus antiquus* of Roman law had thus been transformed into a *usus modernus pandectarum*.[5] Yet, a string of authors from François Hotman to Hermann Conring and Christian Thomasius had started to shake the authority of Roman law: of a law that had given rise to intricate doctrinal disputes, that was wedded to outdated and impracticable subtleties, and that had been enacted by the despotic rulers of past ages. Also, since Roman law was applicable only *in subsidio*, countless more specific territorial or local laws could govern a particular dispute. The great number and complexity of legal sources contributed to a widespread feeling of legal uncertainty and inefficiency as far as the administration of justice was concerned. The codifications were supposed to tidy up this messy situation: they were to provide a systematic regulation of the entire private law, ousting all rival sources including, in particular, the *ius commune*. Thus, Article 1 of the Dutch Abrogation Act (*Afschaffingswet*) provided, in a phrase suffused with fear, relief, and elation: 'The legal validity of Roman law is and remains abrogated.'[6]

II. The German Civil Code as a Late Fruit of the Codification Movement

The German Civil Code is a comparatively late fruit of the codification movement. The three great natural law codifications in Prussia, France, and Austria had been prepared in the late eighteenth and early nineteenth centuries. They were intended to satisfy the desire for territorial legal unity. The *Code civil*, in

---

[4] The standard account is Franz Wieacker, *A History of Private Law in Europe* (1995) (transl. Tony Weir); cf. also Paul Koschaker, *Europa und das römische Recht*, 4th edn. (1966) (on the significance of Roman law for European legal culture); Helmut Coing, *Europäisches Privatrecht*, vol. I (1985); vol. II (1989) (on the history of private law doctrine); Peter Oestmann, *Rechtsvielfalt vor Gericht* (2002) (on early modern German court practice). For an overview, see Reinhard Zimmermann, 'Roman Law and the Harmonization of Private Law in Europe', in Arthur Hartkamp *et al.* (eds.), *Towards a European Civil Code*, 3rd edn. (2004), 21 ff.

[5] The expression took root as a result of Samuel Stryk's work *Specimen usus moderni pandectarum*, Halae (1690–1712); see Klaus Luig, 'Samuel Stryk (1640–1710) und der "Usus modernus pandectarum" ', in *Die Bedeutung der Wörter: Studien zur europäischen Rechtsgeschichte, Festschrift für Sten Gagnér* (1991), 219 ff.

[6] The *Afschaffingswet* was dated 16 May 1829; for all details, see Hendrik Kooiker, *Lex Scripta Abrogata: De derde renaissance van het romeinse recht*, vol. I (1996).

particular, had thus become a potent symbol for the one undivided nation that had emerged from the upheavals following 1789. In the course of the nineteenth century, however, most of the other states of central, southern, and western Europe had codified their private law. Predominantly, the *Code civil* had been the source of inspiration. It continued to apply in Belgium and became the basis of the Dutch *Burgerlijk Wetboek* of 1838.[7] It provided the point of departure for the Italian *Codice civile* of 1865 (which could thus be enacted a mere four years after the kingdom of Italy had come into being), for the Portuguese *Código civil* of 1867, the Spanish *Código civil* of 1888–89 and the Romanian Civil Code of 1865.[8] The Serbian Civil Code of 1844, on the other hand, had been influenced mainly by the Austrian Code.

Increasingly, therefore, the legal position prevailing in nineteenth-century Germany was bound to look odd and anachronistic. The Prussian territories (including Westphalia, Bayreuth, and Ansbach) were governed by the *Preußisches Allgemeines Landrecht*. In the Rhine-Province, Alsace, and Lorraine the *Code civil* applied.[9] The Grand Duchy of Baden had adopted the *Badisches Landrecht* which was based on a translation of the *Code civil*.[10] The Kingdom of Saxony enacted its own Civil Code in 1865. Some places in Bavaria lived according to Austrian law, while in parts of Schleswig-Holstein Danish law prevailed. Most of the remaining German territories (comprising, in 1890, close to 30 per cent of the population of the *Deutsches Reich*) still administered justice according to the *ius commune*. But the *ius commune* only applied *in subsidio*. Countless more specific territorial or local laws could therefore govern a particular dispute: from thirteenth-century texts like Eike von Repgow's famous *Sachsenspiegel* to Baron von Kreittmayr's *Codex Maximilianeus Bavaricus Civilis* of 1756, from the *Neumünsterische Kirchspielgebräuche* to the *Nassau-Katzenelnbogensche Landesordnung*.[11] Thus, for example, there were all in all more than one hundred different regulations concerning succession upon death. None the less, in the German territories, a fundamental intellectual unity had continued to persist throughout the nineteenth century. That unity

[7] Jan Lokin, 'Die Rezeption des Code Civil in den nördlichen Niederlanden', (2004) 12 *Zeitschrift für Europäisches Privatrecht* 932 ff.

[8] Generally on the reception of the French *Code civil*, see Konrad Zweigert and Hein Kötz, *An Introduction to Comparative Law*, 3rd edn. (1998) (transl. Tony Weir), 98 ff.

[9] See the contributions in Reiner Schulze (ed.), *Französisches Zivilrecht in Europa während des 19. Jahrhunderts* (1994), and in Reiner Schulze (ed.), *Rheinisches Recht und Europäische Rechtsgeschichte* (1996); see also Elmar Wadle, *Französisches Recht in Deutschland* (2002).

[10] Elmar Wadle, 'Rezeption durch Anpassung: Der Code Civil und das Badische Landrecht: Erinnerung an eine Erfolgsgeschichte', (2004) 12 *Zeitschrift für Europäisches Privatrecht* 947 ff.

[11] For an overview of the laws applicable in Germany at the end of the nineteenth century, see 'Anlage zur Denkschrift zum BGB', in Benno Mugdan (ed.), *Die gesammten Materialien zum Bürgerlichen Gesetzbuch für das Deutsche Reich*, vol. I (1899), 844 ff.; and see *Allgemeine Deutsche Rechts- und Gerichtskarte*, 1896 (re-edited in 1996 by Diethelm Klippel).

was forcefully promoted by Savigny's Historical School of Law and the pandectist legal scholarship that emerged from it.[12] Thus, the contemporary version of Roman law did not apply only in the areas still governed by the *ius commune*; even in the countries of codified law it provided the underlying legal theory.[13] It provided the self-evident point of reference for understanding and assessing the codifications and territorial statutes. Therefore, it remained perfectly possible for a law professor to be called from Königsberg to Strasbourg, from Gießen to Vienna, or from Heidelberg to Leipzig. Nor were law students, as far as choice and change of universities were concerned, confined to the institutions of the state in which they later wanted to practise. Neither the Prussian Code, nor the *Code civil* or the Saxonian Civil Code, became the focal point for the legal training offered in the universities of the respective states.[14] Just as the codified laws had at first been neglected, and subsequently been pandectified, by contemporary legal scholarship, they constituted hardly more than an appendix to the courses on Roman private law in the curricula of nineteenth-century law faculties.[15]

III. The Programme of 'Historical Legal Science'

Our perception of nineteenth-century pandectist 'legal science' has been coloured, for a long time, by the exaggerations of those who attempted to break away from it and from the 'conceptual jurisprudence' established on that basis. Thus, a scholar like Georg Friedrich Puchta is only slowly beginning to emerge from the shadow cast by the pre-eminence of Savigny.[16] Jhering's work cannot be apportioned as easily, as once thought, into two different periods, separated by a 'conversion' from conceptual to functional jurisprudence. And even Bernhard Windscheid, the embodiment of pandectist scholarship in the second half of the nineteenth century ('Legal scholarship means pandectism, and pandectism means Windscheid') not only regarded himself as the servant, but also as the master of the concepts.[17] True law, for Windscheid, was 'strict but, at the same time, lenient; fixed and yet free; firm but also flexible' (that corresponded to the ideal of classical Roman law), and the true jurist, in his view, was able, like the Roman jurists, 'to serve his concepts and freely to rise

---

[12] For details, and references, see Reinhard Zimmermann, *Roman Law, Contemporary Law, European Law: The Civilian Tradition Today* (2001), 11 ff.   [13] Koschaker (n. 4) 292.

[14] Emil Friedberg, *Die künftige Gestaltung des deutschen Rechtsstudiums nach den Beschlüssen der Eisenacher Konferenz* (1896), 7 ff.   [15] Zimmermann (n. 12) 3 ff.

[16] Hans-Peter Haferkamp, *Georg Friedrich Puchta und die 'Begriffsjurisprudenz'* (2004).

[17] Ulrich Falk, *Ein Gelehrter wie Windscheid: Erkundungen auf den Feldern der sogenannten Begriffsjurisprudenz* (1989).

above them'.[18] The programme of 'historical legal science', as it had been developed by Savigny at the beginning of the century, had also been characterized by a certain tension. For while the emphasis of an organic connection between contemporary law 'and the entire past'[19] led to a discovery of the modern discipline of legal history (previously there had only been 'legal antiquities'),[20] Savigny ultimately aimed at legal (rather than historical) scholarship, i.e. the establishment of a legal doctrine which, though developed 'historically', was in conformity with contemporary requirements.[21] Thus, in the preface to his *System des heutigen Römischen Rechts* (System of Contemporary Roman Law) Savigny emphasized the need 'firstly, to trace and establish, within the entire body of our law, what is . . . of Roman origin, in order not to be unconsciously dominated by it; but then our approach aims at eliminating, among these Roman elements of our intellectual formation, whatever has in fact withered away and merely continues to lead a troublesome shadow life as a result of our misunderstanding'.[22] The main task of a scholar in private law, he writes at another place, 'is the intellectual penetration, adaptation and rejuvenation' of the legal material as it has come down to us.[23] Savigny's vision of an 'organically progressive' legal scholarship,[24] based on a uniform body of sources, guided by the same methodological convictions, and common to the whole nation—for Windscheid this was 'a revelation'[25]—led to a heyday of legal scholarship in Germany. It constituted the intellectual foundation for the emergence of a national community of scholars, of German legal unification on a scholarly level. At the same time, pandectism secured the leading place for Germany in the world of nineteenth-century legal scholarship; it was much admired by lawyers all over Europe and exercised significant influence on the legal development in countries such as France, Italy, and Austria.[26]

[18] Bernhard Windscheid, 'Das römische Recht in Deutschland' (1858), in *idem, Gesammelte Reden und Abhandlungen*, ed. Paul Oertmann (1904), 48 ff.

[19] Friedrich Carl von Savigny, 'Ueber den Zweck dieser Zeitschrift', (1815) 1 *Zeitschrift für geschichtliche Rechtswissenschaft* 3.

[20] Koschaker (n. 4) 269. On the 'discovery of legal history' in the nineteenth century, see Wieacker (n. 4) 330 ff.

[21] On Savigny's conception of legal science, see Joachim Rückert, *Idealismus, Jurisprudenz und Politik bei Friedrich Carl von Savigny* (1984).

[22] Friedrich Carl von Savigny, *System des heutigen Römischen Rechts*, vol. I (1840), xv.

[23] Savigny, (1815) 1 *Zeitschrift für geschichtliche Rechtswissenschaft* 6.

[24] Friedrich Carl von Savigny, *Vom Beruf unserer Zeit für Gesetzgebung und Rechtswissenschaft*, 1814, easily accessible in Hans Hattenhauer (ed.), *Thibaut and Savigny: Ihre programmatischen Schriften*, 2nd edn. (2002), 126.

[25] Bernhard Windscheid, 'Recht und Rechtswissenschaft' (1854), in *idem* (n. 18) 16.

[26] For France, see Alfons Bürge, *Das französische Privatrecht im 19. Jahrhundert* (1991); for Austria: Werner Ogris, *Der Entwicklungsgang der österreichischen Privatrechtswissenschaft im 19. Jahrhundert* (1968); for Italy: the contributions in Reiner Schulze (ed.), *Deutsche Rechtswissenschaft und Staatslehre im Spiegel der italienischen Rechtskultur während der zweiten Hälfte des 19. Jahrhunderts* (1990).

An obvious paradox inherent in Savigny's programme that has repeatedly been noted consisted in the emphasis on Roman law as the basis for a contemporary theory of private law. It ill matched the idea of law as being the product of the spirit of the people (*Volksgeist*). The phenomenon of the 'reception' could only be explained in a very tortuous way on that basis.[27] A second problem arose from Savigny's partiality for the pure and undiluted Roman law, corresponding to the educational principles of contemporary humanism and the aesthetic ideas of classicism.[28] It entailed a somewhat disdainful attitude towards the immediately preceding period of the *usus modernus pandectarum* and a negative, and essentially unjust, evaluation of the work of the medieval Commentators whose *mos italicus* had paved the way for the *usus modernus*. This attitude was not easily reconcilable with a programme that was fundamentally based upon the notion of 'organic growth' and insisted on 'the even and dispassionate recognition of the value and individuality of every age'.[29]

IV. 'Historical Legal Science' and Codification

Moreover, there was, within the Historical School, an ambivalence towards the question of codification that was never quite resolved. The 'founding manifesto'[30] of the Historical School was Savigny's reply to A.F.J. Thibaut's call to end the intolerable and inconvenient diversity of private laws prevailing in Germany by adopting a General German Civil Code, modelled on the French *Code civil*.[31] In his famous essay entitled *Vom Beruf unserer Zeit für Gesetzgebung und Rechtswissenschaft* (Of the Vocation of our Time for Legislation and Legal Science) Savigny not only rejected the idea of a codification to be drafted and enacted *hic et nunc*, but criticized the very notion of a codification as inorganic, unscientific, arbitrary, and hostile to tradition. At best, it was unnecessary; at worst it would distort and stifle 'organic' legal development.[32]

None the less it was widely accepted, from about the middle of the nineteenth century, that a codification of private law in Germany was about to come and was to end the direct application of Roman law. Theodor Mommsen in 1848 voiced the German nation's desire for the creation of a uniform and national law,[33] and Rudolf von Jhering predicted in 1852 that his own generation of

---

[27] Wieacker (n. 4) 309 ff.   [28] Wieacker (n. 4) 290 ff.   [29] Savigny (n. 22) xiv ff.

[30] Bernhard Windscheid, 'Die geschichtliche Schule in der Rechtswissenschaft' (1878), in *idem* (n. 18) 66.

[31] A.F.J. Thibaut, *Über die Notwendigkeit eines allgemeinen bürgerlichen Rechts für Deutschland* (1814), easily accessible today in Hattenhauer (n. 24) 37 ff.   [32] Savigny (n. 24) *passim*, for example, 79 ff.

[33] Theodor Mommsen, 'Die Aufgabe der historischen Rechtswissenschaft', in *idem, Gesammelte Schriften*, vol. III (1907), 587.

lawyers would see the demise of Roman law in its present form.[34] The editorial of the first volume of the *Zeitschrift für Rechtsgeschichte* (Journal of Legal History, 1861), while professing to continue the plan and the aims of Savigny's *Zeitschrift für geschichtliche Rechtswissenschaft* (Journal of Historical Legal Science) gave expression to the prevailing conviction that the historical development of the law could now sufficiently clearly be assessed 'for the results of the historical inquiry to be employed in the legislative process'. And even one of Savigny's most faithful disciples, who had sat at his feet in the University of Berlin and who had never ceased to see in him his own scholarly ideal, Bernhard Windscheid,[35] was among the most influential proponents of a German codification. Among the German lawyers, he wrote in 1878, 'there are probably relatively few who have not, with all the strength of soul available to them, yearned for the great work of a German code of private law'.[36] Thus, it is small wonder that the codification's entry into force on the first day of the new century was greeted with strong feelings of national pride. 'The new century brings to fruition the greatest feat achieved in German legal life', as it was put in one of the two leading law journals for practitioners,[37] while the other one, the *Deutsche Juristenzeitung* (German Lawyers' Journal) opened its January issue for the year 1900 with an ornamental page carrying the heading 'One People. One Empire. One Law'. For the first time, the notion of legal unity had become reality on German soil and for the first time, therefore, the energies of scholars and practitioners alike could focus on the interpretation of one and the same authoritative text.

V. Legal Unity by Way of Legislation

The way towards legal unity by means of a code of private law had been long and arduous. In the first half of the nineteenth century, the various states joined in the *Deutscher Bund* (German Federation) had already started to accommodate the needs of an expanding economy that was operating increasingly on a supraregional level. The advent of machinery and urbanization facilitated the production processes and the rising *bourgeoisie* favoured open markets promoting

---

[34] *Geist des römischen Rechts auf den verschiedenen Stufen seiner Entwicklung*, 1st edn., vol. I (1852), 2; cf. also Walter Wilhelm, 'Das Recht im römischen Recht', in Franz Wieacker and Christian Wollschläger (eds.), *Jherings Erbe* (1970), 228 ff.; Horst Heinrich Jakobs, *Wissenschaft und Gesetzgebung im bürgerlichen Recht nach der Rechtsquellenlehre des 19. Jahrhunderts* (1983), 76 ff.
[35] See, for example, his address in memory of Savigny: 'Festrede zum Gedenken an Savigny' (1879), in *idem* (n. 18) 81 ff. On Windscheid's attitude towards Savigny, see Oertmann (in his preface to the volume just mentioned, XXVII ff.); Jakobs (n. 34) 101 ff.; Falk (n. 17) 174 ff.
[36] Windscheid (n. 30) 70.   [37] [1900] *Juristische Wochenschrift* 1.

the free interplay of economic forces. Legal unification therefore was required, first and foremost, in the trade-related fields of law. A first significant step in this direction was the establishment of a German Customs Union in 1833. In 1848 the law of negotiable instruments was unified by means of the *Allgemeine Deutsche Wechselordnung*,[38] and between 1861 and 1866 nearly all the states of the *Deutscher Bund* adopted the draft of a General German Commercial Code (*Allgemeines Deutsches Handelsgesetzbuch*) that had been completed in 1861.[39] A draft law of obligations (*Dresdener Entwurf*) was published in 1865. Although it was never adopted, it significantly influenced the German Civil Code.

After the creation of the *Deutsches Reich* a streamlined procedural and organizational framework for the uniform and efficient administration of justice was established: the four *Reichsjustizgesetze*[40] concerned the unification of the court system (*Gerichtsverfassungsgesetz*), the law of bankruptcy (*Konkursordnung*), civil procedure (*Zivilprozeßordnung*), and criminal procedure (*Strafprozeßordnung*). They all came into force in October 1879. While they have been amended on various occasions, three of these acts remain upon the statute book today; the *Konkursordnung* was replaced by a new insolvency code (*Insolvenzordnung*) in 1999. The first of October 1879 also saw the opening of a supreme appeal court for the entire *Reich* in all civil and criminal matters: the *Reichsgericht*.[41] Its seat was Leipzig, a city with a distinguished legal tradition which had the advantage of not being identical with, but still sufficiently close to, the political capital of the *Reich* (Berlin). Its first president was Eduard von Simson, a Prussian lawyer of Jewish descent who had been baptized in his early youth. He had presided over the German National Assembly of 1848 that had met in the Frankfurt *Paulskirche* and had also been president of the Imperial Parliament.[42]

---

[38] See Ulrich Huber, 'Das Reichsgesetz über die Einführung einer allgemeinen Wechselordnung für Deutschland vom 26. November 1848', [1978] *Juristenzeitung* 785.

[39] Christoph Bergfeld, 'Preußen und das Allgemeine Deutsche Handelsgesetzbuch', (1987) 14 *Ius Commune* 101 ff.; and see Karsten Schmidt, *Das HGB und die Gegenwartsaufgaben des Handelsrechts* (1983). For the modernization of commercial law in the nineteenth century in general, see Karl Otto Scherner (ed.), *Modernisierung des Handelsrechts im 19. Jahrhundert* (1993); Arnold J. Kanning, *Unifying Commercial Laws of Nation-States* (2003), 46 ff.

[40] On which see Peter Landau, 'Die Reichsjustizgesetze von 1879 und die deutsche Rechtseinheit', in *Vom Reichsjustizamt zum Bundesministerium der Justiz: Zum 100jährigen Gründungstag des Reichsjustizamtes* (1977), 161 ff.

[41] On which see, on the occasion of its 100th anniversary, Arno Buschmann, '100 Jahre Gründungstag des Reichsgerichts', [1979] *Neue Juristische Wochenschrift* 1966 ff.; Elmar Wadle, 'Das Reichsgericht im Widerschein denkwürdiger Tage', [1979] *Juristische Schulung* 841 ff. On the *Reichsgericht's* predecessor, the Supreme Commercial Court, first of the *Norddeutscher Bund* and later of the *Reich* (it existed from 1870–79), see Herbert Kronke, 'Rechtsvergleichung und Rechtsvereinheitlichung in der Rechsprechung des Reichsoberhandelsgerichts', (1997) 5 *Zeitschrift für Europäisches Privatrecht* 735 ff.

[42] On Eduard von Simson, see James E. Dow, *A Prussian Liberal: The Life of Eduard von Simson* (1981); Bernd-Rüdiger Kern and Klaus-Peter Schroeder (eds.), *Eduard von Simson (1810–99)* (2001).

The scene was thus set for what was to be the crowning symbol of German legal unity: a code of private law. Its gestation period was close to thirty years. The starting shot was fired by the *lex* Miquel Lasker of 1873, by means of which the power to legislate concerning the entire field of private law was conferred on the Imperial Parliament. The details of the way in which the BGB has been prepared have often been recounted:[43] appointment of a preliminary commission and, subsequently, of the First Commission, preparation of preliminary drafts by the reporters appointed for the five books of the projected code, publication of the First Draft with the attendant motivations (entitled *Motive zu dem Entwurfe eines Bürgerlichen Gesetzbuches für das Deutsche Reich*), vigorous and very controversial public debate, deliberations of an internal commission of the Imperial Department of Justice, appointment of the Second Commission, publication of the Second Draft, again with the attendant motivations (this time entitled *Protokolle der Kommission für die Zweite Lesung des Entwurfs des Bürgerlichen Gesetzbuches*), revision of the Second Draft by the Federal Council (*Bundesrat*), the debates in the Imperial Parliament (both in committee and in plenary sessions), the taking of the final vote (with the Social Democrats voting against the code because it did not deal with labour relations), promulgation in the Government Gazette of 1896, and entry into force a little less than three and a half years later, on 1 January 1900. In 1897 the librarian of the *Reichsgericht*, Georg Maas, published a little-known bibliography of the official documents relating to the Civil Code;[44] two years later a very useful collection of many important (though not, as was claimed in the title of the work, all) documents was edited by Benno Mugdan.[45] In the meantime, the genesis of each individual rule contained in the BGB has been traced and

On the rise of Jewish lawyers and lawyers of Jewish descent in nineteenth-century Germany, see Peter Landau, 'Juristen jüdischer Herkunft im Kaiserreich und in der Weimarer Republik', in Helmut Heinrichs, Harald Franzki, Klaus Schmalz and Michael Stolleis (eds.), *Deutsche Juristen jüdischer Herkunft* (1993), 133 ff.; Reinhard Zimmermann, ' "Was Heimat hieß, nun heißt es Hölle": The emigration of lawyers from Hitler's Germany: political background, legal framework and cultural context', in Jack Beatson and Reinhard Zimmermann (eds.), *Jurists Uprooted: German-speaking Emigré Lawyers in Twentieth Century Britain* (2004), 9 ff.

[43] See, in particular, Werner Schubert, in Horst Heinrich Jakobs and Werner Schubert (eds.), *Die Beratung des Bürgerlichen Gesetzbuchs in systematischer Zusammenstellung der unveröffentlichten Quellen, Materialien zur Entstehungsgeschichte des BGB* (1978), 27 ff.; Barbara Dölemeyer, 'Das Bürgerliche Gesetzbuch für das Deutsche Reich', in Helmut Coing (ed.), *Handbuch der Quellen und Literatur der neueren europäischen Privatrechtsgeschichte*, vol. III/2 (1982), 1572 ff.; Michael John, *Politics and the Law in Late Nineteenth Century Germany: The Origins of the Civil Code* (1989); Fritz Sturm, 'Der Kampf um die Rechtseinheit in Deutschland—Die Entstehung des BGB und der erste Staudinger', in Michael Martinek and Patrick Sellier (eds.), *100 Jahre BGB—100 Jahre Staudinger* (1999), 24 ff. Cf. also the table by Stefan Stolte, printed in Mathias Schmoeckel, Joachim Rückert and Reinhard Zimmermann (eds.), *Historisch-kritischer Kommentar zum BGB*, vol. I (2003), xxvii ff.

[44] *Bibliographie der amtlichen Materialien zum Bürgerlichen Gesetzbuche für das Deutsche Reich und zu seinem Einführungsgesetze* (1897).   [45] Mugdan (n. 11).

made available in an easily-accessible manner by Horst Heinrich Jakobs and Werner Schubert.[46] In addition, Werner Schubert has organized a reprint of the preliminary drafts of the reporters appointed for the First Commission and their motivations.[47] They contain a wealth of comparative material and are an outstanding source for the state of contemporary doctrinal discussion.

The BGB was supposed to be, in Bernhard Windscheid's words, 'a cathedral of national splendour',[48] and Windscheid himself became one of its principal architects. Neither the design nor the details of its construction, however, could be taken to have been lifted from 'among the treasures deeply hidden in the people's soul'.[49] The general public in Germany has never developed any enthusiasm for the BGB, in spite (or, possibly, because) of all of its technical qualities. And even among lawyers, the code was not universally greeted with feelings of elation or joy. The publication of the First Draft had initiated a persistent stream of criticism. 'A tornado broke loose. It rained, it poured books and pamphlets ... The project was criticized from every point of view ... One might have thought that the whole scheme would perish': thus Maitland, from the perspective of a foreign observer.[50] This criticism was taken into account only to a limited extent. Eventually, German lawyers began to resign themselves to the idea that perhaps too much had been expected of the Civil Code.

VI. The BGB as a 'Prison Cell'?

At the same time, there had also been widespread feelings of apprehension in the years before 1900 as to how the codification would influence the administration of justice.[51] Many lawyers realized that, in view of the special nature of the Roman legal sources, they had enjoyed a great degree of freedom. The richness and complexity of those sources had allowed wide scope for doctrinal development and innovation, and the pandectist scholars had thereby become the high priests of legal scholarship.[52] The new code, it was feared, would reduce the

---

[46] Horst Heinrich Jakobs and Werner Schubert (eds.), *Die Beratung des Bürgerlichen Gesetzbuchs in systematischer Zusammenstellung der unveröffentlichten Quellen*, 16 vols. (1978–2002).

[47] Werner Schubert (ed.), *Die Vorlagen der Redaktoren für die erste Kommission zur Ausarbeitung des Entwurfs eines Bürgerlichen Gesetzbuches*, 15 vols. (1980–86).

[48] Windscheid (n. 18) 48.

[49] See, however, Ernst von Wildenbruch in his impassioned poem 'Das deutsche Recht', [1900] *Deutsche Justiz* 1.

[50] Frederic William Maitland, 'The Making of the German Civil Code', in H.A.L. Fisher (ed.), *The Collected Papers of Frederic William Maitland*, vol. III (1911), 480.

[51] In this regard, see Thomas Honsell, *Historische Argumente im Zivilrecht* (1982), 22 ff., with references.

[52] See James Q. Whitman, *The Legacy of Roman Law in the German Romantic Era* (1990).

judge to a mere 'subsumption machine' (*Subsumtionsautomat*),[53] and would constitute a prison cell for legal scholarship.[54] There was great concern about an impending 'cult of literalism'.[55] These anxieties prompted some authors to attribute to the BGB merely the status of a 'restatement';[56] they stimulated renewed attempts to search for criteria of justice beyond the positive law;[57] and they contributed substantially to the rise of the 'free-law movement' (*Freirechtsschule*).[58]

Looking at the way in which private law developed in the course of the twentieth century, it appears that the BGB did in fact prove to be a kind of prison cell in one respect. For, while the draftsmen of the code had still based their proposals on remarkably comprehensive comparative legal research,[59] private law legislation in the new century, in the words of Ernst Rabel, became enamoured with the example of the Great Wall of China.[60] A similar observation could be made as far as legal doctrine and the study of law are concerned. By the time the BGB entered into force, an avalanche of legal literature had started to sweep across the German legal landscape.[61] Textbooks[62] and commentaries[63] on the BGB had been appearing since as early as 1897. In 1899 a bibliography was published that listed approximately 4,000 titles of over 324 pages.[64] This literature, however, was almost exclusively exegetical in character, focused on the wording of the statute.[65] Many authors at first did hardly more than

[53] On the notion of a judge as a 'subsumption machine', see Regina Ogorek, *Richterkönig oder Subsumtionsautomat? Zur Justiztheorie im 19. Jahrhundert* (1986), 1 ff.

[54] Hans Wüstendörfer, 'Die deutsche Rechtswissenschaft am Wendepunkt', (1913) 110 *Archiv für die civilistische Praxis* 224.

[55] See, for example, Ernst Zitelmann, *Die Gefahren des Bürgerlichen Gesetzbuches für die Rechtswissenschaft* (1896), 14.

[56] See, for example, Rudolph Sohm, 'Das Studium des römischen Rechts', [1908] *Deutsche Juristenzeitung* 39 and the references in Honsell (n. 51) 24.

[57] See Wieacker (n. 4) 463 ff.; Honsell (n. 51) 25.

[58] On which see, for example, Wieacker (n. 4) 457 ff.

[59] On the tradition of *legislation comparée* in the nineteenth century, see, for example, Helmut Coing, 'Rechtsvergleichung als Grundlage von Gesetzgebung im 19. Jahrhundert', (1978) 7 *Ius Commune* 168 ff.; idem, *Europäisches Privatrecht*, vol. II (1989), 56 ff.

[60] This quotation is from an article published in 1913/14; the relevant passage is cited in Ernst Rabel, 'Aufgabe und Notwendigkeit der Rechtsvergleichung', in *idem, Gesammelte Aufsätze*, vol. III (1967), 13 ff.

[61] See Paul Laband, [1906] *Deutsche Juristenzeitung*, col. 2 ff. (who states that the literature in the area of private law broke forth 'with the suddenness and violence of a cloudburst').

[62] See Sibylle Hofer, 'Haarspalten, Wortklauben, Silbenstechen? 100 Jahre Lehrbücher zum BGB: Eine Lebensbilanz', [1999] *Juristische Schulung* 112 ff.

[63] On which, see Heinz Mohnhaupt, 'Die Kommentare zum BGB als Reflex der Rechtsprechung (1897–1914)', in Ulrich Falk and Heinz Mohnhaupt (eds.), *Das Bürgerliche Gesetzbuch und seine Richter: Fallstudien zur Reaktion der Rechtspraxis auf die Kodifikation des deutschen Privatrechts (1896–1914)* (2000), 495 ff.   [64] See Mohnhaupt (n. 63) 495.

[65] For early criticism, see Ludwig Kuhlenbeck, *Von den Pandekten zum Bürgerlichen Gesetzbuch: Eine dogmatische Einführung in das Studium des Bürgerlichen Rechts*, Part I (1898), vii; and cf. Mohnhaupt (n. 63) 495 ff.

paraphrase the statutory provisions. They waited to see how these provisions would be applied in practice[66] and then began to integrate the rapidly emerging case law into the new editions of their works.

Thus, very soon, the letter of the law was filled with life. At first glimpse, at least, it appeared to be a new and youthful life. Since the codification, according to contemporary opinion, contained a comprehensive and closed system of legal rules,[67] it constituted an autonomous interpretational space. Thus, on the one hand, 'the recollection of pandectist scholarship, one of the supreme achievements of the German legal mind',[68] faded remarkably quickly from both the doctrine and the practice of German law; Savigny, Dernburg, Jhering, Windscheid, and many other of the leading authors of the nineteenth century were hardly cited any longer, not to mention the earlier literature of the *ius commune* or the Roman legal sources themselves. The 'historical' interpretation was largely reduced to a perusal of the materials and motivations produced by the draftsmen of the code.[69] Of considerable significance, in that respect, had been the decision of the German law teachers in 1896, at a conference in Eisenach, to assign to the BGB the central position in the law curriculum; this was quite contrary to the way in which the codifications prevailing in parts of nineteenth-century Germany had been treated.[70] On the other hand, everything which lay outside the territorial scope of application of the national codification also vanished from the intellectual horizon of legal academics and practitioners. German law was to be understood and developed from within itself: Italian and French legal literature, let alone English case law, could contribute nothing to it. The codification thus promoted not only a vertical, but also a horizontal, isolation of legal scholarship. '[I] simply do not believe that contemporary law has really grown from the old law, but I regard it as something new, created by the need of the present day and the sovereign will of the modern legislature', wrote Konrad Cosack, the author of a modern textbook,[71] and he therefore refused to develop the law historically. At the same time, the organic point of departure for the incorporation of comparative law was lost. The legal horizon was limited by the rules and principles contained in the BGB. Within this framework, judges and legal writers strove to determine 'the concept' of impossibility,[72] to distinguish the different types of damage

---

[66] See the characteristic comment in (1900) 29 *Juristische Wochenschrift* 4.

[67] See, for example, Heinz Hübner, *Kodifikation und Entscheidungsfreiheit des Richters in der Geschichte des Privatrechts* (1980), 67. [68] Koschaker (n. 4) 190.

[69] See Kuhlenbeck (n. 65) vii. Generally on the 'historical argument' in contemporary legal thinking and practice, see Honsell (n. 51) 47 ff. [70] Friedberg (n. 14).

[71] Konrad Cosack, in Hans Planitz (ed.), *Die Rechtswissenschaft der Gegenwart in Selbstdarstellungen*, vol. I (1924), 16.

[72] On which see, most recently, Ulrich Huber, *Leistungsstörungen*, vol. I (1999), 97 ff.

that can arise as a result of the delivery of non-conforming objects,[73] or to penetrate the labyrinth of the 'owner-possessor-relationship'.[74] According to prevailing, contemporary ideology the codification represented *the* turning point of German legal history.[75]

VII. The Reaction of the Courts

And the courts? Even in the course of the nineteenth-century legal practice had not conformed to the ideas usually associated with the terms 'conceptual jurisprudence' and 'scholarly positivism'. Self-confident courts like the Supreme Appeal Courts of Kassel, Jena, or Munich, the Supreme Appeal Court of the four free cities in Lübeck, the Prussian Supreme Court, or later the Imperial Supreme Court in Commercial Matters and, from 1879, the Imperial Supreme Court, were able without any difficulty to procure for themselves 'the freedom of movement which is so indispensable for a judge' (and which was indeed conceded to them by clear-sighted authors like Windscheid).[76] An example can perhaps illustrate this assertion. At the beginning of the nineteenth century Gustav Hugo had stated very pointedly that Aquilian liability could, essentially, be reduced to the principle: whoever unlawfully injures another is bound to pay compensation. This assertion, he added, gave offence to 'the exact scholars' and was, therefore, not to be found in any of the textbooks, even although it correctly reflected the practice of nearly all courts in Germany.[77] But it was quite in tune with the tradition of the *ius commune*[78] and was to lead, in the course of the following decades, to decisions where compensation was granted for pure economic loss.[79] Essentially, therefore, the *lex Aquilia* was applied in a very similar way as the famous general provision of delictual liability in French law (Article 1382 *Code civil*) was interpreted by the

[73] *Infra* p. 92.
[74] Dirk A. Verse, *Verwendungen im Eigentümer-Besitzer-Verhältnis* (1999), has recently demonstrated, with regard to compensation for improvements, the specific value of an historical and comparative approach.
[75] This view was expressed, for example, by one of the most influential early commentators on the BGB, A. Achilles (judge of the *Reichsgericht*): cf. Mohnhaupt (n. 63) 502.
[76] Bernhard Windscheid and Theodor Kipp, *Lehrbuch des Pandektenrechts*, vol. I, 9th edn., § 28, note 4; and see the revisionist works by Falk and Ogorek (nn. 17 and 53).
[77] Gustav Hugo, *Lehrbuch des heutigen Römischen Rechts*, 7th edn. (1826), 282.
[78] Reinhard Zimmermann, *The Law of Obligations: Roman Foundations of the Civilian Tradition* (1996), 1022 ff., 1031 ff.; Jan Schröder, 'Die zivilrechtliche Haftung für schuldhafte Schadenszufügungen im deutschen usus modernus', in Letizia Vacca (ed.), *La responsabilità civile da atto illecito nelle prospettiva storico-comparatistica* (1995), 147 ff.
[79] See, for instance, the references in Windscheid and Kipp (n. 76) § 451, note 1 (concerning loss resulting from unlawful arrest).

courts.[80] There were many other developments which an 'exact scholar' must have observed with alarm. Thus, as far as liability among neighbours was concerned, pandectist legal literature tended to insist on fault.[81] At the same time, however, the courts displayed a remarkable willingness to abandon the axiomatic fixation on the *culpa* requirement as a foundation for extracontractual liability. When, from the middle of the nineteenth century onwards, industrialization led to a significant increase in neighbour disputes, they realized that an owner of property has to be granted protection, at least in some situations, even beyond the general principles of Aquilian liability. The *actio negatoria* was among the remedies liberally extended in this context.[82] The possibility of sanctioning wrongs by means of private law had vanished from legal practice long before it had vanished from the textbooks.[83] And that an owner has to make sure that his property does not constitute a danger to the public was recognized long before the concept of *Verkehrssicherungspflicht* had found its way into legal literature.[84] Many more examples could presumably be found by closely analysing nineteenth-century court practice. The Imperial Supreme Court in Commercial Matters displayed a great deal of creativity in the nine years of its existence, and in the reasons for its decisions it relied surprisingly often on comparative observations.[85] The *Reichsgericht* interpreted the codes and statutes which it had to apply not in a literalist manner but in the spirit of the historical school, i.e. with reference to the general thinking patterns of pandectist legal scholarship.[86]

This comparatively flexible approach towards the applicable sources of law did not significantly change after the enactment of the BGB. For, contrary to a widely held opinion, the first decades of the twentieth century were not marked by conceptual jurisprudence, statutory positivism, and the fine art of the 'legal game of chess'.[87] Thus, for example, the *Reichsgericht* continued to apply the *exceptio doli* in the tradition of the *ius commune*;[88] soon after 1900, it

---

[80] This enabled Zachariae von Lingenthal to discuss the French law of delict in a way which hardly differed from German law: *Handbuch des Französischen Civilrechts*, vol. II, 6th edn. (1875), § 444.

[81] See, for example, Heinrich Dernburg, *Pandekten*, vol. I, 5th edn. (1896), § 199, 4.

[82] Regina Ogorek, 'Actio negatoria und industrielle Beeinträchtigung des Grundeigentums', in Helmut Coing and Walter Wilhelm (eds.), *Wissenschaft und Kodifikation des Privatrechts im 19. Jahrhundert*, vol. IV (1979), 40 ff.; Andreas Thier, 'Zwischen actio negatoria und Aufopferungsanspruch: Nachbarliche Nutzungskonflikte in der Rechtsprechung des 19. und 20. Jahrhunderts', in Falk and Mohnhaupt (n. 63) 407 ff.

[83] Nils Jansen, *Die Struktur des Haftungsrechts: Geschichte, Theorie und Dogmatik außervertraglicher Ansprüche auf Schadensersatz* (2003), 361 ff.

[84] Detlef Kleindiek, *Deliktshaftung und juristische Person* (1997), 63 ff.

[85] Kronke, (1997) 5 *Zeitschrift für Europäisches Privatrecht* 735 ff.

[86] J. Michael Rainer, 'Zur Rechtsprechung des Reichsgerichts bis zum Inkrafttreten des BGB: Ein Modellfall für den Europäischen Gerichtshof', (1997) 5 *Zeitschrift für Europäisches Privatrecht* 751 ff.

[87] Josef Partsch, *Vom Beruf des römischen Rechts in der heutigen Universität* (1920), 39.

[88] Hans-Peter Haferkamp, 'Die exceptio doli generalis in der Rechtsprechung des Reichsgerichts vor 1914', in Falk and Mohnhaupt (n. 63) 1 ff.

began, from a number of different starting points, to turn the decision of the draftsmen of the BGB not to recognize the doctrines of *culpa in contrahendo*[89] and *clausula rebus sic stantibus*[90] on its head; it granted claims arising from positive malperformance (*positive Forderungsverletzung*) of contracts of sale based on § 276 I 1 BGB in exactly the same way as it had previously done on the basis of the *actio empti* of the *ius commune*;[91] it recognized a right to terminate the contract even in these cases of contractual liability;[92] the judges of the Imperial period had already laid the foundations for the recognition of a contract with protective effect vis-à-vis third parties and the doctrine of transferred loss (*Drittschadensliquidation*);[93] they set in motion the process of a transformation of the law of delict,[94] which was later analysed in a famous article by Ernst von Caemmerer;[95] they established the essential contours of the law of agency as it is practised today,[96] and they determined the boundary between liability for latent defects and the law of mistake[97] which was to hold for the rest of the century. Here, too, many other examples could be given. Where the *Reichsgericht* developed the law, there are usually either overt or covert lines of continuity linking the new law to the old: either because the judges simply perpetuated their earlier case law, or because they extended a line of development which had its origin in the nineteenth century. Except in the ideology of most law teachers, the BGB was certainly not a watershed in German legal development; indeed, rather it bore certain characteristics of a restatement[98] while, at the

---

[89] Tomasz Giaro, 'Culpa in contrahendo: eine Geschichte der Wiederentdeckungen', in Falk and Mohnhaupt (n. 63) 113 ff.

[90] Klaus Luig, 'Die Kontinuität allgemeiner Rechtsgrundsätze: Das Beispiel der clausula rebus sic stantibus', in Reinhard Zimmermann, Rolf Knütel and Jens Peter Meincke (eds.), *Rechtsgeschichte und Privatrechtsdogmatik* (2000), 171 ff.

[91] Hans Peter Glöckner, 'Die positive Vertragsverletzung', in Falk and Mohnhaupt (n. 63) 155 ff.; see also Klaus Luig, 'Die "Privilegierung" des Verkäufers', in *Mélanges en l'honneur de Carlo Augusto Cannata* (1999), 317 ff.; Huber (n. 72) 78 ff.

[92] And thereby continued a development which has its origins in legal scholarship and legislation of the nineteenth century; see Zimmermann (n. 12) 94 ff., with references; Glöckner (n. 91) 167 ff.

[93] Jörg Neuner, 'Die Entwicklung der Haftung für Drittschäden', in Falk and Mohnhaupt (n. 63) 193ff.; cf. also Sybille Hofer, 'Drittschutz und Zeitgeist: Ein Beitrag zur privatrechtlichen Zeitgeschichte', (2000) 117 *Zeitschrift der Savigny-Stiftung für Rechtsgeschichte, Germanistische Abteilung* 377 ff.

[94] Reinhard Zimmermann and Dirk A. Verse, 'Die Reaktion des Reichsgerichts auf die Kodifikation des deutschen Deliktsrechts (1900–14)', in Falk and Mohnhaupt (n. 63) 319 ff.

[95] Ernst von Caemmerer, 'Wandlungen des Deliktsrechts', in *Hundert Jahre deutsches Rechtsleben: Festschrift zum hundertjährigen Bestehen des Deutschen Juristentages 1860–1960*, vol. II (1960), 49 ff.

[96] Mathias Schmoeckel, 'Von der Vertragsfreiheit zu typisierten Verkehrspflichten: Zur Entwicklung des Vertretungsrechts', in Falk and Mohnhaupt (n. 63) 77 ff.

[97] Filippo Ranieri, 'Kaufrechtliche Gewährleistung und Irrtumsproblematik: Kontinuität und Diskontinuität in der Judikatur des Reichsgerichts nach 1900', in Falk and Mohnhaupt (n. 63) 207 ff.

[98] See Horst Heinrich Jakobs, *Wissenschaft und Gesetzgebung im bürgerlichen Recht nach der Rechtsquellenlehre des 19. Jahrhunderts* (1983), 160.

same time, settling a number of deeply-rooted doctrinal disputes.[99] Or, as Bernhard Windscheid wrote in an article in which he attempted, for himself, to resolve the tension between the programme of the Historical School and the impending codification of German private law, or between legal science and legislation: 'As historical jurists we know that the code will be no more than a moment in the development, more tangible, certainly, than the ripple in a stream but, none the less, merely a ripple in the stream'.[100] The great achievement of the *Reichsgericht* lay in the fact that, from the outset, it cautiously developed the law and adapted it to new and changing circumstances while generally avoiding any break in continuity. Among the tools used by the judges were the undisguised appeal to general legal intuition[101] or common sense,[102] the reading of tacit conditions into the contract (a device which has been popular at all times and in many countries),[103] and the construction of fictitious contracts.[104] And in order to satisfy, at least formally, the demands of statutory positivism, even the legislative history was occasionally subjected to a somewhat skewed perspective determined, above all, by the desired result.[105]

VIII. Unity of the System of Private Law?

'But nothing is more certain than that the old society and economic system has irretrievably come to an end' (Thomas Mann in his diary, 15 April 1919). That collapse resulted from the First World War and the upheavals caused by it. At the same time, our perception of the world changed dramatically. 'The modern world began on 29 May 1919', writes Paul Johnson,[106] 'when photographs of a solar eclipse, taken on the island of Principe off West Africa and at Sobral in Brazil, confirmed the truth of a new theory of the universe'. Obviously, the nineteenth century only really ended at around 1920. Thus, unlike the *Code civil*, the BGB did not herald the beginning of the new epoch. In many respects, it still reflected the values of a world that was destined to disappear.[107]

---

[99] See Zimmermann (n. 12) 47 ff.   [100] Windscheid (n. 30) 75 ff.

[101] Cf., for example, RGZ 78, 239 at 240 ff. (the 'linoleum' case, 7 December 1911).

[102] Cf., for example, RGZ 91, 21 at 24 (contaminated residence, 5 October 1917).

[103] See, for example, the references in Luig (n. 91) 181 ff. Generally, see Reinhard Zimmermann, ' "Heard melodies are sweet, but those unheard are sweeter...": Condicio tacita, implied condition und die Fortbildung des europäischen Vertragsrechts', (1993) 193 *Archiv für die civilistische Praxis* 165 ff.   [104] See, for example, the references in Giaro (n. 89) 130 ff.

[105] In this regard, see Thomas Finkenauer, 'Das entstehungsgeschichtliche Argument als Etikettenschwindel: Zwei Beispiele aus der Rechtsprechung des Reichsgerichts zum Bereicherungsrecht', in Falk and Mohnhaupt (n. 63) 305 ff.   [106] Paul Johnson, *History of the Modern World* (1983), 1.

[107] The relationship between private law and German society in the nineteenth and early twentieth centuries is discussed in four studies by Franz Wieacker which have been collected in the

It was a world with a patriarchal family structure, with associations and foundations still firmly under the tutelage of state authorities,[108] and with a comparatively formal concept of freedom of contract;[109] a world in which a regulation on bee swarms was regarded as more important than one on standard terms of business. The typical citizen for the BGB was not the factory worker but rather the moneyed entrepreneur, the landed proprietor, or the public servant.[110] In a number of respects, therefore, the BGB was soon to be regarded as outdated. About 160 statutory amendments and decisions of the Federal Constitutional Court have affected both the text and substance of the code, more than half of them, however, dating from the last quarter of the twentieth century. Family law, in particular, has been subject to fundamental changes; more than thirty important amendments have left hardly any part of it unchanged.[111] Comparatively few changes have been made to text of the other four books. The provisions on lease and employment contracts have been considerably modified and supplemented, but the development of the law of domestic leases[112] has largely, and that of labour relations[113] has completely, taken place outside the framework of the BGB. Other major amendments concern the regulation of contracts relating to package holidays in §§ 651 a ff., the law of land tenure (§§ 585 ff. BGB) and contracts concerning bank transfers, bank payments, and giro accounts (§§ 676 a ff.).[114]

---

volume *Industriegesellschaft und Privatrechtsordnung* (1974): *Das Sozialmodell der klassischen Privatrechtsgesetzbücher und die Entwicklung der modernen Gesellschaft* (1953); *Das Bürgerliche Recht im Wandel der Gesellschaftsordnungen* (1960); *Pandektenwissenschaft und Industrielle Revolution* (1966); *Der Kampf des 19. Jahrhunderts um die Nationalgesetzbücher* (1970). And see now Joachim Rückert, 'Das BGB und seine Prinzipien: Aufgabe, Lösung, Erfolg', in Mathias Schmoeckel, Joachim Rückert and Reinhard Zimmermann (eds.), *Historisch-kritischer Kommentar zum BGB*, vol. I (2003), nn. 92 ff.

[108] See Andreas Richter, *Rechtsfähige Stiftung und Charitable Corporation: Überlegungen zur Reform des deutschen Stiftungsrechts auf der Grundlage einer historisch-rechtsvergleichenden Untersuchung der Entstehung des modernen deutschen und amerikanischen Stiftungsmodells* (2001), 40 ff.

[109] But see now Sibylle Hofer, *Freiheit ohne Grenzen?* (2001).

[110] Zweigert and Kötz (n. 8) 144.

[111] For an overview see Dieter Schwab, *Wertewandel und Familienrecht* (1993); Rainer Frank, '100 Jahre BGB—Familienrecht zwischen Rechtspolitik, Verfassung und Dogmatik', (2000) 200 *Archiv für die civilistische Praxis* 401 ff.

[112] Udo Wolter, *Mietrechtlicher Bestandsschutz* (1984); Heinrich Honsell, *Privatautonomie und Wohnungsmiete*, (1986) 186 *Archiv für die civilistische Praxis* 115 ff. In September 2001, however, the law of domestic leases was re-incorporated into the BGB.

[113] Joachim Rückert, ' "Frei" und "sozial": Arbeitsvertrags-Konzeptionen um 1900 zwischen Liberalismen und Sozialismen', (1992) 23 *Zeitschrift für Arbeitsrecht* 223 ff.; Klaus Adomeit, 'Der Dienstvertrag des BGB und seine Entwicklung zum Arbeitsrecht', [1996] *Neue Juristische Wochenschrift* 1710 ff.

[114] Further examples are provided by § 90a (and, in this connection, a number of other new provisions on the legal status of animals) (on which, see Helmut Heinrichs, in *Palandt, Bürgerliches Gesetzbuch*, 64th edn. (2005), § 90a, n. 1: a 'sentimental pronouncement without any effective legal content') and § 55a (see *Palandt*/Heinrichs (as above) § 55a, n. 1: 'contrary to the system of the law').

Outside the BGB, however, 'a secondary system of private law by way of special statutes'[115] has grown up, by means of which the social model underlying the BGB has been adapted to modern conditions. Apart from competition law and labour law, the law of consumer protection deserves particular mention in this context. Among its core components are the statutes on standard terms of business (1976), doorstep sales and similar transactions (1986), and on consumer credits (1990), but also other statutes like the ones dealing with liability for defective products (1989), time-share agreements (1996) and distance sales (2000). It is often overlooked[116] that this tradition of excluding from the general private law codification subjects which are considered to be of a special nature dates back to the Historical School and that therefore neither the statute concerning instalment sales (1894) nor the one imposing strict liability for personal injuries sustained in the operation of a railway (1871) were included in the code.[117] It has, in fact, remained controversial until today whether, or to what extent, such subjects have attained the kind of structural and conceptual stability required for incorporation into a general code of private law.[118]

IX. The Resilience of the BGB

With the Modernization of the Law of Obligations Act, most of the special statutes in the field of consumer contract law have now found a place in the BGB. In addition, there have been reforms affecting the law of damages,[119] contract of lease,[120] form requirements,[121] package holidays,[122] and foundations.[123] The introduction of same sex partnerships by an act of 16 February

---

[115] Rolf Stürner, 'Der hundertste Geburtstag des BGB—eine nationale Kodifikation im Greisenalter?', [1996] *Juristenzeitung* 742.

[116] But see Karsten Schmidt, *Die Zukunft der Kodifikationsidee: Rechtsprechung, Wissenschaft und Gesetzgebung vor den Gesetzeswerken des geltenden Rechts* (1985).   [117] See *infra* pp. 165 ff., 169.

[118] For all details, see *infra* pp. 159 ff., 205 ff.

[119] For details, see Gerhard Wagner, *Das neue Schadensersatzrecht* (2002).

[120] See Birgit Grundmann, 'Die Mietrechtsreform—Wesentliche Inhalte und Änderungen gegenüber der bisherigen Rechtslage', [2001] *Neue Juristische Wochenschrift* 2497 ff.; Friedrich Klein-Blenkers, 'Das Gesetz zur Neugliederung, Vereinfachung und Reform des Mietrechts (Mietrechtsreformgesetz)', in Barbara Dauner-Lieb, Thomas Heidel, Manfred Lepa and Gerhard Ring (eds.), *Das neue Schuldrecht* (2002), 506 ff.

[121] For details, see Walter Boente and Thomas Riem, 'Das BGB im Zeitalter digitaler Kommunikation—Neue Formvorschriften', [2001] *Jura* 793 ff.; Ulrich Noack, 'Elektronische Form und Textform', in Dauner-Lieb, Heidel, Lepa and Ring (n. 120) 441 ff.

[122] See Ernst Führich, 'Zweite Novelle des Reisevertragsrechts zur Verbesserung der Insolvenzsicherung und der Gastschulaufenthalte', [2001] *Neue Juristische Wochenschrift* 3083 ff.; Mark Niehuus, 'Der Reisevertrag', in Dauner-Lieb, Heidel, Lepa and Ring (n. 120) 322 ff.

[123] Ulrich Burgard, 'Das neue Stiftungsprivatrecht', [2002] *Neue Zeitschrift für Gesellschaftsrecht* 697 ff.

2001[124] has led to more than thirty provisions throughout the BGB being amended. All these changes, however, have happened in the course of the past four years. Up to that time, i.e. for the first one hundred years of its existence, the text of the BGB (apart from the provisions on family law) had been remarkably resistant to change. This resilience throughout all the upheavals of the twentieth century has frequently been commented upon. It is less remarkable for property law, the law of succession, and even for delict or unjustified enrichment, than it is for an inherently dynamic subject such as contract law. The 'evacuation' of important developments (labour law, social lease law, consumer law) provides only part of the explanation. Another reason for the BGB's resilience lies in the character of the code itself. In form and substance it was moulded by nineteenth-century pandectist scholarship. Its draftsmen had, very largely, aimed at setting out, containing, and consolidating 'the legal achievements of centuries'.[125] The BGB was regarded as part of a tradition significantly shaped by legal scholarship. The phenomenon of scholarly 'development' of the law was quite familiar to the draftsmen of the code. Horst Heinrich Jakobs has, therefore, pointedly referred to the BGB as a codification 'which does not contain the source of law in itself but has its source in the legal scholarship from which it was created'.[126] The BGB was designed to provide a framework for an 'organically progressive legal science'. The idea of enacting a prohibition of commenting upon the BGB (as existed with regard to the Prussian Code of 1794)[127] was quite alien to the draftsmen of the BGB: as alien as the equally odd idea that it might be possible to lay down a specific rule for every imaginable situation. Time and again, the *travaux préparatoires* contain express statements to the effect that the solution to a specific problem has to be left to legal scholarship.

Moreover, in spite of having been influenced so strongly by pandectist legal doctrine, the BGB is not doctrinaire in spirit and outlook.[128] Its draftsmen did not feel called upon to provide authoritative definitions for fundamental concepts such as contract, declaration of will, damages, causation, or unlawfulness and thus, in a way, to remove these matters from scholarly discussion. Nor did they

---

[124] See Nina Dethloff, 'Die Eingetragene Lebenspartnerschaft—Ein neues familienrechtliches Institut', [2001] *Neue Juristische Wochenschrift* 2598 ff.   [125] Windscheid (n. 30) 75.

[126] Jakobs (n. 34) 160. He goes on to state that the BGB 'should not, and will not, control legal scholarship, but should be, and will be, controlled by the latter, if such legal scholarship is itself historical, in the full sense of the word'.

[127] Hans-Jürgen Becker, 'Kommentier- und Auslegungsverbot', in *Handwörterbuch zur deutschen Rechtsgeschichte*, vol. II (1978), cols. 963 ff.; Matthias Miersch, *Der sogenannte référé législatif: Eine Untersuchung zum Verhältnis Gesetzgeber, Gesetz und Richteramt seit dem 18. Jahrhundert* (2000).

[128] Okko Behrends, 'Das Bündnis zwischen Gesetzgebung und Dogmatik und die Frage der dogmatischen Rangstufen', in Okko Behrends and Wolfram Henckel (eds.), *Gesetzgebung und Dogmatik* (1989), 9 ff.; Jan Schröder, 'Das Verhältnis von Rechtsdogmatik und Gesetzgebung in der neuzeitlichen Rechtsgeschichte', in Behrends and Henckel (as above) 37 ff.

determine questions of legal construction (what type of legal act is the performance of an obligation?). A number of basic evaluations and doctrinal points of departure were also not specifically spelt out in the code in view of the fact that they could be taken for granted. Thus, for example, there is no explicit reference to freedom of contract. § 119 BGB envisages three different types of mistake which allow a contract to be rescinded; but the intellectual basis for this rule, i.e. that an error in motive is irrelevant in principle, is not mentioned in the code. The BGB sometimes provides hardly more than the conceptual signposts for the development of legal doctrine. The rules contained in it usually attain a considerable level of abstraction, both as far as form and substance are concerned. Contrary to the Prussian Code ('Common chicken, geese, ducks, doves and turkeys are to be counted among the chattels appurtenant to a landed estate')[129] the BGB predominantly does not attempt to provide a careful and detailed regulation of individual situations to be encountered in daily life, but instead makes available a set of rules and concepts which are applicable to a large variety of problems—among them many that could not be envisaged by those who drafted the code. It is hardly surprising that the BGB has come to be regarded as outdated wherever this technique has not been followed and where the code, therefore, confronts its readers with the world of day labourers and coach drivers,[130] or with the merger of migrating bee swarms.[131] In addition, of course, there are open-ended provisions like § 138 I BGB (invalidity of contracts *contra bonos mores*) or § 242 BGB (obligations must be performed in accordance with the precepts of good faith)[132] by means of which the BGB attempts to achieve a balance between doctrinal stability and flexibility.

X. The Development of Private Law under the Code

The foundation was thus laid for courts of law and legal scholarship, in characteristic cooperation, to bring the letters of the law to life, to interpret and develop the provisions contained in the code, and to adapt them to new circumstances.[133] The details of this process are analysed in a new, historical

---

[129] § 58 I 2 PrALR.   [130] § 196, nos. 3 and 9 BGB (old version).   [131] § 963 BGB.

[132] These *Generalklauseln* are a characteristic element of German private law; they constitute the most important as well as the most convenient ports of entry for the values of the community. For a famous warning against the dangers inherent in these provisions, see Justus Wilhelm Hedemann, *Die Flucht in die Generalklauseln: Eine Gefahr für Recht und Staat* (1933).

[133] For a general account of the legal development in twentieth-century Germany, see Karl Kroeschell, *Rechtsgeschichte Deutschlands im 20. Jahrhundert* (1992). For a history of private law during the time of the Weimar Republic, see Knut Wolfgang Nörr, *Zwischen den Mühlsteinen: Eine*

commentary on the German Civil Code.[134] A suitable methodological background was provided by the interest-based approach which was established by Philipp Heck but can ultimately be traced back to Rudolf von Jhering.[135] After 1945, the focus on interests was substituted by an emphasis on the balancing of evaluations.[136] Courts and legal writers attempted to tackle the problems arising from awkwardly formulated, or idiosyncratic, provisions, from a lack of systematic coordination (the relationship between the rules on unjustified enrichment and those on so-called owner-possessor relationships), from individual rules which soon turned out to be unsuitable (the six-month prescription period, running from the moment of delivery, for claims based on latent defects in contracts of sale), or from the fact that the scope of application of a provision came to be seen as too narrow (the *in pari turpitudine* rule, as contained in § 817, 2 BGB) or too wide (*mortuus redhibetur*, as adopted in § 350 BGB). 'Gaps in the law'[137] had to be filled, drafting mistakes had to be corrected, and indeterminate legal concepts had to be specified. Legal solutions had to be found, on the basis of the considerations underlying the regulations in the code, for complex patterns of facts (the various categories of three-party situations in the law of unjustified enrichment). New legal questions, not even imaginable at the beginning of the twentieth century, had to be solved (wrongful birth). New types of contracts which came to be established in business life (such as leasing), had to be brought within the sysem of contracts provided by the BGB. Changes in social mores had to be accommodated, such as the commercialization of ever increasing aspects of life, including holidays and

Privatrechtsgeschichte der Weimarer Republik (1988). There is an extensive literature on the nazification of legal life, and private law, during the 1930s: see Zimmermann (n. 42) 54 ff., 58 ff. with references. Bernd Rüthers, *Die unbegrenzte Auslegung*, 6th edn. (2005), remains of fundamental importance. For the Federal Republic of Germany, see Joachim Rückert, 'Abbau und Aufbau der Rechtswissenschaft nach 1945', [1995] *Neue Juristische Wochenschrift* 1251 ff.; Dieter Medicus, 'Entscheidungen des BGH als Marksteine für die Entwicklung des allgemeinen Zivilrechts', [2000] *Neue Juristische Wochenschrift* 2921 ff.

134 So far, the first volume (covering the General Part of the BGB, i.e. §§ 1–240) has appeared: Mathias Schmoeckel, Joachim Rückert and Reinhard Zimmermann (eds.), *Historisch-kritischer Kommentar zum BGB*, vol. I (2003); the second volume (covering the general part of the law of obligations, i.e. §§ 241–432) is in preparation for 2006.

135 On Philipp Heck, see now Heinrich Schoppmeyer, *Juristische Methode als Lebensaufgabe: Leben, Werk und Wirkungsgeschichte Phillip Hecks* (2001).

136 Jens Petersen, *Von der Interessenjurisprudenz zur Wertungsjurisprudenz* (2001). For a comprehensive analysis of the methods of statutory interpretation in Germany, and their historical development, see Stefan Vogenauer, *Die Auslegung von Gesetzen in England und auf dem Kontinent: Eine vergleichende Untersuchung der Rechtsprechung und ihrer historischen Grundlagen*, vol. I (2001), 28 ff., 430 ff.

137 On which see, generally, Claus-Wilhelm Canaris, *Die Feststellung von Lücken im Gesetz: Eine methodologische Studie über Voraussetzungen und Grenzen der Rechtsfortbildung praeter legem*, 2nd edn. (1983).

leisure time. The law of damages and of unjustified enrichment, as well as other areas, where the BGB contains hardly more than a number of general concepts and provisions, had to be filled with finely nuanced rules and doctrines.

Spacious doctrinal edifices have been created even where the BGB contains hardly more than individual building blocks (*Störung der Geschäftsgrundlage*). Some of these doctrines have been developed in spite of the fact that there does not really exist a 'legal gap' in the BGB, others have been smuggled into the code along side-paths which had not been designed for that purpose (the right to an established and operative business). New systematic schemes have been devised (enrichment by transfer, enrichment based on an encroachment) and new theoretical frameworks came to be established (liability based on reasonable expectations). The 'materialization' of German contract law was evident not only in acts of special legislation outside the BGB—such as the Standard Terms of Business Act, or the rights of revocation contained in a number of consumer protection statutes—but also in the way in which rules like § 138 I BGB came to be applied, for instance, to instalment credit transactions, or to contracts of suretyship entered into by an impecunious wife or child of the main debtor, or in the scope of application given to a doctrine such as *culpa in contrahendo*.[138] The openness and flexibility of the *Generalklauseln* turned out to be a curse under the National Socialist regime, and a blessing under the Basic Law of 1949. The doctrine of the indirectly horizontal effect[139] led to German law being adjusted to the system of values embodied in the fundamental rights provisions of the Basic Law; but it also increasingly placed the Federal Constitutional Court in the position of an irregular supreme court of appeal in private law disputes.[140] Occasionally, even decisions by the Federal Supreme Court which were clearly *contra legem* have been sanctioned by the Federal Constitutional Court in view of certain evaluations derived from the Basic Law.[141]

The American comparative lawyer John P. Dawson has famously referred to a German 'case law revolution'.[142] A large number of 'legal discoveries'[143] has

---

[138] Claus-Wilhelm Canaris, 'Wandlungen des Schuldvertragsrechts—Tendenzen zu seiner "Materialisierung" ', (2000) 200 *Archiv für die civilistische Praxis* 273 ff.

[139] It was developed by Günter Dürig, 'Grundrechte und Zivilrechtsprechung', in *Festschrift für Hans Nawiasky* (1956), 158 ff. and has been adopted by the Federal Constitutional Court in its Lüth decision: BVerfGE 7, 198; on which see David P. Currie, *The Constitution of the Federal Republic of Germany* (1994), 181 ff.

[140] This has been severely criticized: Uwe Diederichsen, 'Das Bundesverfassungsgericht als oberstes Zivilgericht—ein Lehrstück der juristischen Methodenlehre', (1998) 198 *Archiv für die civilistische Praxis* 171 ff.

[141] BVerfGE 34, 269 (14 February 1973; the Soraya case). For details, see Zweigert and Kötz (n. 8) 688 ff.; Basil S. Markesinis and Hannes Unberath, *The German Law of Torts: A Comparative Treatise*, 4th edn. (2002), 415 ff.   [142] John P. Dawson, *The Oracles of the Law* (1968), 432 ff.

[143] Hans Dölle, *Juristische Entdeckungen* (1958), reprinted in Thomas Hoeren (ed.), *Zivilrechtliche Entdecker* (2001), 5 ff.

been made. Much of what has been discovered is new. But often we also find old wine being poured into new vessels. This is true wherever the rules of the BGB constitute pandectist doctrine in statutory form, where we are dealing with rules of interpretation such as the *interpretatio contra eum qui clarius loqui debuisset*, or with general maxims underlying the BGB without specifically having been restated in the code (*dolo agit qui petit quod statim redditurus est*). Wherever a problem has not been decided by the draftsmen of the code but has been left to legal doctrine, the pandectist textbooks also, not rarely, point the way towards the most appropriate solution. We observe the phenomenon of a renaissance of rules and concepts from an ostensibly outdated past (*utile per inutile non vitiatur*).[144] Recourse to the sources of the *ius commune* continues to be of considerable significance for the proper evaluation and interpretation of the provisions contained in the BGB. Ulrich Huber's great monograph on the law of breach of contract[145] can serve as a particularly impressive, as well as comparatively recent, confirmation for the truth of this assertion.

XI. Criticism of the BGB

For more than one hundred years, the BGB has been both a characteristic manifestation and a constituent feature of German legal culture. It has been, and has remained, modern as a result of having provided a framework for an organic development of the law. None the less, there has also always been criticism. This tradition goes back to the period immediately after the publication of the First Draft in 1888. Protagonists of a fundamental line of criticism were then, in particular, the members of the women's movement, the socialists, and the legal Germanists; they regarded the code as patriarchal, insensitive to social issues, not readily comprehensible, and too pervasively Romanist in spirit, form, and substance.[146] Dieter Schwab has recently demonstrated that such criticism continued after the BGB's entry into force and that it was, above all, taken up with renewed vigour in times of upheaval.[147] Thus in 1919, as Otto von Gierke had done around the turn of the new century, Justus Wilhelm

---

[144] Theo Mayer-Maly, 'Die Wiederkehr von Rechtsfiguren', [1971] *Juristenzeitung* 1 ff.; Rolf Knütel, 'Römisches Recht und deutsches Bürgerliches Recht', in Walther Ludwig (ed.), *Die Antike in der europäischen Gegenwart* (1993), 43 ff.; Reinhard Zimmermann, 'Civil Code and Civil Law', (1994/95) 1 *Columbia Journal of European Law* 89 ff.

[145] Ulrich Huber, *Leistungsstörungen*, 2 vols. (1999).

[146] For details, see Dieter Schwab, (2000) 22 *Zeitschrift für Neuere Rechtsgeschichte* 325 ff., with references.   [147] Schwab, (2000) 22 *Zeitschrift für Neuere Rechtsgeschichte* 334 ff.

Hedemann pointed out the BGB's lack of character: 'It is timid and dull, it displays no vigorous spirit, no characteristic personality'.[148] It was oriented towards the conservative and prosperous citizen. This was also disliked by the BGB's critics during the time of National Socialism. The code was thought to be characterized by an exaggerated individualism and to reflect a materialistic world order, it was regarded as 'un-German', removed from the reality of life, and scholastic. The longing for a law that was 'German' now became mixed up with racist ideology.[149] The completion of a 'People's Code', prepared under the auspices of an Academy for German Law by the elite of professors of private law, as far as they were still active in German universities,[150] was prevented by the collapse of the regime. The workers' and farmers' paradise of post-war East Germany found the BGB no more appealing than the Nazi state. In 1965 a family law code was enacted and, in 1976, those parts of the BGB that had still been in force until then were replaced by a socialist civil code. In West Germany, the so-called student revolts from 1967 onwards revived the aversion to the BGB: it was of no use for regulating the 'social processes of our time'.[151]

The ideological bias of a large part of the fundamentalist opposition to the BGB should not be allowed to obscure the fact that the code has never engendered feelings of affection. Nor has it become a popular part of the German cultural heritage, and it has no share in the creation of a national identity comparable to that of the *Code civil* in France, or the common law in England. Most German lawyers, in the words of Hein Kötz, pay their code 'a kind of cool, almost grudging tribute'.[152] Thus, it is hardly surprising that the code's 100th birthday passed without great celebration by either the general public or the legal community. In 1996 and 2000, a number of articles appeared attempting to provide a detached assessment,[153] an occasional colloquium was held,[154] and here and there a series of lectures was

---

[148] In an academic speech in 1919, cited by Schwab, (2000) 22 *Zeitschrift für Neuere Rechtsgeschichte* 337.   [149] Schwab, (2000) 22 *Zeitschrift für Neuere Rechtsgeschichte* 340.

[150] On the project of a 'People's Code', see, for example, Michael Stolleis, 'Volksgesetzbuch', in *Handwörterbuch zur Deutschen Rechtsgeschichte*, vol. V, cols. 990 ff.; Gerd Brüggemeier, 'Oberstes Gesetz ist das Wohl des deutschen Volkes: Das Projekt des "Volksgesetzbuches" ', [1990] *Juristenzeitung* 24 ff.; Hans Hattenhauer, 'Die Akademie für Deutsches Recht (1933–44)', [1986] *Juristische Schulung* 680 ff.

[151] Rudolf Wiethölter in his radio lectures, broadcast by the radio station of Hesse; for details, see Schwab, (2000) 22 *Zeitschrift für Neuere Rechtsgeschichte* 344 ff.

[152] Hein Kötz, in *Verhandlungen des 60. Deutschen Juristentages*, vol. II/1 (1994), K 9.

[153] See, for example, Stürner, [1996] *Juristenzeitung* 741 ff.; Mathias Schmoeckel, '100 Jahre BGB: Erbe und Aufgabe', [1996] *Neue Juristische Wochenschrift* 1697 ff.; Reiner Schulze, 'Ein Jahrhundert BGB—deutsche Rechtseinheit und europäisches Privatrecht', [1997] *Deutsche Richterzeitung* 369 ff.; Norbert Horn, 'Ein Jahrhundert Bürgerliches Gesetzbuch', [2000] *Neue Juristische Wochenschrift* 40 ff.

[154] For example, the symposium 'Das Bürgerliche Gesetzbuch und seine Richter', the contributions to which have been published in the volume edited by Falk and Mohnhaupt (n. 63). The centenaries of the BGB and the Staudinger commentary were celebrated at a symposium in Munich in June 1998;

organized.[155] No *Festschrift* was dedicated to the BGB (quite in contrast, incidentally, to the Federal Supreme Court on the occasion of its 50th birthday, celebrated also in 2000).[156] The general tone of the centenary contributions was not exuberant. The technical quality of the code was praised, as ever, as were its intellectual maturity and the fine sense of legislative self-restraint. German lawyers appreciate the BGB as a stable basis for their work. In other countries, it has always been regarded as a typical product of German legal scholarship ('Never, I should think, has so much first-rate brain power been put into an act of legislation': F.W. Maitland);[157] not surprisingly, therefore, it has had a greater impact on legal theory and legal doctrine in other European countries than on foreign legislation.[158] Still, however, it was received in Greece (with the result that that country is, today, normally regarded as part of the Germanic legal family); it shaped the reform of the Austrian Civil Code in 1914–16; and it influenced the codifications in Italy (1942), Portugal (1966), and the Netherlands (1992). In discussions concerning law reform in the formerly socialist countries and the harmonization of private law in Europe, however, the BGB has often been regarded as outdated. This is, as far as contract law is concerned, largely due to the fact that the Convention on Contracts for the International Sale of Goods has established itself as a more suitable model. Also, a number of the relevant doctrines have been raised by the BGB to a level of abstraction unfamiliar to most lawyers outside Germany: for they are dealt with in the General Part of the BGB, not just the general part of the law of obligations, or of contract law.

Also, of course, it has to be acknowledged that the BGB did in fact contain a number of key provisions that were increasingly regarded as deeply unsatisfactory.

---

on which see the volume edited by Martinek and Sellier (n. 43). The papers presented at the Salzburg conference of the Association of Teachers of Private Law in September 1999 also dealt with the application and further development of the BGB over the last one hundred years; see (2000) 200 *Archiv für die civilistische Praxis* 273 ff. The Association of Young Academics in Private Law had already held a conference on the BGB in 1996; its proceedings are documented in the *Jahrbuch Junger Zivilrechtswissenschaftler* (1996).

[155] Hans Schlosser and Volker Behr (eds.), *Bürgerliches Gesetzbuch 1896–1996* (1997).

[156] No less than three *Festschriften* appeared on this occasion: *50 Jahre Bundesgerichtshof: Festgabe aus der Wissenschaft* (four volumes) (2000); *50 Jahre Bundesgerichtshof: Festschrift aus Anlaß des fünfzigjährigen Bestehens von Bundesgerichtshof, Bundesanwaltschaft und Rechtsanwaltschaft beim Bundesgerichtshof* (2000); *Fortitudo Temperantia, Die Rechtsanwälte am Reichsgericht und beim Bundesgerichtshof: Festgabe zu 50 Jahren Bundesgerichtshof* (2000).

[157] Maitland (n. 50) 484. On the evaluation of the BGB from the point of view of French and English law, see Werner Schubert, 'Das Bürgerliche Gesetzbuch im Urteil französischer Juristen bis zum Ersten Weltkrieg', (1997) 114 *Zeitschrift der Savigny-Stiftung für Rechtsgeschichte, Germanistische Abteilung* 128 ff.; Marcus Dittmann, *Das Bürgerliche Gesetzbuch aus Sicht des Common Law* (2001).

[158] For an overview, see Wieacker (n. 4) 383 ff.; Zweigert and Kötz (n. 8) 154 ff. And see the contributions in (2000) 200 *Archiv für die civilistische Praxis* 365 ff., 493 ff.

They include, as far as the law of obligations is concerned, delictual liability for others in terms of § 831, which is still based on the fault principle in spite of a reversal of the onus of proof, the restrictive attitude with regard to granting compensation for immaterial damage (§§ 847 and 253 BGB), the excessively differentiated law of extinctive prescription, the outdated system of liability for latent defects in relation to contracts of sale and contracts for work, and the badly coordinated restitution regimes contained in §§ 346 ff. and 812 ff. BGB respectively. In one of these cases, the Federal Supreme Court (with the approval of the Federal Constitutional Court)[159] has gone so far as partially to derogate the relevant rule (§ 253 BGB);[160] in another (§ 831 BGB), the courts have attempted to provide workable solutions by extending the regime provided in § 31 BGB[161] and by opening up a wide grey area between delict and contract which they have subjected to the contractual regime;[162] in the other cases they have explored a multitude of subtle ways to get around the problem but have, at the same time, frequently created new difficulties of delimitation or conflicts in evaluation. In the area of liability for latent defects contractual practice has, of course, also helped to find appropriate solutions. The Ministry of Justice intended to deal with two of the problem areas mentioned above and therefore, in 1967, published a draft statute for the amendment and supplementation of provisions dealing with the law of damages. These proposed reforms have, however, never been implemented.[163]

XII. The Modernization of the Law of Obligations

The idea of a comprehensive reform of the law of obligations seems to be attributable to the then Minister of Justice, Hans-Jochen Vogel. He first presented it to the Federal Parliament in 1978 and subsequently also to the 52nd *Deutscher Juristentag* (Meeting of the Association of German Lawyers).[164] The main concerns motivating the reform were (i) the integration of a number of special statutes into the BGB (such as, for example, the Standard Terms of Business Act, the Act on Instalment Sales, and several strict liability statutes),

---

[159] *Supra* n. 141.

[160] Cf., for example, BGHZ 26, 349 ff. (gentleman horse-rider); BGHZ 35, 363 ff. (ginseng roots).   [161] See Kleindiek (n. 84) 314 ff., 340 ff.

[162] See, from a comparative perspective, Zweigert and Kötz (n. 8) 630 ff.; Markesinis and Unberath (n. 141) 701 ff.

[163] For more details on these attempts at reform, see Hermann Lange, *Schadensersatz*, 2nd edn. (1990), 19 ff.; Gottfried Schiemann, in *J. von Staudingers Kommentar zum Bürgerlichen Gesetzbuch*, 13th edn. (1998), preliminary notes to §§ 249 ff., nn. 26 ff.

[164] See the references in Alfred Wolf, 'Weiterentwicklung und Überarbeitung des Schuldrechts', [1978] *Zeitschrift für Rechtspolitik* 249.

(ii) the incorporation of new types of contractual relationships into the BGB (such as doctors' contracts, contracts concluded with old-age and nursing homes, contracts about the supply of energy, and contracts between private clients and their banks), (iii) the reform of a number of specific types of obligations already dealt with in the BGB (sale, contracts for work, the law of unjustified enrichment, delict), and (iv) the need for reshaping the general law of obligations, particularly for adapting it to new developments on the international level.[165]

The Ministry then requested a number of academic opinions, which were published in three large volumes in 1981 and 1983.[166] Each of the reporters had the task of investigating an area of the law of obligations with a view to its need for reform, and of formulating suggestions as to how such reform might be implemented. Almost all areas within the law of obligations were included,[167] with the important exception of the law of lease.[168] The reports were eagerly discussed, both among academics and the various legal professions;[169] thus, for instance, at the beginning of 1983, the Association of Teachers of Private Law devoted a special conference to the reform of the law of obligations.[170] A report on the discussion following the introductory keynote speech[171] referred to a

---

[165] Wolf, [1978] *Zeitschrift für Rechtspolitik* 253 ff.

[166] *Gutachten und Vorschläge zur Überarbeitung des Schuldrechts*, vol. I (1981); vol. II (1981); vol. III (1983).

[167] In particular: recent developments of the law of contract in Europe (Max Planck Institute, Hamburg), extinctive prescription (Frank Peters and Reinhard Zimmermann), law of damages (Gerhard Hohloch), pre-contractual liability (Dieter Medicus), long-term contracts (Norbert Horn), breach of contract (Ulrich Huber), contracts of sale (Ulrich Huber), contracts concerning residence and care in homes for senior citizens (Gerhard Igl), contracts for medical treatment (Erwin Deutsch, Michael Geiger), contracts for work (Hans-Leo Weyers), contracts to take care of a matter for somebody against valuable consideration (Hans-Joachim Musielak), giro account relationships (Franz Häuser), law of negotiable instruments (Ingo Koller), unjustified enrichment (Detlef König), contractual and extra-contractual liability (Peter Schlechtriem), law of delict (Christian von Bar), strict liability (Hein Kötz), consumer protection (Harm Peter Westermann), contracts for the provision of energy (Volker Emmerich), contracts of employment (Manfred Lieb), building contracts (Kurt Keilholz), *negotiorum gestio* (Johann Georg Helm), partnership (Karsten Schmidt), suretyship and guarantee (Walther Hadding, Frank Häuser, and Reinhard Welter). In addition, in 1986 and on behalf of the Hamburg Max Planck Institute, Jürgen Basedow submitted a comparative report on the development of the law of sale: Jürgen Basedow, *Die Reform des deutschen Kaufrechts* (1988).

[168] This was also pointed out by Dieter Medicus, 'Zum Stand der Überarbeitung des Schuldrechts', (1988) 188 *Archiv für die civilistische Praxis* 169 ('striking').

[169] See, for example, the contributions in (1982) 37 *Neue Juristische Wochenschrift* 2017 ff. (by Jürgen Schmude, Helmut Heinrichs, Wolfgang B. Schünemann, Manfred Lieb, Ulrich Hübner and Johannes Denck), and the bibliography included in Wolfgang Ernst and Reinhard Zimmermann (eds.), *Zivilrechtswissenschaft und Schuldrechtsreform* (2001), as appendix II A.

[170] The papers (by Manfred Lieb, Eduard Picker, Max Vollkommer, Hans G. Leser and Klaus J. Hopt) were published in (1983) 183 *Archiv für die civilistische Praxis* 327 ff.

[171] Manfred Lieb, 'Grundfragen einer Schuldrechtsreform', (1983) 183 *Archiv für die civilistische Praxis* 327 ff.

mood of 'sceptical open-mindedness'.[172] One year later, the Federal Minister
of Justice established a Reform Commission[173] headed by the responsible
Director-General; it consisted of four delegates from the justice departments of
the federal states, five judges, one practising lawyer, one notary, and four
professors (Uwe Diederichsen, Hein Kötz, Dieter Medicus, and Peter
Schlechtriem).[174] The problem areas to be dealt with by the Commission were
now limited to the law of breach of contract, liability for defects in contracts of
sale and contracts for work, and liberative prescription. The Commission was
charged with the task of reshaping the law so as to be clearer and 'more in
keeping with the times',[175] taking account of the way in which the law had
developed in practice. Twenty two meetings were held, each of several days'
duration; in 1992, the Commission presented its final report.[176] In addition to
a general section, that report contained specific proposals for legislation in each
of the areas mentioned, as well as the reasoning behind these proposals. As far
as the general law of breach of contract is concerned, the Commission followed
the lead of the UN Convention on the International Sale of Goods (CISG) in
many respects. This was entirely in accordance with the views of the initial
reporter on this subject, Professor Ulrich Huber of the University of Bonn,
who had answered the question: 'Is the introduction of a law of breach modelled
on the Uniform Sales Law to be recommended?' in the affirmative (though he
had still taken his lead from the Convention relating to a Uniform Law on the
International Sale of Goods of 17 July 1973).[177]

At the 60th *Deutscher Juristentag* in September 1994, the Commission's
draft proposals were the subject of the deliberations of the private law
section.[178] In spite of occasional fundamental criticism by distinguished
academics,[179] and outright rejection of the draft by representatives of commerce and industry, the general sentiment towards the draft was favourable.
The report summing up the proceedings of the *Deutscher Juristentag* in one of

---

[172] Gerhard Hönn, 'Diskussionsbericht', (1983) 183 *Archiv für die civilistische Praxis* 366.

[173] See Hans A. Engelhard, 'Zu den Aufgaben einer Kommission für die Überarbeitung des
Schuldrechts', [1984] *Neue Juristische Wochenschrift* 1201 ff.

[174] For details, see Bundesminister der Justiz (ed.), *Abschlußbericht der Kommission zur Überarbeitung
des Schuldrechts* (1992) 13 ff.   [175] Engelhard, [1984] *Neue Juristische Wochenschrift* 1201.

[176] *Abschlußbericht* (n. 174). On the working methods of the Commission, cf. also Medicus,
(1988) 188 *Archiv für die civilistische Praxis* 168 ff. And see the contributions of Walter Rolland, Dieter
Medicus, Lothar Haas and Dieter Rabe to [1992] *Neue Juristische Wochenschrift* 2377 ff.

[177] The UN Convention on the International Sale of Goods of 11 April 1980 only entered into
force in Germany on 1 January 1991.

[178] The reporters were Hein Kötz, Peter Joussen and Gerd Brüggemeier.

[179] See, in particular, the contribution by Werner Flume in *Verhandlungen des 60. Deutschen
Juristentages*, vol. II/2 (1994), K 112 ff. In a similar vein, in the run-up to the conference, cf. also
Wolfgang Ernst, 'Zum Kommissionsentwurf für eine Schuldrechtsreform', [1994] *Neue Juristische
Wochenschrift* 2177 ff.; *idem*, 'Kernfragen der Schuldrechtsreform', [1994] *Juristenzeitung* 801 ff.

the two major general law reviews recorded 'an encouraging result' and appealed to the Government finally to put its words into action;[180] another reporter commented on a discussion that had gone much more smoothly than most participants would have expected.[181] According to Ernst A. Kramer,[182] the discussion displayed 'a fundamentally positive attitude', which also manifested itself in the results of various votes taken at the meeting; by and large they were 'very heartening' for the Commission.[183] Apart from that, however, there was no broadly-based discussion of the draft, either before or after the *Juristentag* in Münster.[184] This was due to an increasingly widespread impression that the draft had disappeared into a drawer in the Ministry of Justice and that its implementation was no longer likely to happen. The excitement associated with an impending reform made way for a general sentiment of indifference. This ended in September 2000 when suddenly something like a bombshell was dropped on the German legal community: the publication of a 630-page 'Discussion Draft' of a statute modernizing the law of obligations.[185] The direct trigger for the Discussion Draft was the enactment of the Consumer Sales Directive and the need for its implementation by 1 January 2002. There can be no doubt that this Directive could have been implemented by effecting a number of comparatively marginal adjustments to German sales law.[186] The Government had, however, decided to use this opportunity finally to carry out the long-postponed reform of the law of obligations. As a result, the entire project was now placed under an enormous pressure of time. This was highly problematic in view of the fact that the Discussion Draft (i) extended the reform agenda that had previously come to be accepted (in particular, it was now proposed to incorporate a number of special statutes concerning consumer protection into the BGB), (ii) even in so far as it dealt with subjects

---

[180] '60. Deutscher Juristentag: Der Tagungsverlauf', [1994] *Neue Juristische Wochenschrift* 3070.

[181] 'Tagungsbericht: Der 60. Deutsche Juristentag in Münster', [1995] *Juristenzeitung* 190.

[182] 'Die Reform des Schuldrechts—Die privatrechtliche Abteilung des 60. Deutschen Juristentags, 20–23. September 1994 in Münster', (1995) 3 *Zeitschrift für Europäisches Privatrecht* 303.

[183] These votes are documented in *Verhandlungen* II/1 (n. 152) K 103 ff.

[184] This has repeatedly been criticized. See, for example, Harm Peter Westermann, [1994] *Monatsschrift für Deutsches Recht* 1. But see the discussion on the occasion of the 24th congress of German notaries, based on papers presented by Günther Brambring and Hermann Amann, as well as the literature listed in Ernst and Zimmermann (n. 169) appendix II B.

[185] The text of the draft rules is easily accessible in Ernst and Zimmermann (n. 169) appendix I; the draft rules plus motivation can be found in Claus-Wilhelm Canaris (ed.), *Schuldrechtsmodernisierung 2002* (2002), 3 ff.

[186] See Wolfgang Ernst and Beate Gsell, 'Kaufrechtsrichtlinie und BGB: Gesetzentwurf für eine "kleine" Lösung bei der Umsetzung der EU-Kaufrechtsrichtlinie', [2000] *Zeitschrift für Wirtschaftsrecht* 1410 ff.; cf. also Wolfgang Ernst and Beate Gsell, 'Nochmals für eine "kleine" Lösung', [2000] *Zeitschrift für Wirtschaftsrecht* 1812 ff.; Andreas Schwartze, 'Die zukünftige Sachmängelgewährleistung in Europa—Die Verbrauchsgüterkauf-Richtlinie vor ihrer Umsetzung', (2000) 8 *Zeitschrift für Europäisches Privatrecht* 544 ff.

covered by the Draft of the Reform Commission, sometimes significantly deviated from that Draft (particularly concerning the law of prescription), and (iii) had not been brought up to date even where it followed the recommendations of that Commission; thus, it failed to take account of recent international initiatives in contract law (the publication of the Principles of European Contract Law and of the UNIDROIT Principles of International Commercial Contracts)[187] and of new studies fundamentally affecting our perception of German contract law.[188] Academic criticism was not, therefore, long in coming. It was articulated particularly strongly at a symposium of German professors in private law held at the University of Regensburg in November 2000.[189] It induced the Government to establish two working groups charged with the task of critically examining the Discussion Draft and the recommendations contained in it. The working group concerning breach of contract consisted mainly of professors;[190] the one looking into the law of prescription, sales law, and other matters was constituted by officials from the Ministries of Justice of the various German *Länder*, judges of the Federal Supreme Court, members of the earlier Reform Commission, practitioners, and one professorial representative.[191] These working groups only had a period of about two months for their deliberations. None the less, they managed to effect a number of substantial changes. In early May 2001 a Government Draft was published which very largely accepted the recommendations of the working groups but also took account of suggestions and requests which had emerged in the course of hearings of interest groups affected by the reform.[192] In the course of summer and autumn 2001 the Government Draft was pushed through Parliament by way

---

[187] Ole Lando and Hugh Beale (eds.), *Principles of European Contract Law*, Parts I and II (2000); Ole Lando, Eric Clive, André Prüm and Reinhard Zimmermann (eds.), *Principles of European Contract Law*, Part III (2003); UNIDROIT (ed.), *Principles of International Commercial Contracts* (1994). For the literature that had appeared, by 2000, on these instruments, see appendix II D in Ernst and Zimmermann (n. 169).

[188] In particular: Ulrich Huber, *Leistungsstörungen*, 2 vols. (1999).

[189] The contributions to this symposium have been published in Ernst and Zimmermann (n. 169). Another symposium was held in January 2001: Reiner Schulze and Hans Schulte-Nölke (eds.), *Die Schuldrechtsreform vor dem Hintergrund des Gemeinschaftsrechts* (2001). On 30/31 March 2001 the Association of German Teachers of Private Law held a special meeting in Berlin to discuss what had by then become the revised version of the Discussion Draft. The lectures delivered at that meeting have been published in a special issue of *Juristenzeitung*: [2001] *Juristenzeitung* 473 ff. The revised version of the Discussion Draft (known as *Konsolidierte Fassung des Diskussionsentwurfs eines Schuldrechtsmodernisierungsgesetzes*) can be found in Canaris (n. 185) 349 ff.

[190] *Kommission Leistungsstörungen*. The names of the members are listed in Claus-Wilhelm Canaris, 'Die Reform des Rechts der Leistungsstörungen', [2001] *Juristenzeitung* 499.

[191] For details, see Canaris (n. 185) x.

[192] 'Entwurf eines Gesetzes zur Modernisierung des Schuldrechts', easily accessible in Canaris (n. 185) 429 ff., 569 ff.

of an accelerated procedure. In the process, it was again repeatedly changed.[193] The Modernization of the German Law of Obligations Act was finally approved by the Federal Parliament in October and by the Council of State Governments in early November 2001, and it was promulgated on 26 November 2001. A little more than five weeks later it entered into force.

The reform legislation has divided the German private law professoriate in an unprecedented manner. Strong language has been used to scold the intellectual immaturity of the new law, and the finger of scorn has been pointed at many of its aspects. Others have emphasized the Government's readiness to listen to academic criticism, to involve leading legal academics in the process of revising the Discussion Draft, and to follow many of their suggestions. In the meantime, German lawyers have had to come to terms with the reform, however critically it may have to be evaluated.[194] An enormous amount of legal literature has appeared, whether in the form of textbooks, commentaries, or even articles. It continues to grow with frightening rapidity. Much more than has hitherto been the case German authors will, however, have to cease to look at German law in isolation. They will have to take account of, and at the same time contribute to, what must be considered to be one of the most important legal developments of our time: the increasing Europeanization of private law.[195]

XIII. The Europeanization of Private Law

From about the mid-1980s, the European Communities began to enact Directives which profoundly affect core areas of the national systems of private law.[196] Milestones of this development were the Directives concerning liability for

---

[193] Thus, for example, the Council of State Governments submitted proposals for 150 amendments, of which the Government accepted about 100; see 'Stellungnahme des Bundesrates (31 August 2001)' and 'Gegenäußerung der Bundesregierung zur Stellungnahme des Bundesrats zum Entwurf eines Gesetzes zur Modernisierung des Schuldrechts', both now easily accessible in Canaris (n. 185) 935 ff., 995 ff.

[194] For an attempt to take stock, see Barbara Dauner-Lieb, 'Das Schuldrechtsmodernisierungsgesetz in Wissenschaft und Praxis—Versuch einer Bestandsaufnahme', in Barbara Dauner-Lieb, Horst Konzen and Karsten Schmidt (eds.), *Das neue Schuldrecht in der Praxis* (2003), 3 ff. For a (largely unfavourable) assessment from the point of view of a foreign observer, see Ole Lando, 'Das neue Schuldrecht des Bürgerlichen Gesetzbuchs und die Grundregeln des europäischen Vertragsrechts', (2003) 67 *Rabels Zeitschrift für ausländisches und internationales Privatrecht* 231 ff.

[195] For an overview, see Nils Jansen, *Binnenmarkt, Privatrecht und europäische Identität* (2004); Reinhard Zimmermann, 'Comparative Law and the Europeanization of Private Law', in Mathias Reimann and Reinhard Zimmermann (eds.), *Oxford Handbook of Comparative Law* (in preparation).

[196] Peter-Christian Müller-Graff, 'EC Directives as a Means of Unification of Private Law', in Arthur Hartkamp *et al.* (eds.), *Towards a European Civil Code*, 3rd edn. (2004), 77 ff.

defective products, contracts negotiated away from business premises, consumer credit, package travel, unfair terms in consumer contracts, and consumer sales.[197] As a result, the requirement of interpreting provisions of national law in conformity with the Directives on which they are based has attained considerable practical importance.[198] In addition, the European Court of Justice, though not a Supreme Court for private law disputes in the European Union, has started to fashion concepts, rules, and principles which are relevant not only for the law of the Union but also for the private laws of its Member States.[199] Several international commissions and groups of experts are busy developing or 'finding' (by means of a type of restatement) common principles of a European law of contract, torts, or even trusts or family law.[200] Ambitious research projects strive to establish the 'common core' of European private law.[201] The codification of European private law has been championed, consistently, by the European Parliament, first in a resolution of May 1989.[202] The Commission of the European Union has, more cautiously, issued an action plan for a more coherent European contract law[203] which, *inter alia*, aims at the development of a 'common frame of reference'. This frame of reference is supposed to provide the basis for further deliberations on an optional instrument in the field of European contract law.[204] The Principles of European Contract Law, drawn up by the so-called 'Lando Commission'[205] constitute a blueprint for such instrument. Among academics across Europe the desirability

[197] These, and the other Directives in the field of private law, can conveniently be found in Oliver Radley-Gardner, Hugh Beale, Reinhard Zimmermann and Reiner Schulze (eds.), *Fundamental Texts on European Private Law* (2003), sub I.

[198] Claus-Wilhelm Canaris, 'Die richtlinienkonforme Auslegung und Rechtsfortbildung im System der juristischen Methodenlehre', in *Im Dienst der Gerechtigkeit: Festschrift für Franz Bydlinski* (2002), 47 ff.

[199] Walter van Gerven, 'The ECJ Case-law as a Means of Private Law Unification', in Hartkamp *et al.* (n. 196) 101 ff.; for the law of delict, see Wolfgang Wurmnest, *Grundzüge eines europäischen Haftungsrechts: Eine rechtsvergleichende Untersuchung des Gemeinschaftsrechts* (2003), 13 ff.

[200] Wolfgang Wurmnest, 'Common Core, Grundregeln, Kodifikationsentwürfe, Acquis-Grundsätze—Ansätze internationaler Wissenschaftlergruppen zur Privatrechtsvereinheitlichung in Europa', (2003) 11 *Zeitschrift für Europäisches Privatrecht* 714 ff.

[201] Mauro Bussani and Ugo Mattei (eds.), *The Common Core of European Private Law* (2002).

[202] On which, see Winfried Tilmann, 'Entschließung des Europäischen Parlaments über die Angleichung des Privatrechts der Mitgliedstaaten vom 26.05.1989', (1993) 1 *Zeitschrift für Europäisches Privatrecht* 613 ff.   [203] COM (2003) 68, OJ 2003, C 63/1.

[204] See, most recently, the 'Communication from the Commission to the European Parliament and the Council on "European Contract Law and the revision of the acquis: the way forward" ', COM (2004) 651 final. The parameters for the academic discussion are analysed by Stephen Weatherill, 'Why Object to the Harmonization of Private Law by the EC?', (2004) 12 *European Review of Private Law* 633 ff.

[205] Lando and Beale (n. 187) and Lando, Clive, Prüm and Zimmermann (n. 187), both quoted above. For comment, see Reinhard Zimmermann, 'The Principles of European Contract Law: Contemporary Manifestation of the Old, and Possible Foundation for a New, European Scholarship of Private Law', in *Essays in Honour of Hein Kötz* (2005), forthcoming.

of a European Civil Code has become a hotly contested issue.[206] Two international initiatives have already embarked on an attempt to devise draft codes for the field of contract law and beyond.[207] In legal education, too, there are signs of a change of perspective.[208] The mobility of law students within the European Union is promoted by the extraordinarily successful Erasmus (now Socrates) programme. More and more law faculties are trying to give themselves a 'European' profile by offering integrated study programmes. Institutes and chairs of European private law, European business law, or European legal history have been established. Models of legal harmonization from Europe's past[209] and from other parts of the world[210] are receiving increasing attention.

Moreover, the national isolation of law and legal scholarship is being overcome by the uniform private law laid down in international conventions. Of central importance, in this respect, is the success story of the Convention on the International Sale of Goods, which is beginning to play an increasingly important role in private law adjudications by national Supreme Courts.[211] The development sketched, so far, in the roughest outline is also reflected in the emergence of a legal literature focusing on European, rather than merely national, law. This began in the fields of comparative law and legal history.[212] Since then, we have seen the publication of a textbook on the European law of contract,[213] delict, and unjustified enrichment,[214] of comparative casebooks,[215]

---

[206] Ewoud Hondius, 'Towards a European Civil Code', in Hartkamp *et al.* (n. 196) 3 ff.

[207] Giuseppe Gandolfi (*coordinateur*), *Code Européen des Contrats: Avant-projet* (2000); Christian von Bar, 'The Study Group on a European Civil Code', in *Festschrift für Dieter Henrich* (2000) 1 ff.

[208] Michael Faure, Jan Smits and Hildegard Schneider (eds.), *Towards a European Ius Commune in Legal Education and Research* (2002).

[209] Reinhard Zimmermann, 'Savigny's Legacy: Legal History, Comparative Law, and the Emergence of a European Legal Science', (1996) 112 *Law Quarterly Review* 576 ff.

[210] Vernon Valentine Palmer (ed.), *Mixed Jurisdictions Worldwide: The Third Legal Family* (2001); Jan Smits, *The Making of European Private Law: Towards a Ius Commune Europaeum as a Mixed Legal System* (2002); Reinhard Zimmermann, Daniel Visser and Kenneth Reid (eds.), *Mixed Legal Systems in Comparative Perspective* (2004).

[211] Reinhard Zimmermann and Kurt Siehr (eds.), 'The Convention on the International Sale of Goods and its Application in Comparative Perspective', (2004) 68 *Rabels Zeitschrift für ausländisches und internationales Privatrecht* 113 ff.

[212] Helmut Coing, *Europäisches Privatrecht*, vol. I (1985); vol. II (1989); Reinhard Zimmermann, *The Law of Obligations: Roman Foundations of the Civilian Tradition* (1990).

[213] Hein Kötz, *Europäisches Vertragsrecht*, vol. I (1996) (English translation under the title *European Contract Law* by Tony Weir, 1997); volume II, to be written by Axel Flessner, has not yet been published.

[214] Christian von Bar, *Gemeineuropäisches Deliktsrecht*, vol. I (1996); vol. II (1999) (English translation under the title *The Common European Law of Torts*, vol. I (1998); vol. II (2000)); Peter Schlechtriem, *Restitution und Bereicherungsausgleich in Europa: Eine rechtsvergleichende Darstellung*, vol. I (2000); vol. II (2001); cf. also Reinhard Zimmermann (ed.), *Grundstrukturen des Europäischen Deliktsrechts* (2003); *idem* (ed.), *Grundstrukturen eines Europäischen Bereicherungsrechts* (2005).

[215] Hugh Beale, Arthur Hartkamp, Hein Kötz and Denis Tallon (general eds.), *Cases, Materials and Text on Contract Law* (2002); Walter van Gerven, Jeremy Lever and Pierre Larouche, *Cases,*

of series of monographs dealing with European legal history and European private law, of at least three legal journals which are devoted to European private law,[216] and of collections of the foundational texts in the field.[217]

At the same time it is clear that we will still be faced, in the foreseeable future, with the co existence of a great number of national systems of private law in Europe. Much would, however, be gained, if these could be assimilated gradually, or organically. This requires the protagonists of national legal development to be aware of what happens in the other national legal systems and on the European level, critically to examine quirks and idiosyncracies of their own legal systems, and to adopt, whenever possible, a harmonizing approach.[218] Those responsible for determining the direction of European private law, on the other hand, have to take account of the national legal experiences which have been gathered by sophisticated courts and legal writers.

It is in this spirit that the studies collected in the present volume attempt to assess the recent reform of German contract law.

Materials and Text on National, Supranational and International Tort Law (2000); Jack Beatson and Eltjo Schrage (eds.), *Cases, Materials and Texts on Unjustified Enrichment* (2003); cf. also Filippo Ranieri, *Europäisches Obligationenrecht*, 2nd edn. (2003).

[216] *Zeitschrift für Europäisches Privatrecht, European Review of Private Law, Europa e diritto privato.*
[217] Radley-Gardner, Beale, Zimmermann and Schulze (n. 197).
[218] See, as far as the judiciary is concerned, Walter Odersky, 'Harmonisierende Auslegung und europäische Rechtskultur', (1994) 2 *Zeitschrift für Europäisches Privatrecht* 1 ff.; and see Zimmermann (n. 205) sub V.

2

Remedies for Non-performance, Viewed against the Background of the Principles of European Contract Law

I. The Path to the New Rules

1. The old law, *Abschlußbericht* and 'Discussion Draft'

Before the revision of the German law of obligations it had been, for a long time, a standard complaint that the German rules concerning breach of contract were far too complex.[1] Moreover, they were taken to be deficient in several important respects. They were based on a classification of various types of breach, i.e. impossibility of performance, delay of performance, and defective performance, rather than structured according to the various remedies available. Central to the understanding of the system, so it was said, was a highly artificial concept of impossibility of pandectist vintage. Moreover, the BGB was thought to be characterized by an axiomatic adherence to the outdated fault principle. One of its core provisions, § 275 BGB (old version), was widely held to be misconceived in so far as the release of the debtor from his obligation to perform in cases of impossibility was confined to the situation where he had not been responsible for his inability to perform. The BGB's insistence on the strict mutual exclusivity of termination of the contract and a claim for damages was regarded as untenable; it was based on outdated conceptual logic. The rule in § 306 BGB, in terms of which a contract the performance of which is impossible was held to be void, was generally criticized as being both conceptually and practically unsound. And, above all, the usually so well-designed BGB was very widely considered to have contained two gaps

---

[1] See, for example, Konrad Zweigert and Hein Kötz, *An Introduction to Comparative Law* (transl. Tony Weir), 3rd edn. (1998), 486 ff.; Reinhard Zimmermann, *The Law of Obligations: Roman Foundations of the Civilian Tradition*, paperback edition (1996), 783, 806 ff.; Basil S. Markesinis, Werner Lorenz and Gerhard Dannemann, *The German Law of Obligations, vol. I: The Law of Contracts and Restitution: A Comparative Introduction* (1997), 398 ff.

which were as central as they were surprising: the code did not deal with the situation where performance was not generally, or objectively, impossible but where it was impossible specifically for the debtor; and it did not contain rules for what already came to be termed—two years after the enactment of the BGB—'positive breach of contract' (*positive Vertragsverletzung*):[2] for situations, *inter alia*, where the creditor had suffered consequential loss as a result of the debtor's deficient performance.

That much of this criticism was fallacious, and that the provisions of the BGB had in fact been based on a well thought-out and logical masterplan—albeit one that had been misunderstood for nearly a century—only became dramatically apparent with the publication of Ulrich Huber's monograph on the German law of breach of contract:[3] a historico-doctrinal study that would probably have had an enormous impact if the reform process had not been catapulted into its decisive round in the very year following the publication of the work. Ironically, the mastermind behind the reform draft, as it had originally been conceived, had also been Ulrich Huber.[4] The study of pandectist literature and of the *travaux préparatoires* of the BGB had, in the meantime, completely transformed his views. As a result, Huber now became one of the fiercest critics of the new system.[5]

That system had been largely inspired by the rules contained in the Convention on the International Sale of Goods (CISG) and its predecessor, the Convention relating to a Uniform Law on the International Sale of Goods of 17 July 1973. Characteristic elements, therefore, of the draft produced by the Commission charged with the revision of the law of obligations, were a system of rules structured primarily under the auspices of the legal remedies available (i.e., in particular, specific performance, damages, termination), a uniform concept of breach of duty (*Pflichtverletzung*) and a shift away from the fault requirement concerning termination of contract.[6] The concept of impossibility that had caused so much doctrinal headache was extirpated. On the other hand, the Commission decided to stick to the fault principle concerning claims for damages while, in terms of CISG, the debtor's liability is excluded

---

[2] See the discussion and the references in Reinhard Zimmermann, *Roman Law, Contemporary Law, European Law* (2001), 92 ff.   [3] Ulrich Huber, *Leistungsstörungen*, 2 vols. (1999).

[4] Ulrich Huber, 'Empfiehlt sich die Einführung eines Leistungsstörungsrechts nach dem Vorbild des Einheitlichen Kaufgesetzes? Welche Änderungen im Gesetzestext und welche praktischen Auswirkungen im Schuldrecht würden sich dabei ergeben?', in Bundesminister der Justiz (ed.), *Gutachten und Vorschläge zur Überarbeitung des Schuldrechts I* (1981), 647 ff.

[5] Ulrich Huber, 'Das geplante Recht der Leistungsstörungen', in Wolfgang Ernst and Reinhard Zimmermann (eds.), *Zivilrechtswissenschaft und Schuldrechtsreform* (2001), 31 ff.

[6] Cf., for example, Rolf Stürner, 'Einige Bemerkungen zum Stand der Schuldrechtsreform', in *Festschrift für Hans Erich Brandner* (1996), 635 ff. On the Reform Commission, and the reform process in general, see *supra* p. 32.

only when the breach is based on an impediment which lies outside the sphere of influence of the debtor and which is not foreseeable by him;[7] moreover, the draft of the Commission required the granting of an additional period of time (*Nachfrist*) before termination of a contract (though exceptions to this requirement were accepted in certain cases of serious breach) whereas, in terms of CISG, termination may be declared immediately in cases of fundamental breach (although a breach of contract can also be made fundamental by the fixing of a *Nachfrist*).[8] In his comparative analysis of both sets of rules, Peter Schlechtriem has, however, come to the conclusion that in both respects the practical differences would not have been very considerable.[9]

2. From the 'Discussion Draft' to the new law

The Discussion Draft of autumn 2001 very largely adopted the Commission's proposals of 1992, as far as the law of breach of contract was concerned. The explanations appended to the Draft were also taken over, often verbatim, from the 1992 proposals. It thus became immediately apparent that the Discussion Draft had missed out on more than ten years of scholarly debate. Neither did it take account of the Dutch *Burgerlijk Wetboek* which had entered into force in 1992, nor of the Principles of European Contract Law by the Lando Commission or UNIDROIT's Principles of International Commercial Contracts which had been published in 1995 and 1994 respectively.[10] This was particularly deplorable in view of the fact that with the reform envisaged by her, the Minister of Justice intended to advance the Europeanization of German law and, at the same time, to promote the BGB as a model for the unification of private law in Europe.

Both sets of international Principles started to be referred to in the ensuing debates about the Discussion Draft.[11] None the less these debates now veered towards a retention of rules and thinking patterns established under the old law, as far as they appeared to have stood the test of time. The rules and concepts used in the Discussion Draft (and in the international Principles) were criticized as being too abstract and too general; a code, it was now argued, should aspire to a significantly higher level of specificity, in order to be workable

---

[7] Art. 79 CISG.   [8] Art. 49 CISG.

[9] Peter Schlechtriem, 'Rechtsvereinheitlichung in Europa und Schuldrechtsreform in Deutschland', (1993) 1 *Zeitschrift für Europäisches Privatrecht* 217 ff., 228 ff., 234 ff.

[10] Ole Lando and Hugh Beale (eds.), *Principles of European Contract Law, Part I* (1995); UNIDROIT (ed.), *Principles of International Commercial Contracts* (1994).

[11] See, concerning breach of contract, particularly the contributions by Huber (n. 5) 31 ff., and Claus-Wilhelm Canaris, 'Die Reform des Rechts der Leistungsstörungen', [2001] *Juristenzeitung* 499 ff.

and to provide the necessary degree of legal certainty. Thus, in particular, the specific types of breach of contract re-entered the scene—albeit under the general umbrella concept of breach of duty.[12] Ulrich Huber and Claus-Wilhelm Canaris emerged as the most prominent critics of the Discussion Draft: the former hammering it with uncompromising severity,[13] the latter adopting an approach more moderate in tone and substance.[14]

The Minister of Justice then decided to appoint a working group charged with a revision of the provisions concerning breach of contract contained in the Discussion Draft.[15] The recommendations made by that working group were subsequently accepted, apparently without exception, and thus decisively shaped the Government Draft of 9 May as well as the Modernization of the Law of Obligations Act based on it. Professor Canaris, the most influential member of the working group, had presented these recommendations to a special meeting of the German Association of Teachers of Private Law at the end of March 2001 in Berlin;[16] his analysis can largely be taken to constitute the *interpretatio authentica* of the new German law of breach of contract.[17] The discussion that follows will have to confine itself to the structural foundations of the new rules.[18] Many details will have to be passed over. On the other hand,

---

[12] In particular, there has been what Barbara Dauner-Lieb has dubbed a 'renaissance' of the concept of impossiblity ('Das Schuldrechtsmodernisierungsgesetz in Wissenschaft und Praxis— Versuch einer Bestandsaufnahme', in Barbara Dauner-Lieb, Horst Konzen and Karsten Schmidt (eds.), *Das neue Schuldrecht in der Praxis* (2003), 15 ff.) which the reformers had originally set out to dethrone. According to Ingeborg Schwenzer, 'Rechtsbehelfe und Rückabwicklungsmodelle im CISG, in den European and UNIDROIT Principles, im Gandolfi-Entwurf und im deutschen Schuldrechtsmodernisierungsgesetz', in Peter Schlechtriem (ed.), *Wandlungen des Schuldrechts* (2002), 39, the opportunity of raising German law to an internationally acceptable level has thus been wasted. Equally critical is Peter Schlechtriem, 'Internationales Einheitliches Kaufrecht und neues Schuldrecht', in Dauner-Lieb, Konzen and Schmidt (as above) 73, who refers to a 'self-referential legal doctrine' having become law.   [13] Huber (n. 5) 31 ff.

[14] Claus-Wilhelm Canaris, 'Zur Bedeutung der Kategorie der "Unmöglichkeit" für das Recht der Leistungsstörungen', in Reiner Schulze and Hans Schulte-Nölke (eds.), *Die Schuldrechtsreform vor dem Hintergrund des Gemeinschaftsrechts* (2001), 43 ff.   [15] *Supra* p. 34.

[16] Claus-Wilhelm Canaris, 'Die Reform des Rechts der Leistungsstörungen', [2001] *Juristenzeitung* 499 ff.

[17] Cf. also Claus-Wilhelm Canaris, 'Das allgemeine Leistungsstörungsrecht im Schuldrechts-modernisierungsgesetz', [2001] *Zeitschrift für Rechtspolitik* 329 ff.; *idem*, 'Einführung', in Claus-Wilhelm Canaris (ed.), *Schuldrechtsmodernisierung 2002* (2002), IX ff.

[18] For a general discussion cf. also Daniel Zimmer, 'Das neue Recht der Leistungsstörungen', [2002] *Neue Juristische Wochenschrift* 1 ff.; Hansjörg Otto, 'Die Grundstrukturen des neuen Leistungsstörungsrechts', [2002] *Jura* 1 ff.; Roland Schwarze, 'Unmöglichkeit, Unvermögen und ähnliche Leistungshindernisse im neuen Leistungsstörungsrecht', [2002] *Jura* 73 ff.; Sonja Meier, 'Neues Leistungsstörungsrecht', [2002] *Jura* 118 ff., 187 ff.; Canaris, 'Einführung' (n. 17) IX ff.; Barbara Dauner-Lieb, 'Das Leistungsstörungsrecht im Überblick', in Barbara Dauner-Lieb, Thomas Heidel, Manfred Lepa and Gerhard Ring (eds.), *Das neue Schuldrecht* (2002), 64 ff.; Stephan Lorenz and Thomas Riehm, *Lehrbuch zum neuen Schuldrecht* (2002), 83 ff.; Peter Huber and Florian Faust, *Schuldrechtsmodernisierung* (2002), 7 ff.; Claus-Wilhelm Canaris, 'Die Neuregelung des

however, an attempt will be made to look at the development of German law from the vantage point of the broader European debate that has led to the formulation of the Principles of European Contract Law.[19]

II. Specific Performance and Exclusion of the Right to Specific Performance

1. Impossibility of performance

The general starting point in German law remains what it has been throughout the twentieth century: the parties to a contract, as a matter of course, are entitled to demand performance of their respective obligations *in specie*. 'The effect of an obligation', says § 241 I at the outset of Book II of the BGB, 'is that the creditor is entitled to claim performance from the debtor.'[20] The implication is: specific performance. Article 9:102 PECL proceeds from the same principle.[21]

The most important exception is laid down in § 275 I BGB: a claim for specific performance is excluded, as far as such performance is impossible. This rule has a very long tradition; it ultimately derives from the Roman principle of

Leistungsstörungs- und des Kaufrechts: Grundstrukturen und Problemschwerpunkte', in Egon Lorenz (ed.), *Karlsruher Forum 2002: Schuldrechtsmodernisierung* (2003), 54 ff.; Dieter Medicus, 'Die Leistungsstörungen im neuen Schuldrecht', [2003] *Juristische Schulung* 521 ff. The first commentary, rule by rule, was Barbara Dauner-Lieb, Thomas Heidel, Manfred Lepa and Gerhard Ring (eds.), *Anwaltkommentar Schuldrecht* (2002); in the meantime many of the standard commentaries on the BGB have appeared in post-reform editions; the most comprehensive of these are Wolfgang Ernst, in *Münchener Kommentar zum Bürgerlichen Gesetzbuch*, 4th edn., vol. IIa (2003) and Hansjörg Otto, in *J. von Staudingers Kommentar zum Bürgerlichen Gesetzbuch*, revised edition (2004).

[19] The rules on non-performance and remedies for non-performance, published first in 1995, are now part of Ole Lando and Hugh Beale (eds.), *Principles of European Contract Law, Parts I and II* (2000). Translations into several other languages have appeared or are about to appear. The UNIDROIT Principles of International Commercial Contracts, 1994, are in broad agreement; discrepancies between both sets of Principles will be noted in the footnotes. Whenever the term 'Principles' is used in the following text, it refers to the Principles of European Contract Law (PECL). The UNIDROIT Principles will be abbreviated as PICC. For a most useful and perceptive comparison between both sets of Principles and the old German rules on non-performance, see Huber (n. 5) 116 ff. That comparison also includes CISG. For a comparison specifically of CISG with the new rules of German law, see Schlechtriem (n. 12) 71 ff.

[20] For historical background, see *Law of Obligations* (n. 1) 770 ff.; Karin Nehlsen-von Stryk, 'Grenzen des Rechtszwangs: Zur Geschichte der Naturalvollstreckung', (1993) 193 *Archiv für die civilistische Praxis* 529 ff.; Wolfgang Rütten, 'Die Entstehung des Erfüllungszwangs im Schuldverhältnis', in *Festschrift für Joachim Gernhuber* (1993), 939 ff.; Tilman Repgen, *Vertragstreue und Erfüllungszwang in der mittelalterlichen Rechtswissenschaft* (1994).

[21] Cf. also Art. 7.2.2 PICC. But see the important qualification of the principle in Art. 9:102 (2)(d) PECL (Art. 7.2.2 (c) PICC): Specific performance cannot be demanded where the aggrieved party may reasonably obtain performance from another source. For comparative observations, see Schwenzer (n. 12) 39 ff.

impossibilium nulla est obligatio and corresponds to the basic principle of moral philosophy, that 'ought implies can'.

§ 275 I BGB, as its wording makes clear, applies to all types of impossibility: objective impossibility (nobody can perform), subjective impossibility (a specific debtor cannot perform),[22] initial impossibility (performance was already impossible when the contract had been concluded), subsequent impossibility (performance has become impossible after conclusion of the contract), partial impossibility, and total impossibility.[23] Exclusion of the right to specific performance does not depend on whether the debtor was responsible for the impossibility or not. The new provision significantly differs from its predecessor in that it places initial and subsequent impossibility on a par; and in that it drops the fault requirement (which had been contained in § 275 I (old version) but which, according to the prevailing opinion under the old law, had to be treated as *pro non scripto*, as far as the right to demand performance was concerned).[24] The Principles also do not, of course, attempt to force a debtor to perform what he is unable to perform. This follows, as far as 'impediments' arising after the conclusion of the contract are concerned,[25] from Article 8:101 (3) read in conjunction with Article 8:108 PECL:[26] where a party's non-performance is excused because it was due to an impediment that was beyond his control and that he could not reasonably have been expected to take into account, or to have avoided or overcome, the creditor may not claim performance. For all

---

[22] Details as to what constitutes 'subjective impossibility' (is performance subjectively impossible wherever the debtor cannot dispose over the object, e.g., because he is not its owner, or only if he cannot reasonably be expected to overcome the impediment, for example by acquiring the object from its owner?) have been disputed under the old law (Huber (n. 3) vol. II, § 60; for a clear summary of the discussion, see Meier, [2002] *Jura* 128 ff.). These details are likely also to be disputed under the new law; cf. *infra* pp. 47 f.

[23] Concerning temporary impossibility, see Arnd Arnold, 'Die vorübergehende Unmöglichkeit nach der Schuldrechtsreform', [2002] *Juristenzeitung* 866 ff.; *Münchener Kommentar*/Ernst (n. 18) § 275, nn. 132 ff.; Manfred Löwisch, in *J. von Staudingers Kommentar zum Bürgerlichen Gesetzbuch*, revised edition (2004), § 275, nn. 42 ff.; Thomas Lobinger, *Die Grenzen rechtsgeschäftlicher Leistungspflichten* (2004), 304 ff.; Wolfgang Däubler, 'Die vorübergehende Unmöglichkeit der Leistung', in *Festschrift für Andreas Heldrich* (2005), 55 ff.; Dieter Medicus, 'Bemerkungen zur vorübergehenden Unmöglichkeit', in *Festschrift für Andreas Heldrich* (2005), 347 ff.

[24] Cf., for example, Helmut Heinrichs, in *Palandt, Bürgerliches Gesetzbuch*, 61st edn. (2002), § 275, n. 24; Manfred Löwisch, in *J. von Staudingers Kommentar zum Bürgerlichen Gesetzbuch*, revised edition (2001), § 275, n. 58. But see the discussion in Huber (n. 3) vol. II, § 58; Christian Knütel, [2001] *Juristische Rundschau* 353 ff.; Hans Stoll, 'Überlegungen zu Grundfragen des Rechts der Leistungsstörungen aus der Sicht des Schuldrechtsmodernisierungsgesetzes', in *Festschrift für Werner Lorenz* (2001), 288 ff.

[25] On the genesis of the notion of an 'impediment' (first used in Art. 79 CISG) and on its interpretation, see Huber (n. 5) 119 ff.; Nicole N. Fischer, *Die Unmöglichkeit der Leistung im internationalen Kauf- und Vertragsrecht* (2001), 55 ff. That Art. 8:108 PECL only deals with impediments arising after conclusion of the contract is stated in the comments: cf. Lando and Beale (n. 19) 379.

[26] Cf. also Art. 7.1.7 PICC.

other cases, i.e. where the remedy of specific performance is not excluded
a limine, Article 9:102 PECL contains the rider that specific performance cannot
be obtained where performance would be impossible.[27]

2. 'Practical Impossibility' and 'Economic Impossibility'

After the revision, therefore, the BGB provides a more streamlined regime, as
far as the exclusion of the right to specific performance is concerned. On the
other hand, however, it now draws a distinction between cases of impossibility
stricto sensu and situations where it would be unreasonable to expect the debtor
to render performance. According to § 275 II BGB the debtor may refuse to
perform insofar as such performance would require an effort which would be
grossly disproportionate to the interest of the creditor in receiving performance, taking into account the content of the obligation and the requirements of
good faith. In determining what can reasonably be required of the debtor,
regard must be had as to whether he was responsible for the impediment or not.

This provision is designed to take account of what was termed, under the old
law, 'practical impossibility' (*faktische Unmöglichkeit*) as opposed to 'economic
impossibility' (*wirtschaftliche Unmöglichkeit*);[28] this is why the effort required
to perform is measured against the interest of the creditor in receiving performance.[29] The paradigmatic example is the ring (worth €100) that has been
dropped into a lake after it has been sold but before it has been transferred to
the purchaser. The cost of draining the lake and recovering the ring would
amount to €100,000. It would obviously be unreasonable to expect the
debtor to incur such vast expenses in view of the fact that the creditor's interest
in the ring is still only €100, i.e. the value of the object.[30] Matters are different

---

[27] Cf. also Art. 7.2.2 (a) PICC. For comparative observations concerning the new § 275 BGB, cf. also *Münchener Kommentar*/Ernst (n. 18) § 275, n. 3.

[28] See, for the old law, *Staudinger*/Löwisch (n. 24) § 275, n. 9 as opposed to n. 10; *Palandt*/Heinrichs (n. 24) § 275, n. 8 as opposed to n. 12; Huber (n. 3) vol. I, § 4 III 4.

[29] Canaris, [2001] *Juristenzeitung* 501 ff.; *idem*, in *Karlsruher Forum* (n. 18) 12 ff.

[30] For details of the application of § 275 II BGB, see Canaris, [2001] *Juristenzeitung* 501 ff.; Meier, [2002] *Jura* 120 ff.; Faust, in Huber and Faust (n. 18) 31 ff.; Lorenz and Riehm (n. 18) 151 ff.; Canaris, in *Karlsruher Forum* (n. 18) 11 ff.; Ulrich Huber, 'Die Schadensersatzhaftung des Verkäufers wegen Nichterfüllung der Nacherfüllungspflicht und die Haftungsbegrenzung des § 275 Abs. 2 BGB neuer Fassung', in *Festschrift für Peter Schlechtriem* (2003), 521 ff.; *Münchener Kommentar*/Ernst (n. 18), § 275, nn. 25 ff., 69 ff., 101 ff. (emphasizing differences in evaluation depending on whether the debtor has been responsible for the impediment or not); Claus-Wilhelm Canaris, 'Die Behandlung nicht zu vertre-tender Leistungshindernisse nach § 275 Abs. 2 BGB beim Stückkauf', [2004] *Juristenzeitung* 214 ff.; *Staudinger*/Otto (n. 18) § 275, nn. 70 ff.; for a critical evaluation, see *Anwaltkommentar*/Dauner-Lieb *et al.* (n. 18) § 275, nn. 7 ff.; Ingo Koller, 'Recht der Leistungsstörungen', in Ingo Koller, Herbert Roth and Reinhard Zimmermann, *Schuldrechtsmodernisierungsgesetz* (2002) 50 ff.; Hans Stoll, 'Notizen zur Neuordnung des Rechts der Leistungsstörungen', [2001] *Juristenzeitung* 591 ff.; Jan Wilhelm, 'Schuldrechtsreform 2001', [2001] *Juristenzeitung* 866 ff. (a 'monstrosity'); Zimmer, [2002] *Neue*

in cases of economic impossibility. If the price of 1,000 barrels of oil that have been sold increases dramatically, the debtor cannot invoke § 275 I, for while it may also be unreasonable in this case to expect the debtor to perform under the changed circumstances, we do not have a gross disproportion between the debtor's effort and the creditor's interest in receiving performance: the latter has not, as in the previous example, remained at the earlier lower level, but has risen to the same extent as the debtor's effort; the object of the sale has become more valuable and the purchaser would, of course, fully benefit from that higher value. The law may still grant some relief to the debtor in this situation. But whether it does so depends on the applicability of the rules on change of circumstances (*Störung der Geschäftsgrundlage*) which is regarded as a conceptually different problem.[31] The rules on change of circumstances had, prior to the reform, been worked out and generally recognized under the auspices of the general good faith rule of § 242 BGB[32] and they had thus constituted one of the most famous examples of a judge-made legal doctrine; they have now found their statutory home in § 313 BGB.[33]

§ 275 II BGB is based on considerations which also find their expression in the Principles; according to Article 9:102 (2)(b) PECL specific performance cannot be obtained where performance would cause the debtor unreasonable effort or expense;[34] and illustration 3 in the comments to Article 9:102 PECL

Juristische Wochenschrift 3 ff.; Otto, [2002] *Jura* 3; Schwarze, [2002] *Jura* 76 ff.; Eduard Picker, 'Schuldrechtsreform und Privatautonomie', [2003] *Juristenzeitung* 1035 ff. ('entirely misconceived'); Lobinger (n. 23) 158 ff., 214 ff., 256 ff.

[31] Canaris, [2001] *Juristenzeitung* 501; Faust, in Huber and Faust (n. 18) 55; Lorenz and Riehm (n. 18) 152; Canaris, in *Karlsruher Forum* (n. 18) 13 ff.; *Münchener Kommentar*/Ernst (n. 18) § 275, nn. 19 ff., 74 ff. The distinction between these two situations, and whether it is sufficiently clearly indicated in the provision of § 275 II BGB, is questioned by *Anwaltkommentar*/Dauner-Lieb *et al.* (n. 18) § 275, n. 14; Wilhelm, [2001] *Juristenzeitung* 866 ff.; Otto, [2002] *Jura* 3; Schwarze, [2002] *Jura* 76 ff.

[32] See Reinhard Zimmermann and Simon Whittaker (eds.), *Good Faith in European Contract Law* (2000), 25 ff., 557 ff. with further references; on the origin of this doctrine, see Zimmermann (n. 2) 80 ff. Most recently, see Bernd Nauen, *Leistungserschwerung und Zweckvereitelung im Schuldverhältnis* (2001) and Christian Reiter, *Vertrag und Geschäftsgrundlage im deutschen und italienischen Recht* (2002).

[33] The German term *Störung der Geschäftsgrundlage* indicates as much as collapse of the basis of the contract. As under the old law, the basis of the contract is seen to consist of those circumstances (i) which the parties have presupposed at the time of conclusion of their contract, (ii) which are so important to one of them that he would not have concluded the contract, or would have concluded it differently, had he known that those circumstances have now materially changed, and (iii) which are of such a nature that that party can now no longer reasonably be expected to comply with the contract. For further discussion, see Bundesminister der Justiz (ed.), *Abschlußbericht der Kommission zur Überarbeitung des Schuldrechts* (1992), 146 ff.; Huber, in Huber and Faust (n. 18) 231 ff.; Lorenz and Riehm (n. 18) 197 ff.; *Anwaltkommentar*/Krebs (n. 18) § 313, nn. 1 ff.; Günter H. Roth, in *Münchener Kommentar zum Bürgerlichen Gesetzbuch*, 4th edn., vol. IIa (2003), § 313; Astrid Stadler, in Othmar Jauernig (ed.), *Bürgerliches Gesetzbuch*, 11th edn. (2004), § 313; Helmut Heinrichs, 'Vertragsanpassung bei Störung der Geschäftsgrundlage—Eine Skizze der Anspruchslösung des § 313 BGB', in *Festschrift für Andreas Heldrich* (2005), 183 ff.   [34] Cf. also Art. 7.2.2 (b) PICC.

demonstrates that the rule is designed to cover the same type of case.[35] As in German law, the problem of change of circumstances is dealt with at a different place and in another systematic context.[36]

3. The problem of 'subjective impossibility'

Under the old law, the rules relating to impossibility were applied to cases of 'practical' impossibility; in other words, no distinction was drawn between situations where performance was factually impossible and where it was merely practically impossible. The new § 275 II does, however, necessitate such distinction—not simply in view of the fact that it contains a special rule concerning practical impossibility, but because that rule provides for a different legal consequence from the one concerning factual impossibility: the debtor's obligation does not automatically fall away, but the debtor is merely granted a right to refuse performance. The law thus wants to leave it open to the debtor to render performance in spite of the unreasonable effort which this may involve.[37]

None the less, this is not a happy solution.[38] For, on the one hand, it places the creditor in an awkward position in cases where the debtor does not perform but does not raise the defence either.[39] On the other hand, the line between the different types of situations may be difficult to draw.[40] This is apparent, particularly in cases of a merely subjective impossibility. Though they are covered by the wording of § 275 I BGB ('. . . as far as performance is impossible *for the debtor*'), they do not usually constitute cases of a factual impossibility. If a person (A) first sells a painting to X and subsequently sells and transfers it to Y,

---

[35] Lando and Beale (n. 19) 396. Canaris, however, draws attention to the fact that the rule contained in the Principles is much less specific than § 275 II BGB: [2001] *Juristenzeitung* 505; *idem*, in *Karlsruher Forum* (n. 18) 16 ff.; while the existence of Art. 9:102 (2) demonstrates the need for a rule of this type, it constitutes, in every other respect, 'a negative example'.

[36] Art. 6:111 PECL; cf. also Arts. 6.2.1 ff. PICC. For an evaluation, from the point of view of German law, see Schlechtriem, (1993) 1 *Zeitschrift für Europäisches Privatrecht* 243 ff.; Reinhard Zimmermann, 'Konturen eines Europäischen Vertragsrechts', [1995] *Juristenzeitung* 486 ff.; Wolfgang Ernst, 'Die Verpflichtung zur Leistung in den Principles of European Contract Law und in den Principles of International Commercial Contracts', in Jürgen Basedow (ed.), *Europäische Vertragsrechtsvereinheitlichung und deutsches Recht* (2000), 147 ff.; Gundula Maria Peer, 'Die Rechtsfolgen von Störungen der Geschäftsgrundlage', in *Jahrbuch Junger Zivilrechtswissenschaftler: Das neue Schuldrecht* (2001), 61 ff.; Fischer (n. 25), 215 ff.; cf. also Huber (n. 4) 123 ff. and Schwenzer (n. 12) 48 ff. (who draw attention to an important point of difference between Art. 6:111 PECL and Art. 6.2.2 PICC).

[37] Canaris, [2001] *Juristenzeitung* 504; cf. also the example provided by Meier, [2002] *Jura* 121.

[38] This is also criticized by Canaris, [2001] *Juristenzeitung* 504. For an account of the legislative history, see *Anwaltkommentar*/Dauner-Lieb *et al.* (n. 18) § 275, nn. 3 ff.

[39] Faust, in Huber and Faust (n. 18) 24; *Münchener Kommentar*/Ernst (n. 18), § 275, n. 100.

[40] Koller (n. 30) 50 ff.

he may well be able to acquire the painting back from Y and will then be in a position to honour his contractual obligation towards X. Whether this may be expected of him is to be determined by applying the requirements of § 275 II BGB. Thus, A may refuse to perform if the painting is worth €10,000 and Y is only prepared to return it at a price of €100,000. Unless the general borderline between § 275 I and II BGB is to be subverted, and unless the debtor is to be denied the benefit of being able to choose whether or not to render performance, this type of case cannot normally be brought under § 275 I BGB.[41] The draftsmen of the new law thus intended § 275 I to apply only where Y is not prepared to return the painting, or where it has been stolen and where neither the thief nor the painting can be found.[42]

Even here, however, it is arguable that performance is not factually impossible and that through an enormous investment of money A might still be able to recover the painting.[43] If, on the other hand, one *does* apply the parameters fixed by § 275 II BGB to cases of subjective impossibility, this may sometimes lead to unsatisfactory results.[44] A dies after he has sold his painting to X for €50,000. A's heir (B), being unaware of the transaction, sells and transfers the painting to Y for €70,000. Y is prepared to return the painting to B for a price of €75,000. If we assume that X, in the meantime, has been able to re-sell the painting for €80,000, B would not have a right to refuse performance under § 275 II, as his expenses (€75,000) could not be said to be grossly disproportionate to the interest of the creditor in receiving performance (€80,000). As a result, B loses €5,000 on account of an impediment for which he was not responsible and which he can, therefore, hardly be expected to overcome. This demonstrates the dangers inherent in any attempt to draw up general rules for exceptional situations.

4. 'Moral impossibility'

There is another situation where German law grants the debtor a right to refuse performance: he has to perform in person, but it would be unreasonable to expect him to perform considering, on the one hand, the impediment that has arisen and, on the other hand, the creditor's interest in receiving performance:

---

[41] See the discussion by Meier, [2002] *Jura* 128 ff.; Zimmer, [2002] *Neue Juristische Wochenschrift* 2 ff.; Faust, in Huber and Faust (n. 18) 25 ff.; *Anwaltkommentar*/Dauner-Lieb *et al.* (n. 18) § 275, nn. 12, 17; Canaris, in *Karlsruher Forum* (n. 18) 17 ff.; *Münchener Kommentar*/Ernst (n. 18) § 275, nn. 52 ff.; *Staudinger*/Otto (n. 18) § 275, nn. 55 ff.

[42] See 'Begründung der Bundesregierung zum Entwurf eines Gesetzes zur Modernisierung des Schuldrechts', in Claus-Wilhelm Canaris (ed.), *Schuldrechtsmodernisierung 2002* (2002), 658.

[43] This is pointed out by Meier, [2002] *Jura* 130.

[44] The following example is taken from Meier, [2002] *Jura* 128, 130.

§ 275 III BGB. This is the case of the soprano who refuses to sing after she has learnt that her son has contracted a disease which threatens his life.[45] Under the old law, this was regarded as a case of 'moral' impossibility to which the rules concerning change of circumstances were applied.[46] The Principles exclude altogether a right to specific performance where the performance consists in the provision of services or work of a personal character;[47] the problem, therefore, does not arise.

The relationship between the new § 275 II and III BGB is not quite clear.[48] Contrary to § 275 II BGB, it does not appear to be a relevant factor, in determining what can reasonably be expected of the debtor, whether she has been responsible for the impediment or not: the soprano may refuse to perform even if she herself has negligently caused her child's disease.[49] Moreover, the creditor's interest in her performance is only one consideration in determining the issue of unreasonableness on the basis of a general balancing of interests; it is not, as under § 275 II BGB, the decisive criterion for establishing whether what the debtor would have to do in order to render performance is excessive and thus unreasonable. § 275 III, in other words, remains a specific manifestation of the general rules concerning change of circumstances, and the inclusion of this rule in § 275 III, in a way, undermines the subtle line the law has drawn in § 275 II between impossibility and change of circumstances.[50]

III. Damages

1. Conceptual foundations

§ 275 BGB only concerns the right to receive specific performance. If the debtor becomes free under § 275 I or is granted a right to refuse to perform

---

[45] 'Begründung' (n. 42) 662; Canaris, [2001] *Zeitschrift für Rechtspolitik* 330; Meier, [2002] *Jura* 121; *Anwaltkommentar*/Dauner-Lieb *et al.* (n. 18) § 275, n. 19; *Münchener Kommentar*/Ernst (n. 18) § 275, nn. 107 ff.; *Staudinger*/Otto (n. 18) § 275, nn. 89 ff.

[46] For a discussion of these cases under the old law, see Volker Emmerich, in *Münchener Kommentar zum Bürgerlichen Gesetzbuch*, vol. II, 4th edn. (2001), § 275, n. 32; Jürgen Schmidt, in *J. von Staudingers Kommentar zum Bürgerlichen Gesetzbuch*, 13th edn. (1995), § 242, nn. 1196 ff.; cf. also Huber (n. 4) 73.   [47] Art. 9:102 (2) (c) PECL; cf. also Art. 7.2.2 PICC.

[48] See, in particular, Faust, in Huber and Faust (n. 18) 56 ff.

[49] *Contra*: *Anwaltkommentar*/Dauner-Lieb *et al.* (n. 18) § 275, n. 20, who argues that the fault requirement was inadvertently dropped when § 275 III BGB became a separate subsection; previously the rule had been included as a second sentence in § 275 II and what is now the second sentence had then been the third sentence; see 'Zusammenstellung des Entwurfs eines Gesetzes zur Modernisierung des Schuldrechts mit den Beschlüssen des Rechtsausschusses', in Canaris (n. 42) 441.

[50] Cf. also the criticism offered by *Anwaltkommentar*/Dauner-Lieb *et al.* (n. 18) § 275, nn. 8, 19; *Münchener Kommentar*/Ernst (n. 18) § 275, nn. 111; Lobinger (n. 23) 65 ff., 173 ff. It also, incidentally,

under § 275 II, III, this does not mean that he may not be exposed to a 'secondary' obligation.[51] The most important secondary obligation is a claim for damages. The BGB now has a core provision concerning damages for non-performance, and that is § 280 I: if the debtor fails to comply with a duty arising under the contract, the creditor is entitled to claim compensation for the loss caused by such breach of his duty. This does not apply if the debtor is not responsible for the breach of duty. Two differences from the Principles are immediately apparent.

(i) The claim for damages, under the BGB, is still based on the notion of fault. The Principles, on the other hand, exclude a claim for damages only in cases where the debtor's non-performance is due to an impediment that is beyond his control and that he could not reasonably have been expected to take into account at the time of the conclusion of the contract, or to have avoided or overcome.[52] The differences between these two regimes may be more apparent than real in practice.[53] For fault is not, strictly speaking, a requirement for the claim; it is the debtor who has to prove that he was not responsible for the breach of duty. This reversal of the burden of proof follows from the negative formulation of § 280 I 2 BGB ('This does not apply, if . . .').[54] Moreover, even under German law, the debtor is not only responsible for fault. This comes out more clearly under the new § 276 than under its predecessor. For while § 276 I 1 BGB (old version) merely stated that the debtor is responsible for fault either in the form of intention or negligence, unless something else is specifically provided, the new rule explicitly affirms that a stricter type of liability may be inferred from the content of an obligation, particularly from the assumption

---

remains unclear what the position is if the debtor does not have to perform in person and the other requirements of § 275 III BGB are met. Presumably, this may be a case of change of circumstances (§ 313 BGB).

[51] For a specific statement to this effect, see § 275 IV BGB.

[52] Arts. 9:501 (1), 8:108 PECL; cf. also Arts. 7.4.1, 7.1.7 PICC. The question whether a claim for specific performance is excluded and whether or not damages may be claimed thus has to be answered according to the same criteria; cf. *supra* p. 44. This is also, as Ulrich Huber has demonstrated, what the draftsmen of the BGB (in its original form) intended to lay down, and it provides the explanation for the way in which § 275 BGB old version was drafted: see Huber (n. 3) vol. II, § 58.

[53] See Schlechtriem, (1993) 1 *Zeitschrift für Europäisches Privatrecht* 228 ff.; Schwenzer (n. 12) 49 ff. The German, fault-based approach is defended by Dieter Medicus, 'Voraussetzungen einer Haftung für Vertragsverletzung', in Basedow (n. 36) 185 ff. Medicus, *inter alia*, discusses the case of a debtor who is prevented from performing his contractual obligation because he has fallen ill; under the Principles, according to Medicus, the debtor would be liable for damages in terms of Art. 9:501 PECL. Contrary to Medicus, however, I think that the illness has to be regarded as an 'impediment beyond [the debtor's] control' and that, therefore, Art. 8:108 (1) would apply; cf. also illustration 6 in the comment (Lando and Beale (n. 19) 382).

[54] But see, for employment relationships, § 619 a BGB (a last-minute amendment to the proposed reform; cf. *Anwaltkommentar*/Dauner-Lieb *et al.* (n. 18) § 619 a, n. 1).

of a guarantee (this is supposed to cover, for example, the promise of a quality in the object sold)[55] or from the assumption of the risk to be able to procure the object in question (this is the case, particularly but not exclusively, if the debtor owes an object described by class).[56] The reform of § 276 BGB was intended primarily to clarify the law.[57] None the less, the way in which the new rule is drafted leaves much leeway for a flexible adjustment of the standard of liability.[58]

(ii) The conceptual cornerstone for a claim for damages is termed 'breach of duty' (*Pflichtverletzung*) in German law, 'non-performance' under the Principles.[59] The main reason for rejecting the term 'non-performance' was that cases of a deficient performance or the infringement of ancillary duties in the course of rendering performance can only awkwardly be accommodated under it.[60] On the other hand, however, the German term *Pflichtverletzung* has a distinctive flavour associating it with the notion of fault—which is inappropriate in view of the fact that fault is an additional element of liability which may or may not be present. An employee who is suffering from pneumonia does not have to go to work. He does not perform his contractual obligation *vis-à-vis* his employer but he can hardly, without some awkwardness, be said to be in breach of a duty in terms of the law of breach of contract.[61]

[55] Faust, in Huber and Faust (n. 18) 75 ff.; Lorenz and Riehm (n. 18) 92 ff.; *Anwaltkommentar/* Dauner-Lieb *et al.* (n. 18) § 276, n. 18; Stefan Grundmann, in *Münchener Kommentar zum Bürgerlichen Gesetzbuch*, 4th edn., vol. IIa (2003) § 276, nn. 173 ff.; Gregor Vollkommer, 'Haftungserweiterung durch Neufassung des § 276 BGB?', in Dauner-Lieb, Konzen and Schmidt (n. 12) 126 ff.; *Staudinger/*Löwisch (n. 23) § 276, nn. 143 ff.

[56] Canaris, [2001] *Juristenzeitung* 518 ff.; Faust, in Huber and Faust (n. 18) 76 ff.; Lorenz and Riehm (n. 18) 93; *Anwaltkommentar/*Dauner-Lieb *et al.* (n. 18) § 276, nn. 22 ff.; *Münchener Kommentar/* Grundmann (n. 55) § 276, nn. 177 ff.; Vollkommer (n. 55) 129 ff.; cf. also *Staudinger/*Löwisch (n. 23) § 276, nn. 148 ff.

[57] *Anwaltkommentar/*Dauner-Lieb *et al.* (n. 18) § 276, n. 3.

[58] The point is also emphasized by Schlechtriem, (1993) 1 *Zeitschrift für Europäisches Privatrecht*, 229; cf. also Faust, in Huber and Faust (n. 18) 74; Vollkommer (n. 55) 123 ff.

[59] This applies to chapters 8 and 9 of PECL as much as to chapter 7 of PICC. The term 'non-performance' is defined in Art. 1:301 (4) PECL as 'any failure to perform an obligation under the contract . . . and includes delayed performance, defective performance and failure to co-operate in order to give full effect to the contract'. Cf. also Art. 7.1.1 PICC.

[60] *Abschlußbericht* (n. 33) 130; 'Begründung' (n. 42) 668 ff.; Helmut Heinrichs, 'Die Pflichtverletzung, ein Zentralbegriff des neuen Leistungsstörungsrechts', in *Festschrift für Peter Schlechtriem* (2003), 515 ff.

[61] For criticism of the term *Pflichtverletzung*, see Huber (n. 3) vol. I, 2 ff.; *idem* (n. 4) 98 ff.; Canaris (n. 14) 59 ff.; Stoll (n. 24) 293 ff.; *idem*, [2001] *Juristenzeitung* 593; Canaris, in *Karlsruher Forum* (n. 18) 29 ff.; *Münchener Kommentar/*Ernst (n. 18) § 280, nn. 9 ff. (who argues that the new law cannot be understood to be based on a uniform concept of *Pflichtverletzung* which would be able to guide its application); *Staudinger/*Otto (n. 18) § 280, nn. C 1 ff. For a defence, see Peter Schlechtriem, 'Entwicklung des deutschen Schuldrechts und europäische Rechtsangleichung', in *Jahrbuch Junger Zivilrechtswissenschaftler* (n. 36) 16 ff. It is widely agreed that *Pflichtverletzung* and non-performance are supposed to be synonymous; see, for example, *Anwaltkommentar/*Dauner-Lieb *et al.* (n. 18) § 280, n. 15; but see *Münchener Kommentar/*Ernst (n. 18) § 280, nn. 19.

Another much more crucial difference between the new BGB and the Principles lies in the different level of complexity of the respective liability regimes. Article 9:501 (1) PECL ('The aggrieved party is entitled to damages for loss caused by the other party's non-performance which is not excused under Article 8:108') provides a general and comprehensive claim for damages covering all forms of failure of performance.[62] § 280 I BGB, on the other hand, only covers cases where the failure to comply with a duty arising under the contract results from conduct which has occurred after conclusion of the contract (subsequent impossibility of performance, delay of performance, defective performance, etc.). This follows from the fact that the BGB provides a special rule for situations in which there is an initial impediment to perform-ance (i.e. cases of initial impossibility): § 311a II BGB.[63] Moreover, even within this limited sphere of application, § 280 I primarily serves as a doctrinal peg for a number of more specific rules establishing further requirements for a claim for damages and is directly applicable only to a residual group of cases. The key to understanding the new liability regime lies in the different types of damages which a creditor may seek to recover, for § 280 BGB distinguishes between 'damages in lieu of performance', damages for delay, and (simple) damages.[64] The most far-reaching of these alternatives, as far as the contractual relationship between the parties is concerned, is the first one: the duty to perform is substituted by a duty to pay damages.

2. Damages in lieu of performance

a) *Impossibility of performance*

'Damages in lieu of performance' (*Schadensersatz statt der Leistung*) is a neolo-gism replacing the familiar term 'damages for non-performance' (*Schadensersatz wegen Nichterfüllung*).[65] It can be claimed only if the additional requirements of § 281, § 282, or § 283 BGB are met (§ 280 III BGB). Here we find, also under the new law, the different types of breach of contract so famil-iar to the German lawyer. In the first place, we have the cases of impossibility of performance, i.e. those situations where the debtor's obligation to perform falls away according to § 275 I BGB, or where the debtor has refused to perform according to § 275 II, III BGB. They are covered by § 283 BGB which, however, merely refers back to the requirements of § 280 I BGB: a doctrinal roundabout

---

[62] Cf. also Art. 7.4.1 PICC.   [63] On which see *infra* VI. 2.

[64] For a lucid analysis, see Hans Christoph Grigoleit and Thomas Riehm, 'Die Kategorien des Schadensersatzes im Leistungsstörungsrecht', (2003) 203 *Archiv für die civilistische Praxis* 727 ff.

[65] For the reasons, see *Abschlußbericht* (n. 33) 131; 'Begründung' (n. 42) 674; *Anwaltkommentar/* Dauner-Lieb *et al.* (n. 18) § 280, n. 36; and see the references in *Münchener Kommentar/*Ernst (n. 18) § 281, n. 1.

which is intended to clarify the law.[66] The upshot is that the creditor may claim his positive interest in all cases of subsequent impossibility unless the debtor proves that he was not responsible for his impossibility to perform. This, at any rate, is the rule the draftsmen of the new law intended to lay down,[67] though it is not easily reconcilable with the way the law is drafted. For since a debtor who does not comply with a duty of which § 275 BGB has specifically relieved him can hardly be said to be acting in breach of the very same duty, the fact that performance has not been made cannot be regarded as the breach of duty required for a claim for damages. Strictly speaking, therefore, it would have to be asked whether the debtor has infringed a duty by causing the event which has led to the impossibility of performance. This alternative perspective would, however, have detrimental consequences for the creditor, who would not merely have to prove the impossibility of performance as such, but also the reason for the impossibility.[68] This would constitute a deviation from what was recognized under the old law that was clearly not intended.[69] The entire problem could have been avoided if 'non-performance' rather than 'breach of duty' had been used as the conceptual pillar for the claim for damages.[70]

b) Delay of performance and deficient performance

Secondly, the cases of a delay of performance and of deficient performance. If the debtor does not perform, or does not perform properly, at the time when he has to effect performance (due date), the creditor may claim damages in lieu of performance, provided the requirements of § 280 I are met and he has fixed, to no avail, a reasonable period for effecting performance (or remedying the defective performance): § 281 I BGB. At first blush, therefore, German law appears to be more lenient towards a debtor who does not perform, or does not perform properly, than the Principles, for in terms of Article 9:501 ff. PECL[71] there is no requirement for the creditor to fix a period, by notice to his debtor, before he can recover damages: a debtor who does not perform in time is liable for breach of contract and is moreover immediately exposed to a claim for damages. It must be kept in mind, however, that the type of damages to which

[66] For criticism cf. also *Anwaltkommentar*/Dauner-Lieb *et al.* (n. 18) § 283, n. 4; Berthold Kupisch, 'Schuldrechtsreform und Kunst der Gesetzgebung', [2002] *Neue Juristische Wochenschrift* 1401 ff.

[67] See 'Begründung' (n. 42) 672: the breach of duty 'quite simply' lies in the fact that performance has not been rendered.

[68] The point has been made by Faust, in Huber and Faust (n.18) 113 ff. The reversal of the onus of proof mentioned above under III. 1 merely relates to the issue of fault. Cf. also Canaris, [2001] *Juristenzeitung* 512; Stoll (n. 24) 295 ff.; *Münchener Kommentar*/Ernst (n. 18) § 283, n. 4; *Staudinger*/Otto (n. 18) § 283, nn. 11 ff.

[69] Faust, in Huber and Faust (n. 18) 114; *Staudinger*/Otto (n. 18) § 283, n. 13.

[70] See the proposal submitted by Canaris, [2001] *Juristenzeitung* 523.

[71] Cf. also Arts. 7.4.1 ff. PICC.

§ 281 BGB applies are damages in lieu of performance. The creditor loses his right to performance (this is specifically stated in § 281 IV BGB) and may claim damages on the basis of not having received performance at all. This includes, in particular, his expenses for procuring a substitute performance.[72] In a way, therefore, the contract is terminated, and the effect of claiming damages in lieu of performance does indeed correspond in many respects to what is termed 'termination' under the Principles.[73]

Consequently, Article 9:506 PECL, i.e. the provision dealing with recovery of the costs for substitute transactions,[74] presupposes that the aggrieved party has terminated the contract. A right to termination, however, is only granted if the debtor's non-performance is fundamental, or, in the case of a delay in performance which is not fundamental, if the creditor has given a notice fixing an additional period of time of reasonable length.[75] Since the BGB also does not insist on the fixing of an additional period for performance in certain cases of a serious breach of contract[76] the differences between both sets of rules are somewhat reduced. They do exist, however, insofar as the recovery of damages other than the difference between the contract price and that of a substitute transaction is concerned,[77] and also, with regard to the costs for a substitute performance, in cases where the debtor has made a defective performance which does not constitute a serious breach.[78]

c) Infringement of ancillary duties which do not affect the performance as such

The third situation where the BGB is prepared to grant a claim for damages in lieu of performance is dealt with in §§ 280 III, 282 BGB. A contractual

---

[72] See, for example, *Anwaltkommentar*/Dauner-Lieb *et al.* (n. 18) § 280, nn. 49 ff.; Faust, in P. Huber and Faust (n. 18) 137 ff.; *Münchener Kommentar*/Ernst (n. 18) Vor § 281, nn. 56 ff.; Grigoleit and Riehm, (2003) 203 *Archiv für die civilistische Praxis* 735 ff.; *Staudinger*/Otto (n. 18) § 281, B 152 ff.; Helmut Heinrichs, in *Palandt, Bürgerliches Gesetzbuch* 64th edn. (2005), § 281, n. 26.

[73] See the note to Art. 8:102 PECL in Lando and Beale (n. 19) 363 ff.

[74] Cf. also Art. 9:507 PECL (for situations where the creditor has not made a substitute performance but where there is a current price for the performance contracted for). These rules correspond to Arts. 7.4.5 and 7.4.6 PICC and they have been inspired by Arts. 75 and 76 CISG. For a comparative assessment of the notion of 'damages for non-performance', in this context, see Hans Stoll, in Peter Schlechtriem (ed.), *Kommentar zum Einheitlichen UN-Kaufrecht*, 3rd edn. (2000), Art. 74, nn. 3, 14; Schlechtriem (n. 61) 22; *idem* (n. 12) 81.

[75] Arts. 9:301 (1), 8:106 (3) PECL; cf. also Arts. 7.3.1 (1), 7.1.5 (3) PICC.   [76] § 281 II BGB.

[77] Cf. the items listed in the comment to Art. 9:502 PECL (Lando and Beale (n. 19) 438 ff.) as compared to what are regarded as damages in lieu of performance in German law (see the references above, n. 72).

[78] Under the Principles, the creditor does not have the possibility, by way of fixing a grace period, to elevate this type of breach to the level of a fundamental one (with the result of being able to terminate the contract).

relationship, according to German law, does not only give rise to duties for performance but may also oblige both parties to be considerate with regard to each other's rights and legal interests (§ 241 II BGB).[79] A wide variety of ancillary duties find their basis in this general principle.[80] Infringement of one of these duties leads to a claim for damages in lieu of performance if the creditor can no longer reasonably be expected to receive performance. This applies, for instance, if a painter immaculately carries out the painting job that he has undertaken but repeatedly damages the door, the chandelier, and other pieces of furniture in his creditor's flat with his ladder.[81] Or: a babysitter tenderly looks after the children entrusted to him but repeatedly attempts to debit too many hours to his employer's account. Under the old law, the doctrine of positive malperformance was applied to these cases. As the examples demonstrate, §§ 280 III, 282 BGB only apply to ancillary duties which do not affect the performance as such (*nicht leistungsbezogene Nebenpflichten*): the main performance owed under the contract is not deficient but it has been rendered under circumstances which the creditor does not have to tolerate. Infringement of ancillary duties directly affecting the performance (*leistungsbezogene Nebenpflichten*)—a doctor fails to provide a step-by-step documentation of the treatment administered by him; the seller does not properly wrap the object sold so that it gets damaged—are covered by §§ 280 III, 281 rather than §§ 280 III, 282 BGB: we are dealing with a case of deficient performance.[82]

The Principles do not have any special rules concerning ancillary duties; presumably, termination is available, provided the painter's or the babysitter's action can be regarded as fundamental non-performance.[83] Apart from that, a claim for damages under Article 9:501 PECL (Article 7.4.1 PICC) may be available. Article 1:301 (4) and the comments to Article 8:101 PECL specifically state that the violation of an accessory duty, or failure to fulfil the duty to cooperate in order to give full effect to the contract, is covered by the term 'non-performance'.[84] None the less it is doubtful whether the claim for damages would not, by many lawyers outside Germany, be regarded as belonging to the province of the law of delict.

---

[79] The same applies even at the pre-contractual stage; see §§ 241 II, 311 II BGB.

[80] See, for example, Ernst A. Kramer, in *Münchener Kommentar zum Bürgerlichen Gesetzbuch*, 4th edn., vol. IIa (2003), § 241, nn. 31 ff.; *Münchener Kommentar*/Ernst (n. 18) § 280, nn. 93 ff.; *Palandt*/Heinrichs (n. 72) § 280, nn. 28 ff.

[81] This is the case mentioned in 'Begründung' (n. 42) 682; cf. also *Anwaltkommentar*/Dauner-Lieb *et al.* (n. 18) § 282, n. 1; Faust, in Huber and Faust (n. 18) 132.

[82] For the differentiation between *leistungsbezogene* and *nicht leistungsbezogene Nebenpflichten* see, for example, Koller (n. 30) 61 ff.; Zimmer, [2002] *Neue Juristische Wochenschrift* 6; *Staudinger*/Otto (n. 18) § 280, C 15 ff., § 282, nn. 19 ff.; but cf. also *Münchener Kommentar*/Ernst (n. 18) § 281, n. 8, § 282, n. 2.   [83] Art. 9:301 (1) PECL; Art. 7.3.1 (1) PICC.

[84] Lando and Beale (n. 18) 123, 359.

3. Damages for delay of performance

a) Mora debitoris

Contrary to damages in lieu of performance, damages for delay leave the debtor's duty to render performance unaffected. They cover the loss that has arisen because the debtor has not performed in time, and this includes gains lost or expenses incurred as a result of the delay as well as a decline in value of the subject matter during the period of delay.[85] They can be recovered if the debtor has defaulted in the technical sense of the word, i.e. if he is in *mora debitoris* (§§ 280 II, 283 BGB). The requirements have been taken over, largely unchanged, from the old law. Due date must have arrived, the creditor must have served a special warning (*Mahnung*) on the debtor, and the latter must still not have performed.[86] In a number of situations, the warning is dispensable, particularly if a time for performance has been fixed with reference to the calendar (*dies interpellat pro homine*).[87] An important change that has been implemented relates to payments which have to be rendered under a bilateral contract. Here the German Government had passed, in March 2000, an Acceleration of Payments Act[88] which was apparently intended to constitute an anticipated implementation of the EU Directive on combating late payments in commercial transactions.[89] This Act had brought about an amendment of the rules on *mora debitoris*[90] which was rightly described as 'infinitely ill-conceived and inappropriate':[91] it had had exactly the opposite effect to the one intended.

---

[85] *Anwaltkommentar/*Dauner-Lieb *et al.* (n. 18) § 280, nn. 47, 62; Faust, in Huber and Faust (n. 18) 100 ff.; *Münchener Kommentar/*Ernst (n. 72) § 286, nn. 117 ff., § 281, nn. 110 ff.; Grigoleit and Riehm, (2003) 203 *Archiv für die civilistische Praxis* 747 ff.; Claus-Wilhelm Canaris, 'Begriff und Tatbestand der Verzögerungsschaden im neuen Leistungsstörungsrecht', [2003] *Zeitschrift für Wirtschaftsrecht* 321 ff.; *Staudinger/*Otto (n. 18) § 280, nn. E 3, E 16 ff.; *Staudinger/*Löwisch (n. 23) § 286, nn. 170 ff.; *Palandt/*Heinrichs (n. 72) § 286, nn. 43 ff.; *Jauernig/*Stadler (n. 33) § 280, nn. 49 ff.; Guenther H. Treitel, *Remedies for Breach of Contract: A Comparative Account* (1988), n. 108. As a general guideline it may be said that damages for delay are those damages which would also have arisen if the debtor had still performed at the end of the delay for which damages are sought. On conceptual problems arising under the new law, see *Münchener Kommentar/*Ernst (n. 18) Vor § 275, nn. 12 ff.

[86] On the requirements for *mora debitoris*, see Faust, in Huber and Faust (n. 18) 81 ff.; *Münchener Kommentar/*Ernst (n. 18) § 286, nn. 18 ff.; *Staudinger/*Löwisch (n. 23) § 286, nn. 5 ff.; *Palandt/*Heinrichs (n. 72) § 286, nn. 11 ff.; *Jauernig/*Stadler (n. 33) § 286, nn. 10 ff.

[87] On *dies interpellat pro homine*, see *Law of Obligations* (n. 1) 798. For a discussion of all cases in which a warning is dispensable, see *Münchener Kommentar/*Ernst (n. 18) § 286, nn. 55 ff.; *Staudinger/*Löwisch (n. 23) § 286, nn. 67 ff.; *Jauernig/*Stadler (n. 33) § 286, nn. 27 ff.

[88] *Bundesgesetzblatt* 2000 I, 330 ff.

[89] See the remarks by Jürgen Schmidt-Räntsch, 'Gedanken zur Umsetzung der kommenden Kaufrechtsrichtlinie', (1999) 7 *Zeitschrift für Europäisches Privatrecht* 302.

[90] See, in particular, the third section of what was then § 284 BGB.

[91] Wolfgang Ernst, 'Deutsche Gesetzgebung in Europa—am Beispiel des Verzugsrechts', (2000) 8 *Zeitschrift für Europäisches Privatrecht* 769. For a detailed criticism, see Ulrich Huber, 'Das neue Recht

Hence the need for reforming the reform. The new § 286 III BGB now specifies the lapse of thirty days, following the date of receipt by the debtor of the invoice or an equivalent request for payment, as the latest date when a payment debtor has to be considered to be in default.[92]

b) Excursus: other consequences of mora debitoris

It may be mentioned, in this context, that a claim for the delay interest is not the only legal consequence of *mora debitoris*. Thus, if the delay relates to payment of a sum of money, the creditor is entitled to interest on that sum, which is specified as 8 per cent above the base rate of interest for legal transactions not involving a consumer, and 5 per cent in all other cases (§ 288 I, II BGB). Moreover, while he is in *mora debitoris*, a debtor is responsible for every degree of negligence (this is relevant in situations where he is normally subject to a more lenient standard of liability)[93] and he is also responsible if performance now becomes impossible, even if such impossibility is not due to his fault, unless the damage would have arisen even if he had performed timeously: § 287 BGB.[94] Contrary to the old law, the specific requirements for *mora debitoris* laid down in § 286 BGB are apparently no longer necessary for the claim for damages in lieu of performance or for the right to terminate the contract;[95] the situation, in this respect, seems to be similar to that under the Principles.[96] As the BGB, the Principles grant a claim for interest if payment of a sum of money is delayed (Article 9:508 (1) PECL);[97] they give a right to damages (Article 9:501 PECL);[98] and they specify that a creditor who recovers the interest is not precluded from recovering further damages that may have arisen (Article 9:508 PECL).[99] Unlike the BGB, however, the Principles do not

des Zahlungsverzugs und das Prinzip der Privatautonomie', [2000] *Juristenzeitung* 743 ff.; *idem*, 'Das Gesetz zur Beschleunigung fälliger Zahlungen und die europäische Richtlinie zur Bekämpfung von Zahlungsverzug im Geschäftsverkehr', [2000] *Juristenzeitung* 957 ff.

[92] For details, see *Anwaltkommentar*/Dauner-Lieb *et al.* (n. 18) § 286, nn. 57 ff.; Faust, in Huber and Faust (n. 18) 90 ff.; Lorenz and Riehm (n. 18) 135 ff.; *Münchener Kommentar*/Ernst (n. 18) § 286, nn. 70 ff.; *Staudinger*/Otto (n. 18) § 286, nn. 89 ff.; *Jauernig*/Stadler (n. 33) § 286, nn. 31 ff.

[93] Such as the situations listed in *Palandt*/Heinrichs (n. 72) § 277, nn. 4 and 6.

[94] For the historical background to this rule, see *Law of Obligations* (n. 1) 799 ff.

[95] See §§ 280 I, 281 and 323 BGB; and see, on the problems of coordination, *Münchener Kommentar*/Ernst (n. 18) Vor § 275, n. 14, § 281, n. 112; Petra Pohlmann, 'Vom Verzug zur verspäteten Leistung?', in Dauner-Lieb, Konzen and Schmidt (n. 12) 272 ff. (who argues that the requirements for *mora debitoris* have to be read into § 281 I BGB); cf. also *Staudinger*/Otto (n. 18) § 281, B 3 ff.   [96] Cf. also Medicus (n. 53) 184.

[97] However, Art. 9:508 (1) PECL is confined to primary contractual obligations to pay; the provision does not cover interest on secondary monetary obligations, such as damages or interest: Lando and Beale (n. 19) 451. Cf. also Art. 7.4.9 PICC. On the interpretation of Art. 9:508 (1) PECL see Helmut Koziol, 'Europäische Vertragsrechtsvereinheitlichung und deutsches Schadensrecht', in Basedow (n. 36) 209 ff.   [98] Cf. also Art. 7.4.1 PICC.

[99] Cf. also Art. 7.4.9 (3) PICC.

have the requirement of a special warning for delay of performance.[100] Nor do they contain a rule like § 287 BGB. Yet, the substance of § 287, 2 BGB is probably inherent in Article 8:108 PECL, in that it may be said of a debtor whose performance has become impossible while he was defaulting that he could have avoided even an impediment that was both unforeseeable and beyond his control. His non-performance would then not be excused.

4. 'Simple' damages

What, then, remains for the claim for damages in § 280 I BGB ('simple' damages)? The draftsmen of the new law intended it to cover consequential loss, i.e. damage suffered by the creditor as a result of the breach of contract, with respect to other objects of legal protection:[101] A has sold cattle to B; the cattle, however, are infected with a disease that now spreads to other cattle owned by B; the radiator that has been sold explodes and injures the purchaser; etc. This was a core area of application of what was called positive malperformance (*positive Forderungsverletzung*) under the old law. The old law, insofar, was based on an intricate distinction between the creditor's interest in receiving the kind of performance that he had bargained for (*Mangelschaden*—this interest was protected by special claims available under the law of sale and contract for work) and his interest in not having his other objects of legal protection impaired as a result of the defective performance (*Mangelfolgeschaden*).[102]

Whether, and how far, this distinction, which was supposed to have become redundant, has in fact survived the reform, or whether it has been replaced by another, equally difficult one, is much disputed. On the one hand, it may be argued that all loss, including consequental loss, is covered by damages in lieu of performance (§ 281 BGB).[103] For if the creditor has to be placed in the position in which he would have been had the debtor performed properly, it has to be taken into account that but for the debtor's breach of duty he would not only have had a healthy cow and a radiator which is functioning well but would not have had his other cattle infected and his bodily integrity impaired either. On the basis of this argument, the range of application of § 280 I BGB

---

[100] For criticism, see Eugen Bucher, 'Mora früher und heute, oder auch: die Verdienste der Römer um ein menschengemässes, und der Redaktoren des Obligationenrechts um ein neuzeitliches Vertragsrecht', in *Pacte—Convention—Contrat: Mélanges en l'honneur du Professeur Bruno Schmidlin* (1998), 412 ff., 426 ff. Cf. also Medicus (n. 53) 183 ff.

[101] 'Begründung' (n. 42) 671 ff., 834.

[102] See, for example, Dieter Medicus, *Bürgerliches Recht*, 18th edn. (1999), nn. 351 ff.; Heinrich Honsell, in *J. von Staudingers Kommentar zum Bürgerlichen Gesetzbuch*, 13th edn. (1995), Vorbem. zu §§ 459 ff., nn. 78 ff.; Frank Peters, in *J. von Staudingers Kommentar zum Bürgerlichen Gesetzbuch*, revised edition (2000), § 635, nn. 55 ff.; Medicus, [2003] *Juristische Schulung* 527 ff.

[103] See, for example, Faust, in Huber and Faust (n. 18) 137.

could be very considerably reduced; it would still, however, cover cases where the injury to the creditor's health, property or other interests has not been the result of a defect in the main performance but has occurred in the course of rendering performance (the painter damaging his employer's chandelier while carrying out his painting job; the purchaser slipping on a banana skin that is lying around in the seller's shop; the doctor causing loss to his patient by disclosing confidential information about him) and where the creditor either does not intend to claim, or is unable to claim, damages in lieu of performance.[104] On the other hand, § 281 BGB requires the creditor to grant his debtor an extra period for rendering performance, and this requirement is obviously meaningless in cases of consequential loss. Arguably, therefore, a line has to be drawn between the loss that could have been avoided as a result of (supplementary) performance having been rendered within the extra period (e.g. the cost of repair, or of a covering transaction) and the loss that would have remained unaffected by the possibility of rendering performance within the extra period (the death of the other cattle, or the injury to the purchaser's health, in the cattle and radiator cases mentioned above).[105] The former situation would have to be brought home under §§ 280 III, 281 BGB (damages in lieu of performance), the latter under § 280 I BGB (simple damages).

Conceptually, this distinction differs from the one, recognized under the old law, between *Mangelschäden* and *Mangelfolgeschäden*,[106] even if there is a significant correspondence in its practical effects. It is predicated on the idea that the notion of damages in lieu of performance has to be interpreted in such a way that it does not effectively deprive the debtor of the 'second chance' granted to him by the BGB to comply with his contractual obligations and thus to earn the price that he has bargained for. At the same time, however, it is a distinction that is not easy to apply in practice. Even at this stage, it has become enveloped by a thick layer of dispute.[107] One of them concerns the recoverability of loss

[104] See *supra* p. 55.
[105] See, with many differences in detail, *Anwaltkommentar/*Dauner-Lieb *et al.* (n. 18) § 280, nn. 39 ff., 51; Stephan Lorenz, 'Rücktritt, Minderung und Schadensersatz wegen Sachmängeln im neuen Kaufrecht: was hat der Verkäufer zu vertreten?', [2002] *Neue Juristische Wochenschrift* 2500; Florian Faust, in Heinz Georg Bamberger and Herbert Roth (eds.), *Kommentar zum Bürgerlichen Gesetzbuch*, vol. 1 (2003), § 437, nn. 47, 51 ff.; *Münchener Kommentar/*Ernst (n. 18) § 280, nn. 65 ff.; Grigoleit and Riehm, (2003) 203 *Archiv für die civilistische Praxis* 751 ff.; *Staudinger/*Otto (n. 18) § 280, E 4 ff.; Harm Peter Westermann, in *Münchener Kommentar zum Bürgerlichen Gesetzbuch*, 4th edn., vol. III (2004), § 437, nn. 26 ff.; *Palandt/*Heinrichs (n. 72) § 280, n. 18. That some kind of distinction has to be drawn can hardly be disputed. The different views proposed so far are analysed by Barbara Grunewald, 'Schadensersatz für Mangel- und Mangelfolgeschäden', in Dauner-Lieb, Konzen and Schmidt (n. 12) 313 ff.
[106] But see, for example, Huber, in Huber and Faust (n. 18) 349 ff.; *Palandt/*Heinrichs (n. 72) § 280, n. 18; cf. also *Staudinger/*Otto (n. 18) § 280, nn. 26 ff.; *Münchener Kommentar/*Westermann (n. 105) § 437, n. 33.
[107] See, for example, the discussion by Faust (n. 105) § 437, nn. 50 ff.; *Staudinger/*Otto (n. 18) § 280, nn. E 1 ff.

(classified as *Mangelschaden* under the old law)[108] which results from the fact that a defective object has been delivered which cannot be used until it has been repaired, or another object has been delivered; if the object is a machine that is vital for the operation of a business it may result in a loss of production (*Betriebsausfallschaden*). At least four different solutions have, so far, been proposed: application of the rules on damages in lieu of performance,[109] application of the 'simple damages' provision of § 280 I BGB,[110] a distinction depending on when the loss resulting from the inability, on the part of the purchaser, to use the object has occurred (at a time when the seller could still have cured the defective performance within the extra period or not),[111] or application of the rules on damages for delay of performance (§§ 280 II, 286 BGB).[112]

It is hardly a satisfactory state of affairs (and hardly one that can be recommended as a model for Europe) that every investigation into a damages claim under the new German law has to start with a complex inquiry as to the type of damages which the plaintiff seeks to recover.

IV. Claim for the Substitute in Cases of Impossibility

If performance has become impossible, due to no fault of the debtor, the creditor cannot, of course, claim damages. Still, however, the debtor may have acquired something in the place of the object he was supposed to deliver: compensation from, or a claim against, an insurance company or a third party. German law regards it as obviously equitable for the debtor to have to make over to the creditor whatever benefit he has acquired:[113] since the debtor was under a duty to deliver the object which was destroyed, lost, or stolen, he should not now retain that object's substitute. This was recognized under the old law (§ 281 BGB old version) as much as it is under the new (§ 285 BGB). Obviously, the creditor may also claim that substitute if the debtor has been responsible for the impediment. His claim for damages in lieu of performance is then reduced by the value of the substitute.[114] Oddly, the Principles do not provide this kind of remedy. Nor does the Convention on the International

---

[108] See *Anwaltkommentar*/Dauner-Lieb *et al.* (n. 18) § 280, n. 41.

[109] Huber, in Huber and Faust (n. 18) 351 ff.

[110] Canaris, in *Karlsruher Forum* (n. 18) 37 ff.   [111] Faust (n. 105) § 437, n. 53.

[112] Grigoleit and Riehm, (2003) 203 *Archiv für die civilistische Praxis* 754 ff.; previously also Faust, in Huber and Faust (n. 18) 155 ('the loss has not arisen because the seller has delivered a defective machine but because he has failed to deliver a machine that was not defective').

[113] *Abschlußbericht* (n. 33) 132 ('offenbarer Gerechtigkeitsgehalt').

[114] § 285 II BGB. For a detailed discussion of the problems arising, see Meier, [2002] *Jura* 122 ff.

Sale of Goods. Some German commentators on the Convention attempt to remedy this deficiency either by way of interpretation of the contract or by resorting to an analogy to Article 84 II CISG.[115]

V. Expenses Incurred in the Expectation of Receiving Performance

It sometimes happens that a creditor finds it difficult to quantify his loss or to establish any loss at all. None the less, he may have incurred considerable expenses in reliance on his debtor's promise. B has bought a piece of property from A only to find out that, contrary to the assurances made by the vendor, he is not allowed to run a disco on the property.[116] Any estimate of his loss of profits is based on mere speculation. A much safer peg on which to hang a claim for damages is the expenses incurred by B in the expectation of being able to run the disco. Yet, these expenses have not been caused by A's non-performance; they would also have been incurred had the vendor not failed to honour his promise. The purpose of these expenses has merely been frustrated. Under the old law, the courts used to help B with a presumption that the transaction would have been profitable and would thus have allowed him to earn the amount he had invested. This, so it was argued, justified using the expenses as a yardstick for measuring the positive interest.[117] An insurmountable problem, however, arose in cases where the creditor had never intended to make money but where the transaction (and the expenses incurred in reliance thereon) served to satisfy some immaterial interest. The obstacle in the way towards a claim for damages was § 253 BGB, i.e. the rule preventing the recovery of immaterial interest in contract law.[118] This was widely regarded as inequitable.[119] The new law, therefore, now has a general provision according to which the creditor, instead of claiming damages in lieu of performance, may

---

[115] Hans Stoll and Georg Gruber, in Peter Schlechtriem and Ingeborg Schwenzer (eds.), *Kommentar zum Einheitlichen Kaufrecht*, 4th edn. (2004), Art. 79, n. 44; Ulrich Magnus, in *J. von Staudingers Kommentar zum Bürgerlichen Gesetzbuch, Wiener UN-Kaufrecht*, revised edition (1999), Art. 79, n. 54. For criticism of the Principles as well as CISG for failing to deal with the matter, see Raimund Bollenberger, *Das stellvertretende Commodum: Die Ersatzherausgabe im österreichischen und deutschen Schuldrecht unter Berücksichtigung weiterer Rechtsordnungen* (1999), 153 ff.

[116] See the case of BGHZ 114, 193 ff.

[117] See, for example, the references in Hansjörg Otto, in *J. von Staudingers Kommentar zum Bürgerlichen Gesetzbuch*, revised edition (2001), § 325, nn. 84 ff.; *Palandt*/Heinrichs (n. 24) § 325, n. 15.

[118] The rule has, in the meantime, been reformed but still requires the immaterial harm to have resulted from an infringement of the body or health of the injured party, from the deprivation of his liberty, or from an encroachment upon his sexual self-determination.

[119] Canaris, [2001] *Juristenzeitung* 516.

recover any expenses that he has incurred in the expectation of receiving performance and that he was reasonably entitled to incur, unless the purpose of these expenses would have been frustrated even without the debtor's breach of duty.[120] The Principles do not contain a rule of this kind; it may, however, conceivably be read into Article 9:502 PECL, as was done under the old German law.[121] Significantly, damages under the Principles include non-pecuniary loss (Article 9:501 (2)(a) PECL).[122]

VI. Initial Impediments to Performance

1. Validity of the contract

We now have to turn our attention to initial impediments to performance.[123] According to § 306 BGB (old version) the initial objective impossibility of performance was not regarded as a specific type of breach of contract but as an impediment to the validity of the contract: 'A contract, the performance of which is impossible, is void.' This rule was widely said to have found its origin in Roman law, but this is wrong. For while the Roman lawyers did indeed coin the phrase *impossibilium nulla est obligatio*,[124] for them it merely encapsulated the idea that nobody can be obliged to perform what he cannot perform. This is not identical to the assertion that a contract aimed at an impossible

---

[120] For further background information on the reasoning behind this provision and the controversy preceding its introduction into the code, and for details of its application, see 'Begründung' (n. 42) 684 ff.; *Anwaltkommentar*/Dauner-Lieb *et al.* (n. 18) § 284, nn. 1 ff.; Faust, in Huber and Faust (n. 18) 157 ff.; *Münchener Kommentar*/Ernst (n. 18) § 284, nn. 1 ff.; Beate Gsell, 'Der Aufwendungsersatz nach § 284 BGB', in Dauner-Lieb, Konzen and Schmidt (n. 12) 321 ff.; Jan Stoppel, 'Der Ersatz frustrierter Aufwendungen nach § 284 BGB', (2004) 204 *Archiv für die civilistische Praxis* 81 ff.; *Staudinger*/Otto (n. 18) § 284, nn. 1 ff.; Stephan Lorenz, 'Schadensersatz statt der Leistung, Rentabilitätsvermutung und Aufwendungsersatz im Gewährleistungsrecht', [2004] *Neue Juristische Wochenschrift* 26 ff.
[121] For a comparative discussion, also dealing with CISG, PECL and PICC, see Torsten Schackel, 'Der Anspruch auf Ersatz des negativen Interesses bei Nichterfüllung von Verträgen', (2001) 9 *Zeitschrift für Europäisches Privatrecht* 248 ff., 268 ff. As far as CISG is concerned, the position is controversial; see Stoll and Gruber (n. 115) Art. 74, n. 5; Peter Schlechtriem, *Internationales UN-Kaufrecht* (1996), n. 308.
[122] Cf. also Art. 7.4.2 PICC. This corresponds to an international trend to recognize claims for non-pecuniary loss in an ever increasing range of situations; see Reinhard Zimmermann, 'Principles of European Contract Law and Principles of European Tort Law: Comparison and Points of Contact', in Helmut Koziol and Barbara C. Steininger (eds.), *European Tort Law 2003* (2004), n. 24.
[123] See, in particular, Sonja Meier, 'Neues Leistungsstörungsrecht: Anfängliche Leistungshindernisse, Gattungsschuld und Nichtleistung trotz Möglichkeit', [2002] *Jura* 187 ff.; *Münchener Kommentar*/Ernst (n. 18) § 311a, nn. 1 ff.; Claus-Wilhelm Canaris, 'Grundlagen und Rechtsfolgen der Haftung für anfängliche Unmöglichkeit nach § 311a Abs. 2 BGB', in *Festschrift für Andreas Heldrich* (2005), 11 ff.   [124] Celsus D. 50, 17, 185.

performance is bound to be void and, in fact, the Roman lawyers were quite prepared to grant to the disappointed purchaser the *actio empti* where this appeared appropriate.[125] Following a proposition first submitted by the Natural lawyers, and later taken up by Rudolf von Jhering,[126] the draftsmen of the BGB at least allowed the purchaser to recover his negative interest if the vendor knew or should have known about the impossibility (§ 307 BGB, old version). Such claim, however, is often insufficient. A contract of sale induces in the purchaser a reasonable reliance that he will in due course receive the promised object; if performance turns out to have been impossible from the outset, he may therefore expect to be placed in the position he would have been in had the contract been properly carried out (as opposed to the position he would have been in had he not relied upon the validity of the contract).

That the rules contained in §§ 306 ff. BGB were unsound and unfortunate was pointed out, influentially, by Ernst Rabel[127] and soon became the established view:[128] textbooks and commentaries were full of exhortations to apply § 306 BGB restrictively and to try to avoid the harshness inherent in the unequivocal verdict of invalidity wherever possible. Occasionally, for instance, the undertaking of a specific guarantee was read into the contract, with the effect that the risk of initial impossibility of performance was shifted to the person who had promised such performance. The reform of the BGB has now put an end to this. § 311a I BGB specifically states that a contract is not invalid merely because at the time it was concluded performance of the obligation undertaken in the contract was impossible.[129] This is in line with Article 4:102 PECL.[130]

---

[125] For details, see *Law of Obligations* (n. 1) 686 ff.; Jan Dirk Harke, 'Unmöglichkeit und Pflichtverletzung: Römisches Recht, BGB und Schuldrechtsmodernisierung', in *Jahrbuch Junger Zivilrechtswissenschaftler* (n. 36) 31 ff.

[126] See *Law of Obligations* (n. 1) 694 ff.

[127] Ernst Rabel, 'Unmöglichkeit der Leistung' (1907) and *idem*, 'Über Unmöglichkeit der Leistung und heutige Praxis' (1911), both today in Ernst Rabel, *Gesammelte Aufsätze*, vol. I (1965), 1 ff., 56 ff.

[128] Zweigert and Kötz (n. 1) 488 ff.; Reinhold Thode, in *Münchener Kommentar zum BGB*, 4th edn., vol. II (2001), § 306, n. 3.

[129] None the less, of course, the creditor does not have a claim for specific performance if performance is impossible: § 275 BGB applies; see, for example, Faust, in Huber and Faust (n. 18) 208 ff. The debtor's liability is governed by § 311a II BGB, on which see *infra* under VI. 2. Does § 311a BGB apply to contracts, the content of which is patently absurd (sale of a hippocentaurus)? This was the type of case with regard to which, even under the old law, invalidity was regarded as appropriate; see *Law of Obligations* (n. 1) 696, n. 135, with references; cf. also the interpretation given to § 878, 1 ABGB ('What is downright impossible, cannot be the object of a valid contract'). Often, the contract will be invalid as being *contra bonos mores* (§ 138 I BGB). Where it is not, it has been argued that the contract should, none the less, be regarded as invalid (Lobinger (n. 23) 277 ff.); or, if it is held to be valid, the liability under § 311a II BGB should be confined to the negative interest; see *Münchener Kommentar*/Ernst (n. 18) § 311a, n. 31; *Palandt*/Heinrichs (n. 72) § 311, n. 7 (advocating a 'teleological restriction' of § 311a II BGB). [130] Cf. also Art. 3.3 PICC.

2. Essential elements of the liability regime

Less clear but equally problematic under the old law was the legal position in cases of what used to be termed initial inability (or initial subjective impossibility) of performance: a painting is sold which has been stolen before the contract was concluded, or which turns out to belong to a third person, or to a museum. Predominantly, the vendor was held to be strictly liable, i.e. irrespective of whether he knew or could have known about the impediment.[131] Methodically, this was based on §§ 275, 306 BGB (*argumentum e contrario*), policy-wise the rule was justified as being inherent in the contractual promise. A person who sells a painting implicitly promises to be able to transfer ownership in the painting: 'I will perform' implies 'I am be able to perform'.

§ 311a II BGB now provides for a different liability regime. It is based on the following considerations: (i) Initial objective and subjective impossibility are to be treated alike.[132] (ii) The same liability regime should apply for initial and supervening impossibility. For it would be both awkward and arbitrary to make the standard of liability dependent on whether the painting was stolen just before or just after conclusion of the contract.[133] (iii) It follows that the fault principle should also prevail in cases of initial impediments.[134] (iv) The point of reference, however, for the attribution of fault is different in cases of initial and supervening impediments. If the painting is stolen or destroyed after the conclusion of the contract, the vendor can be blamed for not properly looking after it. Before the contract has come into existence, on the other hand, the vendor can hardly be made responsible for lack of diligence vis-à-vis the purchaser. What he can be blamed for is merely the fact that at the time the contract was concluded he knew, or should have known, that the painting had been stolen or destroyed.[135] (v) According to general principle, an infringement of a duty not to promise to perform even though the person giving that promise knew, or should have known, that he was unable to perform, can only give rise to a claim for the negative interest. This means that a claim for the positive interest can neither simply be based on §§ 280 I, III, 283 BGB (the debtor's fault relates to an informational deficiency at the precontractual stage, not to the breach of a contractual duty) nor on § 280 I (*culpa in contrahendo*; this is not a claim for the positive interest, i.e. damages in lieu of performance).[136]

---

[131] *Staudinger*/Löwisch (n. 24) § 306, nn. 45 ff.; *Palandt*/Heinrichs (n. 24) § 306, nn. 9 ff.; Huber (n. 3) vol. I, § 22. For an excellent overview of the way in which the discussion developed under the old law, see Meier, [2002] *Jura* 189 ff.   [132] See Canaris (n. 123) 17 ff.
[133] Canaris, [2001] *Juristenzeitung* 506; *Palandt*/Heinrichs (n. 72) § 311a, n. 2; Canaris (n. 123) 20 ff.
[134] For a detailed discussion as to why liability in cases of initial impossibility of performance should be based on fault, see Canaris (n. 123) 21 ff.   [135] See Canaris, [2001] *Juristenzeitung* 507.
[136] See Canaris, [2001] *Juristenzeitung* 507; *idem*, [2001] *Zeitschrift für Rechtspolitik* 331 ff.; *idem*, 'Schadensersatz wegen Pflichtverletzung, anfängliche Unmöglichkeit und Aufwendungsersatz im

3. Initial impossibility and the rules on mistake

These are the reasons why § 311a II BGB now contains a separate liability rule concerning initial impediments which entitles the creditor to claim damages in lieu of performance, unless the debtor did not know of the impediment when the contract was concluded, and was not responsible for not having known about it.[137] The latter clause, which refers to § 276 BGB, opens up the possibility of perpetuating the legal regime prevailing under the old law even after the reform of the law of obligations:[138] it would merely have to be argued that a standard of liability stricter than fault follows 'from the content of the obligation', particularly from the assumption of a guarantee.[139] While such argument would certainly be *contra intentionem legislatoris*, it would hardly be *contra legem*. In case, however, the law is going to be applied in the way in which its draftsmen intended it to be applied, the result will be that while a debtor who knew or could have known about the impediment is liable for the positive interest, there is no liability at all, if the debtor could not have had any knowledge.

Should the law countenance such a stark contrast? Under the old law, after all, even in the latter situation the debtor was often held liable for the positive interest. The suggestion has therefore been advanced that a debtor who is not responsible for not knowing about the impediment should at least be liable for the negative interest under the new law.[140] This suggestion is based on an analogy to § 122 BGB, according to which a person who avoids a contract for mistake is bound to compensate the other party for the damage which that other party has sustained in relying upon the validity of the contract. The analogy, in turn, is justified with reference to the fact that cases of an initial impediment essentially deal with a problem of mistake: the seller does not know that his painting has been stolen or destroyed. Yet, as § 122 BGB demonstrates, the BGB normally only allows a party to rid himself of his contractual

Entwurf des Schuldrechtsmodernisierungsgesetzes', [2001] *Der Betrieb* 1817 ff.; Faust, in Huber and Faust (n. 18) 210 ff.; Beate Gsell, 'Der Schadensersatz statt der Leistung nach dem neuen Schuldrecht', in *Jahrbuch Junger Zivilrechtswissenschaftler* (n. 36) 118 ff. But see *Münchener Kommentar*/Ernst (n. 18) § 311a, nn. 4, 19 (who regards § 311a as, essentially, redundant); *contra* Canaris (n. 123) 34 ff.

[137] For criticism, both from the point of view of doctrinal consistency and practicability, see Meier, [2002] *Jura* 188 ff., 191 ff.; cf. also, for example, Schwarze, [2002] *Jura* 80 ff.; Harke (n. 125) 56 ff.; *Palandt*/Heinrichs (n. 72) § 311a, n. 7. For further references, and for a comprehensive defence of § 311a II BGB and its intellectual foundations, see Canaris (n. 123) 11 ff., 23 ff.; cf. also *Münchener Kommentar*/Ernst (n. 18) § 311a, n. 15.
[138] This has been pointed out by Zimmer, [2002] *Neue Juristische Wochenschrift* 3, and Faust, in Huber and Faust (n. 18) 215. But see now Canaris (n. 123) 29 ff.
[139] On the requirements of § 276 BGB, see *supra* III.1.
[140] Canaris (n. 14) 64 ff.; *idem*, [2001] *Juristenzeitung* 507 ff.

obligation for the price of having to pay the negative interest. It would therefore be inconsistent not to apply the same regime in the present situation.[141]

Whether this argument will ultimately prevail—it has not prevailed in the council chamber of the working group revising the Discussion Draft—remains to be seen.[142] Structurally, it would bring the law into line with the approach adopted in the Principles. For they do indeed treat cases of initial impossibility in the same way as other mistakes.[143] The debtor, therefore, may avoid the contract only if he could not have known about the fact that performance was impossible, either for him or objectively, at the moment when the contract was concluded.[144] Unlike the BGB, however, the Principles do not give the creditor a claim for the negative interest in this situation. The position is thus the same as it would be under the BGB if § 122 BGB were *not* to be applied analogously. Where, on the other hand, the debtor could have known about the initial impediment, he cannot escape his liability for the positive interest by invoking his error. His liability is based on non-performance and follows the general rules.[145] A special provision on damages like § 311a II BGB is therefore unnecessary. Alternatively, the creditor can also claim his negative interest;[146] since he, too, has been labouring under a mistake, he merely has to avoid the contract[147] and may then avail himself of the special damages provision of Article 4:117 PECL.[148]

VII. Termination

1. Doctrinal and historical background to the new law

Following CISG, the Principles grant a claim for loss caused by the other party's non-performance, as long as such non-performance is not excused as a

---

[141] Canaris, *loc. cit.*

[142] Canaris's view is rejected by *Anwaltkommentar*/Dauner-Lieb *et al.* (n. 18) § 311a, n. 18 and Faust, in Huber and Faust (n. 18) 220 ff.; *Münchener Kommentar*/Ernst (n. 18) § 311a, n. 41; *Palandt*/Heinrichs (n. 72) § 311a, n. 14; Lobinger (n. 23) 297 ff.

[143] Lando and Beale (n. 19) 234.

[144] Art. 4:103 (2) (b) PECL. The parallel rule of Art. 3.5 (2) (a) PICC is different in this respect. For the legal position under the UNIDROIT Principles, see Huber (n. 3) vol. I, § 22 III.

[145] Arts. 8:101, 9:501 PECL.

[146] He may want to do this, for instance, in cases where he finds it difficult to quantify his positive interest; cf. Huber (n. 4) 129.

[147] This he can do if the requirements of Art. 4:103 (1) PECL are met (i.e., in particular: the other party has made the same mistake) and if his mistake was excusable. That the creditor does not lose his right to claim the positive interest in view of the fact that he is entitled to rescind the contract is specifically stated in Art. 4:119. Cf. also Arts. 3.7 and 3.18 PICC.

[148] Ulrich Huber (who is generally sympathetic to the approach adopted by the Principles in cases of initial impossibility) argues that the rules contained in the *old* BGB were less complex while leading, by and large, to the same results: Huber (n. 4) 128 ff.

result of an impediment beyond the other party's control. This claim for damages leaves the contract unaffected. In many cases, however, the creditor may wish rather to terminate the contract; or he may wish to terminate the contract in addition to claiming damages. Such right to termination is granted only in cases of fundamental non-performance; on the other hand, however, it does not depend on whether or not the non-performance is excused. This is the remedial model which has been gaining ground internationally and which has now found its most recent manifestation in the Principles.[149]

The notion that the remedy of termination is available only if the non-performance attains a certain minimum level of seriousness is also reflected, in some or other form, in most of the more traditional national legal systems; it is based on the consideration that termination, in a way, jeopardizes the fundamental principle of *pacta sunt servanda* and has the effect of throwing back on the defaulting party a risk which, according to the contract, was to have been borne by the aggrieved party.[150] Roman law was even stricter in this regard and never recognized a general right of termination in case of breach of contract.[151] This approach has, for a long time, dominated the *ius commune*, and it has even shaped the BGB.[152] For the code, too, did not contain a general statutory right of termination but used to provide a highly fragmented regime which was conceptually based, in important respects, on a *lex commissoria* that has been tacitly agreed upon:[153] extinction of the duty to perform, if performance becomes impossible as a result of the debtor's fault[154] but also if he has not been responsible for the impossibility of performance;[155] automatic extinction also of the other party's duty to pay the price where the impossibility was not attributable to the debtor,[156] a right of termination, on the part of the creditor, if the impossibility was attributable to the debtor,[157] in cases of *mora debitoris*,[158] and in those of positive malperformance, provided such malperformance

---

[149] See, as far as termination is concerned, Arts. 8:101, 9:301 PECL; cf. also Arts. 7.1.7 (4), 7.3.1 PICC; Art. 49 CISG. On the international development, see Peter Schlechtriem, 'Abstandnahme vom Vertrag', in Basedow (n. 36) 161 ff.; Schwenzer (n. 12) 41 ff.; Schlechtriem, in Dauner-Lieb, Konzen and Schmidt (n. 12) 77 ff.; Walter Rolland, 'Die Aufhebung des Vertrages nach den Vorschlägen zur Schuldrechtsreform auf dem Hintergrund internationaler Entwicklungen', in *Festschrift für Peter Schlechtriem* (2003), 638 ff. For criticism, see Bucher (n. 100) 430 ff.

[150] Treitel (n. 85) nn. 239 ff., 259 ff.; Axel Flessner, 'Befreiung vom Vertrag wegen Nichterfüllung', (1997) 5 *Zeitschrift für Europäisches Privatrecht* 266 ff.

[151] *Law of Obligations* (n. 1) 578 ff., 800 ff.

[152] Reinhard Zimmermann, ' "Heard melodies are sweet, but those unheard are sweeter…": Condicio tacita, implied condition und die Fortbildung des europäischen Vertragsrechts', (1993) 193 *Archiv für die civilistische Praxis* 160 ff.   [153] See Hans G. Leser, *Der Rücktritt vom Vertrag* (1975), 16 ff.

[154] § 275 BGB old version.

[155] Prevailing opinion under the old law; see, for example, *Palandt*/Heinrichs (n. 24) § 275, n. 24.

[156] § 323 BGB old version.   [157] § 325 BGB old version.

[158] § 326 BGB old version.

seriously affected the contractual relationship;[159] a right to redhibition, which was not dependent on fault, in cases of a latent defect in the object sold or in the work performed;[160] restitution partly according to the law of unjustified enrichment,[161] partly according to a special set of rules devised for a situation where one party may avail himself of a contractual right to terminate the contract;[162] an obvious lack of coordination between the two restitution regimes;[163] a strict mutual exclusivity prevailing between the remedies of damages and termination:[164] the rules contained in the BGB were not generally admired for their clarity and ease of operation. On the contrary, it was extremely difficult to comprehend their doctrinal intricacies and to arrive at solutions which were both practicable and logically consistent.

2. Automatic release of the creditor in cases of impossibility of performance on the part of the debtor

The new set of rules after the reform is considerably simpler than the old law, though it is not exactly simple either. It ties in with the rules contained in §§ 275, 280 ff. BGB. This is particularly obvious with regard to § 326 BGB. This provision refers to the situation where the debtor becomes free under § 275, either because his duty to perform falls away as a result of the fact that performance is impossible (§ 275 I BGB), or because he avails himself of his right to refuse performance under § 275 II, III BGB. The legal consequence, as far as the debtor's own claim against the creditor is concerned, is that it falls away (§ 326 I 1 BGB). The creditor, in other words, does not have to avail himself of a right to terminate the contract but is automatically released from his obligation. This rule, which was not contained in the discussion draft (nor in the *Abschlussbericht*), has been introduced for two reasons: (i) A right of termination is pointless in cases where the creditor does not have any alternative: in view of the impossibility of performance he would not be able to hold on to the contract anyway.[165] This argument, however, is not convincing, for it is not logically impossible for the creditor to claim damages in lieu of performance and ask for these damages to be assessed according to what used to be called, under the old law, 'exchange theory' (*Surrogationstheorie*):[166] he would then be

---

[159] Generally recognized under the old law; see, for example, *Palandt*/Heinrichs (n. 24) § 276, n. 124.

[160] §§ 459, 462 and 633, 634 BGB old version.   [161] §§ 323 III, 327, 2 BGB old version.

[162] §§ 346 ff. BGB old version.   [163] See, for example, *Palandt*/Heinrichs (n. 24) § 350, n. 3.

[164] See, for example, *Abschlußbericht* (n. 33) 19.

[165] Canaris, [2001] *Juristenzeitung* 508; cf. also *Anwaltkommentar*/Dauner-Lieb *et al.* (n. 18) § 326, n. 4; *Staudinger*/Otto (n. 18) § 326, B 2.

[166] On the 'difference' and 'exchange' theories of assessing damages for non-performance in German law (*Differenztheorie* and *Surrogationstheorie*), see Treitel (n. 85) n. 106; *Palandt*/Heinrichs

entitled to the full value of the performance promised to him but only on condition of performing his own promise.[167] (ii) More persuasive is the second reason. The remedies for non-performance do not only apply to contracts of sale and contracts for work, but also, for example, to employment contracts. If an employee is prevented from appearing at work—no matter whether he is responsible for the impediment or not—it would be unreasonable to grant his employer the right to terminate the contract, and artificial to regard his right of termination as being confined to the period for which the employee has not performed his duties.[168] The most appropriate solution appears to be that the creditor is released from his obligation insofar as the debtor is released from his.

For cases of impossibility, exclusion *ipso iure* of the other party's duty to perform is the functional equivalent to a right of termination. This applies both in cases where the debtor has, and where he has not, been responsible for the impossibility.[169] If the impossibility was attributable to the *creditor*, or if it has occurred at a time when the creditor had defaulted in accepting performance, the debtor retains his claim. He must, however, deduct what he saves as a result of being released from his own duty to perform, or what he acquires or wilfully omits to acquire by using his capacity to work elsewhere (§ 326 II BGB). This is what used to be laid down in § 324 BGB (old version); in respect

(n. 23) § 325, nn. 9 ff.; *Staudinger*/Otto (n. 117) § 325, nn. 38 ff. The position under the new law is analysed by Faust, in Huber and Faust (n. 18) 142 ff.; Lorenz and Riehm (n. 18) 106 ff.; Meier, [2002] *Jura* 124 ff.; *Münchener Kommentar*/Ernst (n. 18) Vor § 281, nn. 19 ff.; *Palandt*/Heinrichs (n. 72) § 281, nn. 18 ff. Whether in cases where performance has become impossible and where the debtor is responsible for the impossibility (i.e. where both parties are automatically released from their respective obligations under §§ 275 I and 326 I BGB) the creditor may claim damages only according to the 'difference theory' or also according to the 'exchange theory' has become a matter of dispute immediately after the enactment of the new law: Faust, in Huber and Faust (n. 18) 148 ff. as opposed to Schwarze, [2002] *Jura* 82. According to Faust, § 326 I BGB only determines that the creditor does not *have to* render performance, not that he is not *allowed* to render performance. Thus, the creditor is able to claim damages in terms of §§ 280 I, III, 283 or § 311a II BGB and calculate his loss according to the exchange theory (i.e. by claiming the full value of the debtor's performance on condition of offering his own). This, essentially, is the reason inducing Ernst not to apply § 326 I BGB to cases where the debtor is responsible for his impossibility to perform: *Münchener Kommentar*/Ernst (n. 18) § 326, nn. 13 ff. *Contra*: *Staudinger*/Otto (n. 18) § 326, B 5; cf. also *Palandt*/Heinrichs (n. 72) § 326, n. 2a.

[167] According to § 326 V BGB the creditor, incidentally, does not have to rely on being automatically released from his obligation to perform but is also granted the option of terminating the contract. On the rationale of this rule, see *Anwaltkommentar*/Dauner-Lieb *et al.* (n. 18) § 326, nn. 15 ff.; Huber, in Huber and Faust (n. 18) 199 ff.

[168] Huber (n. 4) 102; Canaris (n. 14) 54 ff.; *idem*, [2001] *Juristenzeitung* 508.

[169] Unless, of course, the courts were to agree with *Münchener Kommentar*/Ernst (n. 18) § 326, nn. 13 ff. that § 326 I BGB has to be teleologically restricted to cases where the debtor has not been responsible for his inability to perform; cf. *supra* n. 166. By denying the creditor the possibility of rendering his own performance (by not allowing him to claim damages according to the exchange theory), he would be placed at an unreasonable disadvantage in view of the fact that he has already been disadvantaged, as a result of the debtor's fault, by having lost his right to claim the debtor's performance.

of the second alternative ('...or if it has occurred...') the rule refers to the
requirements for *mora creditoris* as laid down in §§ 293 ff. BGB.[170] Other
details concerning the fate of the creditor's duty to perform have also been
taken over from the old law: if the creditor claims what the debtor has received
as a substitute for the object owed under the contract, the debtor retains his
claim against the creditor; it is, however, diminished insofar as the value of
the substitute is lower than the value of the performance due.[171] In cases where
the creditor has already performed an obligation from which he was released
under § 326 BGB he may ask for restitution.[172]

3. Requirements for, and mechanics of, termination

Where we have a type of breach of contract other than impossibility, a right of
termination is available to the creditor, provided the requirements laid down in
§§ 323 or 324 BGB are met. These requirements largely mirror those contained
in §§ 281 and 282 BGB (concerning damages in lieu of performance). This
assimilation reflects a desire, on the part of the draftsmen of the new law, to
prevent any danger of the requirements for termination of contract effectively
being subverted by the possibility of resorting to the remedy of damages in lieu
of performance.[173] The structure of §§ 323, 324 BGB thus also largely corresponds to the provisions of §§ 281 ff. BGB. The law distinguishes between the
situation (i) where the debtor does not perform, or does not perform properly,
at the time when he has to effect performance (including those cases in which
he infringes ancillary duties directly affecting the performance) and (ii) where
the debtor infringes ancillary duties which do not affect the performance as
such (i.e. duties of care with regard to the creditor's general rights and interests
as mentioned in § 241 II BGB). For the latter situation, § 324 BGB grants the
creditor a right to terminate the contract if he can no longer reasonably
be expected to accept performance. In all cases covered by the former alternative,

---

[170] The legal position in cases where the impossibility to perform has been attributable both to the
debtor and the creditor was much disputed under the old law and continues to be disputed under the
new law; see Urs Peter Gruber, 'Schuldrechtsmodernisierung 2001/2002—die beiderseits zu vertretende Unmöglichkeit', [2002] *Juristische Schulung* 1066 ff.; *Staudinger*/Otto (n. 18) § 326, C 65 ff.;
Jauernig/Stadler (n. 33) § 326, n. 22; *Palandt*/Heinrichs (n. 72) § 326, n. 15; Claus-Wilhelm Canaris,
'Die von beiden Parteien zu vertretende Unmöglichkeit', in *Kontinuität und Wandel des
Versicherungsrechts: Festschrift für Egon Lorenz* (2004), 147 ff.
[171] § 326 III BGB; cf. § 323 II BGB old version.
[172] § 326 IV BGB; cf. § 323 III BGB old version. However, while the BGB used to refer to the law
of unjustified enrichment, the reference is now to the specific restitution regime of §§ 346 ff.
[173] 'Begründung' (n. 42) 757 ff. For a discussion of how far the draftsmen of the new law have
succeeded in synchronizing the remedies of damages and termination, see Gsell (n. 136) 122 ff.; for
a detailed comparison between the new § 323 BGB and § 326 BGB old version, see Meier, [2002]
Jura 194.

the creditor may terminate if he has fixed a reasonable period for effecting performance, or for remedying the defective performance, and such period has lapsed to no avail (§ 323 I BGB).[174] § 323 II BGB specifies a number of situations where the fixing of a period is dispensable;[175] according to § 323 III BGB a warning (*Abmahnung*) takes the place of the fixing of a period for effecting performance where the latter step is impracticable.[176] § 323 VI BGB mirrors § 326 II BGB in that the creditor is prevented from terminating the contract if he was responsible for the debtor's breach of duty, or if the breach has occurred after the creditor has defaulted in accepting performance. There is, of course, one major point of difference between the requirements for termination and those for a claim for damages in lieu of performance: availability of the remedy of termination does not depend on whether or not the debtor has been at fault.[177] At the same time, this is one of the most significant substantive differences between the old and the new German law of breach of contract.[178]

As under the old law, termination is effected by declaration to the other party.[179] Also as under the old law, termination entails that both parties are released from their duties to perform and that they have to render restitution of what has already been performed. Restitution, however, is not to be rendered in terms of the law of unjustified enrichment: the code, rather, makes available

---

[174] On whether the requirements of *mora debitoris* (apart, obviously, from fault) have to be met in cases where the debtor does not perform, before the creditor may terminate the contract, see Pohlmann (n. 95) 283 ff.

[175] These are: (i) the debtor seriously and definitively refuses to perform; (ii) the debtor does not perform at a date fixed in the contract, or within a certain period, and the creditor has tied the continuation of his interest in receiving performance to performance being rendered in time; (iii) there are special circumstances which justify immediate termination of the contract, taking account of the interests of both parties. All these exceptions are taken, with some slight modifications, from what was recognized under the old law: see *Anwaltkommentar*/Dauner-Lieb *et al.* (n. 18) § 323, nn. 15 ff.; Huber, in Huber and Faust (n. 18) 190 ff.; *Münchener Kommentar*/Ernst (n. 18) § 323, nn. 91 ff.; *Staudinger*/Otto (n. 18) § 323, B 81 ff.

[176] The same rule applies, as far as the claim for damages in lieu of performance is concerned: § 281 III BGB. It is supposed to apply to cases where the debtor is under a duty to refrain from doing something: *Anwaltkommentar*/Dauner-Lieb *et al.* (n. 18) § 281, n. 25 and § 323, n. 21; Faust, in Huber and Faust (n. 18) 123; Lorenz and Riehm (n. 18) 105 ff. Both Faust and Lorenz/Riehm draw attention to the fact that the rule is misconceived, since there is no imaginable situation where a warning would be meaningful. If, for example, a person has acted in contravention of a duty not to compete, a warning no longer makes sense as far as that specific contravention (as well as the legal consequences flowing therefrom) is concerned. Cf. also *Münchener Kommentar*/Ernst (n. 18) § 281, n. 41, § 323, n. 79; *Staudinger*/Otto (n. 18) § 281, B 73.

[177] This difference is not in conflict with the policy mentioned above, text to no. 173; since it does not in any way raise the possibility of the rules on termination being subverted by the remedy of damages in lieu of performance.

[178] *Abschlußbericht* (n. 33) 31; Schlechtriem, (1993) 1 *Zeitschrift für Europäisches Privatrecht* 236; Canaris, [2001] *Juristenzeitung* 522; Rolland (n. 149) 631 ff.; for a comparative evaluation, cf. also Flessner, (1997) 5 *Zeitschrift für Europäisches Privatrecht* 296 ff.; and see Schwenzer (n. 12) 41 ff. Cf. also Bucher (n. 100) 421 ff.; Medicus (n. 53) 189.   [179] § 349 BGB (old and new version).

a specific restitution regime for this purpose (§§ 346 ff. BGB). Formally, it applies because it constitutes a set of *leges speciales*. Doctrinally, the existence of this specific restitution regime has always been justified by pointing out that termination does not remove the entire contract (be it *ab initio* or *ex nunc*) and does not, therefore, create a situation where the performance can be said to have been made 'without legal ground',[180] but instead transforms a relationship aiming at the implementation of the contractual programme originally agreed upon into a contractual winding-up relationship.[181] The pertinent legal rules have been subject to fierce criticism[182] and have therefore been revised by the Modernization of the Law of Obligations Act; details concerning the new restitution regime after termination of contract will be discussed elsewhere.[183]

4. Comparison

If we now attempt to assess the major points of discrepancy and agreement between termination according to the revised German law of obligations and the Principles,[184] the picture looks as follows:

(i) The mechanism of termination is the same, at least in general, since according to the Principles a party's right to terminate the contract is to be exercised by notice to the other party (Article 9:303 (1) PECL).[185] Thus, in particular, there is no requirement of court proceedings to effect termination.[186]

(ii) Sometimes, however, even a notice of termination is dispensable because the contract is terminated automatically. The German rule of § 326 BGB relates to cases of impossibility, Article 9: 303 (4) PECL refers to the situation

---

[180] This is the essential prerequisite for the application of § 812 I BGB; for details, see Reinhard Zimmermann, 'Unjustified Enrichment: The Modern Civilian Approach', (1995) 15 *Oxford Journal of Legal Studies* 403 ff.

[181] BGHZ 88, 46 ff.; BGH, NJW 1990, 2068 ff.; Dagmar Kaiser, in *J. von Staudingers Kommentar zum Bürgerlichen Gesetzbuch*, 13th edn. (1995), Vorbem. zu §§ 346 ff., nn. 53 ff.; *Palandt*/Heinrichs (n. 72) § 346, n. 2. For the new law, see Johannes Hager, in *Anwaltkommentar* (n. 18) § 346, n. 13; Reinhard Gaier, in *Münchener Kommentar zum Bürgerlichen Gesetzbuch*, 4th edn., vol. IIa (2003), Vorbem. § 346, n. 40; *Jauernig*/Stadler (n. 33) Vorbem. §§ 346–354, n. 3.

[182] For details, see Reinhard Zimmermann, 'Restitution after Termination for Breach of Contract in German Law', (1997) *Restitution Law Review* 13 ff.

[183] 'Restitution after Termination for Breach of Contract: German Law after the Reform of 2002', in Andrew Burrows and Alan Rodger (eds.), *Mapping the Law: Essays in Memory of Peter Birks*, forthcoming.

[184] For a comparative evaluation against the background of CISG, see Schlechtriem (n. 12) 78 ff.

[185] Cf. also Art. 7.3.2 (2) PICC.

[186] As is the case, for instance, in France and Spain; for a comparative analysis, see Flessner, (1997) 5 *Zeitschrift für Europäisches Privatrecht* 302 ff.; Schlechtriem (n. 149) 172 ff.

where a party is excused under Article 8:108 in view of an impediment which is total and permanent.[187]

(iii) Both under German law and under the Principles, termination of the contract releases both parties from their obligations for the future.[188] As far as past performances are concerned, the comments to the Principles are at pains to make clear that, unlike in French law, termination does not operate retrospectively.[189] The reasons for adopting this position are, essentially, that (a) the creditor should not be precluded from claiming damages for his loss of expectations,[190] (b) there may be a number of provisions in the contract which are clearly intended to apply even if the contract is terminated, such as dispute settlement clauses,[191] and (c) it would be inappropriate to attempt to undo the exchange of performances for the past where a contract is to be performed over a period of time.[192] In all these respects German law adopts the same view. Termination no longer precludes a claim for damages based on the contract.[193] Moreover, termination merely transforms the contractual relationship and therefore does not affect provisions like dispute settlement clauses. And for all contracts to be performed over a period of time the code now contains a special provision granting the aggrieved party a right to terminate the contract 'for a good cause'.[194] This type of termination is called *Kündigung* and merely operates *ex nunc*.[195]

[187] Flessner, (1997) 5 *Zeitschrift für Europäisches Privatrecht* 303 draws attention to the fact that the difference between termination *ipso iure* and by notice to the other party is not great in practice. The UNIDROIT Principles do not have a rule comparable to Art. 9:303 (4) PECL.

[188] Art. 9:305 PECL; cf. also Art. 7.3.5 (1) PICC. In Germany this is not expressly stated in the code but presupposed as being self-evident: Lorenz and Riehm (n. 18) 216; *Münchener Kommentar*/Gaier (n. 181) Vor § 346, n. 41.

[189] Lando and Beale (n. 19) 420, 422. For a comparative assessment of the effects of termination, and especially the limited value of general statements to the effect that termination operates either retrospectively or prospectively, see Treitel (n. 85) nn. 282 ff. [190] Art. 8:102 PECL; Art. 7.4.1 PICC.

[191] See Art. 9:305 (1) PECL; Art. 7.3.5 (3) PICC; these provisions have their origin in Art. 81 (1) 2 CISG. [192] Lando and Beale (n. 19) 420.

[193] This is now specifically stated in § 325 BGB and constitutes a significant change to what had hitherto been recognized. Under the old law, termination and damages were regarded as mutually exclusive remedies. This was, very widely, regarded as unsatisfactory: see, for example, *Abschlußbericht* (n. 33) 19, 31; Zimmermann, [1995] *Juristenzeitung* 485 ff.; Koziol (n. 97) 205 ff.; Meier, [2002] *Jura* 196 ff.; Gsell (n. 136) 122 ff. The intellectual origin of the new approach lies in Art. 45 (2) CISG.

[194] § 314 BGB. The provision merely codifies a rule that had previously been generally recognized by the courts and legal literature; it had been based on an analogy to §§ 626, 723 BGB. See, for example, *Anwaltkommentar*/Krebs (n. 18) § 314, n. 1; Lorenz and Riehm (n. 18) 120 ff.; *Münchener Kommentar*/Gaier (n. 181) § 313, n. 1; Ulrich Wackerbarth, 'Außerordentliche Kündigung von Dauerschuldverhältnissen und Abmahnung—Widersprüchliches in § 314 BGB n.F.', in Dauner-Lieb, Konzen and Schmidt (n. 12) 159 ff.

[195] For comparative discussion, see Treitel (n. 85) n. 283; Schlechtriem, (1993) 1 *Zeitschrift für Europäisches Privatrecht* 240 ff.; Flessner, (1997) 5 *Zeitschrift für Europäisches Privatrecht* 293 ff., 313.

(iv) Concerning the requirements for termination, German law has now also abandoned its insistence on fault; this is in line with the Principles (and international development in general).[196]

(v) Termination under the Principles is available in cases of fundamental breach of contract.[197] The BGB, on the other hand, requires the granting of an additional period of time before the remedy of termination is available.[198] In theory, this looks quite different. It must, however, be kept in mind that there are exceptions to this requirement in certain cases of serious breach.[199] The Principles, on the other hand, allow the creditor to elevate a non-fundamental delay in performance to a fundamental one by means of granting an extra period.[200] This does not, however, apply in cases of a defective performance.[201]

(vi) Both under the Principles and in German law, the creditor normally only loses his right to choose between claiming performance and terminating the contract at the time when he gives notice of termination.[202] Up to that moment, the law thus effectively gives him the right to speculate at his debtor's expense: he may keep the debtor in suspense and make his decision dependent upon the development of the market.[203] The draftsmen of the revised German law of obligations did not regard this as a problem in view of the fact that the debtor, after all, has committed a breach of duty.[204]

---

[196] Flessner, (1997) 5 *Zeitschrift für Europäisches Privatrecht* 296 ff.; Schlechtriem (n. 97) 166 ff.

[197] Art. 9:301 (1) PECL; Art. 7.3.1 PICC. The notion of fundamental non-performance is defined in Art. 8:103 PECL; cf. also Art. 7.3.1 (2) PICC; for comparative discussion, see Flessner, (1997) 5 *Zeitschrift für Europäisches Privatrecht* 266 ff.; Schwenzer (n. 12) 41 ff.; *Münchener Kommentar*/Ernst (n. 18) § 323, n. 5; *Staudinger*/Otto (n. 18) § 323, A 13 ff.

[198] Where the debtor infringes ancillary duties which do not affect the performance as such, the creditor may terminate the contract if he can no longer reasonably be expected to accept performance: see § 324 BGB and *supra* VII. 3. This may be regarded as a form of fundamental breach.

[199] § 323 II BGB; cf. *supra* n. 175.

[200] Arts. 8:106 (3), 9:301 (2) PECL; cf. also Art. 7.1.5 (3) PICC. The rule has been inspired by § 326 BGB old version (see Lando and Beale (n. 19) 377) and had, previously, also been adopted by Arts. 49 (1) (b) and 64 (1) (b) CISG ('*Nachfrist allemand*').

[201] This is stated expressly in Lando and Beale (n. 19) 374 ff. and also follows clearly from the wording of Arts. 8:106 (3), 9:301 (2) PECL. The position, insofar, is the same under CISG, see *Staudinger*/Magnus (n. 115) Art. 49, n. 21. Schlechtriem (n. 149) 167 ff. appears to interpret the Principles differently.

[202] For the Principles, see Art. 8:106 (3) second sentence, where it is stated that the creditor *may* in his notice provide that if the other party does not perform within the period fixed by the notice the contract shall end automatically.

[203] However, under the Principles the creditor loses his right to terminate the contract unless he gives notice within a reasonable time after he has or ought to have become aware of the non-performance: Art. 9:303 (2) PECL; cf. also Art. 7.3.2 (2) PICC. For Germany, see *Münchener Kommentar*/Gaier (n. 181) § 350, n. 2; *Palandt*/Heinrichs (n. 72) § 350, n. 1.

[204] See 'Begründung' (n. 42) 762; Huber, in Huber and Faust (n. 18) 189. For a comparative discussion of the problems relating to the creditor's *ius variandi*, see Flessner, (1997) 5 *Zeitschrift für Europäisches Privatrecht* 305 ff.

VIII. Other Remedies

The remaining remedies for breach of a contractual duty can be dealt with fairly briefly. First, there is the modern German version of the *exceptio non adimpleti contractus* (§ 320 BGB); it has remained unchanged by the reform and finds its equivalent in Article 9:201 (1) PECL.[205] If under a reciprocal contract one party would normally have to perform first, he may refuse to perform if he realizes, after conclusion of the contract, that his claim to the other party's counter-performance is endangered as a result of that other party's lack of ability to perform (§ 321 BGB). This is termed the 'defence of precariousness' (*Unsicherheitseinrede*) and it is new insofar as the defence is no longer confined to a deterioration in the financial circumstances of the other party.[206] The BGB, in this respect, has moved somewhat closer to the provision of Article 9:201 (2) PECL which focuses on situations where it is clear that there will be a non-performance by the other party.[207]

Secondly, and even apart from the provision of § 321 BGB, anticipatory non-performance has now found a place in the new code. Where the debtor has seriously and definitively refused to perform (*Erfüllungsverweigerung*) the creditor does not have to fix an additional period for performance in order to claim damages in lieu of performance (§ 281 II BGB) or to terminate the contract (§ 323 II No. 1 BGB). § 323 IV BGB specifically states that this applies even if such refusal has occurred before the time for performance has arrived, and the same rule has to be read into § 281 II BGB.[208] These rules were recognized even under the old law, though only on the basis of case law and legal doctrine.[209] Also according to Article 9:304 PECL, the contract may be terminated where, prior to performance, it is clear that there will be a fundamental non-performance;[210] and the comments make clear that a party which exercises a right to terminate the contract for anticipatory non-performance has the same rights as on termination for actual non-performance and is therefore entitled to claim damages.[211]

---

[205] Cf. also Art. 7.1.3 PICC. For historical background, see Wolfgang Ernst, *Die Einrede des nichterfüllten Vertrages* (2000); for a comparative discussion, see Treitel (n. 85) nn. 188 ff.

[206] § 321 BGB old version. For comment on the reform, see *Abschlußbericht* (n. 33) 158 ff.; *Anwaltkommentar*/Dauner-Lieb *et al.* (n. 18) § 321, n. 1; Huber, in Huber and Faust (n. 18) 180 ff.; *Staudinger*/Otto (n. 18) § 321, nn. 1 ff.

[207] Cf. also Art. 71 (1) CISG. The rules provided by CISG and PECL are not, however, only applicable in situations where one party has to perform first.

[208] This view is also taken by *Anwaltkommentar*/Dauner-Lieb *et al.* (n. 18) § 281, n. 20; Faust, in Huber and Faust (n. 18) 120; *Münchener Kommentar*/Ernst (n. 18) § 281, n. 62; *Staudinger*/Otto (n. 18) § 281, B 103; *Jauernig*/Stadler (n. 33) § 281, n. 9.

[209] *Palandt*/Heinrichs (n. 24) § 276, n. 124, § 326, nn. 20 ff. For a detailed discussion, see Huber (n. 3) vol. II, §§ 51–53.   [210] Cf. also Art. 7.3.3 PICC and Art. 72 CISG.

[211] Lando and Beale (n. 19) 418. For a comparative assessment, cf. Schlechtriem, (1993) 1 *Zeitschrift für Europäisches Privatrecht* 237 ff.

Thirdly, the right to price reduction is still confined, in German law, to its traditional areas of application, i.e. the law of sale (§ 441 BGB), lease (§ 536 BGB) and contracts for work (§ 638 BGB). Proposals to generalize this remedy[212] have not been implemented. They would have brought German law into line with Article 9:401 PECL.

The rules on *mora creditoris*, fourthly, have only very slightly been adjusted by the reform of the law of obligations.[213] As under the old law, the creditor is not obliged to receive performance but only entitled to do so. Unlike the creditor in the case of *mora debtoris*, the debtor in the event of *mora creditoris* does not have a right to sue for damages or to terminate the contract: by not accepting performance the creditor does not commit a breach of contract. The rules on *mora creditoris* are merely designed, in certain respects, to relieve the position of a debtor who has done whatever the law expects him to do.[214] The position, therefore, is different to the one prevailing in England where a creditor can be held responsible for breach of contract in the same way as a debtor.[215] The approach adopted in the Principles of European Contract Law (but not in the UNIDROIT Principles) is structurally similar to German law though the regulation found in Articles 7:110 and 7:111 PECL is, on the one hand, less specific than §§ 293 ff. BGB; on the other hand, it also deals with matters considered in another systematic context in German law.[216] The Principles also do not provide for a relaxation of the debtor's liability as does § 300 I BGB; nor do they contain a risk rule on the model of § 300 II BGB.

IX. Concluding Observations

It has been said that the most striking feature of the new German law relating to breach of contract is the simplicity of the structure of its rules.[217] This appears to be an exaggeration. None the less it is true that the structure of the

---

[212] See Manfred Lieb, 'Dienstvertrag', in Bundesminister der Justiz (ed.), *Gutachten und Vorschläge zur Überarbeitung des Schuldrechts* vol. III (1983), 209 ff.; cf. also Konrad Rusch, 'Gewinnabschöpfung bei Vertragsbruch—Teil II', (2002) 10 *Zeitschrift für Europäisches Privatrecht* 132 ff.

[213] On the change of § 296 BGB (which is consequent upon that in § 286 II no. 2 BGB), see *Anwaltkommentar/*Dauner-Lieb *et al.* (n. 18) § 296, n. 2; Lorenz and Riehm (n. 18) 175.

[214] §§ 293 ff. BGB; see *Law of Obligations* (n. 1) 817 ff.; Treitel (n. 85) n. 35.

[215] See Treitel (n. 85) n. 36; cf. also the comparative discussion in Uwe Hüffer, *Leistungsstörungen durch Gläubigerhandeln* (1976), 134 ff.

[216] Zimmermann, [1995] *Juristenzeitung* 489 ff.; and see the analysis by Antoni Vaquer Aloy, 'Mora creditoris and the Principles of European Contract Law', in Santiago Espiau Espiau and Antoni Vaquer Aloy (eds.), *Bases de un Derecho Contractual Europeo* (2003), 385 ff.

[217] Zimmer, [2002] *Neue Juristische Wochenschrift* 12.

new rules is more easily comprehensible than that of the old law.[218] Moreover, the new rules have moved considerably closer to the system of remedies which is increasingly recognized internationally and which has found its most modern manifestation in the Principles of European Contract Law and the UNIDROIT Principles of International Commercial Contracts. Both sets of Principles have been taken into consideration during the last stages of the German reform process.[219] They should now much more readily be resorted to as a comparative baseline for evaluating, interpreting, and developing the new German rules.[220] On the other hand, however, German law contains a number of rules and ideas which can, and should, be used to refine the international Principles. This is true, particularly, where the new rules reflect well-established and time-tested experiences of one hundred years of legal development under the old law of obligations. Where the BGB now adopts new thinking patterns, or attempts to tailor new doctrinal tools for solving the old problems, its value within contemporary comparative discourse is considerably reduced: for it will take many years before it can safely be assessed whether these tools and thinking patterns have stood the test of legal practice.[221] There is place for some scepticism, as far as rules like § 275 II or § 311a BGB, or the coordination between the old established types of breach of contract and the new general concept of 'breach of duty' are concerned.[222] Distinguishing the different types of loss envisaged by § 280 BGB is a task of frightening complexity; yet, this is where the investigation into any damages claim will have to start. Already, these issues have come to be surrounded by profound doctrinal controversies.[223]

---

[218] Irritatingly, perhaps for foreign observers, these rules can be found in two different systematic places: Book 2, Section 1 (Content of Obligations) (§§ 275 ff. BGB) and Book 2, Section 3, Title 2 (Synallagmatic Contracts) (§§ 320 ff. BGB). This reflects the traditional desire, as far as possible, to provide rules covering all types of obligations, including unilaterally binding, or imperfectly bilateral, contracts. §§ 275 ff. BGB essentially deal with the transition from the claim to specific performance to a damages claim and are not, therefore, confined to synallagmatic contracts. §§ 320 ff. BGB, on the other hand, deal with the impact of one party's failure to perform, or to perform properly, on the other party's obligation. This has the consequence of obscuring the parallelism of the claim for damages and the right of termination. Both the Principles of European Contract Law and the UNIDROIT Principles of International Commercial Contracts, on the other hand, contain uniform sets of rules relating to non-performance of 'an obligation under the contract' (Art. 8:101 (1) PECL, and see Art. 7.1.1 PICC). [219] Cf. *supra* n. 11.

[220] On the role of the Principles within the system of legal sources in a national legal system like the German one, see Claus-Wilhelm Canaris, 'Die Stellung der "UNIDROIT Principles" und der "Principles of European Contract Law" im System der Rechtsquellen', in Basedow (n. 36) 5 ff.; Reinhard Zimmermann, 'The Principles of European Contract Law: Contemporary Manifestations of the Old, and Possible Foundations for a New, European Scholarship of Private Law', in *Essays in Honour of Hein Kötz* (2005), forthcoming.

[221] Zimmer, [2002] *Neue Juristische Wochenschrift* 12, even predicts that decades will pass before the courts have applied the new rules in a way that re-establishes legal certainty.

[222] Cf. also the evaluation of the new rules by *Münchener Kommentar/Ernst* (n. 18) Vorbem. § 275, nn. 25 ff. [223] Cf., for example, *supra* III.4.

At the same time, German legal doctrine is still in the process of readjusting itself to the new situation. Thus, of the first two textbooks on the new law which appeared simultaneously in Germany's major legal publishing house, one adopts a structure which is essentially remedy-based[224] whereas the other presents the law as if it were structured according to the different forms of breach.[225] This does not necessarily reflect a weakness in German law's attempt to strike a balance between the system established before the reform and the remedy-based structure of the Principles. The clearly structured and easily comprehensible, but very general, provisions contained in the Principles will have to be specified for certain typical forms of breach of contract should they come to be applied in practice. As a result, they will be subject to a considerable degree of doctrinal refinement. The experiences gathered with the new rules of German law will then be very valuable. At any rate, however, the process of a critical evaluation of *both* the new German law of breach of contract and of the rules relating to non-performance under the Principles has only just started.

[224] Huber and Faust (n. 18).   [225] Lorenz and Riehm (n. 18).

3

The Development of Liability for Non-conformity in German Sales Law

I. Introduction

1. The old approach

Sale has always been, and continues to be, the central type of transaction in a developed economy.[1] It is equally important as a commercial and as a consumer transaction.[2] At the same time, there are still many sales in everyday life which fall into neither of these modern categories.[3] Every purchaser, no matter whether he is a merchant, or a consumer, is interested in receiving an object that is free from defects. Usually, this is his central concern. Of course, a legal system may say: *caveat emptor*; or: let the eye be the purchaser's chapman; or: *qui n'ouvre pas les yeux doit ouvrir la bourse*.[4] It is a harsh but healthy attitude of the law to prevent a purchaser from challenging the contract if he had had a chance to examine the object of the sale.[5] For if that object turns out to be defective, it is often difficult to establish whether the defect existed already at the time when the contract was concluded, or when the object was handed over,[6] or whether it only came about after the object had left the seller's sphere of

---

[1] Matters were different in the days of an early subsistence economy; see Paul. D. 18, 1, 1, 1; Gai. III, 141.

[2] Modern German law has special rules for both of these manifestations of the contract of sale; see §§ 373 ff. HGB and §§ 474 BGB. Both sets of rules are not self-contained; they must be read against the background of the general rules on the law of sale in §§ 433 ff. BGB.

[3] For instance, cases where a 'consumer' (as defined in § 13 BGB) does not buy a movable object from an entrepreneur (as defined in § 14 BGB) but from another 'consumer'. Contracts relating to land provide another example.

[4] Old proverb, see Hamilton, (1931) 40 *Yale LJ* 1164. See Reinhard Zimmermann, *The Law of Obligations: Roman Foundation of the Civilian Tradition*, paperback edition (1996), 306 ff. with references; for English law cf. also Nicole Schneider, *Uberrima fides: Treu und Glauben und vorvertragliche Aufklärungspflichten im englischen Recht* (2004), 111 ff.

[5] For England, see Patrick S. Atiyah, *The Rise and Fall of Freedom of Contract* (1979), 179 ff.: 'But when householders bought most of their commodities at local markets or fairs, when they were able to examine what they bought by look and feel, and haggle over the price, it may be that they "would be more likely to feel ashamed of being outwitted than outraged at being swindled" '.

[6] The former was the relevant moment in Roman law, the latter is relevant in modern German law: §§ 434 I, 446 BGB.

influence. Even in Republican Rome, however, contracts of sale were no longer necessarily concluded and executed at one and the same time. Thus, the purchaser did not always have the object of the transaction 'before his eyes'. And even if he had, he could hardly be expected to discover whether a slave was prone to committing suicide, or had the habit of roving about.[7] Every developed legal system, therefore, provides the disappointed purchaser with remedies for defects as to quality. Continental legal systems traditionally provided a special set of remedies that was distinguished by the following features: the purchaser could either undo the contract by claiming back his purchase price, or ask for a reduction of the purchase price. Damages could only be claimed in exceptional situations, viz. if a promised quality in the object sold was absent, or if the vendor had fraudulently concealed a defect. Except in cases of fraud, these claims were subject to short prescription periods, the commencement of which did not depend on whether the purchaser knew of, or could reasonably discover, the defect.[8] There were, of course, many differences in detail between the various national legal systems. But the general structure of the liability rules was remarkably similar in all the codes up to, and including, the Italian *Codice Civile* of 1942.

2. The Consumer Sales Directive

The widespread acceptance of a set of rules which do not strike the unbiased observer as the only imaginable, perhaps not even as an obvious, solution to the problem of defects as to the quality of the object sold, represents a remarkable degree of traditionalism. Liability for latent defects[9] was, until comparatively recently, decisively determined by an edict issued in the early part of the second century BC by the Roman magistrates responsible for policing the sale of slaves and cattle on an open market.[10] German law has adhered to this tradition particularly faithfully and in spite of the fact that coordination of the special rules concerning latent defects with the system of contractual and delictual liability in general has thrown up intractable problems of great complexity. The

---

[7] For these defects of character (which the Roman market police placed on the same level as diseases or physical defects), see Ulp. D. 21, 1, 1, 1; Ulp. D. 21, 1, 23, 3; Ulp. D. 21, 1, 17, 14.

[8] For a comprehensive comparative analysis, see Andreas Schwartze, *Europäische Sachmängelgewährleistung beim Warenkauf* (2000), 174 ff. (redhibition), 220 ff. (reduction of purchase price), 261 ff. (promised quality), 272 ff. (fraud), 493 ff. (prescription period), 496 ff. (commencement of prescription period).

[9] All legal systems exclude the purchaser's right to claim in cases where he was aware of, or could easily become aware of, the defect; for details see Schwartze (n. 8) 120 ff. The seller's liability in Roman law referred to latent defects *stricto sensu*. Most closely following Roman law, in this respect, are French law ('Le vendeur n'est pas tenu des vices apparents...': Art. 1642 *Code civil*) and Austrian law (§ 928, 1 ABGB: defects must not be apparent).

[10] See generally Max Kaser, *Das römische Privatrecht*, vol. I, 2nd edn. (1971), 557 ff.; *Law of Obligations* (n. 4) 311 ff.; Eva Jakab, *Praedicere und cavere beim Marktkauf: Sachmängel im griechischen und römischen Recht* (1997), 125 ff.; *eadem*, 'Diebische Sklaven, marode Balken: Von den römischen Wurzeln der Gewährleistung für Sachmängel', in Martin Schermaier (ed.), *Verbraucherkauf in Europa* (2003), 27 ff.

necessity of implementing the Consumer Sales Directive of 25 May 1999[11] has given the German government an opportunity to effect a radical reform. This reform was, *inter alia*, intended to advance the Europeanization of private law. It is therefore legitimate to ask whether the new German sales law may indeed be regarded as an exponent of an emerging European sales law. This chapter will discuss key features of the new approach adopted in the German Civil Code and to place them in historical and comparative perspective. It confines itself to liability for latent defects[12] and, within this area, to the remedies available to disappointed purchasers.[13]

[11] *Supra* p. 1. For a comprehensive analysis of how the Consumer Sales Directive has been implemented in the Member States of the European Union, see Heinz-Peter Mansel, 'Kaufrechtsreform in Europa und die Dogmatik des deutschen Leistungsstörungsrechts', (2004) 204 *Archiv für die civilistische Praxis* 408 ff.

[12] As to the question when an object is defective, § 434 I BGB states that an object is free from defects as to quality if, upon the passing of the risk, it is of the quality agreed upon between the parties. If there is no such agreement, the object is free from defects (i) if it is fit for the use presupposed in the contract, and otherwise (ii) if it is fit for the normal use and its quality is such as is usual in objects of the same kind and can be expected by the purchaser by virtue of its nature. Thus, the code now endorses what used to be known, under the old law, as the 'subjective' concept of a defect: in the first place the agreement of the parties determines whether an object is defective or not; for a discussion, see Ulrich Huber, in *Soergel*, *Bürgerliches Gesetzbuch*, vol. III, 12th edn. (1991), Vorbem. § 459, nn. 20 ff. Contrary to Art. 2 of the Directive (which uses the notion of 'conformity with the contract') § 434 I BGB does not merely lay down presumptions as to when an object is free from defects (i.e. 'in conformity with the contract'). The approach adopted in the Directive, as Florian Faust points out, is unfortunate, in that if an object is not presumed to be in conformity with the contract this does not mean that it *is* not in conformity with the contract (i.e. defective): Florian Faust, in Georg Bamberger and Herbert Roth (eds.), *Kommentar zum Bürgerlichen Gesetzbuch*, vol. I (2003), § 434, n. 7. This deviation from the Directive is admissible in terms of Art. 8 (2) of the Directive since it is advantageous to the purchaser. For details of the interpretation of Art. 2 of the Directive, see Peter Huber, 'Kaufrecht—made in Europe! Die EG-Richtlinie über den Verbrauchsgüterkauf und ihre Folgen für das deutsche Gewährleistungsrecht', in *Festschrift für Dieter Henrich* (2000), 298 ff.; Stefan Grundmann, in Massimo C. Bianca and Stefan Grundmann (eds.), *EU Sales Directive: Commentary* (2002), Art. 2 (nn. 117 ff.); for the interpretation of § 434 I BGB, see Hans-Christoph Grigoleit and Carsten Herresthal, 'Grundlagen der Sachmängelhaftung im Kaufrecht', [2003] *Juristenzeitung* 118 ff.; Faust (as above) § 434, nn. 1 ff.; Harm Peter Westermann, in *Münchener Kommentar zum Bürgerlichen Gesetzbuch*, 4th edn., vol. III (2004), § 434, nn. 1 ff.; Annemarie Matusche-Beckmann, in *J. von Staudingers Kommentar zum Bürgerlichen Gesetzbuch*, revised edition (2004), § 434, nn. 1 ff. The concept of 'conformity' (with the contract) has been received into the Directive from Art. 35 of the United Nations Convention on Contracts for the International Sale of Goods (CISG); it illustrates the tendency of the draftsmen of the Directive to coordinate the two instruments: see Dirk Staudenmeyer, 'Die EG-Richtlinie über den Verbrauchsgüterkauf', [1999] *Neue Juristische Wochenschrift* 2394 ff.; Ulrich Magnus, 'Die Verbrauchsgüterkauf-Richtlinie und das UN-Kaufrecht', in Stefan Grundmann, Dieter Medicus and Walter Rolland (eds.), *Europäisches Kaufgewährleistungsrecht* (2000), 79 ff.; *idem*, 'The CISG's Impact on European Legislation', in Franco Ferrari (ed.), *The 1980 Uniform Sales Law: Old Issues Revisited in the Light of Recent Experiences* (2003), 129 ff. Ultimately, the notion of 'conformity', as contained in Art. 35 CISG, derives from the common law; see Ernst Rabel, *Das Recht des Warenkaufs*, vol. II (1958), 107, 161 ff.; for a comparison with conformity according to the UCC, see Richard Hyland, 'Liability of the Seller for Conformity of the Goods under the UN-Convention (CISG) and the Uniform UCC', in Peter Schlechtriem (ed.), *Einheitliches Kaufrecht und nationales Obligationenrecht* (1987), 305 ff.; cf. also Denis Tallon, 'La consécration de la notion de conformité après la Convention des Nations-Unies sur les contrats de vente internationale de merchandises', in *Rechtsvergleichung, Europarecht und Staatenintegration, Gedächtnisschrift für Léontin-Jean Constantinesco* (1983), 753 ff.

[13] The lecture on which this chapter is based was dedicated to the memory of John Kelly (1931–1991; Professor of Roman Law and Jurisprudence in the Faculty of Law at University College

II. Liability for Latent Defects: The Old BGB and its Historical Background

1. Roman law

The aedilitian remedies provided a fair and balanced solution[14] to problems that had arisen with regard to certain individualized commodities which were (i) regularly sold on open markets, (ii) notoriously prone to suffer from defects which even vigilant purchasers were unable to discover on sight, and (iii) offered for sale by persons who had a questionable reputation.[15] The purchaser could avail himself of the *actio quanti minoris* or the *actio redhibitoria*. Thus, he could either claim *quanto ob id vitium minoris fuerit*,[16] i.e. the difference in value between what the slave, or piece of cattle, was actually worth and what that object would have been worth had it been free from defects or possessed the promised qualities; or he could demand repayment of the entire price in return for restoring the slave, or piece of cattle.[17] The first of these remedies could be brought within a year of *prima potestas experiundi vitium*,[18] the latter within six months.[19] The purchaser could not claim damages; on the other hand, however, the seller was liable irrespective of whether he had been at fault or whether he had made specific assertions as to the quality of the object sold. Apart from that, of course, the *actio empti* was available with regard to all types of objects of sale where the seller had acted in such a way that it would have seemed to be in conflict with good faith were he not to be held liable.[20] Two groups of cases fell into this category: the vendor was liable, first, where he had fraudulently failed to disclose a defect known to him and, secondly, where he had specifically assured the purchaser, in the course of concluding the contract, that the object was free from defects or that it possessed certain qualities.[21]

Dublin, and subsequently Member of Parliament, Senator, Minister for Industry and Commerce, and Attorney General), a man deeply learned both in Roman law and modern law. He was a keen proponent of an historical approach to law and must therefore have disliked to see rules or ideas of the past unfitly surviving in a changed environment. Kelly took an active interest in Germany, having spent two formative years at the University of Heidelberg.

[14] For the same evaluation see, for example, Jakab, in Schermaier (n. 10) 37.

[15] See, for instance, Paul. D. 21, 1, 44, 1; Aulus Gellius, *Noctes Atticae*, Lib. IV, II, 5; cf. also Ulp. D. 21, 1, 38 pr.   [16] Aulus Gellius (n. 15); cf. also Ulp. D. 21, 1, 38 pr.

[17] 'Iulianus ait iudicium redhibitoriae actionis utrumque, id est venditorem et emptorem, quodammodo in integrum restituere debere': Ulp. D. 21, 1, 23, 7; cf. also Ulp. D. 21, 1, 21 pr.

[18] Ulp. D. 21, 1, 38 pr.; and cf. Pap. D. 21, 1, 55.

[19] Ulp. D. 21, 1, 19, 6; Pap. D. 21, 1, 55. See Christian Baldus, 'Una actione experiri debet? Zur Klagenkonkurrenz bei Sachmängeln im römischen Kaufrecht', (1999) 5 *Orbis Iuris Romani* 36 ff.

[20] On the role of *bona fides* in Roman contract law and, in particular, concerning *emptio venditio* (the prime example of a type of transaction giving rise to *iudicia bonae fidei*), see Martin Schermaier, 'Bona fides in Roman contract law', in Reinhard Zimmermann and Simon Whittaker (eds.), *Good Faith in European Contract Law* (2000), 63 ff.   [21] See Kaser (n. 10) 557 ff.; *Law of Obligations* (n. 4) 308 ff.

2. *Ius commune*

This was the point of departure for a development which was to culminate in
the modern codifications. Even in the course of classical Roman jurisprudence
there was already an energetic move towards a generalized liability for latent
defects. The aedilitian remedies appear to have been regarded as sufficiently
equitable and well-balanced to be read into the *oportere ex fide bona* clause of
the *actio empti* and thus they were received, eventually, into the *ius civile*.[22] A
more refined interpretation of what was owed, in good faith, under the general
action on sale had thus, effectively, made the original, aedilitian creation
redundant as a self-contained and independent set of remedies. In view of this,
Justinian might have been expected to abolish it. In fact, however, the aedilitian
remedies *proprio sensu* were not only retained,[23] but their range of application
was extended, beyond slaves and cattle, to cover the sale of all objects 'tam
earum quae soli sint quam earum quae mobiles aut se moventes'.[24] The continued existence of two sets of remedies, both dealing with latent defects in the
thing sold, could not but cause difficulties.[25] Generations of lawyers wondered
about its hidden rationale and attempted to find differences between the
praetorian and civilian ways of dealing with redhibition or assessing *quanti
minoris*.[26] Eventually, however, it became clear that the remedies had to be
merged, as far as they overlapped. *Digesta* 21, 1 (*De aedilicio edicto et redhibitione
et quanti minoris*) was usually regarded as *sedes materiae* and the appropriate
place to discuss the rules relating to latent defects. Whether, under these
circumstances, the *actio empti* gradually faded away and finally disappeared
from the scene[27] or whether, the other way round, the aedilitian remedies were
fitted into the general framework of the *actio empti* and the corresponding
duties arising from sale[28]—the practical result was the same: the whole complex

---

[22] Kaser (n. 10) 558; *Law of Obligations* (n. 4) 319 ff.; Baldus, (1999) 5 *Orbis Iuris Romani* 40 ff.
For a more cautious assessment of the development, see Jakab, in Schermaier (n. 10) 37 ff.

[23] Cf. *Constitutio Omnem 4, Constitutio Tanta* 5; Ernst Levy, *Weströmisches Vulgarrecht: Das
Obligationenrecht* (1956), 223 ff.

[24] Ulp. D. 21, 1, 1 pr. (interpolated); cf. further, for example, C. 4, 58, 4, 1; Max Kaser, *Das römische
Privatrecht*, vol. II, 2nd edn. (1975), 393 ff.

[25] *Law of Obligations* (n. 4) 322 ff. (with references to the older literature); Eltjo Schrage, 'Die
Gewährleistung beim Kauf im Mittelalter', in Schermaier (n. 10) 55 ff.; Paolo Maria Vecchi, 'La
garanzia nella vendita in diritto comune', in Schermaier (n. 10) 67 ff.

[26] 'Miretur vel aliquis, Cur Aediles introduxerint actiones, Redhibitoriam et Aestimatoriam, cum
ex iisdem causis competant actiones Civiles. . . . Sed mirari desinat, Differentiae inter illas actiones
Aedilitias et Civiles multae sunt': Johannes Jacobus Wissenbach, *Exercitationes ad Quinquaginta
Libros Pandectarum*, 4th edn., Lipsiae (1673), Disp. XLI, n. 9.

[27] See, for example, Ulrich Huber, *Praelectiones juris civilis*, 4th edn., Francofurti et Lipsiae (1749),
Lib. XXI, Tit. I, nn. 4 ff.

[28] See, for example, Wolfgang Adam Lauterbach, *Collegium theoretico-practicum*, Tubingae (1723 ff.),
Lib. XXI, Tit. I, XXXIV.

was governed by a single set of rules (sometimes referred to as *actio empti quanti minoris/actio empti redhibitoria*). This was also the easiest way to cope with the one major difficulty arising in the practical application of the law; for however much the actions had become assimilated, there always remained one characteristic difference: the *actiones redhibitoria* and *quanti minoris* could only be brought within six months and one year respectively, whereas the *actio empti* was subject to the general prescription period of thirty years.[29] The greater the identity between the remedies, the more unsatisfactory this divergence. In the end, therefore, it came to be accepted that the claims for redhibition and reduction of the purchase price had to be subjected to the strict temporal limitation envisaged by the *aediles*, irrespective of the doctrinal basis for these claims.[30] By the time the BGB was drafted, the streamlined form of liability for latent defects derived from Roman law was both well-established and regarded as well-tested,[31] and it was thus perpetuated in the Code.

3. The sale of unascertained goods

a) Roman law

The most important, and at the same time most problematic, aspect of this process of generalization was that the Roman system of remedies for latent defects, tailored originally for the sale of specific goods,[32] had become applicable to the sale of objects described as being of a particular kind, or belonging to a particular class (unascertained goods). *Emptio venditio*, the Roman contract of sale, was an obligatory act in that it gave rise to obligations on the part of the seller (to deliver the object sold) and on the part of the purchaser (to pay the purchase price agreed upon). At the same time, however, it also had the effect of allocating the object, as far as the relationship between the two parties was concerned, to the purchaser.[33] This explains a number of peculiarities of the

---

[29] Based on C. 7, 39, 3, 1 (Honor. et Theodos.).

[30] See, for example, Christian Friedrich Glück, *Ausführliche Erläuterung der Pandecten nach Hellfeld*, vol. XX (1819), 153 ff. Otherwise the *actio empti* would entirely have cut away the ground for the aedilitian actions; see, for example, Hugo Donellus, 'Commentaria ad titulum, de aediliticio edicto', in *Opera Omnia*, vol. X, Maceratae (1832), Cap. V, n. 4.

[31] See, for example, Heinrich Dernburg, *Pandekten*, vol. II, 6th edn. (1900), §§ 100 and 101; Bernhard Windscheid and Theodor Kipp, *Lehrbuch des Pandektenrechts*, 9th edn. (1906), §§ 393–395; Franz Philipp von Kübel, 'Vorlage des Redaktors', in Werner Schubert (ed.), *Die Vorlagen der Redaktoren für die erste Kommission zur Ausarbeitung des Entwurfs eines Bürgerlichen Gesetzbuches, Recht der Schuldverhältnisse*, Part 1 (1980), 411 ff. ('The draft, in this field, essentially follows the principles of Roman law which have been tested in commercial practice and which have, nearly without exception, been accepted in modern legislation': 412).   [32] Rabel (n. 12) 101 ff.

[33] Frank Peters, 'Die Verschaffung des Eigentums durch den Verkäufer', (1979) 96 *Zeitschrift der Savigny-Stiftung für Rechtsgeschichte, Romanistische Abteilung* 185 ff.; *Law of Obligations* (n. 4) 239 ff.;

Roman law of sale, among them the famous risk rule (*emptione perfecta periculum est emptoris*).[34] It also explains the fact that the Roman *emptio venditio*, according to the very structure of this transaction, could not refer to unascertained goods.[35] For while it is perfectly possible to create an obligation to deliver twenty barrels of a specific type of white wine, or of five units of winter grain, it is not conceivable to allocate twenty barrels or five units to the purchaser, as long as they have not been specified. However, once they have been specified, we are no longer dealing with the sale of unascertained goods. This did not, of course, mean that Roman tradesmen could not engage in what effectively amounted to a sale of goods by description. A whole variety of alternative avenues was available to accommodate the need for such transactions.[36] But it did mean that they could not be accommodated by way of *emptio venditio*. It also meant that all the rules developed by the Roman lawyers within the framework of this type of contract, as a matter of course, related to the sale of specific objects, and were developed from this perspective. The aedilitian remedies provide a good example. If a specific slave was sold who was short-sighted[37] or blind during parts of the day,[38] who suffered from epileptic fits[39] or any other chronic disease,[40] or who could only give birth to dead children,[41] it could not possibly be demanded of the seller to remove the defect; nor was it imaginable to give the seller another chance to earn his purchase price by supplying another slave free from defects. Claims for redhibition, reduction of the purchase price, and damages were thus the only realistic options in the remedial armoury, and they were, in fact, the ones on which the Roman lawyers focused their attention.

b) Tensions

Since it had followed from the structure of the Roman *emptio venditio* that unascertained goods could not become the object of this type of transaction,

Martin Bauer, *Periculum Emptoris: Eine dogmengeschichtliche Untersuchung zur Gefahrtragung beim Kauf* (1998), 75 ff.; Wolfgang Ernst, 'Die Vorgeschichte der exceptio non adimpleti contractus', in *Festgabe für Werner Flume* (1998), 36 ff.; Ralf Michaels, *Sachzuordnung durch Kaufvertrag* (2002), 70 ff.

[34] On which see Wolfgang Ernst, 'Periculum est emptoris', (1982) 99 *Zeitschrift der Savigny-Stiftung für Rechtsgeschichte, Romanistische Abteilung* 216 ff.; *Law of Obligations* (n. 4) 281 ff.; Bauer (n. 33) 26 ff., 72 ff.

[35] Peters, (1979) 96 *Zeitschrift der Savigny-Stiftung für Rechtsgeschichte, Romanistische Abteilung* 189; *Law of Obligations* (n. 4) 240.

[36] Wolfgang Ernst, 'Kurze Rechtsgeschichte des Gattungskaufs', (1999) 7 *Zeitschrift für Europäisches Privatrecht* 600 ff. (drawing attention to the use of penalty clauses—by means of which a promise to deliver goods described by class could be made indirectly enforceable—to the *stipulatio triticaria*, to obligatory instruments of Hellenistic provenance, to the *constitutum debiti*, to the *fenus nauticum*, and to other devices). [37] Ulp. D. 21, 1, 10, 3.

[38] Ulp. D. 21, 1, 10, 4. [39] Jav. D. 21, 1, 53. [40] Ulp. D. 21, 1, 6 pr.
[41] Ulp. D. 21, 1, 14 pr.

the *corpus iuris* did not, of course, contain a specific prohibition to this effect. It did, however, contain examples of the sale of unascertained goods from a specific supply. This was the *emptio ad mensuram* ('ten amphorae of wine from my cellar'). It was, strangely perhaps from our modern point of view, conceptualized as a sale of the specific quantity that was to be allocated by way of *adpendere, adnumerare,* or *admetiri,* from that supply.[42] At the same time, the *emptio ad mensuram* could easily be taken to constitute a first, and very significant, step towards recognition of the sale of unascertained goods. This was the perspective adopted by the medieval Glossators who could not see a difference, in principle, between what came to be termed *venditio in genere limitato* and *venditio in genere generalissimo*: 'sic fit venditio in quantitate, sive in genere: quod idem est'.[43] Such equation was facilitated by the fact that Justinian's compilation emphasized the obligatory aspects of the consensual contract of sale.[44] That it also constituted an act of allocation was no longer very obvious. As a result, the rules relating to *emptio venditio* became applicable, in medieval law, to the sale of unascertained goods: a type of transaction which had become increasingly important in the buzzing economic climate of the twelfth and thirteenth centuries.[45]

The subjection of what soon emerged as economically the most important form of sale to a set of rules tailored for an act allocating a specific object to the purchaser was to cause doctrinal tensions in a number of fields, among them, most prominently, the question of risk[46] and liability for latent defects.[47] Occasionally, alternative approaches were developed. A number of authors conceptualized the sale of unascertained goods as relating to incorporeal objects.[48] The draftsmen of the Prussian Code of 1794 devised a specific set of rules to cover the purchase for future delivery (*Lieferungskauf*) and thus, effectively,

---

[42] Wolfgang Ernst, 'Gattungskauf und Lieferungskauf im römischen Recht', (1997) 114 *Zeitschrift der Savigny-Stiftung für Rechtsgeschichte, Romanistische Abteilung* 303 ff., 315 ff.; on the *emptio ad mensuram* cf. also *Law of Obligations* (n. 4) 236 ff.; Ernst, (1999) 7 *Zeitschrift für Europäisches Privatrecht* 597 ff.; Thomas Rüfner, *Vertretbare Sachen? Die Geschichte der res, quae pondere numero mensura constant* (2000), 49 ff.

[43] *Glossa vaeneant* ad C. 4, 48, 2; for details, see Bauer (n. 33) 98 ff.; Ernst, (1999) 7 *Zeitschrift für Europäisches Privatrecht* 612 ff.

[44] Ernst, (1997) 114 *Zeitschrift der Savigny-Zeitschrift für Rechtsgeschichte, Romanistische Abteilung* 343 ff.; cf. also Helmut Coing, 'A Typical Development in the Roman Law of Sales', in *idem, Gesammelte Aufsätze zu Rechtsgeschichte, Rechtsphilosophie und Zivilrecht,* vol. I (1982), 71 ff.; Kaser (n. 24) § 264 I 2.

[45] See, for example, Harold J. Berman, *Law and Revolution: The Formation of the Western Legal Tradition* (1983), 99 ff., 333 ff.

[46] Bauer (n. 33) 113 ff. (concerning Roman-Dutch law); Ernst, (1999) 7 *Zeitschrift für Europäisches Privatrecht* 624 ff.   [47] Ernst, (1999) 7 *Zeitschrift für Europäisches Privatrecht* 627 ff.

[48] See Rüfner (n. 42) 96 ff.; Ernst, (1999) 7 *Zeitschrift für Europäisches Privatrecht* 630 ff., both with references.

introduced a two-track approach to the law of sale.[49] Predominantly, however, the sale of specific as well as unascertained goods continued to be treated as instances of one and the same type of transaction with a uniform set of rules. This was facilitated by the rise of the modern, generalized concept of contract.[50] Every contract is based on two promises, or declarations of intention, and it gives rise to obligations to carry out these intentions. Sale is the paradigmatic case of a contract engendering mutual obligations on the part of both the seller and the purchaser. But it engenders only these obligations and does not, in addition, allocate the object to the purchaser. Obviously, therefore, any remaining obstacle to the recognition of the sale of unascertained goods as part and parcel of the general law of sale had been removed.[51] At the same time, this change of conceptual basis accentuated the problems in the application of the Roman rules relating to *emptio venditio* even further. For some of these rules were now, strictly speaking, no longer suitable even for the sale of specific goods.[52] Why the risk of accidental destruction of the object of sale should have to be borne by the purchaser from the moment of conclusion of a contract of purely obligatory character has remained a mystery.[53] The writers and codificatons of the Age of Enlightenment, therefore, were hostile to the Roman rule of *emptione perfecta periculum est emptoris*,[54] and so were the draftsmen of the BGB.[55]

c) Controversy and compromise

The traditional regime of liability for latent defects, on the other hand, continued to be regarded as well suited for the sale of specific goods. What became controversial among nineteenth-century authors, however, was whether it could also adequately govern the sale of unascertained goods.[56] For it was recognized,

---

[49] Wolfgang Ernst, 'Das Lieferungsgeschäft als Vertragstyp seit dem Preussischen Allgemeinen Landrecht', in *Festschrift für Wolfgang Zöllner*, vol. II (1998), 1097 ff.

[50] Helmut Coing, *Europäisches Privatrecht*, vol. I (1985), 398 ff.; Klaus-Peter Nanz, *Die Entstehung des allgemeinen Vertragsbegriffs im 16–18. Jahrhundert* (1985); *Law of Obligations* (n. 4) 537 ff.; John Barton (ed.), *Towards a General Law of Contract* (1990); Robert Feenstra, 'Die Klagbarkeit der pacta nuda', in Robert Feenstra and Reinhard Zimmermann (eds.), *Das römisch-holländische Recht: Fortschritte des Zivilrechts im 17. und 18. Jahrhundert* (1992), 123 ff.

[51] Ernst, (1999) 7 *Zeitschrift für Europäisches Privatrecht* 632 ff.

[52] This is emphasized by Ernst, (1999) 7 *Zeitschrift für Europäisches Privatrecht* 634.

[53] See Bauer (n. 33) 261 who, correctly, states that it is impossible to find a convincing doctrinal justification for the Roman risk rule given the modern concept of contract; cf. also Eugen Bucher, 'Die Eigentums-Translativwirkung von Schuldverträgen: Das "Woher" und "Wohin" dieses Modells des Code Civil', (1998) 6 *Zeitschrift für Europäisches Privatrecht* 651 and *passim*.

[54] See, for example, *Law of Obligations* (n. 4) 283, 291.

[55] 'Motive', in Benno Mugdan, *Die gesammten Materialien zum Bürgerlichen Gesetzbuch für das Deutsche Reich*, vol. II (1899), 113 ff.; and see § 446 BGB (which has, substantially, remained unchanged by the 'modernization' of the German Law of Obligations).

[56] See Ernst, (1999) 7 *Zeitschrift für Europäisches Privatrecht* 635 ff.

increasingly, that the Roman contract of *emptio venditio* had only related to specific goods and that its extension to cover unascertained goods had been, historically, incorrect.[57] This paved the way towards reconceptualizing the latter type of transaction. Of course, in view of the fact that *emptio venditio* had become, essentially, a *pactum de trahendo et solvendo*, there was no longer anything intrinsically opposed to acknowledging that unascertained goods could be a proper object of a contract of sale. But what did the seller promise? He did not promise to deliver a specific object (with the result that if he delivered that object, he had, arguably, complied with his contractual obligation even if that object turned out to be defective) but he implicitly promised to deliver an object of average kind or quality or, at least, not one which was unfit for the use envisaged by the parties, or for ordinary use. This meant that the seller of unascertained goods who eventually delivered defective goods had not complied with his contractual obligations. The result was obvious: he was liable for non-performance in the same way as in any other case of non-performance. He was still exposed to the *actio empti* which the purchaser could use to claim performance and/or his interest.[58] An additional liability regime based on a statutory warranty was thus redundant. At the same time, it was inappropriate and inadequate. It did not give the purchaser the right to claim delivery of an object of an average kind and quality. And it allowed him, by keeping the defective object and bringing the *actio quanti minoris*, to accept delivery as due performance of the seller's obligation and to treat it as a case of non-performance at one and the same time.[59]

But there were other writers who defended the application of the aedilitian remedies to the sale of unascertained goods.[60] Most prominent among them was Levin Goldschmidt, the founding father of modern German scholarship in the field of commercial law.[61] He argued that the act of delivery restricts the seller's obligation to the particular object chosen by him: what has originally been the sale of unascertained goods is then turned into the sale of specific goods to which, as a matter of course, the aedilitian remedies apply.[62] Since

---

[57] See, for example, Alois Brinz, *Lehrbuch der Pandekten*, vol. II/2, 2nd edn. (1882), 730 ff.; August Bechmann, *Kauf nach gemeinem Recht*, vol. II (1884), 330 ff.

[58] Bechmann (n. 57) 333; Heinrich Thöl, *Das Handelsrecht*, vol. I/2, 5th edn. (1876), § 275; cf. also Windscheid and Kipp (n. 31) § 394, 5.

[59] See Carl Gareis, *Das Stellen zur Disposition nach modernem deutschen Handelsrecht* (1870), 153 ff. (emphasizing also that application of the *actio quanti minoris* was inimical to the interests of commerce and commercial certainty).   [60] Dernburg (n. 31) § 101, 3.

[61] Karsten Schmidt, 'Levin Goldschmidt (1829–1897): Der Begründer der modernen Handelsrechtswissenschaft', in Helmut Heinrichs, Harald Franzki, Klaus Schmalz and Michael Stolleis (eds.), *Deutsche Juristen jüdischer Herkunft* (1993), 215 ff.; Lothar Weyhe, *Levin Goldschmidt: Ein Gelehrtenleben in Deutschland* (1996).

[62] Levin Goldschmidt, 'Ueber die Statthaftigkeit der aedilitischen Rechtsmittel beim Gattungskauf', (1874) 19 *Zeitschrift für das gesammte Handelsrecht* 105 ff.

Goldschmidt served as a judge of the Commercial Supreme Court, first of the North German Federation, and later of the German Empire, he was able to imprint his views on contemporary legal practice;[63] the Imperial Supreme Court followed suit.[64] The contest between these two approaches was eventually reflected in § 480 BGB. Its draftsmen followed Goldschmidt in that, in principle, they placed the sale of specific and unascertained goods on a par: *actio redhibitoria, actio quanti minoris* and a claim for damages in cases of fraud and specific promise were available. In addition, however, the purchaser was granted a right to claim delivery of an object free from defects in the place of the defective one. This right did not enjoy priority over any of the others: the purchaser was given the choice to claim either redhibition, or reduction of the purchase price, or delivery of another object (or damages, where appropriate). This entailed that the seller was not granted a second chance: he could not avert the purchaser's other remedies by offering to deliver another object which was free from defects.

All in all, therefore, the traditional thinking patterns largely prevailed in the BGB of 1900. Pride of place was given to the sale of specific goods. The sale of unascertained goods was still regarded as a deviation from the norm that could be dealt with by way of special provisions modifying the general law of sale.[65] Liability for latent defects thus continued to be governed by a special set of rules which had been generalized in its scope of application but had otherwise only slightly been adjusted.[66]

III. Problem Areas

An examination of this special set of rules, as contained in the BGB until 31 December 2001, reveals three obvious deviations from the general liability regime laid down in that code. They have all given rise to problems.[67]

---

[63] Decision of the Full Bench of the Imperial Commercial Supreme Court (*Reichsoberhandelsgericht*) of 16 April 1872, apparently unpublished, but mentioned by Goldschmidt, (1874) 19 *Zeitschrift für das gesammte Handelsrecht* 98 ff.

[64] RGZ 6, 189 ff. (28 February 1882); RGZ 12, 78 (84 ff.) (25 November 1884). On the development of the Imperial Court practice both under the *ius commune* and under the Prussian Code of 1794, see Christoph Seiler, *Vom Allgemeinen Landrecht zum Bürgerlichen Gesetzbuch* (1996), 181 ff., 187 ff., 190 ff. [65] See, apart from § 480, § 243 II BGB.

[66] The temporal limitations of the *actiones quanti minoris* and *rehibitoria* were even tightened; cf. *infra* III.3. *in fine.*

[67] See, particularly, Dieter Medicus, 'Zur Geschichte der Sachmängelhaftung', in Reinhard Zimmermann, Rolf Knütel and Jens Peter Meincke (eds.), *Rechtsgeschichte und Privatrechtsdogmatik* (2000), 307 ff.

1. Supplementary performance

In the first place, as has just been mentioned, the seller was not given a second chance to earn the purchase price by either removing the defect or supplying another object free from defects. Had the delivery of the defective object been regarded as an ordinary instance of non-performance, the purchaser would only have been able to terminate the contract, or to claim damages for non-performance, if he had fixed, to no avail, an additional period of time for the seller to fulfil his primary obligation.[68]

The *supply of another object* free from defects is impractical, probably even conceptually inconceivable, as far as the sale of specific objects is concerned. After all, it is the specific object that has been promised, and the seller cannot, therefore, comply with his obligation by delivering another object.[69] Even with regard to the sale of unascertained goods it was only in the last two decades of the nineteenth century that the question had become controversial whether a purchaser could avail himself of the *actio redhibitoria* if the seller was prepared to make amends by way of a substitute delivery.[70] The courts had indeed affirmed the purchaser's right to redhibition and it is hardly surprising, in view of this, and also in view of the fact that the seller's right to cure his defective performance had not been established by any previous codification,[71] that the Second Commission charged with the preparation of the BGB saw and discussed, but ultimately rejected, a proposal to deviate from the established thinking pattern.[72] This was done in spite of the fact that the *purchaser* had been granted the right to demand delivery of another object free from defects[73] and that his position now appeared to be unusually strong in comparison with that of the seller.

Supplementary performance by way of *removal of the defect*, i.e. repair, is imaginable both with regard to the sale of specific and unascertained goods. Again, the Second Commission discussed, but rejected, a proposal according to which the seller was to be granted a right to repair as being apt to lead to unnecessary problems and complexities.[74] Whether the *purchaser* should be

---

[68] § 326 BGB (old version).　　[69] 'Protokolle', in Mugdan (n. 55) 684.

[70] Hans Großmann-Doerth, *Die Rechtsfolgen vertragswidriger Andienung* (1934), 34 ff.

[71] See Großmann-Doerth (n. 70) 44 ff.

[72] 'Protokolle', in Mugdan (n. 55) 684 ff.; *Soergel*/Huber (n. 12) Vorbem. § 459, n. 14.

[73] *Supra* II.3.c) *in fine*.

[74] 'Protokolle', in Mugdan (n. 55) 675 ff. Subsequently, this decision was often justified by pointing out that a seller who was not identical with the producer of the object usually lacked the ability and the means to effect a repair. While it is in line with this argument that § 633 II BGB (old version) granted the customer the right to demand removal of a defect from the contractor under a contract of work, it can hardly be reconciled with the fact that under a contract of lease the lessor has to keep the object of the lease in good repair even though he is also not normally identical with its producer: § 536 BGB (old version) (= § 535 I 2 BGB new version).

given a respective claim to have the object repaired was not even contemplated.[75] Again, the Roman legal thinking patterns prevailed. The aedilitian remedies had been tailored, originally, for slaves and cattle, i.e. for objects with regard to which a corporeal defect or a defect of character could not normally simply be removed by the seller.[76]

After the BGB had entered into effect, it soon became clear that the traditional approach towards liability for defects under a contract of sale, as it had been perpetuated in the code, was unduly disadvantageous to the seller. Where complex technical equipment is sold, redhibition is much too severe a sanction if the defect can easily be remedied by replacing, or repairing, the defective part. The same applies to everyday transactions: a purchaser who has bought a defective specimen of a standard object in a shop can reasonably be expected to accept another object.[77] Where the purchaser avails himself of the codified version of the *actio redhibitoria*, he often does so because he regrets the purchase. This interest does not deserve to be protected. Occasionally, the courts have helped by falling back on the general good faith provision (§ 242 BGB).[78] More often, however, sellers have helped themselves by getting a right to supplementary performance accepted in their contracts. Standard contract terms proved to be a particularly convenient way of achieving this.[79] At the same time, of course, they were a welcome excuse *to reduce* the purchaser to the right of supplementary performance and thus to opt out of the statutory regime of remedies available under §§ 459 ff. BGB. In addition, they provided an opportunity for ensuring that any expenses associated with the removal of the defect had to be borne by the purchaser. Extended litigation eventually led to the inclusion into the Standard Contract Terms Act of two provisions prohibiting these types of terms,[80] and also to an amendment of the BGB.[81]

Purchasers, too, sometimes have a reasonable interest in having the defect repaired rather than being forced to resort to the standard remedies of redhibition or reduction of the purchase price. That no such right was granted to them was also very widely perceived as an inadequacy of the old code.[82]

---

[75] *Soergel*/Huber (n. 12) Vorbem. § 459, n. 16 with a discussion of possible reasons why the matter was not raised.   [76] Medicus (n. 67) 310.

[77] Ulrich Huber, 'Kaufvertrag', in Bundesminister der Justiz (ed.), *Gutachten und Vorschläge zur Überarbeitung des Schuldrechts*, vol. I (1981), 915 ff. For a comparative discussion, see Schwartze (n. 8) 158 ff.

[78] Heinrich Honsell, in *J. von Staudingers Kommentar zum Bürgerlichen Gesetzbuch*, 13th edn. (1995), § 462, n. 12; § 480, n. 9; *Soergel*/Huber (n. 12) § 462, n. 73.

[79] The origins of this development are traced and analysed by Grossmann-Doerth (n. 70) 61 ff., who refers to a modern form of *lex mercatoria* (*selbstgeschaffenes Recht der Wirtschaft*).

[80] § 11 no. 10 b) and c) ABGB.   [81] § 476 a BGB (old version).

[82] Huber (n. 77) 915. Some of the natural law codifications had been more progressive in this respect; cf. §§ 325, 331 I 5 of the Prussian Code of 1794 and § 932 ABGB (1811). The Austrian Code

2. Damages

Secondly, damages could only be claimed if a promised quality in the object sold had been absent, or if the seller had fraudulently concealed a defect: § 463 BGB (old version); the latter alternative was soon extended by the courts to other forms of fraudulent behaviour.[83] But what about the liability of a seller who has negligently caused damage? Normally, a claim for 'positive malperformance' should have been available. That doctrine that had been established in order to cover the situation where a party to a contract had been at fault in not complying with a duty arising under the contract (unless, of course, the rules relating to delay, or impossibility, of performance were applicable).[84] Unrestricted application of the rules relating to positive malperformance would, however, have rendered the regime contained in § 463 BGB nugatory. At the same time, however, there appeared to be no rational justification for reduced protection of a purchaser's health or property, merely because the other party's negligent act consisted in the delivery of a defective object which was apt to explode, or to cause fire. The courts, therefore, attempted to find a compromise solution. They applied the rules concerning 'positive malperformance' in principle, but limited them to the recovery of consequential loss (i.e. damage done to any of the purchaser's objects of legal protection other than the object of sale itself).[85] But the distinction between consequential loss (*Mangelfolgeschaden*) and loss pertaining to the object itself (*Mangelschaden*) has proved to be elusive.[86] Difficult problems of delimitation could also arise as a result of the courts' willingness to grant claims for positive malperformance covering the purchaser's *entire* loss in cases where the seller had infringed ancillary duties arising under the contract of sale, no matter whether these ancillary duties were related to a defect or not.[87]

used to grant the purchaser a right to repair (*Verbesserung*), provided the defect can be removed by way of repair; the purchaser's right to redhibition was excluded under these circumstances. For a comparative discussion, see Rabel (n. 12) 251 ff.; Schwartze (n. 8) 137 ff. Schwartze points out that only five national legal systems in Europe used to recognize a right to removal of the defect prior to the Directive on Consumer Sales: Austria, Portugal, Sweden, Finland and the Netherlands.

[83] *Soergell*Huber (n. 12) § 463, nn. 26 ff.

[84] On the doctrine of 'positive malperformance' in German law, devised by the well-known commercial lawyer Hermann Staub in 1902 (i.e. a mere two years after the BGB had come into existence), see Reinhard Zimmermann, *Roman Law, Contemporary Law, European Law* (2001), 92 ff.; Basil S. Markesinis, Werner Lorenz and Gerhard Dannemann, *The Law of Contracts and Restitution: A Comparative Introduction* (1997), 418 ff. On Hermann Staub, see Günter Elschner, 'Hermann Staub und die Lehre von den positiven Forderungsverletzungen', in Thomas Hoeren (ed.), *Zivilrechtliche Entdecker* (2001), 191 ff.

[85] Dieter Medicus, *Bürgerliches Recht*, 17th edn. (1996), nn. 361 ff.; *Soergell*Huber (n. 12) Vorbem. § 459, nn. 38 ff.; *Staudinger*/Honsell (n. 78) Vorbem. zu §§ 459 ff. nn. 78 ff.

[86] See the casuistry reported by *Soergell*Huber (n. 12) Anh. § 463, nn. 21 ff.

[87] Max Vollkommer, in Othmar Jauernig (ed.), *Bürgerliches Gesetzbuch*, 7th edn. (1994), § 459, IV, 6, b). For the range of these duties, see *Soergell*Huber (n. 12) Anh. I § 433, nn. 1 ff.

3. Extinctive prescription

Thirdly, of course, there was the temporal limitation for the statutory claims arising from latent defects in terms of §§ 459 ff. BGB, as long as they were not based on the seller's fraudulent behaviour: six months in the case of movables and one year with regard to land.[88] Even a six month period is not necessarily unreasonably short, as long as the purchaser has either discovered, or has at least had a fair chance of discovering, the defect. What made the periods contained in § 477 BGB particularly troublesome was the fact that they started to run with delivery (movables) or transfer of the object of the sale (land). Often, therefore, the purchaser's claims were barred by prescription before he had had any chance to know about them. That was regarded, very widely, as manifestly unfair.[89] Also, it was never quite clear why the seller of defective objects should have been blessed with such an advantageous prescription regime. After the object of the sale has been delivered, so the draftsmen of the BGB had argued, it becomes increasingly difficult to determine whether the defect had already existed at the time of delivery, or whether it had only arisen at a later stage.[90] Also, the seller was seen to have a reasonable interest in being able to close his books relating to the transaction.[91] The second of these arguments, however, is as valid for the seller of a defective object as it would be for any other debtor; and in evaluating the first of them it has to be kept in mind that it is the purchaser who has to prove that the object was defective at the moment of delivery; thus, the onus is not on the seller to prove that the object was free of defects at that time.[92]

None the less, of course, for the core area of application of §§ 459 ff. BGB this was a case of *dura lex sed lex*. Indeed, § 477 BGB even had to be applied to claims for consequential loss based on 'positive malperformance', as long as the policy considerations underlying the short prescription period were taken seriously and as long as grave inconsistencies of evaluation were to be avoided.[93] Thus, in this instance, the courts were ready to sacrifice the hallowed principle that every claim has to be dealt with in terms of the rules applicable to it and quite independent of any rules applicable to other claims (*Anspruchskonkurrenz*).[94]

---

[88] § 477 BGB (old version); for the first draft of which, see von Kübel (n. 31) 421 ff.

[89] *Soergel*/Huber (n. 12) § 477, nn. 3 ff.; Frank Peters and Reinhard Zimmermann, 'Verjährungsfristen', in Bundesminister der Justiz (n. 77) 187 ff.; Bundesminister der Justiz (ed.), *Abschlußbericht der Kommission zur Überarbeitung des Schuldrechts* (1992), 23 ff., 28.

[90] 'Protokolle', in Mugdan (n. 55) 660 ff.   [91] See *Soergel*/Huber (n. 12) § 477, n. 2.

[92] Medicus (n. 67) 309.

[93] RGZ 53, 200 (203) (19 December 1902); RGZ 117, 315 (316) (24 June 1927); BGHZ 60, 9 (12) (29 November 1972); BGHZ 77, 215 (219 ff.) (2 June 1980); *Staudinger*/Honsell (n. 78) § 477, n. 22.

[94] On which see, in general, Heinz-Peter Mansel, in Othmar Jauernig (ed.), *Bürgerliches Gesetzbuch*, 11th edn. (2004), § 241, n. 14.

Matters were different, as far as claims for positive malperformance based on the infringement of ancillary duties arising under the contract of sale were concerned. These, after all, did not depend on proof of a defect in the object sold and were thus taken to be subject to the general prescription period of thirty years.[95] It has, however, never been easy to see why the six-month period of § 477 BGB was applied where a purchaser of adhesive claimed compensation for the damage that had arisen as a result of incorrect advice about the adhesive's resistance to water,[96] whereas the thirty-year period was held to prevail where charged batteries were delivered in an unpacked state and therefore caused a fire.[97] The two examples demonstrate that the line to be drawn between a defect and the infringement of an ancillary duty can become very thin.[98]

The principle of *Anspruchskonkurrenz* has, incidentally, enabled German courts to explore subtle ways of escaping the inequitable rule of § 477 BGB. Thus, for example, they have maintained that where the object sold is destroyed by a 'functionally separable' part of it that was defective, a damages claim can be based on the law of delict because the seller can be seen to have infringed the purchaser's property in terms of § 823 I BGB.[99] This claim used to be subject to a three-year period of prescription running from the moment when the injured party learnt about the injury and the identity of the person bound to make compensation: § 852 I BGB (old version). A delictual claim was granted, for example, where the purchaser's car had been damaged as a result of a collision caused by a defective accelerator pedal.[100] Effectively, therefore, the courts have used the law of delict to devise an additional remedy for damages arising from latent defects in order to subvert the six-month period of § 477 BGB.

It should be noted that while the prescription period contained in § 477 BGB imitated the temporal limitation of the Roman *actiones quanti minoris* and *redhibitoria*,[101] the latter had originally only applied to slaves and cattle. Strictly

---

[95] RGZ 144, 162 ff. (16 March 1934); BGHZ 66, 208 (213 ff.) (28 April 1976); *Staudinger*/Honsell (n. 78) § 477, n. 31.   [96] BGHZ 88, 130 (136 ff.) (13 July 1983).

[97] BGHZ 66, 208 (214) (28 April 1976).

[98] For a discussion of the case law, see *Soergel*/Huber (n. 12) § 477, nn. 12 ff.; for an overview of the prescription problems in English, see Reinhard Zimmermann, 'Extinctive Prescription in German Law', in Erik Jayme (ed.), *German National Reports in Civil Law Matters for the XIVth Congress of Comparative Law* (1994), 168 ff.

[99] This line of decisions started with BGHZ 67, 359 ff. (24 November 1976) (the 'floater-switch' case); see further Hartwig Sprau, in *Palandt, Bürgerliches Gesetzbuch*, 64th edn. (2005), § 823, nn. 177 ff.; Dieter Medicus, *Bürgerliches Recht*, 20th edn. (2004), n. 650 b; Erich Steffen, 'Die Bedeutung der "Stoffgleichheit" mit dem "Mangelunwert" für die Herstellerhaftung aus Weiterfresserschäden', [1988] *Versicherungsrecht* 977 ff.; and see now the monograph by Beate Gsell, *Substanzverletzung und Herstellung* (2003).   [100] BGHZ 86, 256 ff. (18 January 1983).

[101] There was a slight deviation from Roman law which had had two different periods (six months and one year, respectively) for the two actions, whereas the draftsmen of the BGB, following a number of earlier codifications, and draft codifications, treated both actions alike but drew a distinction between movable objects and land; see von Kübel (n. 31) 421.

speaking, therefore, they should have provided a model for the regulation of the sale of livestock for which the draftsmen of the BGB, however, devised a special regime.[102] In their German statutory version, the Roman rules were thus applied to objects for which they had never been intended to apply. Moreover, the BGB considerably tightened the Roman limitation rules. Both under Roman law and the *ius commune*, commencement of the period had depended on whether the purchaser knew or could have known about the defect. Also, it had not applied to claims for damages. And finally, the *actio quanti minoris* had only been barred after the lapse of a year, even with regard to movables.[103]

4. Other precarious borderlines

Many other problems associated with the special regime for latent defects might be mentioned. Subtle distinctions had to be drawn between cases where the object that had been delivered was merely defective (§§ 459 ff. BGB) and where it *differed* from the object sold (normal remedies for non-performance). Even with regard to the sale of specific objects the borderline was not always easily determinable (a violin is sold as a solo instrument but turns out to be an instrument to be used by an orchestra player);[104] in cases involving unascertained goods it could become entirely elusive.[105] Difficult problems of delimitation could also arise as a result of the fact that the special rules of §§ 459 ff. BGB only related to defects as to the quality of the object sold, whereas for defects of title a different regime prevailed (§ 440 read with §§ 320–327 BGB (old version)).[106] According to the complex construction adopted in §§ 462, 465 BGB (old version) the purchaser could not simply terminate the contract, or reduce the purchase price; he was granted a claim against the seller to get the latter to agree to redhibition, or reduction.[107] Strictly speaking, therefore, the

---

[102] § 490 BGB (old version), operating with a period of six weeks for 'principal defects'; see *Law of Obligations* (n. 4) 326 ff.

[103] Dernburg (n. 31) § 101, 1 f.) and 2 c); Windscheid and Kipp (n. 31) § 393; cf. also Medicus (n. 67) 310 ff.

[104] *Staudinger*/Honsell (n. 78) § 459, nn. 25 ff.; *Soergel*/Huber (n. 12) Vorbem. § 459, nn. 132 ff.; Medicus (n. 85) nn. 332 ff.

[105] RGZ 86, 90 (18 December 1914) (Kawamatta silk); *Staudinger*/Honsell (n. 78) § 459, nn. 44 ff.; *Soergel*/Huber (n. 12) Vorbem. § 459, nn. 106 ff.; Medicus (n. 85) nn. 335 ff.

[106] For the casuistry surrounding this question, see *Soergel*/Huber (n. 12) § 459, nn. 29 ff.; *Abschlußbericht* (n. 89) 21 ff.

[107] That the purchaser was not, as might have appeared natural, given the right unilaterally to terminate the contract, or to reduce the purchase price, but that he was merely granted a 'claim' (*Anspruch*) against the seller, was a decision based on a technical consideration: claims, according to § 194 I BGB are subject to extinctive prescription: 'Motive', in Mugdan (n. 55) 131, whereas *Gestaltungsrechte* do not prescribe. The reasons why the draftsmen of the BGB chose such a complex, two-layered system, are explained by *Soergel*/Huber (n. 12) § 462, nn. 33 ff.

purchaser had to institute two actions if he wanted to recover his purchase price, or part of it: the first in order to effect the legal act of redhibition, or reduction, and the second to claim what was due to him once this act had been effected. The Imperial Court (*Reichsgericht*) soon found a much more practicable solution which, however, remained difficult to conceptualize.[108]

IV. Reform

1. Characteristic features

All in all, therefore, reform was very widely regarded as overdue.[109] Incorporation of §§ 459 ff. had led to the irrational survival of an antiquated doctrine. This was very clearly recognized by Ernst Rabel in his great monograph concerning the law of sale of goods.[110] Delivery of an object with a defect as to its quality can be regarded as one of many instances of non-performance to which the normal rules on non-performance can very largely be applied. The matter thus requires, in the words of Ernst Rabel, 'only a moderate degree of explicit statutory attention'.[111] This was a fundamentally important insight which has shaped, first the (Hague) Uniform Law on the International Sale of Goods (ULIS) of 1964, and then the (Vienna) Convention on Contracts for the International Sale of Goods (CISG) of 1980.[112] The latter Convention has now been ratified by more than sixty states[113] and has given rise to close to 1,000 decisions by courts of law worldwide.[114] More than a quarter of these

---

[108] RGZ 58, 423 (425) (16 September 1904); for the theories developed by academic writers to conceptualize redhibition (and reduction), and for comment, see *Staudinger*/Honsell (n. 78) § 465, nn. 2 ff.; *Soergel*/Huber (n. 12) § 462, nn. 48 ff.

[109] Huber (n. 77) 915 ff.; *Abschlussbericht* (n. 89) 20 ff.; Christian Baldus, *Binnenkonkurrenz kaufrechtlicher Sachmängelansprüche nach Europarecht* (1999), 37 ff.

[110] Rabel (n. 12) 101. This view is widely shared today wherever the aedilitian remedies still survive in statutory form; for Italy see, for example, Luigi Garofalo, 'L'attuazione della direttiva 1999/44/CE in Italia', in Martin Schermaier (n. 10) 245 ff. with references.

[111] Rabel (n. 12) 132.

[112] See Peter Schlechtriem, 'Bemerkungen zur Geschichte des Einheitskaufrechts', in *idem* (ed.), *Einheitliches Kaufrecht und nationales Obligationenrecht* (1987), 27 ff.; Ulrich Magnus, in *J. von Staudingers Kommentar zum Bürgerlichen Gesetzbuch, Wiener UN-Kaufrecht* (1999), Einl. zum CISG, nn. 20 ff.

[113] For a complete list of states, as per 1 March 2003, see Burghard Piltz, 'Neue Entwicklungen im UN-Kaufrecht', [2003] *Neue Juristische Wochenschrift* 2056 ff.; cf. also the list in Oliver Radley-Gardner, Hugh Beale, Reinhard Zimmermann and Reiner Schulze (eds.), *Fundamental Texts on European Private Law* (2003), 240 ff.

[114] See Ulrich Magnus, 'Das UN-Kaufrecht—aktuelle Entwicklungen und Rechtsprechungspraxis', (2002) 10 *Zeitschrift für Europäisches Privatrecht* 524; Kurt Siehr and Reinhard Zimmermann (eds.), 'Symposium: The Convention on the International Sale of Goods and its application in comparative perspective', (2004) 68 *Rabels Zeitschrift für ausländisches und internationales Privatrecht* 427 ff.

decisions have been handed down by German courts.[115] Thus, via CISG, the modern approach to non-performance has become an important part of German sales law. But it has also, from the beginning, greatly influenced all efforts to reform the German law of obligations.[116] Breach of contract and liability for latent defects in contracts of sale and contracts for work have remained, together with the law of extinctive prescription, at the top of the reform agenda ever since a comprehensive reform of the law of obligations was first mooted in 1978.[117] The reform was eventually triggered by the enactment of the European Consumer Sales Directive. But it went far beyond what was required by that Directive.[118] Thus, a set of special rules concerning liability for defects and guarantees in *consumer* sales could have been enacted.[119] The Federal Minister of Justice, however, wanted to preserve the integrity of the German law of sale as much as possible. One of the two main features characterizing the reform of German sales law,[120] therefore, is a determined effort to extend the requirements of the Directive to all types of sale, including commercial sales.[121] The second characteristic trait of the reform is the attempt to integrate liability for latent defects, as far as possible, into the general regime governing breach of contract under the revised German law of obligations which, in turn, has also largely followed the lead provided by CISG.[122] It therefore appears to be legitimate, when discussing the new structure of the remedies concerning liability for defects in the German law of sale, to ask how

[115] Magnus, (2002) 10 *Zeitschrift für Europäisches Privatrecht* 524.

[116] *Abschlußbericht* (n. 89) 19 ff.; Peter Schlechtriem, 'Rechtsvereinheitlichung in Europa und Schuldrechtsreform in Deutschland', (1993) 1 *Zeitschrift für Europäisches Privatrecht* 217 ff. Ulrich Huber, 'Leistungsstörungen', in Bundesminister der Justiz (n. 77) 647 ff. and *idem* (n. 77) 911 ff. had still been guided by ULIS.   [117] *Supra* pp. 30 ff.

[118] The options available to the German legislature with respect to the implementation of the Directive are discussed in the contributions by Dieter Medicus, Axel Flessner, Harm Peter Westermann, Stefan Grundmann and Wolfgang Ernst, all in Stefan Grundmann, Dieter Medicus and Walter Rolland (eds.), *Europäisches Kaufgewährleistungsrecht* (2000), 219 ff., 233 ff., 251 ff., 281 ff., 325 ff.; cf. also Huber (n. 12) 311 ff.

[119] As has happened, for example, in Italy: Arts. 1519-bis ff.; see Garofalo (n. 110) 237 ff.

[120] Claus-Wilhelm Canaris, 'Die Neuregelung des Leistungsstörungs- und des Kaufrechts: Grundstrukturen und Problemschwerpunkte', in Egon Lorenz (ed.), *Karlsruher Forum 2002: Schuldrechtsmodernisierung* (2003), 54 ff.

[121] This leads to a methodological problem insofar as it has to be asked whether rules of German sales law have to be interpreted in accordance with the provisions of the Consumer Sales Directive only for consumer sales, or also for other types of sale; see Ulrich Büdenbender, 'Die Bedeutung der Verbrauchsgüterkaufrichtlinie für das deutsche Kaufrecht nach der Schuldrechtsreform', (2004) 12 *Zeitschrift für Europäisches Privatrecht* 36 ff.; Josef Drexl, 'Die gemeinschaftsrechtliche Pflicht zur einheitlichen richtlinienkonformen Auslegung hybrider Rechtsnormen und deren Grenzen', in *Festschrift für Andreas Heldrich* (2005), 67 ff., and the literature quoted *infra* n. 227. On the precept of interpreting national legal rules in conformity with the provisions of directives of European law which they seek to implement, see Claus-Wilhelm Canaris, 'Die richtlinienkonforme Auslegung und Rechtsfortbildung im System der juristischen Methodenlehre', in *Im Dienste der Gerechtigkeit: Festschrift für Franz Bydlinski* (2002), 47 ff.   [122] See *supra*, Chapter 2.

far it reflects the requirements laid down in the Directive (though laid down in that Directive only for consumer sales) and to what extent it is in line with international developments, evidenced particularly by CISG.[123]

2. The basic structure

The new German Law of sale, most importantly perhaps, takes as a model for its regulation the sale of unascertained goods. The draftsmen of the new code even went so far as to regard the distinction between the sale of specific and unascertained goods as redundant.[124] Since, however, it is not an arbitrary legal construct but based on the way in which the parties devise the content of their transaction, it continues to determine details of the application of the new rules.[125] Thus, for instance, supplementary performance by way of supply of another object free from defects cannot be demanded in contracts for the sale of a specific object.[126] The new approach (a uniform regulation geared towards the sale of unascertained goods but also including the sale of specific objects)[127]

---

[123] In addition, the Principles of European Contract Law (PECL) and the UNIDROIT Principles of International Commercial Contracts (PICC) will be referred to as exponents of the international development. Both sets of Principles, however, do not specifically deal with the contract of sale and are thus, in the present context, only of limited value. On the impact of CISG on PECL and PICC, see Harry M. Flechtner, 'The CISG's Impact on International Unification Efforts: The UNIDROIT Principles of International Commercial Contracts and the Principles of European Contract Law', in Franco Ferrari (ed.), *The 1980 Uniform Sales Law: Old Issues Revisited in the Light of Recent Experiences* (2003), 169 ff.

[124] 'Begründung der Bundesregierung zum Entwurf eines Gesetzes zur Modernisierung des Schuldrechts', in Claus-Wilhelm Canaris (ed.), *Schuldrechtsmodernisierung 2002* (2002), 596 and 844.

[125] Faust (n. 12) Vorbem. § 433, n. 4; Roland Michael Beckmann, in *J. von Staudingers Kommentar zum Bürgerlichen Gesetzbuch*, revised edition (2004), Vorbem. zu §§ 433 ff. Martin Schermaier, 'Rechtsangleichung und Rechtswissenschaft im kaufrechtlichen Sachmängelrecht', in *idem* (n. 10) 16 ff. criticizes the fact that the new rules insufficiently take account of contracts of sale concerning specific objects.

[126] Peter Huber, 'Der Nacherfüllungsanspruch im neuen Kaufrecht', [2002] *Neue Juristische Wochenschrift* 1006; *idem*, in Peter Huber and Florian Faust, *Schuldrechtsmodernisierung* (2002), 321 ff.; Stephan Lorenz and Thomas Riehm, *Lehrbuch zum neuen Schuldrecht* (2002), n. 505; Faust (n. 12) § 439, n. 27; Matthias Jacobs, 'Die kaufrechtliche Nacherfüllung', in Barbara Dauner-Lieb, Horst Konzen and Karsten Schmidt (eds.), *Das neue Schuldrecht in der Praxis* (2003), 377 ff.; for CISG, see Markus Müller-Chen, in Peter Schlechtriem and Ingeborg Schwenzer (eds.), *Kommentar zum Einheitlichen UN-Kaufrecht*, 4th edn. (2004), Art. 46, n. 18; *Staudinger*/Magnus (n. 112) Art. 46, n. 33. *Contra*: 'Begründung' (n. 124) 806; Hans Putzo, in *Palandt, Bürgerliches Gesetzbuch*, 64th edn. (2005), § 439, n. 15; Canaris (n. 120) 79 ff.; *idem*, 'Die Nacherfüllung durch Lieferung einer mangelfreien Sache beim Stückkauf', [2003] *Juristenzeitung* 831 ff.; OLG Braunschweig, [2003] *Neue Juristische Wochenschrift* 1053 (with comment by Pammler, [2003] *Neue Juristische Wochenschrift* 1992 ff.); and see the controversy between Thomas Ackermann and Claus-Wilhelm Canaris, [2003] *Juristenzeitung* 1154 ff.); *Münchener Kommentar*/Westermann (n. 12) § 439, nn. 11 ff.; *Staudinger*/Matusche-Beckmann (n. 12) § 439, nn. 28 ff.; Christian Berger, in Othmar Jauernig (ed.), *Bürgerliches Gesetzbuch*, 11th edn. (2004), § 439, n. 13.

[127] 'Inklusiver Einheitstyp, orientiert am Gattungskauf', in the typology of Wolfgang Ernst, (1999) 7 *Zeitschrift für Europäisches Privatrecht* 586.

is in conformity with CISG; it had been implemented in Germany, as early as 1861, in the General German Commercial Code of the German Federation,[128] and it has been espoused by Ernst Rabel.[129] It also forms the basis of the Consumer Sales Directive.[130]

It follows from this change of perspective that the seller is under an obligation to deliver an object free from defects. Under the old law it was argued that the seller of a specific object could only be seen to be under an obligation to deliver that specific object. If it turned out to be defective, this was not a case of non-performance. Rather, the seller was held to be liable as the result of an additional, statutory warranty imposed upon him by §§ 459 ff. BGB.[131] The new § 433 I 2 puts it beyond doubt that the contrary view, forcefully propagated under the old law by Ernst Rabel,[132] Ulrich Huber[133] and a number of other authors,[134] and generally accepted for the sale of unascertained goods,[135] now provides the theoretical basis for liability for latent defects: the seller is not only bound to hand over the object to the purchaser and to transfer ownership; he also has to procure the object free from defects of quality and of title.[136]

V. Supplementary Performance

1. Repair or replacement

Again, it follows logically from this change of perception that delivery of a defective object does not affect the purchaser's right to claim specific performance of the seller's obligation: delivery of the defective object, after all, constitutes an act of *non*-performance.[137] In this situation, however, specific performance can

---

[128] Ernst, (1999) 7 *Zeitschrift für Europäisches Privatrecht* 584 ff.

[129] Ernst Rabel, *Das Recht des Warenkaufs*, vol. I (1936), 65.

[130] See, for example, Gert Brüggemeier, 'Zur Reform des deutschen Kaufrechts—Herausforderungen durch die EG-Verbrauchsgüterkaufrichtlinie', [2000] *Juristenzeitung* 531 ff.

[131] Karl Larenz, *Lehrbuch des Schuldrechts*, vol. II/1, 13th edn. (1986), § 41 II e); *Staudinger*/Honsell (n. 78) Vorbem zu §§ 459 ff., nn. 9 ff.   [132] Rabel (n. 12) 104 ff.

[133] *Soergel*/Huber (n. 12) Vorbem. § 459, nn. 169 ff.

[134] See, for example, *Jauernig*/Vollkommer (n. 87) § 459, I 1 b); for a comprehensive discussion, see *Soergel*/Huber (n. 12) Vorbem. § 459, nn. 145 ff.

[135] *Soergel*/Huber (n. 12) Vorbem. § 459, nn. 156 ff.

[136] This is in accordance with the Directive (see Art. 2 I Consumer Sales Directive and Grundmann (n. 12) Art. 2, n. 1) and also with CISG (Art. 35 (1) CISG). Cf. also Art. 7.1.1 PICC ('Non-performance is failure by a party to perform any of its obligations under the contract, including defective performance or late performance'); Art. 8:101 PECL must be understood in the same sense: Ole Lando and Hugh Beale (eds.), *Principles of European Contract Law, Parts I and II* (2000), 359. For a comparative overview, see Schwartze (n. 8) 38 ff.

[137] This is the term most widely used internationally; see, for example, Art. 1:301 (4) PECL and Art. 7.1.1 PICC. The term chosen by the draftsmen of the new German Law of Obligations is 'breach of duty' (*Pflichtverletzung*); see *supra* p. 51.

now take one of two forms. The purchaser may demand the supply of an object which is free from defects; this is imaginable only with regard to the sale of unascertained objects.[138] Or he may ask for removal of the defect, a right which applies both to the sale of specific objects and of unascertained goods. The BGB does indeed grant the purchaser these rights (§§ 437 I no. 1, 439 BGB) implementing, thereby, Article 3 (2) of the Consumer Sales Directive.[139] Article 46 (2), (3) CISG also provides the purchaser with a right to require the seller to remedy the lack of conformity by repair or to request delivery of substitute goods (though the latter right is limited to cases where the lack of conformity constitutes a fundamental breach of contract).[140] According to § 439 I BGB it is the purchaser who may choose between these two forms of supplementary performance. Again, the draftsmen of the new BGB followed the Consumer Sales Directive,[141] even though, as far as contracts for work are concerned, they decided the matter differently: here it is the contractor, not the customer, who has the choice between removal of the defect and the production of new work.[142] The solution adopted for the law of sale is unconvincing in view of the fact that the seller's position can be affected very seriously by the choice made by the purchaser whereas the purchaser's position is safeguarded by the consideration that the seller would, in any event, only be able to choose a form of supplementary performance which completely removes the defect and thus satisfies the purchaser's reasonable interests. At the same time, it is usually the seller who can more easily assess the chances, and determine the effectiveness, of the different forms of supplementary performance.[143]

---

[138] *Supra* n. 126.

[139] For a comparison with the way in which the Directive has been implemented, in this respect, in English law, see Thomas Zerres, 'Recht auf Nacherfüllung im deutschen und englischen Kaufrecht', (2003) *Zeitschrift für Wirtschaftsrecht* 746 ff.

[140] See Müller-Chen (n. 126) Art. 46, n. 4; cf. also Florian Schulz, *Der Ersatzlieferungs- und Nachbesserungsanspruch des Käufers im internen deutschen Recht, im UCC und im CISG* (2002), 234 ff. A note on terminology: German law now distinguishes between 'removal of the defect' (*Beseitigung des Mangels*) and 'supply of a thing free from defects' (*Lieferung einer mangelfreien Sache*) as two different forms of 'supplementary performance' (*Nacherfüllung*). The Directive refers to 'repair' (*Nachbesserung*) and 'replacement' (*Ersatzlieferung*) as two different forms of the goods being brought 'into conformity' (*Herstellung des vertragsgemäßen Zustands*). The terms chosen by CISG are 'repair' (*Nachbesserung*; for Austria the translation is *Verbesserung*) and 'delivery of substitute goods' (*Ersatzlieferung*); there is no *nomen collectivum*. For the terminology chosen in other national legal systems, see Schwartze (n. 8) 136.

[141] See recital 10 of the Consumer Sales Directive. The Directive, in this respect, deviates from CISG, where the seller is given the choice; see Arts. 37, 48 (1) CISG and Müller-Chen (n. 126) Art. 48, n. 6; Heiko Lehmkuhl, *Das Nacherfüllungsrecht des Verkäufers im UN-Kaufrecht* (2002), 18 ff.; *contra*: Staudinger/Magnus (n. 112) Art. 48, n. 32.   [142] § 635 I BGB.

[143] For criticism, see Daniel Zimmer, 'Das geplante Kaufrecht', in Wolfgang Ernst and Reinhard Zimmermann (eds.), *Zivilrechtswissenschaft und Schuldrechtsreform* (2001), 199; Huber, [2002] *Neue Juristische Wochenschrift* 1005; Faust (n. 12) § 439, n. 8; Jacobs (n. 126) 375; cf. also Canaris (n. 120) 75 ff. (who refers to a 'somewhat irriating contrast' between the law concerning sales and

2. Details

Conceptually, the right to supplementary performance is regarded as a continuation, in modified form, of the original right to specific performance.[144] The transformation occurs at the moment when the risk passes to the purchaser, i.e., according to German law (§ 446 BGB), when the object sold is handed over (*Übergabe*).[145] Whether this is tantamount to delivery (*Lieferung*) in terms of Article 3 (1) Consumer Sales Directive remains to be seen; it depends on the way in which the European Court of Justice is going to interpret the latter term.[146] Article 3 (1) Consumer Sales Directive, incidentally, deviates from Article 36 (1) CISG which, like German law, refers to 'the time when the risk passes to the buyer'.[147] According to § 439 II BGB the seller has to bear all expenses associated with the supplementary performance, in particular the costs of carriage, transport, labour and materials.[148]

The right to supplementary performance is excluded, according to general principle, in cases of factual impossibility, practical impossibility, or moral impossibility (§ 275 I-III BGB).[149] In addition, the seller may refuse the form

contracts for work). As the law now stands, the reasonable interests of the seller must be safeguarded by a liberal interpretation of the seller's right to refuse the form of supplementary performance chosen by the purchaser 'if that form of supplementary performance is possible only with unreasonable expense'. In that connection, *inter alia*, regard must be had as to whether the defect can be remedied 'by the other form of supplementary performance without material detriment to the purchaser': § 439 III; cf. Art. 3 (3) Consumer Sales Directive.

[144] On the right to specific performance in historical and comparative perspective, see *Law of Obligations* (n. 4) 770 ff.; Konrad Zweigert and Hein Kötz, *An Introduction to Comparative Law* (transl. Tony Weir), 3rd edn. (1998), 470 ff.; Andrea Sandrock, *Vertragswidrigkeit der Sachleistung* (2003), 170 ff.; cf. also Art. 46 CISG and Müller-Chen (n. 126) Art. 28, nn. 1 ff., Art. 46, nn. 1 ff.; Arts. 9:102 ff. PECL and Lando and Beale (n. 136) 394 ff. For the proposition that the right to supplementary performance is a continuation, in modified form, of the right to specific performance, see Huber, [2002] *Neue Juristische Wochenschrift* 1005; *idem*, in Huber and Faust (n. 126) 319 ff.; Lorenz and Riehm (n. 126) n. 504; Faust (n. 12) § 439, n. 6; Jacobs (n. 126) 373 ff.; Canaris (n. 120) 77 ff.; *Staudinger*/Matusche-Beckmann (n. 12) § 439, n. 1; Jürgen Oechsler, 'Praktische Anwendungsprobleme des Nacherfüllungsanspruchs', [2004] *Neue Juristische Wochenschrift* 1825 ff.

[145] Huber, [2002] *Neue Juristische Wochenschrift* 1005; *idem*, in Huber and Faust (n. 126) 331 ff.; Lorenz and Riehm (n. 126) n. 497; Canaris (n. 120) 72 ff.; for the old law (concerning the sale of unascertained goods, § 480 I BGB (old version)), see *Soergel*/Huber (n. 12) § 480, nn. 11 ff. *Contra*: Faust (n. 12) § 439, n. 6 and § 437, nn. 4 ff.   [146] Canaris (n. 120) 73.

[147] On the discrepancy between the Directive and CISG, see Massimo C. Bianca, in Bianca and Grundmann (n. 12) Art. 3, nn. 13 ff.

[148] See Art. 3 (2) Consumer Sales Directive ('free of charge'); for CISG (which does not expressly deal with the matter) see Ulrich Huber, in Peter Schlechtriem (ed.), *Kommentar zum Einheitlichen UN-Kaufrecht*, 3rd edn. (2000), Art. 46, n. 54.

[149] On the significance of § 275 II BGB (practical impossibility), in the present context, see Ulrich Huber, 'Die Schadensersatzhaftung des Verkäufers wegen Nichterfüllung der Nacherfüllungspflicht und die Haftungsbegrenzung des § 275 Abs. 2 BGB neuer Fassung', in *Festschrift für Peter Schlechtriem* (2003), 542 ff. The right to supplementary performance is excluded only 'insofar' as supplementary performance is impossible; thus, for example, if the purchaser so desires, the seller has to repair the

of supplementary performance chosen by the purchaser if it is possible only with unreasonable expense (§ 439 III BGB). The expense can be unreasonable in comparison either with the other form of supplementary performance (relatively unreasonable) or with the general interest of the purchaser in receiving supplementary performance (absolutely unreasonable).[150] § 439 III BGB covers both situations, even though only the former is envisaged, apart from the case of impossibility, by the Consumer Sales Directive.[151] In order to avoid a conflict between § 439 III BGB and the Directive, absolute unreasonableness may only be taken into account, under § 439 III BGB, if it is tantamount to impossibility in terms of Article 3 (3) 1 Consumer Sales Directive.[152] The notion of 'impossibility' not being specified in the Directive, the rules of national law have to provide some guidance. According to § 275 II BGB the debtor may refuse to perform insofar as such performance would require an effort which would be grossly disproportionate to the interest of the creditor in receiving performance, taking into account the content of the obligation and the requirements of good faith.[153] The requirement of interpreting German law in accordance with the Directive will thus, presumably, prevent German courts from introducing a significantly lower threshold via the notion of absolute unreasonableness.[154] Of course, the purchaser has to return the defective object if the seller delivers an object free from defects by way of supplementary performance.[155]

3. Open questions

It is already apparent that a number of practically important questions have not been regulated by the new law. Thus, it is not clear whether the purchaser is bound by his choice between the two different types of supplementary performance available to him[156] or whether, for example, he may still choose the supply of

object sold even if the defect cannot completely be removed by that repair. See Faust (n. 12) § 439, n. 34. On the distinction between factual, practical and moral impossibility, and on the exclusion of 'economic' impossibility from the ambit of § 275 BGB, see supra pp. 43 ff.

[150] See the distinction drawn by Faust (n. 12) § 439, n. 36; *Münchener Kommentar*/Westermann (n. 12) § 439, n. 21; *Staudinger*/Matusche-Beckmann (n. 12) § 439, n. 40.

[151] See Art. 3 (3) Consumer Sales Directive; and see Recital 11 of the Directive. Concerning CISG, see Art. 46 (3) (relating to the right of repair) and Müller-Chen (n. 126) Art. 46, nn. 40 ff.; Schulz (n. 140) 299 ff.

[152] Faust (n. 12) § 439, n. 38; *Staudinger*/Matusche-Beckmann (n. 12) § 439, n. 41; a different solution is adopted by *Münchener Kommentar*/Westermann (n. 12) §439, n. 21.

[153] § 439 III read in conjunction with §§ 346 ff. BGB.

[154] For details, see Faust (n. 12) § 439, n. 50; cf. also *Münchener Kommentar*/Westermann (n. 12) § 439, n. 26; *Staudinger*/Matusche-Beckmann (n. 12) § 439, n. 42.

[155] § 439 III read in conjunction with §§ 346 ff. BGB.

[156] His right of choice would then be governed by § 263 II BGB; this is the view proposed by Ulrich Büdenbender, in Barbara Dauner-Lieb, Thomas Heidel, Manfred Lepa and Gerhard Ring (eds.), *Anwaltkommentar Schuldrecht* (2002), § 438, n. 5; *Jauernig*/Berger (n. 126) § 439, n. 9.

another object free from defects if the seller has failed to comply with his original request to repair the object delivered.[157] Also, while § 439 I BGB gives the purchaser the right to choose between the two types of supplementary performance (removal of the defect, or supply of another object free from defects), the code does not deal with the situation of a defect which can be *removed* in one of two different ways: a defective part of an object can either be repaired, or it can be substituted by a new one. While the seller is in a much better position to assess the merits of these alternatives, and should thus be granted the right to choose between them,[158] the gap can also, arguably, be filled by extending the evaluation underlying § 439 I BGB and thus giving the right of choice to the purchaser.[159] Whether, and if so under which circumstances, the purchaser may himself remove the defect, is disputed.[160]

Difficult problems also arise from the fact that the code does not specify the scope, or extent, of supplementary performance. Thus, the defect which has existed at the time of transfer of the risk may, in the meantime, have spread to other parts of the object sold. Or it may have caused damage to other pieces of the purchaser's property. Equally, the purchaser may, in the meantime, have painted, or otherwise improved, the object he had bought, or he may have joined it with other objects. In these and other cases the basic proposition has to be that the purchaser cannot merely request an object as it should have been at the time of transfer of the risk but can ask, as far as the object of the sale itself is concerned, to be placed in the position in which that

---

[157] He would then have, in principle, a *ius variandi* (the exercise of which is, of course, subject to the principle of good faith): see Andreas Spickhoff, 'Der Nacherfüllungsanspruch des Käufers: Dogmatische Einordnung und Rechtsnatur', [2003] *Betriebs-Berater* 589 ff.; Jacobs (n. 126) 376 ff.; Faust (n. 12) § 439, nn. 9 ff.; *Münchener Kommentar*/Westermann (n. 12) § 439, nn. 4 ff.; *Staudinger*/Matusche-Beckmann (n. 12) § 439, n. 7.

[158] This is the view expressed by Huber, in Huber and Faust (n. 126) 323; *idem*, [2002] *Neue Juristische Wochenschrift* 1006; *Münchener Kommentar*/Westermann (n. 12) § 439, n. 4; *Staudinger*/Matusche-Beckmann (n. 12) § 439, n. 10.

[159] Jacobs (n. 126) 377. For criticism concerning the rule of § 439 I BGB insofar as it grants the right of choice to the purchaser, see *supra* V.1.

[160] Such right to self-help is recognized with regard to contracts for work (§ 637 BGB) and used to be granted under the old law, according to the prevailing opinion, also to purchasers (*Soergel*/Huber (n. 12) § 462, n. 68). For the new law, see *Jauernig*/Berger (n. 126) § 439, n. 8; *contra*: *Anwaltkommentar*/Büdenbender (n. 156) § 437, n. 14; Faust (n. 12) § 439, n. 4; *Staudinger*/Matusche-Beckmann (n. 12) § 439, n. 25. Stephan Lorenz, 'Selbstvornahme der Mängelbeseitigung im Kaufrecht', [2003] *Neue Juristische Wochenschrift* 1417 ff. discusses the legal consequences resulting from the purchaser's resort to self-help under the new law. According to Lorenz, the purchaser thus makes supplementary performance by the seller impossible. As a result, he remains bound to pay the (full) purchase price; he loses his right to terminate the contract, to reduce the purchase price or to claim damages in lieu of performance. On the other hand, he can ask for reimbursement of whatever the seller has saved as a result of no longer having to make supplementary performance (§ 326 II 2 BGB *per analogiam*). Cf. also *Münchener Kommentar*/Westermann (n. 12) § 439, n. 10. *Contra*: Oechsler, [2004] *Neue Juristische Wochenschrift* 1826 ff.

object would *now* have been, had it been free from defects at the time of transfer of the risk.[161]

4. Second chance

Purchasers of a defective object, at least in consumer transactions, often prefer to be able to get another object free from defects, or to have the defective object repaired rather than having to resort to reduction of the purchase price or redhibition.[162] The new BGB, however, not only grants purchasers a right to these two types of supplementary performance, in addition to the other remedies available to them under the old law. It has introduced a graded system of remedies in that the purchaser is, in the first place, *confined* to his right to supplementary performance. It is his primary right. This is not clearly spelt out in §§ 437 ff. BGB, but follows from the fact that all the other rights of the purchaser (termination of the contract, reduction of the purchase price, and damages) generally require an additional period for the seller to effect performance, or supplementary performance, to have been fixed by the purchaser, and to have lapsed to no avail.[163] Once again, the priority given to supplementary performance is in accordance with the Consumer Sales Directive which states in Article 3 (3) that the consumer may *in the first place* require the seller to repair the goods or to replace them, and which grants the rights to reduction and rescission only if the consumer is entitled neither to repair nor to replacement, if the seller has not completed the remedy within a reasonable time, or if the seller has not completed the remedy without significant inconvenience to the consumer (Article 3 (5) Consumer Sales Directive).[164]

---

[161] This is the approach suggested by Faust (n. 12) § 439, nn. 14 ff.; cf. also the discussion by *Münchener Kommentar/*Westermann (n. 12) § 439, n. 9; *Staudinger/*Matusche-Beckmann (n. 12) § 439, nn. 10 ff. In principle, therefore, supplementary performance has to cover all the eventualities mentioned above except for damage caused to other pieces of the purchaser's property. As far as the first eventuality is concerned (defect having spread to other parts of the object sold), this interpretation is supported by Art. 3 (2) Consumer Sales Directive (which does not merely state that the defect has to be removed but that the goods must be brought into conformity).

[162] See 'Begründung' (n. 124) 844.

[163] Termination: § 323 I BGB; reduction of the purchase price: § 441 I 1 BGB read in conjunction with § 323 I BGB; damages in lieu of performance: § 281 I 1 BGB. See Lorenz, [2003] *Neue Juristische Wochenschrift* 1417 ff.; Lorenz and Riehm (n. 126) n. 504; Jacobs (n. 126) 386 ff.; Faust (n. 12) § 439, n. 2; *Staudinger/*Matusche-Beckmann (n. 12) § 439, n. 5.

[164] See Brigitta Jud, 'Die Rangordnung der Gewährleistungsrechtsbehelfe: Verbrauchsgüterkaufrichtlinie, österreichisches, deutsches und UN-Kaufrecht im Vergleich', in *Jahrbuch Junger Zivilrechtswissenschaftler. Das neue Schuldrecht* (2001), 205 ff. Use of the term 'remedy' in the Directive is unfortunate because it is ambiguous. 'Remedy', in the present context, does not refer to the purchaser's avenues of redress in general but is used as a *nomen collectivum* for repair and replacement (remedying the defect). Strange also is the use of the past tense in the latter two alternatives of Art. 3 (5) Consumer Sales Directive; see *infra* text to n. 194.

Effectively this means that the seller is granted a right to cure the defective performance: he has a second chance to comply with his contractual obligations. This right is limited, both under the Directive and under the BGB, by considerations focusing on whether the purchaser can reasonably be expected to accept supplementary performance;[165] moreover, the way in which it may be exercised (i.e. by repair or replacement) is determined by the purchaser.[166] Article 48 CISG even specifically grants the seller the right to remedy, at his own expense, any failure to perform his obligation:[167] a provision which has its main significance in cases of delivery of non-conforming goods.[168] Article 44 (1) ULIS had contained a substantially similar rule.[169] It did not have a model in the then-existing national codifications but appears to have been introduced at the prompting of Ernst Rabel as being in conformity with commercial practice.[170] Rabel, in turn, drew support from a monograph on the seller's right to have a second chance to comply with his contractual obligations which had been published in 1934 by Hans Großmann-Doerth.[171] The new system of remedies, introduced by CISG, by the Consumer Sales Directive, and in the new German law of sale in structurally similar ways[172] reflects a desire to strengthen the principle of *pacta sunt servanda* by keeping the contract going as far as reasonably possible.[173] Purchasers are not supposed immediately to terminate the contract, or to claim damages for non-performance, if they have received non-conforming goods. The delivery of a defective object can thus no longer provide a welcome excuse for getting rid of a contract which the purchaser has started to regret. At the same time, the position of the consumer in Germany has arguably been weakened by the new approach.[174] Under the

---

[165] For a detailed discussion, see Jacobs (n. 126) 387 ff.   [166] *Supra* V.1.

[167] For a detailed discussion, see Lehmkuhl (n. 141). The seller's right is, of course, subject to the standard of reasonableness; see Müller-Chen (n. 126) Art. 48, nn. 13 ff.; Lehmkuhl (n. 141) 19 ff.

[168] Müller-Chen (n. 126) Art. 48, n. 1.

[169] For a comparison, see *Staudinger/Magnus* (n. 112) Art. 48, n. 4.

[170] Rabel (n. 12) 252 ff., 373. For a modern comparative overview, see Schwartze (n. 8) 242 ff.

[171] Großmann-Doerth (n. 70). The Max Planck Institute in Hamburg owns Ernst Rabel's copy of this work (the book mark is Rvgl. 14786 2. Ex.). It is heavily annotated, partly in shorthand. Many of these annotations are hardly of a complimentary character. On p. 19 Großmann-Doerth muses on the differences in character between (North-)Germans and Austrians and states, *inter alia*, that the latter do not take many things as seriously as the former do; 'pure nonsense', according to Rabel's pencilled gloss. Rabel was Austrian by birth.

[172] Cf. also Art. 7.1.4 PICC. Structurally different is the solution adopted in Art. 8:104 PECL: the seller is only given a right to cure if the purchaser has rejected the defective goods. This is similar to the regulation in the UCC; see Lehmkuhl (n. 141) 55 ff., 87 ff.

[173] See, for example, Stephan Lorenz, 'Schadensersatz wegen Pflichtverletzung—ein Beispiel für die Überhastung der Kritik an der Schuldrechtsreform', [2001] *Juristenzeitung* 743; Jacobs (n. 126) 372; Faust (n. 12) § 440, n. 2.

[174] Barbara Dauner-Lieb, 'Die geplante Schuldrechtsmodernisierung—Durchbruch oder Schnellschuss?', [2001] *Juristenzeitung* 13; Westermann, [2001] *Juristenzeitung* 537; Jacobs (n. 126)

old BGB, the purchaser immediately had a very strong and—from the point of view of the seller—inconvenient right at his disposal: the *actio redhibitoria*. Thus, he was able to terminate his contract with a seller in whose ability to perform properly he had lost confidence. On the other hand, he could use it as a bargaining tool to get the seller to agree to the kind of supplementary performance that was favourable to him. Now he faces the prospect of protracted negotiations and attempts to remedy the defect before he can get away from the contract. It has even been argued that under the new law the purchaser no longer has the right to reject delivery of a defective object in cases where supplementary performance can only take the form of repair.[175]

VI. Secondary Rights

Apart from supplementary performance, a purchaser who has received a defective object is granted the right (i) to terminate the contract; (ii) to claim damages; (iii) to claim any expenses incurred in the expectation of receiving performance; and (iv) to reduce the purchase price.[176] Even though the Consumer Sales Directive only deals with the rights to termination and price reduction, it does not prevent the legal systems of the EU member states from giving additional rights to purchasers and thus strengthening their position.[177] All these rights, however, (except for 'simple damages')[178] are secondary rights for, as a rule, they are available only if a reasonable period has been fixed by the purchaser, and has lapsed to no avail.[179] There are a number of exceptions to this rule. A period for performance does not have to be fixed if supplementary performance is impossible;[180] if the seller seriously and definitively refuses to make supplementary performance;[181] if there are special circumstances which, after the interests of both parties have been weighed up against each other, justify the immediate assertion of any of the secondary rights;[182] if the seller fails to perform by a date specified in the contract, or within a specified period

---

372. For a balanced evaluation of the advantages and disadvantages of the new regime for the seller and the purchaser see Faust (n. 12) § 440, n. 5; cf. also Schulz (n. 140) 446 ff.

[175] Nils Jansen, 'Gewährleistung trotz Annahmeverzugs und Untergangs der Kaufsache?', [2002] *Zeitschrift für Wirtschaftsrecht* 877 ff. The purchaser would, therefore, be exposed to the consequences of *mora creditoris* if he does not accept the defective object. *Contra* (i.e., a general right of rejection, as under the old law): Philipp Lamprecht, 'Nochmals: Gewährleistung trotz Annahmeverzugs und Untergang der Kaufsache?', [2002] *Zeitschrift für Wirtschaftsrecht* 1790 ff.; Faust (n. 12) § 433, n. 14; *Münchener Kommentar*/Westermann (n. 12) § 437, n. 16.   [176] § 437 BGB.
[177] See Art. 8 (1) Consumer Sales Directive.   [178] On which see *infra* VIII.2.
[179] *Supra* V.4.
[180] §§ 283, 311 a, 326 V BGB, provided performance is impossible in terms of § 275 I BGB.
[181] §§ 281 II, 323 II no. 1 BGB.   [182] §§ 281 II, 323 II no. 3 BGB.

and the purchaser has intimated in the contract that his interest in receiving performance is limited to receiving it in time;[183] if the seller has refused both forms of supplementary performance in cases where they are possible only by incurring unreasonable expense;[184] if the form of supplementary performance to which the seller is entitled has failed;[185] or if the purchaser cannot reasonably be expected to accept supplementary performance.[186] These exceptions, which overlap to some extent,[187] are contained partly in the general rules relating to breach of contract and partly in a specific provision introduced into the law of sale. While only some of them are based on the Consumer Sales Directive,[188] the others are also in conformity with that Directive since they are favourable to the purchaser.[189]

VII. Termination

The right to termination which is granted to the purchaser under § 437 I no. 2 BGB takes the place of the old claim for redhibition. This reflects the desire of the draftsmen of the new law to streamline the remedies for breach of contract and, in particular, to integrate the rules relating to the law of sale as far as possible with the general remedial armoury for breach of contract. It means that the general rules contained in §§ 323, 326 V BGB apply;[190] they are modified only by the special provision of § 440 BGB. Termination, unlike redhibition under the old law, is effected by declaration to the other party.[191] Article 3 (2) of the Consumer Sales Directive states that the purchaser shall be entitled 'to have the contract rescinded'. The Directive thus appears to envisage that the purchaser has a claim for termination and cannot simply terminate the contract by his own act. Once again, however, the German rule does not contravene the Convention since it facilitates termination of the contract on the part of the purchaser.[192]

---

[183] § 323 II no. 2 BGB. This rule is applicable to termination and, via § 441 I 1 BGB, also to reduction of the purchase price (though it hardly makes sense in that respect; Faust (n. 12) § 440, n. 23, therefore proposes a teleological restriction). On the other hand, it does not apply to the right to claim damages; some authors have thus argued in favour of an analogous application of § 323 II no. 2 BGB (see the discussion by Faust (n. 12) § 440, n. 24).

[184] § 440 I 1 read in conjunction with § 439 III BGB.

[185] § 440, 1 BGB. A repair is deemed to have failed, as a rule, after two unsuccessful attempts: § 440, 2 BGB.   [186] § 440, 1 BGB.

[187] For a detailed discussion, see Faust (n. 12) § 440, nn. 18 ff.

[188] Art. 3 (3) and (5) Consumer Sales Directive.   [189] Faust (n. 12) § 440, n. 7.

[190] On which see *supra* pp. 68 ff.   [191] § 349 BGB.

[192] Art. 8 (2) Consumer Sales Directive; see Faust (n. 12) § 437, n. 8. The problem that extinctive prescription only refers to *claims* (*Ansprüche*) has been solved by § 218 BGB: termination for non-performance or for failure to perform in accordance with the contract is ineffective if the claim for performance, or the claim for supplementary performance, has prescribed and if the debtor raises this defence.

More problematic is another discrepancy between the Directive and the new rules of German law. According to § 323 I the purchaser may terminate the contract, 'if he has fixed, to no avail, an additional period of time for performance'. Article 3 (5) of the Directive, on the other hand, states that the consumer can have the contract rescinded 'if the seller has not completed the remedy within a reasonable time'. Here German law requires more of the purchaser than the Directive since even after the lapse of a reasonable period he cannot simply terminate the contract unless he has previously fixed such period. Whether § 323 I BGB can be interpreted in conformity with the Directive is doubtful.[193] Moreover the Directive, in the passage just cited, appears to enable the purchaser to terminate the contract even in cases where the object sold has been successfully repaired, or replaced by another one free from defects, though not within a reasonable time ('. . . has not completed . . .').[194] Again, therefore, it is doubtful whether German law, which does not allow termination under these circumstances, conforms to the Directive.[195] On the other hand, it has been suggested that the Directive should be interpreted restrictively; for it is hardly reasonable to allow a purchaser to terminate the contract at a time when he has a flawless object at his disposal.[196]

VIII. Damages

Consideration of the claim for damages opens up a quagmire of subtle distinction. This is so in spite of the fact that, as in the case of termination, the draftsmen of the new law of sale attempted to integrate the claim for damages into the general rules concerning breach of contract;[197] and also in spite of the fact that the Consumer Sales Directive does not deal with the claim for damages and so, unlike in the case of termination, does not provide an added level of complexity. Three different types of damages must be distinguished; no less than six

---

[193] The problem is discussed, with great ingenuity, by Faust (n. 12) § 437, nn. 17 ff. Faust refers to § 323 II no. 3 BGB, a rule which, under special circumstances, even allows the purchaser to terminate the contract immediately.

[194] Cf. also the third alternative contained in Art. 3 (5) of the Directive (the consumer may have the contract rescinded 'if the seller *has* not completed the remedy without significant inconvenience to the purchaser'; emphasis added).

[195] See Wulf-Henning Roth, 'Die Schuldrechtsmodernisierung im Kontext des Europarechts', in Wolfgang and Zimmermann (n. 143) 243 ff.; Beate Gsell, 'Kaufrechtsrichtinie und Schuldrechtsmodernisierung', [2001] *Juristenzeitung* 70; Tobias Tröger, 'Zum Systemdenken im europäischen Schuldvertragsrecht—Probleme der Rechtsangleichung durch Richtlinien am Beispiel der Verbrauchsgüterkauf-Richtlinie', (2003) 11 *Zeitschrift für Europäisches Privatrecht* 531 ff.

[196] Harm Peter Westermann, 'Das neue Kaufrecht einschließlich des Verbrauchsgüterkaufs', [2001] *Juristenzeitung* 537; Faust (n. 12) § 437, n. 24; *Staudinger*/Matusche-Beckmann (n. 12) § 441, n. 44.   [197] § 437 no. 3 BGB, referring to the general liability rules for breach of duty.

different bases for a claim for damages have to be taken into account; and the key feature of a claim for damages, the breach of duty, can appear in a number of different guises.[198] The three different types of damages are damages in lieu of performance, damages for delay of performance, and 'simple' damages.[199]

1. Damages in lieu of performance

a) The concept explained

The key concept for comprehending the structure of the relevant provisions is the notion of damages in lieu of performance.[200] Here the purchaser is to be placed, *qua* damages, in the position in which he would have been had the seller performed in conformity with his contractual obligation. The duty to perform is substituted by a duty to pay damages. Since, however, the seller has not failed to perform altogether but has in fact delivered a defective object, two alternatives are imaginable, and it is generally agreed that they are both available to the purchaser: either the purchaser may keep the defective object and claim as damages the difference between the situation as it is and as it should have been (i.e., the difference between having the defective object and having an object in conformity with the seller's obligation), or he may return the defective object and ask to receive compensation in money for the value of the entire performance owed to him.[201] Thus, in the latter alternative, he may either claim the value of the object without any defect, or the costs incurred for a covering transaction. Damages arising from the fact that the purchaser was unable to use the object, transportation costs, compensation for improvements, damage to other pieces of the purchaser's property, or to his bodily integrity, etc., can be claimed *sub voce* damages in lieu of performance

---

[198] For an exceptionally clear analysis, see Faust (n. 12) § 437, nn. 41 ff.; see also Huber (n. 149) 521 ff.; Hans Christoph Grigoleit and Thomas Riehm, 'Die Kategorien des Schadensersatzes im Leistungsstörungsrecht', (2003) 203 *Archiv für die civilistische Praxis* 727 ff.; *Münchener Kommentar*/Westermann (n. 12) § 437, nn. 21 ff.

[199] For these distinctions, see *supra* pp. 52 ff.

[200] Neither CISG nor the Principles of European Contract Law recognize the concept of damages in lieu of performance; see Huber (n. 149) Art. 45, n. 41; Hans Stoll, in Peter Schlechtriem (n. 148), Art. 74, n. 3 (both pointing out that a purchaser, under the Convention, has to combine termination and a claim for damages in order to achieve the same practical effect as damages in lieu of performance under German law); and see Lando and Beale (n. 136) 363 ff. (note to Art. 8:102 PECL). As far as the other national legal systems in Europe are concerned, see the comparative overview by Schwartze (n. 8) 312 ff.

[201] This is the distinction between what in German doctrine is called *kleiner Schadensersatz* and *großer Schadensersatz*; see Lorenz and Riehm (n. 126) nn. 206 ff.; Faust, in Huber and Faust (n. 126) 137 ff.; *idem* (n. 12) § 437, n. 125; Wolfgang Ernst, in *Münchener Kommentar zum Bürgerlichen Gesetzbuch*, vol. 2a, 4th edn. (2003), § 281, nn. 123 ff.; *Münchener Kommentar*/Westermann (n. 12) § 437, n. 35; *Jauernig*/Berger (n. 126) § 281, n. 21. For the old law, see *Soergel*/Huber (n. 12) § 463, nn. 38 ff., 53 ff.

only insofar as they would not have arisen had the purchaser rendered supplementary performance at the latest possible moment.[202] If they would have arisen at any rate, i.e. even if the seller had made supplementary performance within the additional period fixed by the purchaser, they have to be qualified as 'simple' damages.

b) When can they be claimed?

Damages in lieu of performance can be claimed under §§ 280 I, III, 281 I 1 BGB, because the seller has delivered a defective object (and has, thus, 'failed to perform properly': § 281 I 1 BGB). Of course, he must have been responsible for the breach of his contractual duty (this is a general requirement for damages claims under the German law relating to breach of contract)[203] and he must have fixed, to no avail, a reasonable period for supplementary performance (this is an additional requirement relating specifically to damages in lieu of performance).[204] Delivery of the defective object is not, however, the only breach of duty for which a seller may be held responsible. He can also have failed to render supplementary performance, or he may not have rendered supplementary performance properly. Again, the purchaser can claim damages in lieu of performance (§§ 280 I, III, 281 I BGB), provided the general requirements for a claim for damages and the special requirements for a claim for damages in lieu of performance are met.[205] Of course, the purchaser may not claim damages in lieu of performance twice over. This does not, however, mean that the claim based on failure to render supplementary performance, or to render it properly, is of a purely academic nature. For it is easily imaginable that a seller who is responsible for his breach of duty concerning supplementary performance, has not been responsible for having delivered a defective object in the first place, or the other way round.[206]

Damages in lieu of performance can also be claimed if, at the time of conclusion of the contract, it was impossible (§ 275 I BGB), or if the seller was entitled to refuse to perform (§ 275 II, III BGB) in conformity with the contractual obligation. This claim, however, is based on § 311a II BGB.[207] Here, too, the

---

[202] Damages in lieu of performance can only be claimed, in principle, if a reasonable period has been fixed by the purchaser and has lapsed to no avail. Thus, for the purposes of distinguishing damages in lieu of performance and simple damages, it has to be asked whether the detrimental consequences in question would have been avoided had the seller performed in time, i.e. within the present context, had the seller made supplementary performance within the reasonable period fixed by the purchaser: see Faust (n. 12) § 437, nn. 47, 51 ff. The question of where the borderline between damages in lieu of performance, 'simple' damages (and damages for delay of performance) has to be drawn is much disputed; see *supra* pp. 58 ff.   [203] § 280 I 2 BGB; see *supra* pp. 50 f.

[204] § 281 I 1 BGB.   [205] For details, see Faust (n. 12) § 437, nn. 90 ff.; Huber (n. 149) 528 ff.

[206] Faust (n. 12) § 437, n. 67.   [207] For details, see Faust (n. 12) § 437, nn. 102 ff.

fault principle normally prevails, though the point of reference for the attribution of fault is different: the seller is not blamed for delivering a defective object but for having concluded the contract in spite of the fact that he knew, or should have known, that he would not be able to honour his obligation. Obviously, the granting of an additional period is not required in this situation. Impossibility of performance can arise not only before the conclusion of the contract but also afterwards. In the present context, two types of situation are imaginable:[208] the object of the sale is not defective at the time of conclusion of the contract; however, before it is handed over, a defect occurs which cannot, or does not have to, be removed in view of § 275 BGB; or the object is defective at the time of conclusion of the contract but the removal of the defect only becomes impossible subsequently. In both situations different legal consequences arise depending on whether removal of the defect becomes impossible before[209] or after the object has been handed over. In the latter situation, the claim for damages in lieu of performance (§§ 280 I, III, 283) can be based either on the fact that the seller has rendered a defective performance, or that (supplementary) performance has become impossible.[210]

Finally, damages in lieu of performance can be claimed under §§ 280 I, III, 282 BGB (in spite of the fact that the draftsmen of the new sales law forgot to include a reference to § 282 in § 437 no. 3 BGB) if the seller infringes an ancillary duty which does not affect the performance as such.[211] This can be relevant in cases where the seller is not responsible for having delivered a defective object but where he has infringed a duty to inform the purchaser about the defect. Apart, of course, from fault, the claim requires that the purchaser can no longer reasonably be expected to abide by the contract and to receive supplementary performance.

2. Simple damages

The notion of 'simple' damages covers all financially detrimental consequences resulting from the delivery of the defective object which could not have been averted by supplementary performance at the latest possible moment and with regard to which the granting of an additional period would not, therefore, make sense.[212] Thus, for example, damage done by the defective product to other pieces of the purchaser's property, or to his bodily integrity, has to be classified as 'simple' damage, if it occurred at a time when the seller was still in

---

[208] For what follows, see the exposition by Faust (n. 12) § 437, nn. 107 ff.
[209] Here the purchaser is discharged from his obligation to deliver an object that is free from defects: § 275 BGB. [210] For details, see Faust (n. 12) § 437, nn. 109, 112 ff.
[211] See Faust (n. 12) § 437, nn. 118 ff. On the concept of *nicht leistungsbezogene Nebenpflichten*, see *supra* p. 55. [212] *Supra* text to n. 202.

a position to make supplementary performance. If it arose at a time when supplementary performance could no longer be rendered, it forms part of the damages in lieu of performance since it would not have arisen in case of supplementary performance at the latest possible moment.[213] 'Simple' damages may be claimed under § 280 I BGB if there is a breach of duty for which the seller is responsible. The breach of duty can lie either in the handing over of a defective object or in the infringement of an ancillary duty which does not affect the performance as such (the seller fails to draw the purchaser's attention to the defect).[214] The claim for 'simple' damages is not affected by the fact that subsequently a claim for damages in lieu of performance arises.[215]

3. Damages for delay of performance

Since all damages can either be prevented by supplementary performance or not, they are covered either by the notion of simple damages or by that of damages in lieu of performance. None the less, the third type of loss envisaged by § 280 BGB, i.e. damages for delay of performance (§§ 280 II BGB),[216] can also be relevant in the present context.[217] It applies in situations where the seller cannot be held responsible for having handed over to the purchaser a defective object (and where, therefore, the requirements for a claim for simple damages, or damages in lieu of performance, have not been met) but where the purchaser wishes to claim his loss resulting from, and arising in the course of, the debtor's delay in rendering supplementary performance.[218] For the latter claim the requirements of *mora debitoris*, as set out in § 286 BGB have to be met. One of these requirements, once again, is that the seller has been responsible for the delay in rendering supplementary performance.

---

[213] Faust (n. 12) § 437, n. 54. Predominantly, however, damage to other pieces of the purchaser's property, or to his bodily integrity, is classified as 'simple damages', no matter at which time it arose (see, for example, Barbara Dauner-Lieb, in *Anwaltkommentar Schuldrecht* (n. 156) § 280, n. 55; Lorenz and Riehm (n. 126) 548; Huber, in Huber and Faust (n. 126) 351 ff.; Dieter Medicus, 'Die Leistungsstörungen im neuen Schuldrecht', [2003] *Juristische Schulung* 528; Grigoleit and Riehm, (2003) 203 *Archiv für die civilistische Praxis* 727 ff.; Horst Ehmann and Holger Sutschet, 'Schadensersatz wegen kaufrechtlicher Schlechtleistungen—Verschuldens- und/oder Garantiehaftung?', [2004] *Juristenzeitung* 68 ff.; *Jauernig/Berger* (n. 126) § 437, n. 15. On the recoverability of such consequential loss under CISG, see *Staudinger/Magnus* (n. 112) Art. 74, nn. 29, 45 ff.; cf.: Schwartze (n. 8) 323 ff.

[214] For details, see Faust (n. 12) § 437, n. 133 ff.   [215] Faust (n. 12) § 437, n. 62.

[216] On which see *supra* pp. 56 f.

[217] Very widely, however, the claim for damages for delay of performance under §§ 280 II, 280 BGB is attributed a greater scope of application; see, for example, Grigoleit and Riehm, (2003) 203 *Archiv für die civilistische Praxis* 754 ff.; *Palandt/Putzo* (n. 126) § 437, n. 36; *Jauernig/Berger* (n. 126) § 437, nn. 16 ff.

[218] *Münchener Kommentar/Ernst* (n. 201) § 280, n. 71. For details, see Faust (n. 12) § 437, nn. 48, 63 ff., 141 ff. He refers to a 'second track' of liability.

The frightening level of complexity of this system of rules will, presumably, render it unfit to serve as a source of inspiration in the current debates surrounding European contract law.

4. Appendix: claim for the substitute in cases of impossibility

If performance has become impossible, due to no fault of the debtor, the creditor cannot claim damages. Still, however, the debtor may have acquired something in the place of the object he was supposed to deliver: compensation from, or a claim against, an insurance company or a third party. German law regards it as equitable for the debtor to have to make over to the creditor whatever benefit he has acquired: § 285 BGB.[219] In spite of the fact that § 285 is not mentioned in § 437 BGB, the rule also applies to a purchaser who has received a defective object from the seller.[220] If supplementary performance has become impossible, the purchaser may well wish to have transferred to him a claim for damages which may have accrued to the seller against the seller's supplier. Oddly, neither CISG nor the Principles of European Contract Law provide for this kind of remedy. The Consumer Sales Directive, too, does not deal with it.

IX. Reduction of the Purchase Price

Termination, damages and the claim for the substitute in cases of impossibility are general remedies for breach of contract which also apply to the purchaser.[221] Reduction of the purchase price, on the other hand, retains its character as a specific remedy available to purchasers.[222] It is a right which is, in principle, subject to the same requirements as termination since, according to § 441 I BGB, it is granted 'instead of termination'. Like termination, reduction is effected by unilateral declaration to the other party: the purchaser may not merely demand reduction from the other party but may himself reduce the price.[223] The mechanism for effecting the reduction thus differs from the one available under the old German law of sale.[224] At the same time, it is more favourable to the purchaser than the system envisaged by the Consumer Sales

---

[219] *Supra* pp. 60 f.   [220] Faust (n. 12) § 437, nn. 147 ff.

[221] The same is true with regard to the purchaser's right to claim whatever expenses he may have incurred in the expectation of receiving performance in conformity with the contractual promise: § 437 no. 3, 2nd alternative BGB. On this right—which is not envisaged in the Consumer Sales Directive—see Faust (n. 12) § 437, nn. 144 ff. and, more generally, *supra* pp. 61 f.

[222] For a comparative analysis, see Rabel (n. 12) 232 ff.; Schwartze (n. 8) 220 ff.; Sandrock (n. 144) 209 ff.; and see Art. 50 CISG; Art. 9:401 PECL.

[223] Cf. also Art. 50 CISG; for a comparative analysis, see Sandrock (n. 144) 222 ff.

[224] *Supra* text to n. 107.

Directive (the purchaser 'may require' an appropriate reduction of the price). As in the case of termination, and for the same reason, this does not bring German law into conflict with the Directive.[225] Like termination, but unlike the claim for damages, reduction of the purchase price does not depend on fault. As in the case of both termination and the claim for damages, the purchaser must, as a rule, have fixed, to no avail, an additional period of time for performance (§§ 441 I, 440, 437 no. 2, 323 BGB). As far as consumer sales is concerned, this is not in conformity with the Consumer Sales Directive; it can be saved, possibly, by a somewhat strained interpretation of a provision contained in § 323 II no. 3 BGB: from the moment when the purchaser requests the seller to make supplementary performance, a reasonable period of time automatically starts to run, even if it has not been fixed by the purchaser.[226] Such interpretation in conformity with the Directive, incidentally, leads to two problematic consequences: with regard to termination and reduction, consumer sales are treated differently from other contracts of sale; and with regard to consumer sales, termination and reduction are treated differently from the claim for damages (which is not covered by the Consumer Sales Directive).[227] There is one major difference between termination and reduction in that reduction is, but termination is not, available in cases of an immaterial breach of duty.[228] This is in conformity with the Directive,[229] and reflects the fact that reduction affects the contractual relationship much less severely than termination.[230]

As far as the extent of the reduction is concerned, the Directive merely states that it has to be 'appropriate'.[231] The draftsmen of the new law of sale, after some intellectual contortions,[232] eventually decided to maintain the formula recognized under the old law: the purchase price after reduction has to relate to

---

[225] *Supra* text to n. 192.   [226] *Supra* n. 193.

[227] On the question of a split interpretation, which should be avoided, as far as possible, see Mathias Habersack and Christian Meyer, 'Die überschiessende Umsetzung von Richtlinien', [1999] *Juristenzeitung* 913 ff.; Peter Hommelhoff, 'Die Rolle der nationalen Gerichte bei der Europäisierung des Privatrechts', in *Festschrift für den Bundesgerichtshof*, vol. II (2000), 914 ff.; York Schnorbus, 'Autonome Harmonisierung in den Mitgliedstaaten durch die Inkorporation von Gemeinschaftsrecht', (2001) 65 *Rabels Zeitschrift für ausländisches und internationales Privatrecht* 654 ff.; Grundmann (n. 12) Einl., n. 39; Helmut Heinrichs, in *Palandt, Bürgerliches Gesetzbuch* 64th edn. (2005), Einl., n. 44; Büdenbender, (2004) 12 *Zeitschrift für Europäisches Privatrecht* 36 ff.; Drexl (n. 121) 67 ff.   [228] See § 441 I 2 BGB.

[229] Art. 3 (6) Consumer Sales Directive.

[230] For the same reason, the scope of application of the *actio redhibitoria* had been restricted by many authors of the *ius commune*; see *Law of Obligations* (n. 4) 325 ff. The old BGB had gone even further and had excluded the seller's liability altogether in cases of an insignificant diminution in value or fitness for use: § 459 I 2 BGB (old version). For details, see Baldus (n. 109) 37 ff.

[231] Art. 3 (5) Consumer Sales Directive.

[232] For criticism see Claus-Wilhelm Canaris, 'Das allgemeine Leistungsstörungsrecht im Schuldrechtsmodernisierungsgesetz', [2001] *Zeitschrift für Rechtspolitik* 335; Heinrich Honsell, 'Die EU-Richtlinie über den Verbrauchgüterkauf und ihre Umsetzung ins BGB', [2001] *Juristenzeitung* 281 ff.

the original purchase price agreed upon by the parties as the true value of the object does to the value of the object free from defects (§ 441 III BGB).²³³ The most controversial question so far, concerning reduction of the purchase price, has its origin in two innocuous-looking words contained in the Directive: the consumer may require an appropriate reduction of the price 'if the seller *has not* completed the remedy within a reasonable time' or 'without significant inconvenience to the consumer'.²³⁴ According to the Directive, therefore, the purchase price may be reduced even if supplementary performance has taken place, provided only that it has been rendered too late or has entailed significant inconvenience to the purchaser. There are good reasons to assume that German law (which only allows the purchaser to reduce the price as long as the defect has not been remedied) is not in conformity with the Directive as far as the second of these alternatives is concerned.²³⁵

Sale is not the only contract with regard to which the BGB recognizes a remedy of reduction of the purchase price in cases of defective performance. The code contains similar rules for contracts of lease and contracts for work.²³⁶ It may be useful also for contracts of services.²³⁷ In other countries, too, there is a tendency to generalize this remedy.²³⁸ The Dutch BW has, therefore, abandoned the specific provisions concerning price reduction and has moved the remedy to the general part of the law of obligations, though in the form of a partial termination (*gedeeltelijke ontbinding*) of the contract.²³⁹ Article 9:401 PECL also provides a general remedy of price reduction, applicable to all contracts where a price is paid for a performance.²⁴⁰ Given the general desire of

²³³ For details see Faust (n. 12) § 441, nn. 8 ff.; *Münchener Kommentar*/Westermann (n. 12) § 441, nn. 12 ff.; *Palandt*/Putzo (n. 126) § 441, nn. 12 ff. For the old law, see § 472 BGB (old version) and *Soergel*/Huber (n. 12) § 472, nn. 1 ff. This is also the formula chosen in Art. 50 CISG (on the model of § 472 BGB; see Huber (n. 149) Art. 50, n. 2) and Art. 9:401 PECL. For a comparison of the national legal systems in Europe, see Schwartze (n. 8) 228 ff.; Sandrock (n. 144) 225 ff.

²³⁴ Art. 3 (5) second and third alternatives Consumer Sales Directive (emphasis added). For the parallel problem concerning termination, see *supra* VII. *in fine*.

²³⁵ See Peter Schlechtriem, 'Das geplante Gewährleistungsrecht im Licht der europäischen Richtlinie zum Verbrauchgüterkauf', in Ernst and Zimmermann (n. 143) 219 ff.; for a detailed argument along these lines, see Faust (n. 12) § 441, nn. 30 ff.; cf. also *Staudinger*/Matusche-Beckmann (n. 12) § 441, nn. 45 ff. Others argue that German law does not comply with the requirements of the Directive as far as both alternatives are concerned; see Roth (n. 195) 243 ff.; Gsell, [2001] *Juristenzeitung* 70. Cf. also *Münchener Kommentar*/Westermann (n. 12) § 442, n. 19.   ²³⁶ §§ 536, 638 BGB.

²³⁷ Manfred Lieb, 'Dienstvertrag', in Bundesminister der Justiz (ed.), *Gutachten und Vorschläge zur Überarbeitung des Schuldrechts*, vol. III (1983), 219 (§ 614 III).   ²³⁸ Sandrock (n. 144) 209 ff.

²³⁹ For comment, see Sandrock (n. 144) 210 ff. For the consequences of the right to reduction of the purchase price in terms of Art. 3 (5) of the Consumer Sales Directive for Dutch law, see Jan Smits, 'Wie is er bang voor de actio quanti minoris? Over een onvermijdelike Europese ontwikkeling', [2000] *Weekblad voor privaatrecht, notariaat en registratie* 685 ff.; *idem*, 'De richtlijn consumentenkoop en het Nederlandse rechts', in *idem* (ed.), *De richtlijn consumentenkoop in perspectief* (2003), 1 ff.

²⁴⁰ See Lando and Beale (n. 136) 430 ff.; this approach is welcomed by Schlechtriem, (1993) 1 *Zeitschrift für Europäisches Privatrecht* 242 ff.

the draftsmen of the new law of obligations to integrate liability for latent defects, as far as possible, with the general regime governing breach of contract, it is surprising to see that the fractured regulation of price reduction has been retained in the new BGB.

X. Unsolved Problems

Much more important, practically, is another characteristic of liability for defects as to quality that has not been abandoned in the new law, even though it has caused considerable problems under the old: the special prescription regime[241] laid down in § 438 BGB.[242] It will continue to give rise to a number of problems of delimitation, among them the vexed question whether a defect relates to a 'functionally separable' part of the object of sale only, or to the object as a whole (in the former case a delictual claim, governed by the regular prescription period, would be available if the object is subsequently destroyed as a result of the defect).[243]

But this is only one of the issues which the draftsmen of the new law failed to resolve, even though they had specifically set out to tackle them.[244] To a certain extent, this also applies to the question of how to deal with cases where the seller does not deliver a defective object but one that is different from the one envisaged in the contract.[245] According to § 434 III BGB, delivery by the seller of a different object is equivalent to a defect as to quality. This rule is intended to avoid the necessity of distinguishing between the two types of cases. But does this mean that a seller who has promised a painting by Picasso and proceeds, in fulfilment of this contract, to deliver a bag of coal, has to be treated as if he had delivered a defective painting by Picasso: with the result that the buyer would not retain his original claim to specific performance, which is subject to the regular prescription regime of §§ 195, 199 I BGB, but could only avail himself of the rights listed in § 437 BGB (including supplementary

---

[241] For details, see *infra* pp. 133 ff. Under the old law, § 477 BGB was applicable; see *supra* III.3.

[242] It relates to all claims based on the seller's liability for defects as to quality (as well as defects of title), whether or not they are listed in § 437 BGB: Faust (n. 12) § 438, nn. 1, 8; for two claims not listed in § 437 BGB (*supra* text to nn. 211 and 220), see Faust (n. 12) § 437, nn. 118, 149. The provision of § 438 BGB is in line with the Consumer Sales Directive; see Faust (n. 12) § 438, n. 5. The draftsmen of the new German law have not, as they could have done (Art. 5 (2) Consumer Sales Directive), adopted a rule according to which, in order to benefit from his rights, the purchaser has to inform the seller of the lack of conformity within a period of two months from the date on which he detected such lack of conformity.   [243] *Supra* text to n. 99.

[244] See, for example, Hansjörg Geiger (director general in the Federal Department of Justice), 'Einführung: Zum Stand des Gesetzgebungsverfahrens', [2001] *Juristenzeitung* 473 ff.

[245] *Supra* text to nn. 104 and 105.

performance), which are governed by the prescription period contained in § 438 BGB?[246] Whoever regards this as absurd, or inappropriate,[247] is faced, once again, with problems of delimitation, though on a different level and subject to other criteria than under the old law. Another problem which the new law intended to obviate is the need to distinguish between defects as to quality and defects of title.[248] Even though both types of defect are still dealt with in two different provisions,[249] they have, in principle, been placed on a par: §§ 437 ff. BGB also apply to defects of title. There is one rule, however, the reversal of the burden of proof contained in § 476 BGB,[250] which only refers to defects as to quality.[251] In this respect, the distinction will therefore still retain some significance.[252]

XI. Conclusion

The aedilitian edict was a practically important instrument of what would be called, in modern parlance, consumer protection.[253] The remedies provided by the Roman market police soon came to be merged with the general sales law. The scene was thus set for a breathtaking extension of the aedilitian rules of liability for latent defects. The generalized form of aedilitian liability became part and parcel of the *ius commune* and it even distinctively shaped the national codifications in Europe. It took a long time before it was realized that what was

[246] This is the view adopted, for example, by Huber, in Huber and Faust (n. 126) 308 ff. (from whom the example is taken; Huber explicitly states that the bag of coal is, so to speak, a defective Picasso); cf. also Faust (n. 12) § 434, n. 108; Hans-Joachim Musielak, 'Die Falschlieferung beim Stückkauf nach dem neuen Schuldrecht', [2003] *Neue Juristische Wochenschrift* 89 ff.; Klaus Tiedtke and Marco Schmidt, 'Die Falschlieferung durch den Verkäufer', [2004] *Juristenzeitung* 1092 ff.; *Staudinger*/Matusche-Beckmann (n. 12) § 434, n. 115; *Palandt*/Putzo (n. 126) § 434, n. 52a. This is in line with the approach adopted by CISG and the Consumer Sales Directive; see Ernst A. Kramer, 'Abschied von der aliud-Lieferung?', in *Besonderes Vertragsrecht—aktuelle Probleme: Festschrift für Heinrich Honsell* (2002), 247 ff.
[247] See, for example, Canaris (n. 120) 68 ff.; Andreas Thier, 'Aliud- und Minus-Lieferung im neuen Kaufrecht des Bürgerlichen Gesetzbuches', (2003) 203 *Archiv für die civilistische Praxis* 399 ff.; *Jauernig*/Berger (n. 126) § 434, n. 21 (delivery of a toy car in the place of a real motor car); cf. also Medicus (n. 99) n. 288.   [248] *Supra* text to n. 106.
[249] § 434 as opposed to § 435 BGB.   [250] This is based on Art. 5 (3) Consumer Sales Directive.
[251] Whether the Directive only applies to defects as to quality or also to defects of title, is disputed; see Ernst and Gsell, [2000] *Zeitschrift für Wirtschaftsrecht* 1411 on the one hand, and Grundmann (n. 12) Art. 2, nn. 14 ff. on the other.
[252] Thus, the problem continues to be discussed; see Faust (n. 12) § 435, nn. 9 ff.; *Jauernig*/Berger (n. 126) § 435, nn. 3 ff.; *Palandt*/Putzo (n. 126) § 435, nn. 5 ff. The distinction also continues to have some relevance for CISG; see Ingeborg Schwenzer, in Schlechtriem and Schwenzer (n. 126) Art. 35, n. 5 and Art. 41, nn. 3 ff.
[253] Max Kaser and Rolf Knütel, *Römisches Privatrecht*, 17th edn. (2003), 270; Jakab, in Schermaier (n. 10) 33.

appropriate for the sale of slaves and cattle on an open market did not present the ideal solution for commercial sales in the industrial era. First attempts by the Natural lawyers to devise liability rules based on reason rather than on the peculiarities of Roman law did not have a lasting influence.[254] It was only towards the end of the nineteenth century that the dominant thinking pattern started to change for good. The decisive insight triggering this change was based on a simple observation. Modern commercial life is dominated by the sale of unascertained goods. This has to be reflected in the rules of modern sales law. If the object of the sale has merely been described by kind or class, the delivery of a defective individual species of this kind or class is a straightforward case of non-performance. In principle, therefore, the normal remedies for non-performance should apply.

In modern European law we are faced, once again, with a piece of legislation dealing with the problem of liability for defects in the object sold and also serving the end of consumer protection. Once again, this piece of legislation has an inherent potential for generalization. It constitutes the foundation for a new approach prevailing throughout Europe which will eventually govern sales law in general.[255] There is one decisive difference, however. Unlike the aedilitian remedies, the rules contained in the Consumer Sales Directive are not geared specifically towards the type of sale with which they purport to deal. The enactment of the Consumer Sales Directive, though based formally on Article 95 of the Treaty establishing the European Community, also relies on Article 153 (1) and (3) of the EC Treaty[256] and is therefore motivated, *inter alia*, by the desire to achieve a high level of consumer protection by adopting 'a uniform minimum

---

[254] Walter Jürgen Klempt, *Die Grundlagen der Sachmängelhaftung des Verkäufers im Vernunftrecht und Usus modernus* (1967), 26 ff.

[255] As is evident from modern codifications such as the one applicable in the Netherlands since 1992. As a result, implementation of the Consumer Sales Directive has not deeply affected the Dutch law of sale (apart from the fact that the *actio redhibitoria* has been re-introduced). For a comparative assessment of Dutch law before the transformation of the Directive, see Schwartze (n. 8) 139 (right of repair), 161 (replacement), 183 (termination), 225 (reduction of the price), 268 ff. (damages) and *passim*; for the transformation of the Directive into Dutch law, see Ewoud Hondius and Christoph Jeloschek, 'Die Kaufrichtlinie und das niederländische Recht: Für den Westen kaum etwas Neues', in Grundmann, Medicus and Rolland (n. 12) 197 ff.; A.J.B. Sirks, 'Die Umsetzung der Richtlinie 1999/44/EG in den Niederlanden', in Schermaier (n. 10) 275 ff.; the contributions by Jan Smits and Jaap Hijma, both in Smits (n. 239) 1 ff., 29 ff. On the fate of the *actio quanti minoris* in Dutch law, see *supra* n. 239. For other national legal systems whose law of sale, or consumer sale, no longer conforms to the model of the old *ius commune*, see Grundmann (n. 12) Einl., n. 10; and see the detailed comparative discussion by Schwartze (n. 8) *passim*.

[256] See recital 1 of the Consumer Sales Directive; for commentary, see Dirk Staudenmeyer, 'EG-Richtlinie 1999/44/EG zur Vereinheitlichung des Kaufgewährleistungsrechts', in Grundmann, Medicus and Rolland (n. 12) 28 ff.; Grundmann (n. 12) Einl., nn. 16 ff.; Luca Serrano, in Bianca and Grundmann (n. 12) Art. 1, nn. 1 ff.; Andreas Schwartze, 'Sachprobleme für die Umsetzung aus Genese, Inhalt und Dogmatik der Richtlinie über Verbraucherkäufe', in Schermaier (n. 10) 130 ff.

set of fair rules governing the sale of consumer goods'.[257] Yet, the rules contained in the Consumer Sales Directive are generally fair not only for the sale of consumer goods but also for all other types of contracts.[258] This applies, in particular, to the concept of conformity and to the remedies provided by the Directive. In both respects the Directive largely mirrors the provisions of the Convention on the International Sale of Goods which applies to commercial transactions and even specifically excludes consumer sales from its range of application.[259] The correspondence between these two international instruments will significantly contribute to the emergence of a common framework of reference for the discussion and development of the general sales law in Europe.[260] Germany has gone further than most other legal systems in tailoring its general sales law to the new international pattern.[261] Since it is a jurisdiction with a large incidence of litigation and a vigorous academic community, German case law and academic discussion should be of considerable interest also to courts and lawyers outside Germany.

This chapter has attempted to provide a basis for the comparative assessment of developments in Germany. Core features of the new German liability regime, which reflect the international state of the discussion, are the purchaser's right to supplementary performance (which constitutes a continuation, in modified form, of his original right to specific performance and which can take the form of removal of the defect or supply of an object free from defects), his right to termination, to price reduction and to damages. The latter three rights are only available on a secondary level for, in principle, the purchaser first has to seek supplementary performance. Effectively this means that the seller is granted a right to cure the defective performance. Sadly, however, this picture is marred by a number of unfortunate features concerning both the Directive and internal German law. Some of the decisions taken in the Directive are unconvincing.[262] Moreover, the Directive adopts an overly paternalistic approach in that it does not allow the parties to consumer sales to contract out of the liability regime provided in it.[263] The new German law of sale, on the other hand, has been hastily drafted and does not display the intellectual maturity and the

---

[257] Recital 2 of the Consumer Sales Directive.

[258] This point is also strongly emphasized by Grundmann (n. 12) Einl., nn. 6, 24 ff.

[259] Art. 2 a) CISG.

[260] For the contours of a set of Principles of European Sales Law, as currently drafted by the Study Group on a European Civil Code, see Viola Heutger, 'Konturen des Kaufrechtskonzeptes der Study Group on a European Civil Code—Ein Werkstattbericht', (2003) 11 *European Review of Private Law* 155 ff.

[261] See Schermaier (n. 125) 21 ff. and the country reports in the same volume; and see Mansel, (2004) 204 *Archiv für die civilistische Praxis* 396 ff.   [262] See, for examples, *supra* V.1., VII. *in fine*.

[263] Art. 7 (1) Consumer Sales Directive; for critical comment, see Michael Martinek, 'Unsystematische Überregulierung und kontraintentionale Effekte im Europäischen Verbraucherschutzrecht oder: Weniger wäre mehr', and Hans-Bernd Schäfer, 'Grenzen des Verbraucherschutzes und adverse

technical precision for which the BGB was once renowned. A number of
its provisions are unclear or difficult to understand;[264] sometimes it is also
questionable whether the requirements of the Directive have been properly
implemented.[265] The rules concerning the claim for damages perpetuate a
number of peculiarities of German law and entail so many subtle distinctions
that, like the rules governing the recovery of contractual damages under the *ius
commune*, they may well be described as comprising 'mare amplissimum, in
quo pauci sine periculo navigarunt'.[266] That the draftsmen of the new German
law decided to extend the system of remedies provided in the Directive to all types
of sale, including commercial sales, is to be welcomed.[267] Equally commendable
is their decision to integrate liability for non-conformity, as far as possible, with
the remedies for non-performance in general. However, the more the liability
rules for non-conformity and for non-performance in general coincide, the more
questionable is the single most important feature that continues to distinguish
the two liability regimes: the different rules concerning extinctive prescription. If
non-conformity is, essentially, merely one instance of non-performance, it is
difficult to see why it should not also be governed by the same, i.e. the regular,

Effekte des Europäischen Verbraucherrechts', both in Stefan Grundmann (ed.), *Systembildung und
Systemlücken in Kerngebieten des Europäischen Privatrechts* (2000), 530 ff., 559 ff.; Grundmann (n. 12)
Einl., n. 33; Fernando Gomez, in Bianca and Grundmann (n. 12) Einl., nn. 116 ff.; Roger van den
Bergh, 'De richtlijn consumentenkoop in rechtseconomisch perspectief', in Smits (n. 239) 79 ff.

[264] See, for example, *supra* nn. 202, 242. Another example of a rule, the rationale of which is
unclear and which has consequently given rise to dispute, is § 444 BGB ('The seller may not rely on
an agreement excluding or restricting the purchaser's rights in respect of defects if the seller... has
guaranteed the quality of the object'); see Huber, in Huber and Faust (n. 126) 369; Canaris
(n. 120) 84 ff.; Faust (n. 12) § 444, nn. 16 ff.; Barabara Dauner-Lieb and Jan Thiessen,
'Garantiebeschränkungen in Unternehmenskaufverträgen nach der Schuldrechtsreform', [2002]
Zeitschrift für Wirtschaftsrecht 108 ff.; Dirk Looschelders, 'Beschaffenheitsvereinbarung, Zusicherung,
Garantie, Gewährleistungsausschluss', in Dauner-Lieb, Konzen and Schmidt (n. 126) 405 ff.; Jan
Dirk Harke, '§ 444 BGB und die Beschaffenheitsgarantie: Verwechslung von Tatbestand und
Rechtsfolge', [2003] *Juristische Rundschau* 404 ff.; *Münchener Kommentar/*Westermann (n. 12) § 444,
nn. 13 ff.; *Staudinger/*Matusche-Beckmann (n. 12) § 444, nn. 51 ff. As a result of the widespread criti-
cism, § 444 BGB has, in the meantime, been changed: Art. 1 no. 6 *Gesetz zur Änderung der Vorschriften
über Fernabsatzverträge bei Finanzdienstleistungen, Bundesgesetzblatt* I 2004, 3102. The new § 444
BGB merely substitutes the word 'if' ('... if the seller... has guaranteed the quality of the object') by
the words 'insofar as'. It is unclear, and consequently disputed, whether the reform (in effect from
8 December 2004) has resolved the problem: Christoph H. Seibt, 'Rechtssicherheit beim
Unternehmens-, Beteiligungs- und Anlagenverkauf: Analyse der Änderungen bei §§ 444, 639 BGB',
[2004] Neue *Zeitschrift für Gesellschaftsrecht* 801 ff.

[265] See, for example, *supra* text to nn. 151 ff., 193 ff.; cf. also, concerning the definition of when an
object is defective, Tröger, (2003) 11 *Zeitschrift für Europäisches Privatrecht* 529 ff. (with references).

[266] Sigismundus Scaccia, quoted by Wilhelm Endemann, *Studien in der romanisch-kanonistischen
Wirtschafts- und Rechtslehre bis gegen Ende des 17. Jahrhunderts*, vol. II (1883), 244; cf. also Helmut
Coing, *Europäisches Privatrecht*, vol. I (1985), 438; *Law of Obligations* (n. 4) 833.

[267] Cf. also Tröger, (2003) 11 *Zeitschrift für Europäisches Privatrecht* 527 ff. (who, in this context,
refers to Austria and Greece).

prescription rules. That German law continues to subscribe to the old approach, in this respect, is likely to be a continuing source of irritation and distortion. Significantly, English and Irish law apply the general prescription regime to breach of contract for damages claims resulting from the delivery of non-conforming goods.[268] The English Law Commission now proposes to introduce a regular limitation period of three years running from the date of reasonable discoverability. No special period for claims based on the delivery of non-conforming goods is envisaged.[269] Dutch law does have a special rule but one that does not significantly differ from the *general* regime provided in the German code.[270] By retaining a rule which is less favourable to purchasers who have received defective goods than to other creditors (and particularly, other creditors of damages claims) the new German law still remains a prisoner of past ages.

[268] See Schwartze (n. 8) 495.
[269] The Law Commission, Limitation of Actions, Law Com No. 270, 2001.
[270] Art. 7:23 (2) BW; on which see Schwartze (n. 8) 498 ff.

4

The New German Law of Prescription and Chapter 14 of the Principles of European Contract Law

I. Introduction

The Principles of European Contract Law of the so-called 'Lando Commission' constitute the most advanced, and internationally most widely noted, project on the way towards a harmonization of contract law in Europe.[1] These Principles are designed to facilitate cross-border trade within Europe by making available a set of neutral rules, detached from the peculiarities of any one national legal system, to which parties can subject their transactions. Moreover, they can be regarded as a modern formulation of a *lex mercatoria* which may be referred to, for instance, by arbitrators who have to decide a case before them according to 'internationally accepted principles of law'. These are very practical purposes. In a longer-term perspective, the Principles can be seen to provide a conceptual and systematic infrastructure for community legislation concerning contract law; at the same time, they can even be taken to constitute a first step on the way towards a European Civil Code.[2]

Of central significance in the immediate future appears to be yet another aspect: the Principles as a source of inspiration for national legislatures, courts of law, and legal doctrine.[3] They constitute a yardstick, established on the basis of comparative research and international cooperation, against which the peculiarities of the existing national legal systems can be assessed. Thus, they should be taken into consideration not only by comparative lawyers but, particularly, by those who are engaged in shaping the development of national law.

---

[1] Ole Lando and Hugh Beale (eds.), *Principles of European Contract Law*, Parts I and II (2000); Ole Lando, Eric Clive, André Prüm and Reinhard Zimmermann (eds.), *Principles of European Contract Law*, Part III (2003).   [2] See Lando and Beale (n. 1) xxi ff.

[3] Reinhard Zimmermann, 'The Principles of European Contract Law as Contemporary Manifestation of the Old, and Possible Foundation for a New, Scholarship of European Private Law', in *Essays in Honour of Hein Köt* (2005), forthcoming.

By intellectually relating the national laws and the Principles to each other, legal scholarship can create an awareness of the Principles as a model for legislative reform and as a guideline for judicial interpretation of the law. The present chapter on prescription has been written in this spirit.

The law of liberative prescription[4] has been, for a long time and in many European countries, in dire need of reform.[5] In Germany, the first comprehensive reform proposals were tabled in 1981.[6] However, it was only twenty-one years later, and as a result of the Modernization of the Law of Obligations Act,[7] that a new regime finally entered into effect. In the final stages of the reform process, a draft version of Chapter 14 of the Principles of European Contract Law, Part III, was brought to the attention of the working group charged by the German Minister of Justice with the task of revising the Discussion Draft, as far as it related to the law of prescription, and did indeed significantly influence the deliberations of that committee.[8] The German government subsequently specifically acknowledged that it 'had adopted, in large parts, the model proposed by the [Lando]Commission'.[9] This is an additional reason for comparing the new German law with Chapter 14 of the Principles and highlighting divergences between the two regimes. In assessing my own attitude, it should perhaps be kept in mind that within the Lando Commission I have been responsible for the drafting of Chapter 14[10] and for tracing its comparative

---

[4] The term 'liberative prescription' is chosen here in preference to the more common term 'extinctive prescription' in view of the fact that neither in German law nor under the Principles is the claim affected by prescription extinguished: see *infra* IX. The UNCITRAL Principles of International Commercial Contracts refer to 'limitation periods'; see *infra* n. 42.

[5] For details, see Reinhard Zimmermann, *Comparative Foundations of a European Law of Set-Off and Prescription* (2002), 66 ff.

[6] Frank Peters and Reinhard Zimmermann, 'Verjährungsfristen: Der Einfluss von Fristen auf Schuldverhältnisse; Möglichkeiten der Vereinfachung von Verjährungsfristen', in Bundesminister der Justiz (ed.), *Gutachten und Vorschläge zur Überarbeitung des Schuldrechts*, vol. I (1981), 77 ff. For a discussion of the old German law of prescription in English, see Reinhard Zimmermann, 'Extinctive Prescription in German Law', in Erik Jayme (ed.), *German National Reports in Civil Law Matters for the XIVth Congress of Comparative Law in Athens 1994* (1994), 153 ff. One of the main criticisms of the old law related to the great diversity of prescription periods with some of them being very widely regarded as inordinately short while others (particularly the general period of prescription) were excessively long. For the prescription 'labyrinth' of the old German law of prescription cf. also, for example, Hans-Georg Hermann, in Mathias Schmoeckel, Joachim Rückert and Reinhard Zimmermann (eds.), *Historisch-kritischer Kommentar zum BGB (HKK)*, vol. I (2003), §§ 194–225, 'Verjährung', nn. 27 ff.

[7] *Bundesgesetzblatt* 2001 I, 3138.

[8] The essential elements of a modern prescription regime had previously been outlined by Reinhard Zimmermann, ' "... ut sit finis litium": Grundlinien eines modernen Verjährungsrechts auf rechtsvergleichender Grundlage', [2000] *Juristenzeitung* 853 ff.

[9] 'Bericht des Rechtsausschusses', BT-Drucksache 14/7052, easily accessible in Claus-Wilhelm Canaris (ed.), *Schuldrechtsmodernisierung 2002* (2002), 1051 ff. (1066); cf. also 'Begründung der Bundesregierung zum Entwurf eines Gesetzes zur Modernisierung des Schuldrechts', BT-Drucksache 6857, in Canaris, in the volume just quoted, 569 ff. (600, 612 ff.).

[10] Lando, Clive, Prüm and Zimmermann (n. 1) x.

foundations.[11] I was also a member of the working group in charge of the reform of the law of prescription[12] and drew that Commission's attention to the Principles of European Contract Law.[13]

II. The Development of the Law of Prescription

1. The reform process in Germany

The law of extinctive prescription,[14] though of the greatest practical significance, has long been marginalized both in domestic and comparative legal literature. In Germany, this only started to change with the publication of the two-volume treatise by Karl Spiro in 1975[15] and with the project to reform the law of obligations, initiated soon thereafter.[16] In the meantime, a considerable amount of legal literature has been produced in Germany and also in other jurisdictions.[17] This has been stimulated not least by the fact that a number of countries have reformed their law of prescription, whether by means of a simple act (as, for example, in South Africa), or as part of a comprehensive re-codification of private law (as in the Netherlands, Québec, and Russia).[18] The English Law Commission

---

[11] See Chapters 2 and 3 of *Comparative Foundations* (n. 5); these chapters are revised versions of my 'position papers' presented to the Commission.

[12] See Canaris (n. 9) x. The working group met on 15/16 January and 23 March 2001 in Berlin. As a result of an unexpected wildcat strike of *Lufthansa* pilots, I was unable to attend the second of these meetings at which many details of the new regime were discussed.

[13] In the German translation of the then existing draft by Ulrich Drobnig and myself, published in (2001) 9 *Zeitschrift für Europäisches Privatrecht* 400 ff.; what eventually became Chapter 14 was, at that stage, Chapter 17.

[14] For historical background, see Helmut Coing, *Europäisches Privatrecht*, vol. I (1985), 183 ff.; David Johnston, *Prescription and Limitation* (1999), 1.13; *HKK*/Hermann (n. 6) §§ 194–225, 'Verjährung', nn. 7 ff.

[15] Karl Spiro, *Die Begrenzung privater Rechte durch Verjährungs-, Verwirkungs- und Fatalfristen*, 2 vols. (1975).   [16] *Supra* pp. 30 ff.

[17] See, for example, Gerhard Dannemann, Fotios Karatzenis and Geoffrey V. Thomas, 'Reform des Verjährungsrechts aus rechtsvergleichender Sicht', (1991) 55 *Rabels Zeitschrift für ausländisches und internationales Privatrecht* 697 ff.; M.W.E. Koopmann, *Bevrijdende verjaring* (1993); Ewoud Hondius (ed.), *Extinctive Prescription: On the Limitation of Actions* (1995); M.M. Loubser, *Extinctive Prescription* (1996); Neil Andrews, 'Reform of Limitation of Actions: The Quest for Sound Legal Policy', (1998) 57 *Cambridge Law Journal* 589 ff.; David Johnston, *Prescription and Limitation* (1999); Antonella Bata, Vincenzo Carbone, Maria Vittoria de Gennaro and Giacomo Travaglino, *La Presczione e la Decandenza* (2001); Anne Danco, *Die Perspektiven der Anspruchsverjährung in Europa: Eine rechtsvergleichende Untersuchung unter besonderer Berücksichtigung der Sachmängelgewährleistungsfristen im Kaufrecht* (2001); Terence Prime and Gary Scanlan, *The Limitation of Actions*, 2nd edn. (2001); for Germany, see nn. 6, 21, 24, 26.

[18] For references, see *Comparative Foundations* (n. 5) 67 ff. In addition, see Martin Käerdi, 'Regulation of Limitation Periods in Estonian Private Law: Historical Overview of Prospects', (2001) 6 *Estonian Civil Code in European Private Law Context, Juridica international (Law Review of the University of Tartu)* 66 ff. (referring specifically to the German reform debate).

has issued a Consultation Paper in 1998.[19] After completion of the consultation process, a revised draft was laid before Parliament and is now waiting for its implementation.[20]

In Germany, the reform process was set in motion by the Peters/Zimmermann draft, submitted in 1981 at the request of the then Minister of Justice.[21] The Reform Commission,[22] which was subsequently established and which eventually tabled a report in 1992,[23] proposed a regime differing in significant respects from the one envisaged by Peters and Zimmermann. Thereafter, the discussion soon appeared to peter out[24] as a result of an increasingly widespread impression that a reform of the German law of obligations was no longer very likely to happen. Thus, it was only the publication of the Discussion Draft[25] in September 2000 that initiated a heated debate.[26] One of the striking features of the Discussion Draft was that the prescription regime proposed in it neither followed the recommendations submitted by Peters/Zimmermann nor

[19] Consultation Paper No. 151 ('Limitation of Actions') (1998).

[20] The Law Commission, Limitation of Actions, Law Com No. 270, 2001.

[21] *Supra* (n. 6). For discussion, see Helmut Heinrichs, 'Reform des Verjährungsrechts', [1982] *Neue Juristische Wochenschrift* 2021 ff.; Wolfgang Grunsky, 'Vorschläge zu einer Reform des Schuldrechts', (1982) 182 *Archiv für die civilistische Praxis* 453 ff.; Karl Spiro, 'Zur Reform der Verjährungsbestimmungen', *Festschrift für Wolfram Müller-Freienfels* (1986), 617 ff.; Helmut Heinrichs, 'Überlegungen zum Verjährungsrecht, seine Mängel, seine Rechtfertigung und seine Reform', in Ernst Klingmüller (ed.), *Karlsruher Forum* (1991), 10 ff.; Dieter Rabe, 'Vorschläge zur Überarbeitung des Schuldrechts: Verjährung', [1992] *Neue Juristische Wochenschrift* 2395 ff. [22] *Supra* p. 32.

[23] Bundesminister der Justiz (ed.), *Abschlußbericht der Kommission zur Überarbeitung des Schuldrechts* (1992).

[24] But see the report by Gert Brüggemeier on the reform of the German law of prescription in 'Verhandlungen des sechzigsten Deutschen Juristentages Münster' 1994, vol. II/2, *Sitzungsberichte* (1994), K 47–K 102; Matthias Unterrieder, *Die regelmässige Verjährung: Die §§ 195–202 BGB und ihre Reform* (1998); Henner Haug, *Die Neuregelung des Verjährungsrechts: eine kritische Untersuchung des Verjährungsrechts im Entwurf der Kommission zur Überarbeitung des Schuldrechts* (1999).

[25] On which, see *supra* p. 33.

[26] See especially Heinz-Peter Mansel, 'Die Reform des Verjährungsrechts', in Wolfgang Ernst and Reinhard Zimmermann (eds.), *Zivilrechtswissenschaft und Schuldrechtsreform* (2001), 333 ff.; Peter Bydlinski, 'Die geplante Modernisierung des Verjährungsrechts', in Reiner Schulze and Hans Schulte-Nölke (eds.), *Die Schuldrechtsreform vor dem Hintergrund des Gemeinschaftsrechts* (2001), 381 ff.; Horst Eidenmüller, 'Zur Effizienz der Verjährungsregeln im geplanten Schuldrechtsmodernisierungsgesetz', [2001] *Juristenzeitung* 283 ff.; Detlef Leenen, 'Die Neuregelung des Verjährungsrechts', [2001] *Juristenzeitung* 552 ff.; Helmut Heinrichs, 'Entwurf eines Schuldrechtsmodernisierungsgesetzes: Neuregelung des Verjährungsrechts', [2001] *Der Betriebs-Berater* 1417 ff.; Reinhard Zimmermann, Detlef Leenen, Heinz-Peter Mansel and Wolfgang Ernst, 'Finis Litium? Zum Verjährungsrecht nach dem Regierungsentwurf eines Schuldrechtsmodernisierungsgesetzes', [2001] *Juristenzeitung* 684 ff.; Andreas Piekenbrock, 'Reform des allgemeinen Verjährungsrechts: Ausweg oder Irrweg?', in *Jahrbuch Junger Zivilrechtswissenschaftler. Das neue Schuldrecht* (2001), 309 ff.; Armin Willingmann, 'Reform des Verjährungsrechts', in Hans-W. Micklitz, Thomas Pfeiffer, Klaus Tonner and Armin Willingmann (eds.), *Schuldrechtsreform und Verbraucherschutz* (2001), 1 ff.; Heinz-Peter Mansel and Christine Budzikiewicz, *Das neue Verjährungsrecht* (2002); Thomas Finkenauer, 'Das neue Verjährungsrecht', in Horst Ehmann and Holger Sutschet (eds.), *Modernisiertes Schuldrecht* (2002), 289 ff.

those of the Reform Commission.[27] A symposium at the University of Regensburg, in the course of which very serious and substantial criticism was levelled against the Draft,[28] led to the appointment of two working groups, one of which was charged, *inter alia*, to look into the law of prescription.[29] It only had a period of about two months for its deliberations. None the less, four new drafts were produced in quick succession, each often radically different from its predecessor.[30] In May 2001 a Government Draft was published.[31] Though it was pushed through Parliament by way of an accelerated procedure, the Draft was again repeatedly changed. The final text of the reform bill was approved by the Federal Parliament in October and entered into force on 1 January 2002.

2. The UNCITRAL Convention, the Principles of European Contract Law and the UNIDROIT Principles

On the international level the United Nations' Commission on International Trade Law (UNCITRAL) drafted, in the early 1970s, a convention for a uniform prescription regime governing international sales; it was adopted in 1974, amended in 1980, and came into effect in 1988.[32] However, this Convention has been conspicuously less successful than the Convention on the International Sale of Goods, since it has been ratified (in its amended form) by only seventeen states, none of them belonging to the European Union.[33] As it was tailored to fit a specific type of claim, the prescription regime laid down in the Convention cannot be taken to constitute a model for a general law of prescription.[34]

The first international draft for a general prescription regime, therefore, is the one adopted by the Lando Commission at its final meeting in February 2001 and published, with commentary and comparative notes, in the course of 2003.[35] In spite of the fact that it appears as part of a set of 'Principles' of

---

[27] *Infra* III, text to n. 58.

[28] Wolfgang Ernst and Reinhard Zimmermann (eds.), *Zivilrechtswissenschaft und Schuldrechtsreform* (2001); see, in particular, the contributions by Heinz-Peter Mansel and Wolfgang Ernst.   [29] For details, see *supra* p. 34.

[30] For the details, see Zimmermann, Leenen, Mansel and Ernst, [2001] *Juristenzeitung* 684 ff.

[31] 'Entwurf eines Gesetzes zur Modernisierung des Schuldrechts', easily accessible in Canaris (n. 9) 429 ff., 569 ff.

[32] The text of the Convention is easily accessible in Oliver Radley-Gardner, Hugh Beale, Reinhard Zimmermann and Reiner Schulze (eds.), *Fundamental Texts on European Private Law* (2003), 269 ff. See also (1979) 10 *UNCITRAL Yearbook* 145 ff.; Karl Spiro, 'Befristung und Verjährung der Ansprüche aus dem Wiener Kaufrechtsübereinkommen', in Hans Hoyer and Willibald Posch (eds.), *Das einheitliche Wiener Kaufrecht* (1992), 195 ff.; K. Boele-Woelki, 'De verjaring van vorderingen uit internationale koopovereenkomsten', [1996] *Europees Privaatrecht* 99 ff.

[33] For details, see n. 1 in Radley-Gardner, Beale, Schulze and Zimmermann (n. 32) 269.

[34] See *Comparative Foundations* (n. 5) 68, 84 ff.; Danco (n. 17) 333.

[35] Lando, Clive, Prüm and Zimmermann (n. 1).

European Contract Law (PECL), we are dealing here with draft legal rules that could, if enacted on a national or European level, be applied by courts of law. Chapter 14 of PECL does not contain general standards that are to be observed because it is just, or fair, to do so; the provisions contained in it set out legal consequences that follow when all of their conditions have been met. Strictly speaking, and considering the distinction between rules and principles in general methodological discourse,[36] the use of the term 'Principles' is a misnomer in the present context. Apart from that, the title 'Principles of European Contract Law' is misleading also in another respect. Most of the topics covered in Part III of the Principles (including prescription) relate not only to contractual obligations but to obligations in general.[37] If the Lando Commission thus decided to extend its (self-imposed) brief, it did so in recognition of the fact that the various branches of the law of obligations are inter-related with each other in so many ways that the isolated consideration of merely one of its components is bound to lead to an imperfect perception; at the same time, it entails the danger of inconsistencies in result and evaluation. Nowhere is this more obvious than in the law of prescription.[38] It has to be remembered, in this context, that the title of the German Modernization of the Law of Obligations Act is equally misleading,[39] for prescription in German law is not only confined to claims within the law of obligations but to all types of claims, whether they are based on an obligation or not.[40] This is why the matter is dealt with in the General Part of the BGB (§§ 194 ff. BGB).

In the course of 2004 UNIDROIT published an amended version of its Principles of International Commercial Contracts (PICC)[41] containing, *inter alia*, a new chapter on the law of prescription (or, as the draftsmen of the UNIDROIT Principles decided to say: limitation periods).[42] In many respects,

---

[36] Ronald Dworkin, *Taking Rights Seriously* (1977), 22 ff.

[37] Lando, Clive, Prüm and Zimmermann (n. 1) xvi.   [38] *Comparative Foundations* (n. 5) 81 ff.

[39] *Supra* p. 2.

[40] This is contrary to the position in many other countries and also contrary to the approach adopted by the Principles; see *Comparative Foundations* (n. 5) 85 ff. (n. 97); Danco (n. 17) 89 ff.; Lando, Clive, Prüm and Zimmermann (n. 1) 158 ff.

[41] UNIDROIT (ed.), *Principles of International Commercial Contracts* (2004) (replacing UNIDROIT (ed.), *Principles of International Commercial Contracts*, 1994). For comment, see Michael Joachim Bonell, 'UNIDROIT Principles 2004—The New Edition of the Principles of International Commercial Contracts adopted by the International Institute for the Unification of Private Law', (2004) 9 *Uniform Law Review* 6 ff.; Eckart Brödermann, 'Die erweiterten UNIDROIT Principles 2004: Ein willkommenes "Werkzeug" für die Vertragsgestaltung und für Schiedsverfahren', (2004) 50 *Recht der Internationalen Wirtschaft* 721 ff.

[42] The term 'prescription' appears to have an odd ring for a common lawyer: see Andrew McGee, 'England', in Ewoud H. Hondius (ed.), *Extinctive Prescription: On the Limitation of Actions* (1995), 135. He rather refers to 'limitation of actions', thus also making it clear that the English institution is procedural in nature. In order to disassociate from these procedural connotations itself the UNCITRAL Prescription Convention merely referred to 'limitation periods'. The draftsmen of the Principles of

the UNIDROIT Principles are remarkably similar to the Principles of European Contract Law.[43] This is true both generally and specifically of the law of prescription. Most importantly, Chapters 14 of PECL and 10 of PICC implement the same policy considerations in very similar ways.[44] Both Chapters are based on the same conceptual framework, and both contain legal rules rather than 'principles'. Contrary to Article 14:101 PECL, however, Article 10.1 ff. PICC appear to be restricted to the law of contract in their scope of application.[45] Also, it should be noted that under the Principles of European Contract Law (as under German law, both old and new: § 194 I BGB) 'claims' (*Ansprüche*) are subject to prescription,[46] while Article 10.1 PICC, more broadly, refers to 'rights' governed by these Principles.[47]

3. A common framework

If we look at the development of the law of prescription, at new enactments and proposed drafts over the past hundred years, we find a number of characteristic trends. (i) There is a clear tendency towards uniform periods of prescription.[48] (ii) Such uniform period must neither be particularly short (six months), nor excessively long (thirty years); it has to be fixed somewhere between two and five years. A period of three years appears to be regarded as reasonable internationally.[49] (iii) The running of this relatively short general period of prescription should not be tied to an objective criterion, such as due date, accrual of the claim, delivery, acceptance, completion (of a building), etc.; it should rather depend on whether the creditor knew (or ought reasonably to

International Commercial Contracts decided to follow suit (even if the chapter heading is now imprecise in that the chapter does not only determine periods of prescription, or limitation, but also lays down rules concerning renewal, suspension, agreements concerning prescription, etc.). Since, however, both PICC and PECL regard prescription, or limitation, as a matter of substantive law, the difference in terminology does not have any practical implications.

[43] For details, see Reinhard Zimmermann, 'Die UNIDROIT-Grundregeln der internationalen Handelsverträge 2004 in vergleichender Perspektive', (2005) 13 *Zeitschrift für Europäisches Privatrecht* 268 ff.

[44] For an analysis, see Michael Joachim Bonell, 'Limitation Periods', in Arthur Hartkamp and Martijn Hesselink *et al.* (eds.), *Towards a European Civil Code*, 3rd edn. (2004), 517 ff.; Reinhard Zimmermann, (2005) 13 *Zeitschrift für Europäisches Privatrecht* 273 ff.

[45] This appears from Art. 10.1 ('The exercise of rights governed by these Principles . . .').

[46] A claim is defined in Art. 14:101 as 'a right to performance of an obligation'.

[47] This is to indicate that 'not only the right to require performance or the right to another remedy for non-performance can be barred, but also the exercise of rights which directly affect a contract, such as the right of termination or a right to price reduction . . .': UNIDROIT (n. 41) 312. For comparative comment, see Zimmermann, (2005) 13 *Zeitschrift für Europäisches Privatrecht* 276.

[48] For details, see *Comparative Foundations* (n. 5) 89 ff.

[49] For details, see *Comparative Foundations* (n. 5) 86 ff. The more recent history of the law of prescription is, essentially, the history of a shortening of the periods of prescription. On the phenomenon of an 'acceleration' of time see, in this context, *HKK*/Hermann (n. 6) §§ 194–225, 'Verjährung', n. 41.

have known) of the identity of his debtor and of the facts giving rise to his claim.[50] (iv) Prescription must not be deferred indefinitely; at some stage, the parties have to be able to treat an incident as indubitably closed. This is why a relative period (the running of which depends on the discoverability criterion) has to be supplemented by a maximum period ('long stop'), tied to an objective criterion, at the expiry of which a claim must be barred regardless of the creditor's knowledge. For this long stop a period of between ten and thirty years may be chosen; increasingly, however, choice of the upper end of this range is regarded as reasonable only for personal injury claims.[51] (v) It is internationally widely recognized that prescription should only have a 'weak' effect: once the period of prescription has run out, the creditor's right is not extinguished, but the debtor is merely granted a right to refuse performance. Prescription, in other words, constitutes a defence which the debtor may or may not choose to raise.[52]

III. Subjective or Objective System

The Principles of European Contract Law, the new German law of prescription, and the reform bill drafted by the English Law Commission all reflect these tendencies.[53] They constitute variations of a fundamentally uniform model (which, from a German perspective, can be regarded as a generalization of the prescription regime laid down, under the old law, for delictual claims).[54] The establishment of this model, both on a national and international level, is to be welcomed. At the same time, it has to be kept in mind that a perfect prescription regime does not exist. A delicate balancing of interests is required[55] which may induce a legal system to opt either for uniformity based on the criterion of discoverability (relative, or subjective, system of prescription), or

---

[50] For details, see *Comparative Foundations* (n. 5) 92 ff.

[51] For details, see *Comparative Foundations* (n. 5) 99 ff.

[52] For details, see *Comparative Foundations* (n. 5) 72 ff.; for historical background, see *HKK*/Hermann (n. 6) §§ 194–225, 'Verjährung', nn. 21 ff.

[53] The same is true of the rules on limitation in the revised UNIDROIT Principles of International Commercial Contracts; see Arts. 10.1 ff. For Swiss law, see the proposal by Peter Loser-Krogh, 'Kritische Überlegungen zur Reform des privaten Haftpflichtrechts—Haftung aus Treu und Glauben, Verursachung und Verjährung', (2003) 137 *Referate und Mitteilungen des Schweizerischen Juristenvereins* 197 ff.

[54] § 852 BGB (old version). The new, uniform model was first proposed by Peters and Zimmermann (n. 6) 315 ff.

[55] See Hartmut Oetker, *Die Verjährung* (1994), 33 ff.; Danco (n. 17) 71 ff.; Piekenbrock (n. 26) 314 ff.; Willingmann (n. 26) 16 ff.; *Comparative Foundations* (n. 5) 76 ff. For the interests to be served by a prescription regime cf. also Mansel (n. 26) 342 ff.; Mansel and Budzikiewicz (n. 26) 30 ff.; *HKK*/Hermann (n. 6) §§ 194–225, 'Verjährung', nn. 12 ff.; Helmut Grothe, in *Münchener Kommentar zum Bürgerlichen Gesetzbuch*, vol. 1a, 4th edn. (2003), Vorbem. § 194, nn. 6 ff.

for objectively determinable but necessarily differentiated periods (absolute, or objective, system of prescription). The key for organizing the law of prescription, in other words, lies in the criterion determining commencement of the running of the period of prescription. Both models have their specific advantages and drawbacks. The objective system permits the choice of the most suitable period for each type of claim. However, such a differentiated system almost inevitably leads to problems of delimitation and to doctrinal fault lines, to conceptual distortions and an unnecessary increase in litigation. The explosive potential inherent in a differentiated prescription regime is clearly apparent in the history of the old German law of prescription.[56] Proponents of the subjective system accept, from the outset, a certain degree of uncertainty, for a period tied to an objective date can be more easily calculated than a period based on the discoverability criterion.[57] On the other hand, however, a uniform prescription period can only be established in terms of a subjective system.

With the Peters/Zimmermann proposals and those of the Commission charged with the reform of the law of obligations, the Federal Ministry of Justice had at its disposal two model regulations, one of them following the subjective, the other the objective system. The authors of the Discussion Draft took the most unfortunate decision imaginable, under the circumstances, in that they did not follow either of the two models but attempted to combine elements of both of them.[58] They decided, contrary to the Commission's Draft,[59] to re-introduce a (short) general period of prescription, the commencement of which did not depend on knowledge or discoverability. This kind of regime, however, is unacceptable as an act effectively amounting, in many cases, to an expropriation[60] and might even have been in conflict with the requirements of constitutional law.[61] In the course of the deliberations of the working group established subsequent to the Regensburg symposium, a fundamental change of regime was therefore agreed upon: the general period of prescription is now

[56] For all details, see Peters and Zimmermann (n. 6) 196 ff. The arguments in favour of uniformity are summarized in *Comparative Foundations* (n. 5) 79 ff.

[57] This is highlighted by Heinrichs, *Karlsruher Forum* (n. 21) 8 ff.; Heinrich Honsell, 'Einige Bemerkungen zum Diskussionsentwurf eines Schuldrechtsmodernisierungsgesetzes', [2001] *Juristenzeitung* 20; Wolfgang Zöllner, 'Das neue Verjährungsrecht im deutschen BGB—Kritik eines verfehlten Regelungssystems', in *Besonderes Vertragsrecht—Aktuelle Probleme: Festschrift für Heinrich Honsell* (2002), 163 ff. The reasons why the Commission charged with the reform of the law of obligations preferred the objective system are set out in *Abschlußbericht* (n. 23) 54 ff.; cf. also Unterrieder (n. 24) 271 ff.; Haug (n. 24) 44, 88 ff., 150 ff. For a principled and policy-based argument in favour of a differentiated system (though quite a different one from that proposed by the German Commission), see Andrews, (1998) 57 *Cambridge Law Journal* 589 ff.

[58] §§ 194 ff. BGB (Discussion Draft).   [59] §§ 194 ff. BGB in *Abschlußbericht* (n. 23) 283 ff.

[60] See also Wolfgang Ernst, 'Zum Fortgang der Schuldrechtsmodernisierung', in Ernst and Zimmermann (n. 28) 581.

[61] Thus, for instance, in Belgium there has been doubt about the constitutionality of short prescription periods, which start to run before the damage manifests itself; see *Comparative Foundations* (n. 5) 79, n. 78 (with references); Lando, Clive, Prüm and Zimmermann (n. 1) 179.

based on the subjective system.[62] None the less, the new German law of prescription is marked by a distinctive, and unhappy, air of compromise.[63] The working group had to operate under an extreme pressure of time and, as a result, was unable carefully to discuss and consider many matters of detail. Time and again, new proposals were put forward and adopted, without any thorough consideration of the impact that these changes would have on the system of prescription in its entirety, or of the practicalities of their implementation.[64] This is alarming, particularly, if the most important drawback of the subjective system, mentioned above,[65] is kept in mind. It is acceptable only in view of the advantages gained by uniformity. If, however, the subjective system is not implemented as consistently as possible, the danger exists that the resulting regime will combine the disadvantages, rather than the advantages, of both systems. This, I fear, will become apparent once the new rules start to be applied in practice.[66]

IV. The Thirty-year Prescription Period

If we compare individual aspects of the new German law of prescription with Chapter 14 of the Principles of European Contract Law, it has to be noted, in

---

[62] §§ 195, 199 I and II BGB.

[63] See Zimmermann, Leenen, Mansel and Ernst, [2001] *Juristenzeitung* 698 ff.; cf. also Piekenbrock (n. 26) 333; Heinz-Peter Mansel and Michael Stürner, in Barbara Dauner-Lieb, Thomas Heidel and Gerhard Ring (eds.), *Anwaltkommentar BGB*, vol. I (2005), Vorbem. § 194–218, n. 4.

[64] One commentator thus expressed the view that, with its monthly change of paradigm, the law of prescription was swinging 'like reed in the wind': Herbert Roth, 'Die Reform des Werkvertragsrechts', [2001] *Juristenzeitung* 544; *HKK*/Hermann (n. 6) §§ 194–225, n. 3 refers to a 'hastily staged competition of drafts'.   [65] *Supra* text to n. 57.

[66] Litigation concerning the new law has not yet reached the level of the Federal Supreme Courts. German commentators, however, have started to interpret and elucidate the new provisions; see, as far as the general provisions (§§ 194 ff. BGB) are concerned, the work by Mansel and Budzikiewicz (n. 26); Werner Niedenführ, in *Soergel, BGB, Allgemeiner Teil 3* (2002); *Münchener Kommentar zum Bürgerlichen Gesetzbuch*/Grothe (n. 55); Wolfgang Henrich and Gerald Spindler, in Heinz Georg Bamberger and Herbert Roth (eds.), *Kommentar zum Bürgerlichen Gesetzbuch* (2003); Helmut Heinrichs, in *Palandt, Bürgerliches Gesetzbuch*, 64th edn. (2005); Frank Peters, in *J. von Staudingers Kommentar zum Bürgerlichen Gesetzbuch*, revised edition (2004); Othmar Jauernig, in Othmar Jauernig (ed.), *Bürgerliches Gesetzbuch*, 11th edn. (2004); Heinz-Peter Mansel, Michael Stürner and Christine Budzikiewicz, in Barbara Dauner-Lieb, Thomas Heidel and Gerhard Ring (eds.), *Anwaltkommentar BGB*, vol. I (2005). This literature is largely exegetical in character and accepts, rather than critically evaluates, the new rules. That is, of course, entirely justified. Occasionally, however, it is suggested that much of what has been written, in a critical spirit, before the reform, is now no longer of any value and can be disregarded: Helmut Heinrichs, in *Palandt, Bürgerliches Gesetzbuch*, 61st edn. (2002), Einl. v. § 241, n. 32 ('. . . will become wastepaper on 1 January 2002'). This curiously ahistorical attitude, which seems to assume that a new code provides an autonomous interpretational space, cut off from the debates leading up to its enactment, is coupled with a skewed account of these debates (*Palandt*/Heinrichs (as above) Einl. v. § 241, n. 32). It is noticeable, at any rate, that the critical debate concerning the new prescription regime (see *supra* II., n. 26) has largely died down. For a spirited attack of the new core regime see, however, Zöllner (n. 57) 153 ff.

the first place, that the scope of application of §§ 194 ff. BGB extends much beyond the law of obligations.[67] This is problematic even with regard to a claim as centrally important within the system of German private law as the *rei vindicatio* which is subjected by § 197 I no. 1 to a thirty-year period of prescription. The *rei vindicatio* is a claim designed to give full effect to the absolute right of ownership. It should not, therefore, be affected by prescription but should rather perish with the absolute right itself.[68] Otherwise we would be faced with the legal construct of *dominium sine re* and its undesirable consequences: there would be a person who is owner of an object but is unable to assert his right against whoever happens to be in possession of the object. Whether, and under which circumstances, the interests of someone who has been in possession of an object for a long time may prevail over those of the owner—whether, and under which circumstances, in other words, the public interest requires acknowledgment of the *status quo*: this is a question requiring a uniform answer. The Code provides that answer, in an entirely satisfactory manner, by means of its provisions on acquisitive prescription (§§ 935 II, 937 ff. BGB). The additional threat of prescription to the owner's claim to recover his object from the possessor primarily protects persons who do not deserve to be protected.[69] It is interesting to note, in this context, that in a case concerning the restitution of a painting that had got lost in the turmoil of the Second World War the Federal Republic of Germany took the view that prescription was in conflict with the (English) *ordre public*.[70]

§ 197 I BGB (new version) not only contains a special thirty-year prescription period for claims for the recovery of an object based on ownership or other rights *in rem* (no. 1), but also for 'claims under family law or the law of succession' (no. 2) and for claims conclusively established by legal proceedings (no. 3). With regard to no. 2, the authors of the new rules did not ask themselves which claims will still be covered by this provision[71] in view of the special prescription rules contained in books 4 (family law) and 5 (succession) of the BGB.[72] They did not take up proposals to tidy up these special rules and to achieve uniformity, as far as possible, also in these areas of

---

[67] *Supra* text following n. 38.   [68] Peters and Zimmermann (n. 6) 186, 287.

[69] See Kurt Siehr, 'Verjährung der Vindikationsklage?', [2001] *Zeitschrift für Rechtspolitik* 346 ff.; Christian Armbrüster, 'Privatrechtliche Ansprüche und Rückführung von Kulturgütern ins Ausland', [2001] *Neue Juristische Wochenschrift* 3586 ff.

[70] See Mansel (n. 26) 368 ff.; Kurt Siehr, 'Verjährt ein Anspruch auf Herausgabe des Eigentums? Deutsches Verjährungsrecht vor englischem Gericht' in Michael H. Carl, Herbert Güttler and Kurt Siehr (eds.), *Kunstdiebstahl vor Gericht: City of Gotha v Sotheby's* (2001), 78 ff.

[71] For all details concerning 'claims under the law of succession' (*erbrechtliche Ansprüche*) see now Martin Löhnig, 'Die Verjährung der im fünften Buch des BGB geregelten Ansprüche', [2004] *Zeitschrift für Erbrecht und Vermögensnachfolge* 267 ff.

[72] See, for example, §§ 1302, 1378 IV, 1390 III 1, 2287 II, 2232 BGB.

the law.[73] Nor did they appreciate that a thirty-year period is almost certainly much too long for a number of the claims that *are* to be covered by no. 2; the right to claim a legacy provides an example.[74] As far as no. 3 is concerned, a thirty-year period no longer appears to be internationally acceptable. Article 14:202 PECL lays down a period of ten years. This is in line with a number of the existing national legal systems. Considering that the English Limitation Act 1980 provides for a period of six years,[75] and that the Law Commission even proposes to apply the regular period of three years to these claims (counting from discoverability)[76] ten years appear to be a reasonable compromise solution.[77]

V. Liability for Non-conformity

1. The law of sale

Special prescription rules of very considerable practical significance are contained in §§ 438, 634 a BGB (new version). They relate to claims arising from liability for non-conformity under contracts of sale[78] or contracts for work. Concerning contracts of sale, the regular period of three years has been reduced to two years.[79] More importantly, however, this two-year period has been tied to an objective date: it begins to run with the delivery of the object sold. The establishment of a special prescription regime in the case of liability for non-conformity can only be justified as a device that may be necessary to limit the seller's risk.[80] In Germany, this applies particularly to the remedies of supplementary performance, termination, and price reduction since they do not depend on the seller's fault. A special regime is inappropriate, however, with regard to the claim for damages. Here, according to German law, it is the fault requirement that provides an equitable distribution of the risk that the

---

[73] Peters/Zimmermann (n. 6) 330 ff. (with reference to the legal position in 1980).

[74] See Zimmermann, Leenen, Mansel and Ernst, [2001] *Juristenzeitung* 694; Piekenbrock (n. 26) 327 ff.

[75] English Limitation Act 1980, s. 24.

[76] Law Com No. 270 (n. 20) 155. Eighty per cent of all institutions and persons consulted were in agreement with this proposal.

[77] For a comparative overview, see *Comparative Foundations* (n. 5) 112 ff.; Lando, Clive, Prüm and Zimmermann (n. 1) 167.   [78] On which see *supra* Chapter 3.

[79] For criticism (from the consumer protection perspective) see Willingmann (n. 26) 19 ff.; 43 (according to whom the change has been brought about by 'massive interventions on the part of the business sector').

[80] Cf., in particular, Detlef Leenen, '§ 477 BGB: Verjährung oder Risikoverteilung?', 1997; *idem*, [2001] *Juristenzeitung* 553 ff. with further references. For a comprehensive comparative discussion, see Danco (n. 17) in the third part of her work (202 ff.); cf. also Andreas Schwartze, *Europäische Sachmängelgewährleistung beim Warenkauf* (2000), 492 ff.

object sold may turn out to be defective. An additional device in the form of a short prescription period is not only unnecessary, but would even counteract the reasonable risk allocation.[81] Also, it is impossible to see why a seller who injures the purchaser's body, health or property, should be better off merely because his fault relates to the delivery of a defective object which subsequently explodes. If the seller could be expected to know about the defect, and to protect the purchaser from the damage arising from that defect, he does not deserve to be in a more favourable position than the one in which he would have been, had he negligently injured his contractual partner in another manner.[82] Anything else would indeed be 'downright absurd'.[83]

None the less, this is the solution adopted by the draftsmen of the new law, and the only possibility to limit its practical impact consists in excluding consequential loss from the prescription regime of § 438 BGB (new version). This has, indeed, been proposed.[84] As a result, however, the intricate distinction between damage pertaining to the object itself and consequential loss, which has caused such intractable problems under the old law,[85] would, in some form or another, be perpetuated under the new.[86] But even apart from that, there are other difficult problems of delimitation that will continue to exist as a result of the decision to subject damages claims based on latent defects to a special regime:[87] whether or not the defect relates to a 'functionally separable' part of the object of sale only, or to the object as a whole (in the former case a delictual claim, governed by the regular prescription period, would be available if the object is subsequently destroyed as a result of the defect);[88] whether or not the

---

[81] See also, from the point of view of economic analysis, Eidenmüller, [2001] *Juristenzeitung* 285.

[82] See Leenen, [2001] *Juristenzeitung* 552 ff.; Zimmermann, Leenen, Mansel and Ernst, [2001] *Juristenzeitung* 690; Ernst (n. 60) 584 ff.

[83] Claus-Wilhelm Canaris, 'Das allgemeine Leistungsstörungsrecht im Schuldrechtsmodernisierungsgesetz', [2001] *Zeitschrift für Rechtspolitik* 336.

[84] Canaris, [2001] *Zeitschrift für Rechtspolitik* 335 ff.; cf. also Gerhard Wagner, 'Mangel- und Mangelfolgeschäden im neuen Schuldrecht?', [2002] *Juristenzeitung* 479 ff.; Helmut Rüßmann, 'Mangelschäden und Mangelfolgeschäden nach der Schuldrechtsmodernisierung', in *Recht und Risiko: Festschrift für Helmut Kollhosser* (2004), 571 ff. *Contra*: Heinz-Peter Mansel, 'Die Neuregelung des Verjährungsrechts', [2002] *Neue Juristische Wochenschrift* 95; Florian Faust, in Georg Bamberger and Herbert Roth (eds.), *Kommentar zum Bürgerlichen Gesetzbuch*, vol. I (2003), § 438, n. 9.

[85] See the casuistry reported and discussed by Ulrich Huber, in *Soergel, Bürgerliches Gesetzbuch*, vol. III, 12th edn. (1991), Anh. § 463, nn. 21 ff.; Peters and Zimmermann (n. 6) 202 ff.; for an overview in English, see Zimmermann (n. 6) 168 ff.   [86] Cf. also *supra* pp. 58 f.

[87] Cf. also, for example, Finkenauer (n. 26) 308 ff. As in many other cases, no motivation is given for this decision (apart from a remark that it would 'not make sense' to subject the various claims based on liability for non-conformity to different prescription regimes: 'Begründung der Bundesregierung zum Entwurf eines Gesetzes zur Modernisierung des Schuldrechts', in Canaris (n. 9) 841). But see Heinrichs, [2001] *Betriebsberater* 1423; *idem*, [2001] *Juristenzeitung* 561; for a critical discussion of Heinrich's views see Zimmermann, Leenen, Mansel and Ernst, [2001] *Juristenzeitung* 690.

[88] BGHZ 67, 359 ff.; Johannes Hager, in *J. von Staudingers Kommentar zum Bürgerlichen Gesetzbuch*, 13th edn. (1999), § 823, nn. B 105 ff.; Dieter Medicus, *Bürgerliches Recht*, 20th edn.

purchaser's breach of duty relates to a defect;[89] and whether or not a claim can be based on *culpa in contrahendo* in cases where the seller, in the course of the negotiations preceding the contract, has infringed a duty of disclosure, or has negligently made an untrue statement, concerning the object sold.[90] Since the prescription periods under the new law no longer diverge as extravagantly as under the old (where the choice often was between a period of six months or thirty years), the significance of these problems has been reduced, but they have not disappeared.

A glance across the border into a closely associated legal system would, incidentally, have been of benefit to German law. Like all the other Member States of the EU, Austria had to implement the Consumer Sales Directive by 1 January 2002.[91] Here we find the new § 933 ABGB establishing a special prescription regime, based on the objective system, which only refers to the claims mentioned in § 932 ABGB, i.e. repair, delivery of another object, reduction of the purchase price, and termination of the contract. The damages claim according to § 933 a ABGB, on the other hand, is governed by the general prescription period of § 1489 ABGB (three years, running from the moment of knowledge of tortfeasor and damage).[92]

(2004), n. 650 b; for a comprehensive discussion, see Beate Gsell, *Substanzverletzung und Herstellung* (2003); and see *supra* p. 94. For the new law, see Faust (n. 84) § 437, nn. 188 ff.; Wolfgang Ernst, *Münchener Kommentar zum Bürgerlichen Gesetzbuch*, vol. 2 a, 4th edn. (2003), § 280, n. 78. The problem would be obviated if the proposal by Heinz-Peter Mansel, in *Anwaltkommentar Schuldrecht* (2002), § 195, nn. 50 ff. were to be adopted. He suggested applying the prescription rule of § 438 BGB also to delictual claims as far as they coincide with damages claims under § 437 no. 3 BGB. This would, however, run counter to the principle of *Anspruchskonkurrenz* (on which see *supra* p. 93).

   89   Thus, the case of BGHZ 107, 249 ff. will remain problematical; see Medicus (n. 88) nn. 329 ff.; Zimmermann, Leenen, Mansel and Ernst, [2001] *Juristenzeitung* 692.

   90   BGHZ 60, 319 ff.; see Leenen, [2001] *Juristenzeitung* 555 ff.; Zimmermann, Leenen, Mansel and Ernst, [2001] *Juristenzeitung* 691 ff.; Volker Emmerich, 'Das Verhältnis der Gewährleistungsregeln bei Kauf und Miete zur c.i.c.', in *Besonderes Vertragsrecht—Aktuelle Probleme: Festschrift für Heinrich Honsell* (2002) 209 ff.

   91   For an overview, see Brigitta Jud, 'Umsetzung der Verbrauchsgüterkauf-Richtlinie in Österreich', in Ernst and Zimmermann (n. 28) 743 ff.; Rudolf Welser and Brigitta Jud, *Die neue Gewährleistung, Kurzkommentar* (2001); Michael Gruber, 'Die Umsetzung der Verbrauchgüterkauf-Richtlinie in Österreich', in Martin Schermaier (ed.), *Verbraucherkauf in Europa* (2003), 153 ff.; Heinz-Peter Mansel, 'Kaufrechtsreform in Europa und die Dogmatik des deutschen Leistungsstörungsrechts', (2004) 204 *Archiv für die civilistische Praxis* 396 ff.

   92   According to § 933 a II ABGB the reversal of the onus of proof laid down in § 1298 ABGB is limited to ten years. The Principles of European Contract Law do not contain special rules with regard to claims arising from liability for non-conformity and, therefore, also do not provide for special rules of prescription for such claims. An aggrieved party's general right to terminate the contract in case of non-performance is to be exercised by notice to the other party (Art. 9:303 (1) PECL). Notice has to be given 'within a reasonable time after [the party] has or ought to have become aware of the non-performance'. Art. 9:401 PECL constitutes a generalized right to price reduction. This is not subject to prescription. If the purchaser has received a defective object, he can exercise his right to price reduction when the seller demands payment for that object. This claim for payment is subject to the normal

2. Contracts for work

The prescription of claims based on latent defects under a contract for work used to raise particularly difficult problems under the old law.[93] The uncertainty as to whether, in a particular situation, the special six-month period of § 638 BGB (old version) or the general period of thirty years (§ 195 BGB (old version)) was to be applied could hardly have been greater. The new rule of § 634 a BGB was preceded by protracted and difficult discussions. In the course of the parliamentary proceedings the Government Draft was criticized in no less than five individual points in this respect; subsequently, the rule was entirely restructured by the Federal Ministry of Justice. Still, however, the criticism levelled against § 634 a Government Draft remains valid.[94] Very pointedly, it can be said that a prescription regime tailored for, and specifically applicable to, liability for non-conformity in contracts for work has ceased to exist. For § 634 a BGB (new version) draws a distinction between 'work, the result of which consists in the production, servicing, or alteration of a thing, or in the provision of planning or supervisory services therefore' and other results produced under a contract for work. In the first case, a prescription period of two years applies, as in the law of sale, beginning with the act of acceptance of the work (the period is five years, however, also from the moment when the work is accepted, 'in the case of a building and work the result of which consists in the provision of planning or supervisory services therefor').[95] In the second case, the contractor is completely deprived of the advantages arising from a

rules of prescription. If the purchaser has already paid the purchase price and subsequently claims back the amount by which he would have been able to reduce the price (Art. 9:401 (2) PECL), we are dealing with a claim based on unjustified enrichment, which is also subject to the normal rules of prescription.

[93] Cf. Peters and Zimmermann (n. 6) 206 ff.; Hartwig Sprau, in *Palandt, Bürgerliches Gesetzbuch*, 60th edn. (2001), Vorbem. v. § 633, nn. 22 ff.; Frank Peters, in *J. von Staudingers Kommentar zum Bürgerlichen Gesetzbuch*, revised edition (2000), § 635, nn. 46 ff.; for an overview in English, see Zimmermann (n. 6) 164 ff. A 'contract for work' (defined in § 631 II BGB as a contract the object of which is 'the production or alteration of a thing, or some other result to be brought about by labour or the performance of a service') is the modern equivalent of what used to be called *locatio conductio operis* under the *ius commune*.

[94] What follows is an adapted version of Zimmermann, Leenen, Mansel and Ernst, [2001] *Juristenzeitung* 690 ff.

[95] § 634 a I and II BGB. As a result of the distinction drawn in these two sub-paragraphs of § 634 a, the courts will remain confronted with the problems of delimitation surrounding the interpretation of the phrase 'bei *Bauwerken*' (in the case of a building) in § 638 BGB (old version). See Peters and Zimmermann (n. 26) 197 ff.; *Staudinger*/Peters (n. 93) § 638, nn. 36 ff.; Zimmermann (n. 6) 168. These problems are not resolved, but merely shifted, by the last-minute addition of the words 'and work the result of which consists in the provision of planning or supervisory services therefor'.

specific prescription regime for liability for non-conformity, for according to
§ 634 a I no. 3 BGB the general period of prescription applies, with the
important consequence that its commencement is determined according to the
subjective system. As a result, a contractor of the second category receives
the same treatment, from the point of view of the law of prescription, as a
contractor of the first category who fraudulently conceals a defect (§ 634 a
III BGB (new version)).

The approach adopted in the new § 634 a BGB treats too leniently a
contractor who has promised the production, servicing, or alteration of a
thing, or who has to provide the planning or supervisory services therefor, in
that the special prescription rules, governed by the objective system, also apply
to the claim for damages.[96] On the other hand, however, the new approach
deals with all other contractors too favourably by denying them the advantages
associated with the objective system even for those remedies (like supplementary performance, termination, and reduction of the price) that do not depend
on fault. The distinction drawn in § 634 a BGB essentially constitutes a
compromise between those members of the working group who wanted to
eliminate problems of delimitation by treating contracts of sale and contracts
for work alike, and others (particularly the representatives of the Federal
Supreme Court) who were more worried about the difficulties of drawing a line
between contracts for work and contracts of services.[97] Of course, it can be
awkward to have to draw a line between contracts of sale and contracts for
work, and between contracts for work and contracts for services, merely in
order to determine whether a claim has prescribed or not.[98] But the (internal)
dividing line between two different types of contracts for work, that has now
been introduced, can be at least as awkward. Also, it is to be expected that the
rule concerning fraud (§ 634 a III BGB) will be converted into a safety valve for
the pressure built up as a result of the short prescription period for damages
claims under § 634 a I no. 1.[99]

---

[96] Including all claims for so-called *Mangelfolgeschäden* (consequential loss). No reasons are stated
as to why it should have been necessary, or advisable, to change the legal position recognized, in this
respect, by the courts under the old law; they had correctly, it is submitted, allocated this risk to the
contractor; see Ernst (n. 60) 583 ff.; Leenen, [2001] *Juristenzeitung* 556; Zimmermann, Leenen,
Mansel and Ernst, [2001] *Juristenzeitung* 690.

[97] To contracts for services (§§ 611 ff. BGB) the normal prescription regime applies: there is no
specific liability regime for non-conformity. On the problems of delimitation between contracts for
work and contracts for services see, e.g., Hartwig Sprau, in *Palandt, Bürgerliches Gesetzbuch*, 64th edn.
(2005), nn. 8, 18 ff. and, in the context of the old German law, Peters and Zimmermann (n. 6) 200 ff.

[98] See *Comparative Foundations* (n. 5) 80 ff.

[99] See Ernst (n. 60) 584; Leenen, [2001] *Juristenzeitung* 556; Zimmermann, Leenen, Mansel and
Ernst, [2001] *Juristenzeitung* 692.

VI. Commencement of Prescription

1. Implementing the subjective system

The rules concerning the commencement of prescription were also substantially revised even after the publication of the Government Draft. These changes were not of merely an editorial nature. One key decision, however, has remained unaffected: the subjective system has been confined to the general period of prescription,[100] while with regard to all claims not subject to that general period the objective system has been chosen.[101] Effectively, this means that the general moment of commencement of prescription is the one when the claim comes into being (§ 200 BGB), but that this general rule does not apply to the general period of prescription. In spite of this curiously contorted regulation, the new provision concerning the commencement of the regular period of prescription is structured more clearly than its labyrinthine predecessor contained in the Government Draft.[102] On the substantive level, however, a number of objections raised against the Government Draft remain valid. This applies, in particular, to the systematic position of the discoverability criterion. According to § 199 I no. 2 BGB it determines the commencement of prescription[103] whereas, according to Article 14:301 PECL it constitutes a ground for suspending the running of the period of prescription. The solution adopted in the Principles is superior for a number of reasons.

(i) If a creditor brings an action against his debtor, he has to establish the requirements on which his claim is based. That his claim has not prescribed is not one of those requirements. Prescription is a defence. If it is invoked by the debtor, it is he who has to establish the requirements of that defence. The central requirement, of course, is that the period of prescription applicable to his claim has elapsed. That depends on the date of commencement. If that were the date of discoverability, the debtor would, in many cases, face an unreasonably difficult task. For whether the damage to his creditor's house, the injury to his body, the consequences flowing from defective delivery, etc., were reasonably discoverable, or whether the creditor perhaps even had positive knowledge, are matters within the creditor's sphere and largely removed from the debtor's range of perception.[104] Also, by and large, and considering the full range of possible claims, the creditor

---

[100] § 199 I BGB.   [101] § 200 BGB.
[102] See Zimmermann, Leenen, Mansel and Ernst, [2001] *Juristenzeitung* 688.
[103] Cf. also Art. 10.2 PICC.
[104] Peters and Zimmermann (n. 6) 248, 306; *Anwaltkommtar*/Mansel/Stürner (n. 63) § 199, nn. 6, 9, 103. Cf. also Loubser (n. 17) 112; Law Commission Consultation Paper (n. 19) 398 ('The date of discoverability is concerned with the knowledge of the plaintiff rather than the defendant ... In

will normally know about his claim at the time the latter falls due; at least, he can reasonably be expected to know about it. That, exceptionally, he did not do so, is a matter to be raised, and established to the satisfaction of the court, by the creditor. This comes out more clearly if discoverability is not made a requirement for the commencement of prescription but if the fact that the creditor could reasonably be aware of his claim provides a ground for extending the period of prescription: that prescription is suspended, or otherwise extended, must, according to general principle, normally be proved by the creditor.

(ii) This way of proceeding also considerably simplifies the structure of the prescription regime. Contrary to the BGB, the Principles do not have to operate with a second, separate period of prescription running from a date different to that of the 'normal' period. The three-year period is quite simply the only general period of prescription with due date as the general moment of commencement;[105] in addition, it is merely laid down that prescription is not to be extended to more than ten years, or in the case of claims for personal injuries, for more than thirty years.[106]

(iii) This entails an important difference as to the character of the maximum period. Under the BGB, the ten- and thirty-year periods are normal prescription periods which are subject to the general rules concerning suspension and postponement of expiry.[107] As a result, they do not really constitute 'maximum' periods: prescription can take much longer.[108] Article 14:307 PECL, on the other hand, applies to all grounds of suspension or postponement of expiry, and it also covers situations where two or more of them apply to the same claim. The only exception to this rule is suspension in case of judicial proceedings.[109] The approach adopted by PECL promotes the idea that, at some stage, an incident has to be treated as closed: *interest rei publicae ut sit finis litium*.[110] Inevitably, it will cause hardship in a number of cases. On the other hand, however, not even the more generous (from the point of view of the claimant) rules of German law would have helped the victims of asbestos-related occupational diseases in the cases which have caused so much concern in the Netherlands.[111]

consequence it will commonly be more difficult and expensive for the defendant to provide evidence of the knowledge of the plaintiff at a particular date, than for the plaintiff to provide such evidence'). Generally on onus of proof concerning prescription requirements, see Spiro (n. 15) §§ 359 ff.

[105] Art. 14:203 PECL.   [106] Art. 14:307 PECL.   [107] § 199 II–IV BGB.
[108] See also *Palandt*/Heinrichs, 64th edn. (n. 66) § 199, n. 39; *Anwaltkommentar*/Mansel/Stürner (n. 63) § 199, n. 64.   [109] Art. 14:307, second sentence PECL.
[110] See *Comparative Foundations* (n. 5) 64.
[111] See Michael Faure and Ton Hartlief, 'The Netherlands', in Helmut Koziol and Barbara C. Steininger (eds.), *European Tort Law 2001* (2002), 358; Michael Faure and Ton Hartlief, 'The Netherlands', in Helmut Koziol and Barbara C. Steininger (eds.), *European Tort Law 2003* (2004), 280 ff.; Evelien de Kezel, 'Problematiek van verborgen letselschade en verjaring: reflectie over een speciale vergoedingsregeling n.a. zgv. "Asbest-Schadevorderingen" ', in *Liber Amicorum Tijdschrift voor Privaatrecht en Marcel Storme* (2004), 107 ff.

(iv) That prescription should not run against a creditor who cannot reasonably become aware of his claim is a specific manifestation of a much wider idea: a claim must not prescribe if it is impossible for the creditor to pursue it (*agere non valenti non currit praescriptio*).[112] This is why prescription does not run in cases of *vis maior*,[113] and why expiry is postponed in case of incapacity,[114] and where an estate is without a representative or heir.[115] All these impediments are taken into account by extending the period of prescription. Ignorance should, therefore, be dealt with in the same way.

2. Reasonable discoverability; obligations to refrain from doing something

The rules contained in Articles 14:203, 14:301 PECL are also superior to those in § 199 BGB in certain other respects. Article 14:301 PECL focuses, as far as suspension in case of ignorance is concerned, on reasonable discoverability. Under § 199 BGB, it has to be determined when 'the creditor . . . ought to have become aware [of the circumstances giving rise to the claim and of the identity of the debtor] but for his gross negligence'. The concept of 'gross negligence'[116] implies a duty, on the part of a potential creditor, to find out whether or not he has a claim. Such a duty, however, cannot always plausibly be held to exist, particularly not with regard to claims arising from delict.[117] Furthermore, the point of reference for the discoverability criterion is more precisely defined in Article 14:301 (l) PECL than the point of reference for gross negligence in § 199 BGB ('. . . including, in the case of a right to damages, the type of damage').[118] And prescription in situations where a person is under an obligation to refrain from doing something is also more appropriately dealt with in Article 14:203 (2) PECL than in § 199 V BGB. The German rule ('If one party is entitled to request the other to refrain from doing something, the date of infringement of that obligation takes the place of the date on which the claim comes into being') states something which is obvious (neither the date when the claim comes into being nor due date can be the appropriate moment for commencement of prescription since the creditor's claim has come into existence, and is due, even before the debtor has infringed his obligation; yet, before such

---

[112] *Comparative Foundations* (n. 5) 132 ff.   [113] *Infra* VIII.2.   [114] *Infra* VIII.4.
[115] *Infra* VIII.6.
[116] For a detailed analysis of which see, in the present context, Markus Riedhammer, *Kenntnis, grobe Fahrlässigkeit und Verjährung* (2004).
[117] Zimmermann, Leenen, Mansel and Ernst, [2001] *Juristenzeitung* 687; *Anwaltkommentar/* Mansel/Stürner (n. 63) § 199, n. 57; *contra*: Piekenbrock (n. 26) 325.
[118] For comment, see Zimmermann, Leenen, Mansel and Ernst, [2001] *Juristenzeitung* 687 ff.; cf. also *Comparative Foundations* (n. 5) 148 ff.

infringement has occurred, the creditor does not normally have any reason to sue the debtor so as to stop the period of prescription from running); but it does not address the most important problem raised in this type of situation, i.e. whether in cases of a continuing obligation to refrain from doing something the period of prescription commences, once and for all, with the first act of contravention, or with each new act of contravention.[119]

3. Due date

A comparison with Article 14:203 PECL also reveals that the regulation contained in § 199 BGB is unnecessarily complicated. With regard to claims for damages, prescription begins to run from the time of the act which gives rise to the claim.[120] This is stated both in Article 14:203 (1) PECL and in § 199 II, III BGB, albeit in § 199 II, III BGB only for what, under the BGB, is the long period of prescription which runs irrespective of whether the creditor knew, or could reasonably have known, about the identity of the debtor, or the facts giving rise to the claim (but what is, in terms of PECL, a maximum period for extending the one and only period of prescription applicable to the claim in question). The same can and should, however, apply to the short general period of prescription, for the creditor is sufficiently protected by the discoverability criterion. This kind of regulation would have the added advantage that for all other types of claims, apart from damages, due date could constitute the relevant moment for the commencement of prescription; and that would be in tune with the basic principle that prescription should run only against a creditor who has the possibility of enforcing his claim in court (or of starting arbitration proceedings).[121] This is why, under the old law, the rule of § 198 I BGB (which focused on the moment when the claim has come into being) was taken to have referred to due date;[122] and all reform drafts, from Peters/ Zimmermann via the report of the Reform Commission to the Government Draft had, therefore, proposed expressly to state this in the new law. Strangely, the motivation to a last-minute amendment suggests that the phrase 'when the claim has come into being' conveys more clearly what the law is supposed to be than the term 'due date'.[123] The contrary is true. The only other argument

[119] Art. 14:302 (2) PECL adopts the latter solution. Cf. also Zimmermann, Leenen, Mansel and Ernst, [2001] *Juristenzeitung* 688; *Comparative Foundations* (n. 5) 150 ff.

[120] For the relevant policy considerations, see *Comparative Foundations* (n. 5) 109 ff.

[121] See Art. 14:203 (1) PECL; Art. 10.2 (2) PICC; and see *Comparative Foundations* (n. 5) 105 ff. (with references).

[122] Peters and Zimmermann (n. 6) 172 ff.; Frank Peters, in *J. von Staudingers Kommentar zum Bürgerlichen Gesetzbuch*, 13th edn. (1995), § 198, nn. 1 ff. The same view will be taken under the new law; see, for example, *Anwaltkommentar/*Mansel/Stürner (n. 63) § 199, n. 17.

[123] 'Bericht des Rechtsausschusses', in Canaris (n. 9) 1070.

advanced in favour of the amendment is that reference to the 'due date' would lead to problems with regard to damages claims[124] (the due date of which will, very often, depend on the occurrence of damage). This consideration does not apply to the type of regulation adopted in Article 14:203 (1) PECL.

4. Other peculiarities of the German regulation

Equally unnecessary is the complex double-track regulation contained in § 199 III BGB (new version).[125] In terms of this rule, damages claims not covered by § 199 II BGB (i.e. all damages claims not based on the infringement of life, bodily integrity, health, or liberty) prescribe (i) irrespective of knowledge or grossly negligent lack of knowledge, after a period of ten years from the moment when they arise, (ii) irrespective of the moment when they arose, and irrespective of knowledge or grossly negligent lack of knowledge, after a period of thirty years from the date on which the act, breach of duty, or other event causing the loss has occurred. And § 199 III 2 BGB adds that the period which ends first is decisive. It would be quite sufficient to let the maximum period run from the time of the act which has given rise to the claim. Also, considering the comparative evidence, the thirty-year period laid down in § 199 III no. 2 BGB for damages claims not based on the infringement of life, bodily integrity, health, or liberty is far too long.[126] A period of ten years would appear to be appropriate.[127]

Another important change concerning the commencement of prescription slipped into the new law after the publication of the Government Draft. Since the Council of State Governments does not appear to have suggested it, it is not quite clear at whose prompting this change was made.[128] The (regular) period of prescription does not run from the moment when the claim comes into being, and when the creditor becomes aware of the circumstances giving rise to the claim and of the identity of the debtor, or ought to have become aware of these matters but for his gross negligence, but *from the expiry of the year* in which these events occur.[129] The device of focusing on the end of the year, for the purposes of prescription periods, had been employed, by the draftsmen of

---

[124] 'Bericht des Rechtsausschusses', in Canaris (n. 9) 1070.

[125] On which see also 'Bericht des Rechtsausschusses', in Canaris (n. 9) 1070.

[126] See *Comparative Foundations* (n. 5) 99 ff.

[127] Provided, of course, a legal system draws a distinction between personal injuries and other damage in this respect. Art. 14:307 PECL and the recommendation of the English Law Commission (Law Com No. 270 (n. 20) 65 ff.; the Law Commission, however, does not envisage any long stop at all for personal injury claims) indicate that this corresponds to a widespread view. *Contra*: *Comparative Foundations* (n. 5) 101 ff.; Art. 10.2 (2) PICC; Piekenbrock (n. 26) 321; Willingmann (n. 26) 24.

[128] But see *Anwaltkommentar*/Mansel/Stürner (n. 63) § 199, n. 10 (referring to requests from the legal profession).   [129] § 199 I BGB.

the old BGB, for a range of claims concerning payment for services rendered and goods delivered.[130] This used to be a peculiarity of German law that has not been eagerly received in other jurisdictions.[131] But instead of taking its cue from what is very widely accepted in Europe, the new law has not merely perpetuated the old rule, but has generalized it so as to be applicable to the regular period of prescription.[132] In a sense, this must be welcomed, for any attempt to isolate specific types of claims to which the end-of-the-year rule should apply is bound to create inconvenient problems of delimitation. At the same time, however, it must be said that the generalized rule of § 199 I BGB (new version) now applies to a large number of claims which do not fit the rationale advanced for § 201 BGB (old version), questionable as that rationale was.[133] The only motivation given for § 199 I BGB is a bland reference to 'practical advantages' (for the creditors of claims).[134] No word is lost about the objections that can be (and have been) raised against the rule.[135]

VII. Renewal of the Period of Prescription

The most radical interference with the running of a period of prescription is what used to be called 'interruption' and is now referred to, both in the Principles and in the BGB, as 'renewal' of the period of prescription. It is justified only in two cases: acknowledgment of the claim by the debtor vis-à-vis the creditor, and acts of execution effected by, or at the application of, the creditor.[136] § 212 BGB effectively reflects what was recognized under the old law, and it corresponds to Article 14:401 ff. PECL. A closer comparison, however, reveals one questionable aspect of the German regulation. Acknowledgement of a claim established by judgment sets in motion a new thirty-year period of prescription (§§ 197 I no. 3 read in conjunction with § 212 I no. 1 BGB). According to Article 14:401 (2) PECL the new period is always the general period of prescription, even in cases where the claim was originally subject to the ten-year period laid

---

[130] § 201 BGB (old version).   [131] But see Art. 253 *Astikos Kodikas* (Greek Civil Code).

[132] § 199 BGB at the beginning.

[133] 'Motive', in Benno Mugdan (ed.), *Die gesammten Materialien zum Bürgerlichen Gesetzbuch für das Deutsche Reich*, vol. I (1899), 522 ff.; for comment, see *Comparative Foundations* (n. 5), 152 ff.

[134] 'Bericht des Rechtsausschusses', in Canaris (n. 9) 1069; for comment, see *Münchener Kommentar*/Grothe (n. 55) § 199, n. 40; *Anwaltkommentar*/Mansel/Stürner (n. 63), § 199, n. 10 ff. The motivation to the Government Draft had still severely criticized the rule: 'Begründung des Entwurfs eines Gesetzes zur Modernisierung des Schuldrechts', in Canaris (n. 9) 606.

[135] Spiro (n. 15) § 125; Peters and Zimmermann (n. 6) 247; *Comparative Foundations* (n. 5) 152 ff.; Willingmann (n. 26) 28 ff.; and see previous note.

[136] For background, see *Comparative Foundations* (n. 5) 124 ff.

down in Article 14:202 PECL for claims established by judgment. In the latter case, however, this must not lead to a shortening of the ten-year period which is already running. The rule envisaged in the Principles appears to be preferable. The creditor may rely on the debtor's acknowledgement and refrain from instituting an action. Also, the acknowledgement reduces any uncertainty surrounding the creditor's claim. In both respects, however, the creditor's legal position does not differ according to the nature of the claim to which the acknowledgement relates. It is the acknowledgement, and no longer the original claim, which should determine the appropriate legal regulation.

VIII. Suspension and Postponement of Expiry

1. Judicial and other proceedings

Under the old law the commencement of legal proceedings concerning the claim had the effect of interrupting the running of the period of prescription.[137] That event has now been downgraded to a ground for suspending prescription. This appears to be appropriate and is also in accordance with Article 14:302 PECL.[138] Suspension lasts until a decision has been passed which is final in the sense of having the effect of *res judicata*, or until the case has been otherwise disposed of. In this respect, too, the new German law corresponds to the regime laid down by Article 14:302 (2) PECL. There is one difference, however, in that § 204 II BGB grants the creditor an extra period of six months to bring another action.[139] This is practically relevant in cases where the original action has either been withdrawn or has been dismissed for procedural reasons (i.e. where the proceedings have ended without a decision on the merits of the claim) and where only very little of the old period of prescription is left. There is, however, no good reason why the creditor should be placed in a better position than if he had not brought an action in the first place.[140] Once again, therefore, the rule adopted in the Principles appears to be preferable.

---

[137] §§ 209 ff. BGB. For criticism, see Peters and Zimmermann (n. 6) 260 ff., 308; *Abschlußbericht* (n. 23) 83 ff.

[138] For a comparative analysis and evaluation of the options available—the period of prescription stops running (as in English law: see Andrew McGee, *Limitation Periods*, 3rd edn. (1998) nn. 2.001 ff.; probably also under § 13 of the UNCITRAL Convention), interruption of prescription (this is the solution adopted by all codifications based on Roman law) and suspension of prescription—see *Comparative Foundations* (n. 5) 122 ff. Cf. also Art. 10.5 PICC.

[139] Similar extra periods are granted in a number of other jurisdictions. The periods range from sixty days (Art. 139 Swiss OR (Code of Obligations)) to one year (Art. 17(2) UNCITRAL Convention). For details, see *Comparative Foundations* (n. 5) 122 ff.   [140] See *Abschlußbericht* (n. 23) 86.

The range of other measures which have the same effect on the running of a period of prescription as the commencement of an action has been brought up to date by the new § 209 BGB. However, by attempting to streamline the relevant provisions the draftsmen of the new law have occasionally managed to create new problems. According to § 220 BGB (old version) the provisions concerning the effect of judicial proceedings on the running of a period of prescription were applied, *mutatis mutandis*, to arbitration proceedings. Thus, for example, interruption of prescription could be effected by way of set-off in arbitration proceedings in the same way as in proceedings before an ordinary court of law.[141] The new § 204 BGB specifies in its no. 11 that the beginning of arbitration proceedings suspends prescription (as does the bringing of an action in an ordinary court of law: no. 1). Set-off in proceedings before an ordinary court of law also has the effect of suspending prescription (§ 204 I no. 5 BGB), but set-off in arbitration proceedings the BGB now lacks a provision which deals with. Of course, § 204 I no. 5 BGB can be, and will have to be, applied *per analogiam*[142] but it is remarkable (and not uncharacteristic) that this untoward consequence of an attempt to clarify the law was not noticed.[143]

2. Impediment beyond the creditor's control

The creditor must have a fair chance of pursuing his claim: otherwise prescription would operate unduly harshly.[144] The creditor can hardly, however, be reproached for not pursuing a claim if he does not pursue a claim which he cannot pursue: *agere non valenti non currit praescriptio*.[145] This is why *force majeure* has always been, and still is, recognized as a ground for suspending prescription: § 203 BGB (old version), § 206 BGB (new version). The German rule effectively corresponds to Article 14:303 PECL,[146] even if the formula

[141] § 220 read in conjunction with § 209 I, II no. 3 BGB (old version).

[142] Hans-Clemens Köhne and Sören D. Langner, 'Geltendmachung von Gegenforderungen im internationalen Schiedsverfahren', [2003] *Recht der Internationalen Wirtschaft* 365; Jan Erik Windthorst, 'Die Wirkung des Antrags auf Feststellung der Zulässigkeit eines schiedsrichterlichen Verfahrens (§ 1032 Abs. 2 ZPO) auf die Verjährung', [2004] *Zeitschrift für Schiedsverfahren* 230 ff.

[143] The motivation to the Government Draft contains the somewhat cryptic statement that the new law should 'not merely' provide for an analogous application of the rule concerning commencement of an action in an ordinary court of law in order to avoid uncertainty as to what, in arbitration proceedings, constitutes 'a situation comparable to the commencement of an action': 'Begründung der Bundesregierung zum Entwurf eines Gesetzes zur Modernisierung des Schuldrechts', in Canaris (n. 9) 635.

[144] See *Comparative Foundations* (n. 5) 78 ff. (drawing attention to the fact that an element of *Verwirkung* is always inherent in prescription: a creditor, in a way, is acting against the precepts of good faith if he sits on his rights without exercising them).

[145] For details, see *Comparative Foundations* (n. 5) 132 ff.

[146] Cf. also Art. 21 UNCITRAL Convention; Art. 10.8 PICC. For a comparative overview, see *Comparative Foundations* (n. 5) 129 ff.; Lando, Clive, Prüm and Zimmermann (n. 1) 185.

chosen by the authors of the Principles to define the range of impediments
leading to suspension is somewhat different; it ties in with the way in which
Article 8:108 PECL determines the circumstances under which a party's non-
performance is excused ('. . . an impediment which is beyond the creditor's
control and which the creditor could not reasonably have been expected to
avoid or overcome'). Both § 206 BGB (new version) and Article 14:303 PECL
attempt to limit the impact of this rule on the running of the period of prescription. And indeed, there is no compelling reason to extend the period of
prescription if the impediment preventing the institution of an action has
ceased to exist well before the end of that period: the creditor, under these circumstances, still has ample time to pursue his claim. Both provisions, however,
avail themselves of different techniques to implement that policy. According to
Article 14:303 PECL the impediment only has the effect of suspending the
period of prescription 'if [it] arises, or subsists, within the last six months of the
prescription period'. § 206 BGB, in turn, suspends the running of the period
'for as long as the creditor has, within the last six months of the prescription
period, been prevented by *force majeure* from pursuing his claim'. Thus,
according to German law, the maximum period for which prescription may be
suspended on account of *force majeure* is six months.[147] This may, however, be
too short: cases of kidnapping present an obvious example.[148]

3. Negotiations

Negotiations between the parties to reach a settlement out of court deserve to
be encouraged. They should not be carried out under the pressure of an
impending prescription of the claim. Nor should negotiations be allowed to
constitute a trap for the creditor. The idea of negotiations about the claim, or
about circumstances from which a claim might arise, as a ground for suspending prescription had, therefore, gained considerable support in Germany even
before the modernization of the law of obligations.[149] It had been recognized
in a number of specific provisions, the most important of which was § 852 II
BGB (old version) concerning delictual claims.[150] Ultimately, these provisions

---

[147] Frank Peters, in *J. von Staudingers Kommentar zum Bürgerlichen Gesetzbuch*, revised edition
(2004), § 206, n. 2. But see, for a more equitable interpretation, Heinz-Peter Mansel and Christine
Budzikiewicz, in *Anwaltkommentar BGB*, vol. I (2005), § 206, n. 16.

[148] The UNCITRAL Convention determines that the period of prescription '. . . shall be
extended so as not to expire before the expiration of one year from the date on which the relevant cir-
cumstance ceased to exist' (Art. 21). Effectively, therefore, the creditor is granted a minimum period
of one year during which he must be able to pursue his claim. But this solution goes beyond what is
necessary to protect the reasonable interests of the creditor; cf. *Comparative Foundations* (n. 5) 131 ff.

[149] See, for example, BGHZ 93, 64 (69); Peters and Zimmermann (n. 6) 250 ff., 317.

[150] Cf. also §§ 651g II 3, 639 II BGB (old version).

had to be regarded as manifestations of the principle of good faith (§ 242 BGB),[151] to which the courts used to resort for claims not covered by any of the specific provisions. A generalized rule concerning negotiations is now contained both in § 203 BGB and Article 14:304 PECL.[152] A comparison between the two provisions reveals two differences. (i) Prescription, according to § 203 BGB, is suspended 'until one of the parties refuses to continue the negotiations'. This rule does not sufficiently take account of the possibility that negotiations may simply peter out. The danger thus exists that prescription might be suspended indefinitely.[153] This is why Article 14:304 PECL focuses on the last communication made in the negotiations. (ii) Whereas German law regards negotiations as a ground for suspending prescription, Article 14:304 PECL uses the device of a postponement of expiry of the period of prescription. The Principles thus attempt to minimize the effect of negotiations on prescription. This appears to be appropriate in view of the fact that, once negotiations have failed, the creditor does not need more than a reasonable minimum period in order to decide whether or not to pursue his claim in court. There is no good reason to extend prescription merely because within the first year of a three-year period the parties have, for a number of weeks or months, conducted negotiations about the claim. The notion of prescription is jeopardized unnecessarily if, as under German law, all negotiations, rather than only those conducted within a critical interval before the expiry of the period of prescription, are taken into consideration.[154]

4. Close personal ties and incapacity

The previous paragraph raises an important general issue concerning a prescription regime. *Suspension* of prescription is a time-honoured device well-known to civilian jurisdictions.[155] It extends a given period of prescription: the

---

[151] See, for example, Ursula Stein, in *Münchener Kommentar zum Bürgerlichen Gesetzbuch*, vol. V, 3rd edn. (1997), § 852, n. 67; Karl Schäfer, in *J. von Staudingers Kommentar zum Bürgerlichen Gesetzbuch*, 12th edn. (1986), § 852, nn. 116 ff.

[152] Most of the other national legal systems do not have a provision of this kind. But only very few of them are happy to allow a debtor 'to negotiate himself into prescription'. For details, see case study 20, in Reinhard Zimmermann and Simon Whittaker (eds.), *Good Faith in European Contract Law* (2000), 493 ff. and the comparative evaluation at 530 ff.; cf. also *Comparative Foundations* (n. 5) 142 ff.

[153] For references as to how the German courts attempted to solve this problem in the application of § 852 II BGB (old version), see *Münchener Kommentar*/Stein (n. 151) § 852, n. 69. For the new law, see *Anwaltkommentar*/Mansel/Budzikiewicz (n. 147) § 203, nn. 39, 49 ff. (onus of proof).

[154] See *Comparative Foundations* (n. 5) 144 ff. (fn. 143); Zimmermann, Leenen, Mansel and Ernst, [2001] *Juristenzeitung* 695 ff.

[155] See, for example, Arts. 2251 ff. *Code civil*; §§ 1494 ff. ABGB; §§ 202 ff. BGB (old version); Arts. 255 ff. *Astikos Kodikas*; Arts. 2941 ff. *Codice civile*. Under the *ius commune* it used to be said that prescription was dormant (*praescriptio dormit*): Bernhard Windscheid and Theodor Kipp, *Lehrbuch des Pandektenrechts*, 9th edn. (1906), § 109.

interval during which prescription is suspended is not counted in calculating the period of prescription.[156] *Postponement of expiry* also has the effect of extending[157] a given period of prescription. Here the period of prescription runs its course but is only completed after the expiry of a certain extra period. The latter device is of more recent origin (it appears first in the Prussian code of 1794) but has increasingly gained ground internationally as a milder form of interference with prescription. In Germany it is known as *Ablaufhemmung*;[158] in the new Dutch Code, under the label of *verlenging van de verjaring*, it has completely replaced the traditional concept of suspension (*schorsing*).[159] Even if the Principles of European Contract Law do not go that far, they still attempt to interfere with the running of a period of prescription only to the extent that is absolutely necessary for the protection of the creditor. In case of doubt, therefore, they prefer the device of postponement of expiry to that of suspension. This is apparent not only from a comparison between Article 14:304 PECL and § 203 BGB (i.e. the rules on the effect of negotiations on prescription) but also by contrasting Article 14:305 (2) PECL with § 207 BGB. The latter two rules both cover claims existing between persons who are subject to an incapacity (and who are not, therefore, able to look after their own affairs) and their representatives. Again, postponement of expiry is the more adequate option in this situation.[160] § 207 BGB also suspends claims between spouses, and between life partners, for the period for which the marriage, or the life partnership, persists.[161] The common denominator between the claims covered by § 207 BGB is the family tie which constitutes, in the old-fashioned

---

[156] This is specifically stated in § 209 BGB (= § 205 BGB (old version)).

[157] The term 'extension' is used in the present chapter, as it is in the Principles of European Contract Law, in contrast to 'renewal'. A period of prescription can be extended by way of suspension or postponement of its expiry; see Lando, Clive, Prüm and Zimmermann (n. 1) 174; *Comparative Foundations* (n. 5) 138 ff.

[158] See 'Motive', in Mugdan (n. 133) 528; Spiro (n. 15) §§ 87 ff.

[159] See Arts. 3:320 ff. BW; Arthur S. Hartkamp, *Mr C. Asser's Handleiding tot de Beoefening van het Nederlands Burgerlijk Recht, Verbintenissenrecht*, Deel I, 12th edn. (2004), n. 682; Koopmann (n. 17) 83 ff. Generally, see Danco (n. 17) 193 ff.

[160] *Comparative Foundations* (n. 5) 137. Art. 14:305 (2) PECL thus states: 'The period of prescription of claims between a person subject to an incapacity and that person's representative does not expire before one year has passed after either the incapacity has ended or a new representative has been appointed'. According to § 207 I nos. 2 and 3 BGB prescription of claims between parents and children and the spouse of one parent and the latter's children is suspended during the minority of the children; and prescription of claims between a guardian and his ward is suspended as long as the guardianship continues. The same applies to claims between persons subject to an incapacity and other persons who may have been appointed to look after their affairs (*Rechtliche Betreuung*: §§ 1896 ff. BGB; *Pflegschaft*: §§ 1909 ff. BGB); see § 207 I nos. 4 and 5.

[161] For other national legal systems, see *Comparative Foundations* (n. 5) 139; Lando, Clive, Prüm and Zimmermann (n. 1) 192. On the concept of a life partnership (i.e. a registered marriage-like relationship between persons of the same sex) see the Life Partnership Act of 16 February 2001, *Bundesgesetzblatt* I 2001, 266.

language of the draftsmen of the original BGB, a relationship of piety requiring utmost delicacy.[162] Such a rule, however, appears to be hardly defensible today.[163] It leads to problems being swept under the carpet rather than solved. The death of one of the spouses should not enable the other to surprise disagreeable heirs by presenting claims which would normally have prescribed many years ago. Nor should divorce provide the trigger for settling old scores. Marriage would then have had the effect of removing protection against stale claims: a result which may well be regarded as discriminatory.[164] If, on the other hand, one were to regard the rationale underlying suspension between spouses as sound, it is difficult to see why the rule should not be generalized so as to cover other, closely related persons living in a common household.[165] These considerations have prompted the authors of Article 14:305 PECL to confine their attention to the problem of lack of capacity.[166] Obviously, therefore, Article 14:305 (2) PECL is not motivated by the close personal ties usually existing between persons subject to an incapacity and their representatives but by the fact that the person subject to an incapacity is unable to stop the running of a period of prescription by bringing an action.[167] If German law and the Principles disagree as to whether the period has to be suspended or whether its expiry has to be postponed, both of them accept that suspension or postponement of expiry should work both ways: it affects claims by the person subject to an incapacity against his representative and by the representative against the person subject to an incapacity.[168]

The rules in § 207 BGB and Article 14:305 (2) PECL need to be supplemented by a provision covering the situation that the person subject to an incapacity is without a representative. Both the BGB (§ 210) and Article 14:305 (1) PECL determine that a period of prescription does not expire before a certain interval has passed after either the incapacity has ended, or a representative has been appointed.[169] German law, therefore, in this situation also avails itself of

---

[162] 'Motive' in Mudgan (n. 133) 531.

[163] *Staudinger*/Peters (n. 147) § 207, n. 2; *Comparative Foundations* (n. 5) 139 ff.; Lando, Clive, Prüm and Zimmermann (n. 1) 190.   [164] *Staudinger*/Peters (n. 147) § 207, n. 2.

[165] Generally, see Karl Spiro, 'Verjährung und Hausgemeinschaft', in *Festschrift für Friedrich Wilhelm Bosch* (1976), 975 ff.; cf. also *Anwaltkommentar*/Mansel/Budzikiewicz (n. 147), § 207, nn. 21 ff.

[166] The same is true of the Principles of International Commercial Contracts, even if the approach adopted in Art. 10.8 (2) PICC differs from Art. 14:305 PECL; for comparative comment see Zimmermann, (2005) 13 *Zeitschrift für Europäisches Privatrecht* 282 ff.

[167] See *Staudinger*/Peters (n. 147) § 204, n. 3. For a comparative overview, see *Comparative Foundations* (n. 5) 135; Lando, Clive, Prüm and Zimmermann (n. 1) 191. According to French and English law, prescription does not run against persons subject to an incapacity: *Code civil* Art. 2252 first part; (English) Limitation Act 1980, s. 28.

[168] *Comparative Foundations* (n. 5) 137; Lando, Clive, Prüm and Zimmermann (n. 1) 189.

[169] For a comparative overview and evaluation of the various ways of how to deal with the matter, see *Comparative Foundations* (n. 5) 134 ff.

the device of a postponement of expiry.[170] The relevant interval, however, is only six months, whereas it is one year according to the Principles.

5. Sexual abuse

A novelty for German law is the rule contained in § 208 BGB: suspension of prescription 'in the case of claims for infringement of the right to sexual self-determination'.[171] The provision has its origin in a revised version of the Discussion Draft, where it was cautiously described as a 'rough draft'. None the less, the Government Draft only contained a shortened and simplified version of that draft.[172] Subsequently the provision was changed again in order further to increase the protection of minors who have been victims of sexual abuse. However, a central objection raised against the previous drafts also remains valid against § 208 BGB: the provision does not take the relevant rules of criminal law as its point of departure.[173] Thus, suspension of prescription does not depend on whether a provision has been infringed which serves to protect the right to sexual self-determination, but on whether (in the conviction of the court dealing with the prescription issue) the claim that has been brought is based on the infringement of the right to sexual self-determination. This means that the scope of application of the suspension rule is unnecessarily vague.[174] Furthermore, contrary to the regime laid down in §§ 207, 210 BGB, the minor enjoys an overall protection, irrespective of whether she has a statutory representative who would be able to pursue her claim for damages. It is not clear, however, why the minor should be granted greater protection with regard to claims for the infringement of the right to sexual self-determination than in other cases of physical abuse and cruelty.[175] Finally, it is not satisfactory that claims, according to § 208 BGB, can still be brought after an exceptionally

---

[170] § 210 BGB and Art. 14:305 (1) PECL also correspond to each other in that they apply to prescription periods running for and against a person subject to an incapacity; see *Comparative Foundations* (n. 5) 136 ff.; Lando, Clive, Prüm and Zimmermann (n. 1) 189. This is in contrast to § 206 BGB (old version).

[171] Prescription is suspended until the person whose right to sexual self-determination has been infringed, has reached the age of twenty-one.

[172] For criticism, see Zimmermann, Leenen, Mansel and Ernst, [2001] *Juristenzeitung* 696 ff.

[173] In that respect it differs from Art. 3:310 (4) BW (a provision introduced in 1994). For a discussion of damages claims based on sexual abuse of minors, and of the prescription problems involved, see, both for the new and the old law, Elke Beduhn, *Schadensersatz wegen sexuellen Kindesmißbrauchs* (2004), 283 ff.

[174] This is also criticized by *Münchener Kommentar*/Grothe (n. 55) § 208, n. 4.

[175] The point is also criticized by *Anwaltkommentar*/Mansel/Budzikiewicz (n. 147) § 208, n. 8. The English Law Commission therefore proposes the same regime for both cases; 'sexual abuse' poses no problems which, compared with other instances of 'personal injury', would justify special treatment: Law Com No. 270 (n. 20) 103 ff. (The Law Commission, however, proposes to grant to the courts in cases of 'personal injury' a discretion not to apply the three-year period of prescription; and

long time.[176] In many cases, a fair trial which could also take account of the legitimate interests of the defendant, will hardly be possible any longer. It is important to remember, in this context, what is valid for the law of prescription in general: that well-founded claims may be defeated is the necessary price a legal system has to pay if it wishes to provide the debtor with an easy means to defeat unfounded ones.[177] Of course, particularly with regard to the claims covered by § 208 BGB, the natural sense of justice revolts at the idea that prescription rules may have the effect of depriving the victim of sexual abuse of a well-founded claim. But this must not obscure the fact that, as the years pass by, legal disputes tend to become an ever greater source of uncertainty and unfairness. Not every allegation of sexual abuse, after all, is well founded.

On the other hand, a critical evaluation of § 208 BGB (new version) also has to take into account that even by increasing the age limit to twenty-one years and by adding the provision on the domestic community[178] the draftsmen of the new law have not been able to change the fact that in a number of cases the period of prescription will have expired before the person who has been sexually abused will be able to pursue her rights. Thus, a victim may well be aware of what (for example) her father or uncle has inflicted upon her before

it proposes not to apply the 'long-stop' at all. Such regulation would, in my view, be unacceptable for German law.) But see the *obiter dictum* of the European Court of Human Rights in *Stubbings v. United Kingdom* (1997) 23 *European Human Rights Reports* 213 (234): 'There has been a developing awareness in recent years of the range of problems caused by child abuse and its psychological effects on victims, and it is possible that the rules on limitation of actions applying to Member States of the Council of Europe may have to be amended to make special provision for this group of claimants in the near future'.

[176] Cases such as the following are imaginable. A minor (born on 10 November 1970) is repeatedly sexually abused by her father between November 1974 and October 1977. If the new law were applicable, prescription of her claims is suspended until her twenty-first birthday (1991): § 208, 1 BGB. If the victim of the sexual abuse continues to live in a domestic community with her parents until her thirtieth birthday, prescription is further suspended: § 208, 2 BGB. Thus, it is only at the end of 2000 that the three-year period of prescription starts to run (§ 195 BGB read in conjunction with § 209 BGB). If the victim of the abuse has suppressed her traumatic childhood experiences, or if she is unable to establish a causal link between her childhood experiences and her physical or psychological condition later in life (see, for example, Patty Gerstenblith, 'United States', in Ewoud Hondius (ed.), *Extinctive Prescription: On the Limitation of Actions* (1995), 362 ff.; Alastair C. L. Mullis, 'Compounding the Abuse? The House of Lords, Childhood Sexual Abuse and Limitation Periods', (1997) 5 *Medical Law Review* 24 ff.), this can result in the three-year period only expiring in thirty, forty or even fifty years. Thus, the thirty-year period contained in § 199 II BGB can become relevant. This period runs from the date on which the sexual abuse has been committed (1974–77) and would, therefore, expire in October 2007 at the latest. But since we are dealing here with a prescription period (rather than a maximum period for extending prescription), all grounds of suspension contained in §§ 203 ff. BGB presumably apply. The thirty-year period thus only commences to run from 10 November 2000 and, accordingly, prescription of the claim may only occur on 10 November 2030. By that time the victim of the abuse is sixty years old, and the events, which have to be established in court, have happened fifty-three years ago.

[177] See *Comparative Foundations* (n. 5) 63 ff., 76 ff.

[178] 'If, when the period of prescription commences, the creditor with respect to claims for infringement of the right to sexual self-determination is living with the debtor in a domestic community, prescription is suspended until the domestic community has been terminated'.

she attained the age of twenty-one, and she may also no longer live in the same household as her father or her uncle. None the less, in view of a continuing relationship of psychological dependence, she may not be able, for many years, to bring an action for damages.[179] § 208 BGB, therefore, continues to be a well-intentioned but hardly well-thought-out provision.[180] The Commission on European Contract Law recognized that the relevant issues could not be fully considered in the present context and therefore abstained from rushing into what can only be considered, at this stage, as a legislative experiment.[181]

6. Deceased's estate; right to refuse performance

Both the BGB (§ 211)[182] and the Principles of European Contract Law (Article 14:306) provide for a postponement of expiry of claims by or against a deceased person's estate. Both rules very largely correspond to each other; this is hardly surprising in view of the fact that Article 14:306 PECL has been inspired by German law.[183] Once again, however, there is a difference in the choice of the period which the creditor (i.e. either the heir or representative of the estate, or the person claiming from the heir or representative of the estate) has at his disposal to bring an action, once the claim in question can be enforced (six months according to German law, one year according to the Principles). No counterpart in the Principles of European Contract Law can be found for § 205 BGB.[184] In view of § 212 I no. 1 BGB and Article 14:401 (1) PECL[185] this rule has no independent practical significance.

---

[179] See the decision by the *Hooge Raad* of 23 October 1998, [2000] *Nederlandse Jurisprudentie* 15, where the period of prescription in Art. 3:310 BW was not applied for reasons of 'reasonableness and fairness' (see Art. 6:2 BW): the claimant had not been in a position to institute an action in view of the 'psychological superiority' (*psychische overmacht*) of the person who had committed the sexual abuse (he was, in this case, brother-in-law as well as the employer of the victim; both parties do not appear to have lived in domestic community, however). At the time the victim brought the action, she was 34 years old.

[180] For criticism of the new German rule, cf. also Beduhn (n. 173) 361 ff. For comparative remarks, see Ewoud Hondius, 'General Report', in *idem* (n. 17) 9 ff.; Law Commission Consultation Paper (n. 19) 294 ff. For the Netherlands cf., apart from the decision just mentioned, *Hoge Raad* of 25 June 1999, [2000] *Nederlandse Jurisprudentie*, 16; for England, see the article by Mullis, quoted above (n. 176). On the relevant case material in the United States, see Gerstenblith (n. 176) 361 ff.; David F. Partlett and Barry Nurcombe, 'Recovered Memories of Child Sexual Abuse and Liability: Society, Science and the Law in a Comparative Setting', (1998) 4 *Psychology, Public Policy and Law* 1274 ff.

[181] Lando, Clive, Prüm and Zimmermann (n. 1) 189 ff.

[182] This provision is practically unchanged compared to § 211 BGB (old version).

[183] *Comparative Foundations* (n. 5) 141; Lando, Clive, Prüm and Zimmermann (n. 1) 192.

[184] 'Prescription is suspended for as long as the debtor is entitled, on the basis of an agreement with the creditor, to refuse to perform'.

[185] Renewal of prescription in case of acknowledgement; see Peters and Zimmermann (n. 6) 253 ff., 308; cf. also *Abschlußbericht* (n. 23) 88; *Anwaltkommentar*/Mansel/Budzikiewicz (n. 147) § 205, nn. 2 ff.

IX. Effects of Prescription

The legal consequences of prescription are largely the same under the BGB and the Principles. Prescription does not extinguish the claim (this is why the term 'extinctive prescription' is inappropriate)[186] but only provides the debtor with a right to refuse performance.[187] Whatever has been performed in order to discharge a claim may not be reclaimed merely because the period of prescription had expired;[188] this is expressly stated in Article 14:501 (2) PECL, and § 214 II BGB intends to lay down the same rule.[189] Concerning the effect of prescription on ancillary claims, § 217 BGB and Article 14:502 PECL correspond to each other; again, the same idea[190] has only been formulated differently. According to the new § 215 BGB, prescription does not preclude set-off, provided prescription had not yet occurred at the moment when set-off could first have been effected. The new law thus perpetuates the regime laid down in § 390, 2 BGB (old version) and ignores the criticism raised against it.[191] Article 14:503 PECL has adopted a different rule: a claim in relation to which the period of prescription has expired may none the less be set off, unless the debtor has invoked prescription previously or does so within two months of notification of set-off. As under German law, a right of set-off according to the regime envisaged in the Principles has to be exercised by notice to the other party.[192] Unlike under German law, such notice does not, however, operate retrospectively.[193] This

---

[186] *Supra* n. 4.

[187] § 222 I BGB (old version), § 214 I BGB (new version), Art. 14:501 PECL. The comparative evidence and the relevant policy considerations are discussed in *Comparative Foundations* (n. 5) 72 ff.; cf. also *HKK*/Hermann (n. 6) §§ 194–225, 'Verjährung', nn. 23 ff. and Art. 10.9 (1) and (2) PICC.

[188] It can be reclaimed on other grounds: see *Staudinger*/Peters (n. 147) § 214, n. 35; Lando, Clive, Prüm and Zimmermann (n. 1) 203.

[189] 'What has been performed in satisfaction of a claim that has prescribed may not be reclaimed, even if performance had been made without knowledge of the expiry of the period of prescription.' For the comparative evidence, see Danco (n. 17) 49 ff.; *Comparative Foundations* (n. 5) 73, 154 ff.; Lando, Clive, Prüm and Zimmermann (n. 1) 204; and see Art. 10.11 PICC.

[190] The period of prescription for claims of an ancillary nature should not expire later than the period for the principal claim; see *Comparative Foundations* (n. 5) 157 ff.; Lando, Clive, Prüm and Zimmermann (n. 1) 205.

[191] Peters and Zimmermann (n. 6) 266; Peter Bydlinski, 'Die Aufrechnung mit verjährten Forderungen: Wirklich kein Änderungsbedarf?', (1996) 196 *Archiv für die civilistische Praxis* 193 ff.; *Comparative Foundations* (n. 5) 160 ff. [192] Art. 13:104 PECL.

[193] Art. 13:106 PECL; see *Comparative Foundations* (n. 5) 36 ff.; Reinhard Zimmermann, *Roman Law, Contemporary Law, European Law: The Civilian Tradition Today* (2001), 118 ff.; Pascal Pichonnaz, *La Compensation: Analyse historique et comparative des modes de compenser non conventionnels* (2001), 638 ff.

explains the approach adopted by Article 14:503 PECL.[194] The Principles do not contain a rule dealing with the effect of prescription on real security provided by the debtor or a third party.[195] This is due to the fact that they confine themselves to the law of obligations. The relevant rule in the new German law (§ 216 BGB) preserving the securities for the creditor, corresponds to § 223 BGB (old version); in addition, it now specifically adopts the extension of this rule to cases involving reservation of title that had been recognized by the courts under the old law.[196] It has repeatedly been stressed that the evaluation on which § 216 BGB (new version) is based is open to doubt.[197]

X. Modification by Agreement

To what extent is it possible to modify the prescription regime by agreement? This question is dealt with by § 202 BGB under a misleading heading and at a systematically inappropriate place. The heading ('inadmissibility of agreements concerning prescription') is misleading in view of the fact that agreements concerning prescription are very largely permitted; in particular, the new provision is much more liberal than its predecessor.[198] There are only two restrictions: (i) in the case of liability for deliberate acts or omissions, prescription may not be reduced in advance by way of agreement between the parties (§ 202 I BGB); and (ii) prescription may not be extended, by way of agreement, beyond a period of thirty years from the date of commencement of the general period of prescription (§ 202 II BGB). The upper limit of thirty years fixed by § 202 II BGB conforms to the solution adopted by Article 14:601 (2) PECL and is justified in view of the fact that the public interest[199] would be adversely affected if the parties were allowed effectively to exempt a claim from prescription. Concerning reduction of the period of prescription, the Principles are much stricter than the BGB: they do not allow the parties to agree to a period of less than one year after the time of commencement set out in Article 14:203.[200] This

---

[194] Cf. also Art. 10.10 PICC; for comment, see Zimmermann, (2005) 13 *Zeitschrift für Europäisches Privatrecht* 283.

[195] On the fate of accessory security rights, see the comparative analysis by Danco (n. 17) 55 ff.

[196] Cf., for example, Helmut Heinrichs, in *Palandt, Bürgerliches Gesetzbuch*, 60th edn. (2001) § 223, n. 8.

[197] Mathias Habersack in Ernst and Zimmermann (n. 28) 427; Mansel (n. 26) 402, 427; Zimmermann, Leenen, Mansel and Ernst, [2001] *Juristenzeitung* 697 ff.; *Anwaltkommentar/Mansel/Budzikiewicz* (n. 147) § 216, n. 3; and see *Comparative Foundations* (n. 5) 158 ff.

[198] According to § 225 BGB (old version) the prescription regime was unilaterally mandatory: while the parties were allowed to facilitate prescription, especially by providing for a period that was shorter than the statutory one, they could not render prescription more difficult, particularly by extending the statutory period. For a comparative analysis, see *Comparative Foundations* (n. 5) 162 ff.; Lando, Clive, Prüm and Zimmermann (n. 1) 208 ff.   [199] See *Comparative Foundations* (n. 5) 63 ff., 166.

[200] Art. 14:601 (2) PECL. Cf. also Art. 10.3 (2) (a) PICC.

is to be regretted. Agreements facilitating prescription are much more widely recognized in the existing national legal systems than those rendering prescription more difficult.[201] Moreover, they do not conflict with the public policy-based concerns underlying the law of prescription[202] (nor, of course, with the policy considerations concerning the protection of the debtor). The autonomy of the parties would be curtailed much too severely, and without any good reason, if they were not allowed, by way of individually negotiated agreement, to agree upon a prescription period of six months, or less.[203]

That § 202 BGB is placed at the end of title 1 ('Object and period of prescription') of the BGB's section on the law of prescription creates the mistaken impression that the provision only deals with matters covered in §§ 194–201 BGB, i.e. particularly the period and commencement of prescription. It is, however, intended also to cover agreements concerning other aspects of the prescription regime, such as grounds for suspension or postponement of expiry, or the effect of prescription.[204] Article 14:601 (1) PECL, in turn, permits parties to modify the requirements for prescription and specifically states that shortening or lengthening the period of prescription is only one way of doing so. Article 14:601 (2) PECL, therefore, must also be taken to establish minimum and maximum periods for all types of agreements modifying elements of the prescription regime.

XI. Another Reform

The transition from the old to the new prescription regime was governed by a complex set of rules incorporated in the Introductory Act to the German Civil Code: Article 229 § 6 EGBGB. Wherever the new prescription regime provided for a shorter period than the old one, the new period was also to be applied to claims that had arisen before 1 January 2002, though it was to be calculated from 1 January 2002.[205] Since the new general period is three years, this meant that 31 December 2004 was a particularly important date within the process of

---

[201] *Comparative Foundations* (n. 5) 163; Lando, Clive, Prüm and Zimmermann (n. 1) 209.

[202] See, for example, *Asser*/Hartkamp (n. 159) n. 678.

[203] Standard contract terms interfering with the prescription regime must, of course, be carefully scrutinized. The Unfair Terms in Consumer Contracts Directive provides the necessary tool; see *Abschlußbericht* (n. 23) 100; Art. 4:110 PECL.

[204] See Zimmermann, Leenen, Mansel and Ernst, [2001] *Juristenzeitung* 698. Generally on agreements concerning prescription under the new German law, see Panajotta Lakkis, 'Die Verjährungsvereinbarung nach neuem Recht', (2003) 203 *Archiv für die civilistische Praxis* 763 ff.

[205] Art. 229 § 6 IV 1 EGBGB. For all details concerning the transition rules, see Mansel and Budzikiewicz (n. 26) 253 ff.; *Anwaltkommentar*/Mansel/Budzikiewicz (n. 147) Art. 229 § 6 EGBGB.

transition.[206] By that time, however, the German Parliament had enacted another important piece of reform legislation: the Act on the Adjustment of Prescription Periods to the Modernization of the Law of Obligations Act (Law of Prescription Adjustment Act) of 9 December 2004 which entered into effect on 15 December 2004.[207] It was designed to tackle an important item on the reform agenda that the Modernization of the Law of Obligations Act had failed to deal with. A great variety of individual statutes outside the BGB had contained prescription provisions, usually deviating from the regime provided in the BGB and often ill-adjusted to each other. This was an unsatisfactory state of affairs that had contributed to the complexity of the German law of prescription and to the need for reform. The doctrinal contortions, to which the Federal Supreme Court had felt compelled to resort in order to protect clients of lawyers, tax consultants, and accountants from the effect of the prescription rules of § 51 b *Bundesrechtsanwaltsordnung*, § 68 *Steuerberatungsgesetz* and § 51 a *Wirtschaftsprüferordnung* in professional malpractice suits, provide a well-known example.[208] Back in 1981 Peters and Zimmermann had listed close to eighty statutes and had investigated to what extent they could be brought in line with the new general prescription regime proposed by them.[209] In many cases the amendment would have required nothing more than a repeal of the special prescription provisions; for it is generally agreed that the prescription rules contained in the General Part of the BGB do not only apply to all the other four Books of that Code but also (*per analogiam*) to all claims based on special legislation in the field of private law, unless the relevant statute provides otherwise.[210] Though the Government repeatedly acknowledged the

---

[206] But see Ronald Kandelhard, [2005] *Neue Juristische Wochenschrift* 630 ff.

[207] *Bundesgesetzblatt* I 2004, 3214. For comment, see Heinz-Peter Mansel and Christine Budzikiewicz, 'Verjährungsanpassungsgesetz: Neue Verjährungsfristen, insbesondere für die Anwaltshaftung und im Gesellschaftsrecht', [2005] *Neue Juristische Wochenschrift* 321 ff.; Frank-Michael Goebel, *Die neuen Verjährungsfristen* (2005), 19 ff.

[208] These prescription periods used to follow the objective system, i.e. they commenced to run irrespective of knowledge or discoverability on the part of the clients of the members of these professions. The courts attempted to mitigate the harshness resulting from these provisions by construing 'secondary' damages claims: the lawyer/tax consultant/accountant should have informed his client about the damages claim against himself as well as of the fact that that claim was threatened by prescription. If he failed to do so, he was held liable to his client whom he had to place in the position in which he would have been had the duty of information not been infringed: the client would then have been able to bring his damages claim against the lawyer/tax consultant/accountant. See *Palandt*/Heinrichs (n. 196) § 194, nn. 16 ff.; Helmut Grothe, in *Münchener Kommentar zum Bürgerlichen Gesetzbuch*, 4th edn. (2001), § 194, n. 12. The logic of the courts' arguments can easily be extended to 'tertiary' claims, etc.; see Reinhard Zimmermann, ' "Sekundäre" und "Tertiäre" Schadensersatzansprüche gegen den Rechtsanwalt', [1985] *Neue Juristische Wochenschrift* 720 ff. According to Helmut Heinrichs, in *Palandt, Bürgerliches Gesetzbuch*, 62nd edn. (2003), Überbl. v. § 194, n. 3, that legal position was 'intolerable'.   [209] Peters and Zimmermann (n. 6) 149 ff., 334 ff.

[210] *Münchener Kommentar*/Grothe (n. 55) § 195, n. 11; *Staudinger*/Peters (n. 147) § 194, n. 22; Mansel and Budzikiewicz (n. 26) 44 ff.; *Anwaltkommentar*/Mansel/Stürner (n. 63) § 194, nn. 10 ff.;

need to tidy up this maze of special rules,[211] it only managed to embark on this project after the enactment of the Modernization of the Law of Obligations Act. But even in the Law of Prescription Adjustment Act hardly more than a first step was taken, for that Act affects only nineteen statutes with special prescription provisions.[212] Some of the most serious problems have thus been resolved; in particular, the three provisions concerning the liability of lawyers, tax consultants, and accountants, mentioned above, were repealed.[213] Whether the Government implicitly rejected the need for amendment with regard to the statutes not affected by the Law of Prescription Adjustment Act is not entirely clear, since the Act does not contain a list of statutes that have been critically examined.[214] Also, within the BGB, a number of special prescription provisions continue to exist.[215] Once again, a complex set of rules has been devised to govern the transition from the old regime to the new.[216]

XII. Conclusion

The final evaluation has to be ambivalent. The new German law of prescription is considerably better than the old law and the Discussion Draft. The general direction is right. But can that be sufficient for such an ambitious and centrally important reform project? Consistency of approach is one of the key considerations to be kept in mind in devising a prescription regime. It has not sufficiently been heeded in Germany. In the first half of 2001 a variety of drafts was produced. Even the Government Draft of May 2001 was still

---

Mansel and Budzikiewicz, [2005] *Neue Juristische Wochenschrift* 322 (referring also to the Government motivation to the Law of Prescription Amendment Act). Mansel, however, argues that in individual instances the old general period of thirty years (§ 195 BGB, old version) may have to be applied: Mansel and Budzikiewicz (n. 26) 45; *Anwaltkommentar*/Mansel/Stürner (n. 63) § 194, nn. 13 ff. On the application of §§ 194 ff. BGB in the field of public law, see *Münchener Kommentar*/Grothe (n. 55) § 195, n. 12; *Staudinger*/Peters (n. 147) § 194, n. 22; *Palandt*/Heinrichs, 64th edn. (n. 66) § 195, n. 20; but see *Anwaltkommentar*/Mansel/Stürner (n. 63) § 194, nn. 16 ff.

[211] See, for example, 'Begründung der Bundesregierung zum Entwurf eines Gesetzes zur Modernisierung des Schuldrechts', in Canaris (n. 9) 591.

[212] The motivation to the Government Draft of the Modernization of the Law of Obligations from 2001, however, had referred to more than eighty statutes containing more than 130 prescription rules. Cf. also the list in Mansel and Budzikiewicz (n. 26) 43 ff.

[213] The special prescription rule of § 51a *Wirtschaftsprüferordnung* had already been repealed by another amending act with effect from 1 January 2004. For all details as to the statutes amended by the Law of Prescription Adjustment Act, see Mansel and Budzikiewicz, [2005] *Neue Juristische Wochenschrift* 322.

[214] Cf. also the criticism by Mansel and Budzikiewicz, [2005] *Neue Juristische Wochenschrift* 321 ff.

[215] Such as the ones mentioned above n. 72 (family law and the law of succession).

[216] Art. 229 § 12 EGBGB; for comment, see Mansel and Budzikiewicz, [2005] *Neue Juristische Wochenschrift* 324 ff. (questioning the constitutionality of the transition regime).

changed in several respects. There have been a number of improvements. On the other hand, however, many of the criticisms levelled at the various drafts have not been taken into consideration. Also, so many architects have been involved in the process of construction, that the edifice of the new German law of prescription can hardly be called homogeneous. It does not require much prophetic skill to predict that the German law of prescription will remain a source of doctrinal irritation. Courts and legal literature will still be able to display their ingenuity in ironing out practical problems and conceptual inconsistencies. In part, they will be able to perpetuate devices developed under the old law. Sometimes new doctrinal borderlines will have to be drawn. The new set of provisions can be described as being 'European' in spirit, in that it attempts to implement the same core regime as the Principles of European Contract Law; the latter have in fact provided the immediate source of inspiration for the former. There are, however, a number of important deviations. Whether the draftsmen of the German Code or of the Principles have hit upon the preferable solution can, of course, be open to dispute. The present analysis suggests that, in the large majority of instances, the Principles adopt the sounder view. It is unfortunate, at any rate, that the draftsmen of the BGB did not take the time to consider alternative suggestions and to provide a reasoned motivation for their choices. They have thereby reduced the potential of the BGB's new prescription rules to influence further international developments. For such influence should be based on the persuasive power of the better arguments: on *ratio* rather than *voluntas*.[217]

---

[217] Cf. also, in the same spirit, Mansel (n. 26) 409 who points out that where German law deviates from the European standard it can only claim to be taken seriously within the European legal discourse, if such deviations are based on critical discussion, taking account of what is accepted in other jurisdictions.

5

Consumer Contract Law and General Contract Law

I. Introduction

More than by any other component of the reform process, the face of the BGB has been changed by the incorporation of a number of special statutes aiming at the protection of consumers. The draftsmen of the new law have thus made an effort to streamline, or harmonize, general contract law and consumer contract law. This is the issue that will be discussed in the present Chapter. While it had been on the initial reform agenda of 1978,[1] it had no longer been part of the brief of the Commission charged with the reform of the German law of obligations.[2] The Discussion Draft[3] could not, therefore, be based on previous drafts or detailed academic discussion as to how such integration might be achieved. Nor was the incorporation into the BGB of the special legislation concerning consumer protection required by any fiat on the European level. On the contrary: European law is still itself confronted with the problem of coordinating general contract law and consumer contract law. The issue is very much on the agenda mapped out by the action plan for a more coherent European contract law[4] and it also still has to be considered by the draftsmen of the Principles of European Contract Law[5] who, while providing a blueprint for general contract law, have so far failed to take account of the *acquis communautaire* in the field of consumer contracts.[6] The debates conducted, and

---

[1] *Supra* pp. 30 f.   [2] *Supra* p. 32.   [3] On which see *supra* p. 33.

[4] COM (2003) 68, OJ 2003, C 63/1.

[5] Ole Lando and Hugh Beale (eds.), *Principles of European Contract Law, Parts I and II* (2000); Ole Lando, Eric Clive, André Prüm and Reinhard Zimmermann (eds.), *Principles of European Contract Law, Part III* (2003). For comment, see Reinhard Zimmermann, 'The Principles of European Contract Law: Contemporary Manifestation of the Old, and Possible Foundation for a New, European Scholarship of Private Law', in *Essays in Honour of Hein Köt* (2005), forthcoming.

[6] This has repeatedly been criticized; see Jürgen Basedow, 'The Renascence of Uniform Law: European Contract Law and its Components', (1998) 18 *Legal Studies* 138 ff.; Ralf Michaels, 'Privatautonomie und Privatkodifikation', (1998) 62 *Rabels Zeitschrift für ausländisches und internationales Privatrecht* 589; Wolfgang Wurmnest, 'Common Core, Grundregeln, Kodifikationsentwürfe,

experiences gathered, in Germany may therefore also be instructive as far as the future development of European contract law is concerned.

II. Freedom, Equality, and Social Responsibility at the Time of the Original BGB

1. Protecting the weaker party

One of the characteristic lines of development of contract law over the past four decades, both in Germany and internationally, is the rise of legislation aiming at the protection of consumers who are about to enter, or who have entered into contracts which may be, or turn out to be, against their own best interests. This legislation is widely regarded as unsatisfactory. It is obviously ill-coordinated.[7] Moreover, a certain tension is often seen to exist between the approach embraced by the consumer contract legislation and the fundamental precepts of legal equality and private autonomy underlying the BGB.[8] Also, both the definition of, and focus on, the concept of 'consumer' have been criticized.[9]

Acquis-Grundsätze—Ansätze internationaler Wissenschaftlergruppen zur Privatrechtsvereinheitlichung in Europa', (2003) 11 *Zeitschrift für Europäisches Privatrecht* 729 ff.; Hans-W. Micklitz, 'Verbraucherschutz in den Grundregeln des Europäischen Vertragsrechts', (2004) 103 *Zeitschrift für vergleichende Rechtswissenschaft* 88 ff.; Hannes Rösler, *Europäisches Konsumentenvertragsrecht* (2004), 137 ff.

[7] See, for example, Jürgen Basedow, 'Das BGB im künftigen europäischen Privatrecht: der hybride Kodex', (2000) 200 *Archiv für die civilistische Praxis* 449 ff.; Christian Kirchner, 'Der punktuelle Ansatz als Leitprinzip gemeinschaftsrechtlicher Privatrechtsharmonisierung', in Stefan Grundmann, Dieter Medicus and Walter Rolland (eds.), *Europäisches Kaufgewährleistungsrecht* (2000), 95 ff.; Thomas M.J. Möllers, 'Europäische Richtlinien zum Bürgerlichen Recht', [2002] *Juristenzeitung* 121 ff.; Thomas Pfeiffer, 'Die Integration von "Nebengesetzen" in das BGB', in Wolfgang Ernst and Reinhard Zimmermann (eds.) *Zivilrechtswissenschaft und Schuldrechtsreform* (2001) 481 ff.; Rösler (n. 6) 218 ff.

[8] On the principles underlying the BGB, see Joachim Rückert, 'Das BGB und seine Prinzipien: Aufgabe, Lösung, Erfolg', in Mathias Schmoeckel, Joachim Rückert and Reinhard Zimmermann (eds.), *Historisch-kritischer Kommentar zum BGB*, vol. I (2003), Vorbem. § 1, nn. 1 ff.

[9] See, for example, Dieter Medicus, 'Wer ist ein Verbraucher?', in *Wege zum japanischen Recht: Festschrift für Zentaro Kitagawa* (1992) 471 ff.; Meinrad Dreher, 'Der Verbraucher—Das Phantom in den opera des europäischen und deutschen Rechts?', [1997] *Juristenzeitung* 167 ff. For a discussion of the issues involved on the European and German level, see Wolfgang Faber, 'Elemente verschiedener Verbraucherbegriffe in EG-Richtlinien, zwischenstaatlichen Übereinkommen und nationalem Zivil- und Kollisionsrecht', (1998) 6 *Zeitschrift für Europäisches Privatrecht* 854 ff.; Josef Drexl, *Die wirtschaftliche Selbstbestimmung des Verbrauchers* (1998), 433 ff.; Thomas Pfeiffer, 'Der Verbraucher nach § 13 BGB', in Hans Schulte-Nölke and Reiner Schulze (eds.), *Europäische Rechtsangleichung und nationale Privatrechte* (1999) 133 ff.; Tilman Repgen, *Kein Abschied von der Privatautonomie: Die Funktion zwingenden Rechts in der Verbrauchsgüterkaufrichtlinie* (2001), 30 ff.; Karl Riesenhuber, *System und Prinzipien des Europäischen Vertragsrechts* (2003), 250 ff.; Oliver Remien, *Zwingendes Vertragsrecht und Grundfreiheiten des EG-Vertrages* (2003), 238 ff.; Rösler (n. 6) 101 ff.; Kai-Udo

Does modern consumer law constitute a special branch of private law with its own distinctive features and evaluations (and, some would say, ideology)? Does it perhaps deal with a specific type, or class, of persons who deserve to be protected? But consumers do not constitute a class.[10] Everyone can be a consumer, as long as he acts in a specific role.[11] The inexperienced housewife and the impecunious workman are as much 'consumers' as the wealthy entrepreneur, or the distinguished law professor, as long as they buy a car, or book, or loaf of bread, or carpet, for their private use. Consumers are, however, protected only in specific situations against specific dangers which the law perceives to exist. Obviously, therefore, the law pursues a typological approach:[12] it attempts to grant protection to one contracting party who is considered to be in a weaker position, or at a specific disadvantage, vis-à-vis the other.

Consumer protection is thus a modern manifestation of a much broader concern. The tradition of legislation protecting weaker parties against disadvantageous contract terms has a long pedigree; it reaches back to the maximum interest rates for loans,[13] the *senatus consultum Vellaeanum*,[14] and the *laesio enormis* of Roman law.[15] Commercial life in the Middle Ages was dominated by the prohibition on usury[16] and by countless regulations attempting to fix the *iustum pretium* for various commodities.[17] The aedilitian edict, issued in the early part of the second century BC, essentially served the purpose of what would today be called consumer protection;[18] the generalized form of 'aedilitian liability' became part and parcel of the *ius commune* and also distinctively

Wiedenmann, *Verbraucherleitbilder und Verbraucherbegriff im deutschen und europäischen Privatrecht* (2004), 134 ff.; Bettina Heiderhoff, *Grundstrukturen des nationalen und europäischen Verbrauchervertragsrechts* (2004), 238 ff.; Jochen Mohr, 'Der Begriff des Verbrauchers und seine Auswirkungen auf das neugeschaffene Kaufrecht und das Arbeitsrecht', (2004) 204 *Archiv für die civilistische Praxis* 670 ff.

[10] Dieter Medicus, 'Schlussbetrachtung', in Ernst and Zimmermann (n. 7) 607.

[11] On the notion of 'role' as a point of departure for legal consequences, see Dieter Medicus, 'Eigenschaft oder Rolle als Anknüpfungspunkt für Rechtsfolgen', in *Privatrecht und Methode: Festschrift für Ernst A. Kramer* (2004), 211 ff.

[12] Thomas Duve, in Mathias Schmoeckel, Joachim Rückert and Reinhard Zimmermann (eds.), *Historisch-kritischer Kommentar zum BGB*, vol. I (2003), §§ 1–14, nn. 78 ff.; Heiderhoff (n. 9) 250 ff.; Wiedenmann (n. 9) 113 ff.

[13] Reinhard Zimmermann, *The Law of Obligations: Roman Foundations of the Civilian Tradition*, paperback edition (1996), 166 ff.   [14] *Law of Obligations* (n. 13) 145 ff.

[15] *Law of Obligations* (n. 13) 259 ff.   [16] *Law of Obligations* (n. 13) 170 ff.

[17] See H. Kellenbenz, 'Preisbindung', in *Handwörterbuch zur deutschen Rechtsgeschichte*, vol. III (1984), cols. 1886 ff. Generally on the devices used in medieval and early modern Europe in order to afford what would today be called 'consumer' protection, see Wolfgang Schuhmacher, *Verbraucher und Recht in historischer Sicht* (1981), 11 ff.

[18] See Max Kaser and Rolf Knütel, *Römisches Privatrecht*, 17th edn. (2003), 270; Eva Jakab, 'Diebische Sklaven, marode Balken: Von den römischen Wurzeln der Gewährleistung für Sachmängel', in Martin Schermaier (ed.), *Verbraucherkauf in Europa* (2003), 27 ff.

shaped the national codifications in Europe.[19] The German Civil Code has often been criticized for unduly neglecting this protective dimension and with it, in the words of Otto von Gierke, the 'social task of private law'.[20] It is said to be based on an exaggerated individualism and on a formalistic concept of freedom and equality.[21] This evaluation does not, however, convey an entirely accurate picture of the legal position more broadly conceived.[22] Contemporary lawyers were acutely aware of the limitations of freedom of contract.[23] At the same time, it must be kept in mind that many of the problems with which we are faced today were only beginning to emerge.[24] They were not necessarily tackled by means of private law, and even where they were, the respective rules were enacted by way of special legislation rather than incorporated into the codification of general private law. The scene was thus set for the double-track approach which remained characteristic of German private law until 2002.

2. Economic background

The German Civil Code was promulgated in 1896 and came into effect on 1 January 1900. Its preparation had taken twenty-two years, for the first, 'preliminary', Commission had been appointed in 1874.[25] This was a time when Germany was beginning to experience a period of rapid change. The population of the new *Reich* grew from forty-one million in 1871 to fifty-six million in 1900.[26] More and more of that population lived in towns. While up to 1871 close to two-thirds of all Germans had lived in the countryside, that number had sunk to less than half (45.6 per cent) in 1900.[27] The number of

---

[19] *Law of Obligations* (n. 13) 311 ff., 319 ff.

[20] Otto von Gierke, *Die soziale Aufgabe des Privatrechts* (1889); cf. also, for example, Rudolph Sohm, 'Ueber den Entwurf eines bürgerlichen Gesetzbuches für das Deutsche Reich in zweiter Lesung', (1895) 39 *Gruchots Beiträge zur Erläuterung des deutschen Rechts* 747.

[21] Franz Wieacker, *A History of Private Law in Europe* (1995) (transl. Tony Weir), 376 ff.; Konrad Zweigert and Hein Kötz, *An Introduction to Comparative Law*, 3rd edn. (1996) (transl. Tony Weir), 148 ff.

[22] *HKK*/Rückert (n. 8) vor § 1, n. 96; Rösler (n. 6) 50 ff.; Mohr, (2004) 204 *Archiv für die civilistische Praxis* 660 ff. For a comprehensive discussion, see Tilman Repgen, *Die soziale Aufgabe des Privatrechts* (2001).

[23] See, for example, Gottlieb Planck, 'Die soziale Tendenz des BGB', (1899) 4 *Deutsche Juristenzeitung* 181 ff.; Planck was one of the most influential draftsmen of the BGB. For further discussion, and references, see Repgen (n. 22) 24 ff., 68 ff.; the revisionist view is also supported by Sibylle Hofer, *Freiheit ohne Grenzen?* (2001). For a comparative analysis, see Jean-Louis Halpérin, 'Quelle histoire pour le droit des consommateurs?', (2001) 23 *Zeitschrift für Neuere Rechtsgeschichte* 62 ff.; for Austria, see Schuhmacher (n. 17) 34 ff.   [24] The point is also emphasized by Rösler (n. 6) 50 ff.

[25] See the table prepared by Stefan Stolte, 'Die Entstehung des BGB im Überblick mit Nachweis der Quellentexte', in Mathias Schmoeckel, Joachim Rückert and Reinhard Zimmermann (eds.), *Historisch-kritischer Kommentar zum BGB*, vol. I (2003), xxvii ff.

[26] For details, see Thomas Nipperdey, *Deutsche Geschichte 1866–1918*, vol. I, paperback edition (1998), 9 ff.   [27] Nipperdey (n. 26) 35.

Germans living in big cities (of over 100,000 inhabitants), on the other hand, had risen from 4.8 per cent in 1871 to 16.2 per cent in 1900; by 1910 Germany had forty-eight cities with over 100,000 inhabitants as opposed to merely eight in 1871.[28] At the same time, there was a marked East-West migration; thus, in 1907, 24 per cent of those born in the three north-eastern provinces of Prussia lived in other areas of Germany, many of them in the mining area of the Ruhr.[29] During the last three decades of the nineteenth century Germany turned from a (predominantly) agrarian into a (predominantly) industrialized society. The coal output in the Ruhr area, for example, increased from 11.5 million tons in 1870 to 60.1 million tons in 1900.[30] Transportation facilities and capacities had been improved very considerably by the end of the century. In 1880, 10 per cent of the capital generated in the *Reich* was invested in the railways.[31] In 1913, 7,024 million letters were sent, compared with 269 million in 1867.[32] The invention of the telephone dramatically improved the speed of communication. In 1881 there had been only 1,400 telephone installations; by 1900, the figure had passed 1 million.[33] The years after 1870 saw the rise of the modern interventionist state. At the same time, it was a period of unparalleled economic growth; German national unification, in particular, stimulated the proverbial 'foundational boom'.[34] But there were also setbacks and recessions which highlighted the problems of an industrialized society.[35] An ever larger percentage of the population worked as labourers in trade and industry[36] and thus depended, for their livelihood, on the smooth functioning and growth of these sectors of the economy. Trade unions and strikes for better work conditions became a feature of modern public life.[37]

3. The drops of social oil

The law reacted to these challenges in various ways. Most famously, perhaps, Bismarck created the modern social security system in order to improve the welfare of the workers and, at the same time, to achieve an integration of the 'fourth estate' into the prevailing system of government.[38] The Emperor pronounced the promotion of the welfare of those in need to be one of the noblest tasks of every body politic.[39] The fathers of the BGB saw in the protection of the economically weaker party an important policy objective and

[28] Nipperdey (n. 26) 34.   [29] Nipperdey (n. 26) 40.   [30] Nipperdey (n. 26) 227.
[31] Nipperdey (n. 26) 260.   [32] Nipperdey (n. 26) 263.   [33] Nipperdey (n. 26) 263.
[34] For details, see Nipperdey (n. 26) 283 ff.   [35] See Nipperdey (n. 26) 284, 336.
[36] For details, see Nipperdey (n. 26) 291 ff.   [37] See Nipperdey (n. 26) 319 ff.
[38] Nipperdey (n. 26) 335 ff.; Michael Stolleis, *Geschichte des Sozialrechts in Deutschland* (2003), 52 ff.
[39] Emperor's speech of 17 November 1881, as quoted by Repgen (n. 22) 28.

emphasized the need for social sensitivity.[40] Within the code itself, these considerations manifested themselves in various ways. Thus, of course, there were the famous 'general provisions' like §§ 138, 226, 242 and 826 BGB. They have turned out to be highly pliable devices for the infusion of more than a few drops of social oil into the fabric of the BGB.[41] But there were also a number of other rules, most of them adopted in deviation from contemporary pandectist legal doctrine: sale does not 'break' lease;[42] the restrictions on the lessor's statutory pledge over objects brought onto the premises by the lessee;[43] continuation of payment of wages in cases where an employee is prevented from performing his services 'for a comparatively insignificant time' for a reason 'associated with his person' (such as sickness);[44] the protection of employees against excessively long employment contracts by means of a statutory right to terminate the contract after five years;[45] the judicial power to reduce 'disproportionately high' conventional penalties;[46] or the right of the debtor to terminate a loan after the lapse of six months if an interest rate in excess of six per cent has been agreed upon.[47] These are merely examples. Even the regulation of a technical area of the law not usually in the forefront of political discussion, such as 'extinctive' prescription, was based on social concerns including, particularly, protection of the debtor.[48] More important, however, is another

---

[40] See the quotations from speeches by Gottlieb Planck before the Imperial Parliament, as quoted by Repgen (n. 22) 70.

[41] Otto von Gierke had famously demanded that 'a drop of socialist oil' had to seep through the fabric of private law: Repgen (n. 22) 12 ff. On the pedigree of the oil metaphor (which had also, previously, been used by Bismarck), see Repgen (n. 22) 4 f.; cf. also Tilman Repgen, 'Was war und wo blieb das soziale Öl?', (2000) 22 *Zeitschrift für Neuere Privatrechtsgeschichte* 406 ff. For a historical analysis of the application of §§ 138 and 226 BGB, see now Hans-Peter Haferkamp, in Mathias Schmoeckel, Joachim Rückert and Reinhard Zimmermann (eds.), *Historisch-kritischer Kommentar zum BGB*, vol. I (2003), § 138 and §§ 226–231.

[42] § 571 BGB (old version) (now: § 566 BGB); see *Law of Obligations* (n. 13) 377 ff.; Repgen (n. 22) 231 ff.

[43] §§ 559 ff. BGB (old version) (now: §§ 562 ff. BGB); for an extensive analysis, see Repgen (n. 22) 250 ff.

[44] § 616 BGB; on which see Hartmut Oetker, in *J. von Staudingers Kommentar zum Bürgerlichen Gesetzbuch*, revised edition (2002), § 616, nn. 1 ff.; cf. also Repgen (n. 22) 215 ff.

[45] § 624 BGB; on which see Ulrich Preis, in *J. von Staudingers Kommentar zum Bürgerlichen Gesetzbuch*, revised edition (2002), § 624, nn. 1 ff.

[46] § 343 BGB; on which see Ralf-Peter Sossna, *Die Geschichte der Begrenzung von Vertragsstrafen* (1993), 165 ff.

[47] § 247 BGB (repealed in 1986); on the origin of which see Peter Landau, 'Die Gesetzgebungsgeschichte des § 247 BGB: Zugleich ein Beitrag zur Geschichte der Einführung der Zinsfreiheit in Deutschland', in Gerd Kleinheyer and Paul Mikat (eds.), *Beiträge zur Rechtsgeschichte: Gedächtnisschrift für Hermann Conrad* (1979), 385 ff.; Rolf Geyer, *Der Gedanke des Verbraucherschutzes im Reichsrecht des Kaiserreichs und der Weimarer Republik (1871–1933)* (2001), 71 ff.

[48] For details, see Repgen (n. 22) 179 ff.; for the policy objectives pursued by the law of prescription cf. also, in this context, Reinhard Zimmermann, *Comparative Foundations of a European Law of Set-Off and Prescription* (2002), 63, 77.

point. The BGB was supposed to provide a general framework for parties to regulate their own affairs; it subscribed to the ideals of equal rights, freedom, and self-determination. At the same time, it was not intended to advance the interests of particular groups, or classes, within contemporary society. Its draftsmen did not reject the legitimacy of specific policy concerns militating for special rules of a protective character. But these, by and large, were special concerns which required special legislation outside the general Civil Code.

4. The Act concerning Instalment Sales

The most prominent example of such special legislation is the Act concerning Instalment Sales (*Abzahlungsgesetz*) of 16 May 1894.[49] Its origins have repeatedly been analysed.[50] Mass production and improved distribution facilities had led to the opening up of new markets and a vastly increased range of potential purchasers. Instalment transactions enabled the members of the less affluent classes to obtain goods required for their daily life (such as furniture) or the machinery required to earn their livelihood. By the middle of the 1880s, for example, more than half of the 500,000 sewing machines produced in Germany annually were sold by way of instalment sales; by 1892/93 the percentage even appears to have risen to between 80 and 90 per cent.[51] These sewing machines were bought, very largely, by female homeworkers. Instalment sales had thus become a very widespread type of transaction that was welcomed, in principle, both from the point of view of social policy and national economy. But they also entailed a number of specific risks and disadvantages. One of them was the so-called 'forfeiture clause' (*Verfallklausel*) on which instalment sellers used to insist:[52] if the purchaser failed to pay one of the instalments, the seller was entitled to take back the object and to keep all the instalments that had previously been paid. In the second half of the 1880s the problems associated with instalment sales became the subject of widespread

---

[49] *Reichsgesetzblatt* 1894, 450. Another very important special statute implementing a finely tuned model of protecting contractual parties who were perceived to be in a weaker position, is the Insurance Contract Act of 30 May 1908, *Reichsgesetzblatt* 1908, 263. For discussion, see Wulf-Henning Roth, *Internationales Versicherungsvertragsrecht* (1985), 77 ff.

[50] Hans-Peter Benöhr, 'Konsumentenschutz vor 80 Jahren: Zur Entstehung des Abzahlungsgesetzes vom 16. Mai 1894', (1974) 138 *Zeitschrift für das gesamte Handelsrecht und Wirtschaftsrecht* 492 ff.; Werner Schubert, 'Das Abzahlungsgesetz von 1894 als Beispiel für das Verhältnis von Sozialpolitik und Privatrecht in der Regierungszeit des Reichskanzlers von Caprivi', (1985) 102 *Zeitschrift der Savigny-Stiftung für Rechtsgeschichte (Germanistische Abteilung)* 130 ff.; Geyer (n. 47) 48 ff.

[51] Benöhr, (1974) 138 *Zeitschrift für das gesamte Handelsrecht und Wirtschaftsrecht* 494; Geyer (n. 47) 48.

[52] See, for example, Schubert, (1985) 102 *Zeitschrift der Savigny-Stiftung für Rechtsgeschichte (Germanistische Abteilung)* 146 ff.

debates. In 1891 they were examined at the annual meeting of the German Lawyers' Association, with the young Philipp Heck (subsequently to become one of the most influential German private lawyers and legal theorists) providing the key address.[53] By that time, close to 1,000 petitions had reached the *Reichstag*.[54] Only few of those who voiced their opinions questioned the necessity for intervention by the legislature. Very widely it was agreed that commercial freedom had to be restricted in a situation where one party, as a result of his inferior economic position, was effectively required to accept the conditions fixed by the other:[55] in a situation, in other words, where the principle of *pacta sunt servanda* typically could not be relied upon in order to achieve acceptable results. The Act concerning Instalment Sales prohibited forfeiture clauses;[56] apart from that it introduced mandatory rules protecting purchasers in cases of termination of the instalment sale and in situations of default of payment.[57] Significantly, its range of application was not confined to 'consumers'; it was to cover, above all, small-scale professionals, such as poorly off seamstresses, craftsmen, or piano teachers.[58] This is why a negative formula was chosen: the Act was not to apply, if the recipient of the object in question had been entered as a merchant into the commercial register.[59]

The Act concerning Instalment Sales was prepared between 1890 and 1894, i.e. roughly at the time when the so-called Second Commission revised the draft BGB. The mere chronology of events, in other words, would not have prevented the incorporation of the Act into the BGB. A number of the critics of the first draft of the BGB had in fact urged such inclusion.[60] Both the Department of Justice and the Second Commission, however, decided not to pursue this option.[61] Instalment sales had become both a mass phenomenon and an urgent problem. Since, in the early 1890s, it was not yet clear when the BGB would come into effect, a special Act could be, and was eventually,

---

[53] Philipp Heck, 'Wie ist den Mißbräuchen, welche sich bei den Abzahlungsgeschäften herausgestellt haben, entgegen zu wirken?', Gutachten, in *Verhandlungen des Einundzwanzigsten Deutschen Juristentages*, vol. II (1891), 131 ff.   [54] Eike von Hippel, *Verbraucherschutz*, 3rd edn. (1986), 193.

[55] See the references in Benöhr, (1974) 138 *Zeitschrift für das gesamte Handelsrecht und Wirtschaftsrecht* 499 ff.; Geyer (n. 47) 59.

[56] See §§ 1, 3, 5 *Gesetz betreffend Abzahlungsgeschäfte*.

[57] §§ 2, 4 II *Gesetz betreffend Abzahlungsgeschäfte*. § 4 I gave judges the right to reduce excessive penalty clauses; this rule was subsequently generalized: § 343 BGB.   [58] Geyer (n. 47) 54 ff.

[59] § 8 *Gesetz betreffend Abzahlungsgeschäfte*.

[60] Hermann Jastrow, 'Wie ist den Mißbräuchen, welche sich bei den Abzahlungsgeschäften herausgestellt haben, entgegen zu wirken?', Gutachten, in *Verhandlungen des Zweiundzwanzigsten Deutschen Juristentages*, vol. I (1892), 285 ff.; Wilhelm Hausmann, *Die Veräußerung beweglicher Sachen gegen Ratenzahlung (das sog. Abzahlungsgeschäft) nach dem Preußischen Allgemeinen Landrechte und dem Entwurfe eines bürgerlichen Gesetzbuches für das Deutsche Reich* (1891), 78 ff.; von Gierke (n. 20) 16 and *passim*.

[61] For details, see Benöhr, (1974) 138 *Zeitschrift für das gesamte Handelsrecht und Wirtschaftsrecht* 501 f.; Geyer (n. 47) 65 ff.; *HKK*/Duve (n. 12) §§ 1–14, n. 70.

adopted considerably earlier. Equally important was probably another consideration which was expressed by Gottlieb Planck in reply to Otto von Gierke. The BGB was supposed, by and large, to restate, rather than change, the existing law. Social innovation was to be left to special legislation, particularly if it was contemplated in response to very specific problems that had arisen comparatively recently with the result that the approach to be adopted was still a matter of political dispute and a well-established and time-tested set of rules that could be expected to last was not available.[62] The regulation of instalment sales, in other words, had not attained the level of doctrinal stability required for inclusion into a code that was envisaged to be something more than a permanent building site.

5. Early 'doorstep' legislation

Instalment transactions have, in fact, remained a major policy concern; the relevant regulations have repeatedly been amended, and the protection of the purchaser has been extended in the course of time.[63] Another important issue on the modern consumer protection agenda has been doorstep sales (or, to quote the language of the relevant European Union Directive,[64] contracts negotiated away from business premises). It was prefigured, in the late nineteenth century, by the problems associated with contracts concluded with pedlars.[65] Once again, the matter was dealt with by special legislation: the Act concerning Trade and Industry.[66] When it came into effect, in October 1869, it was designed, mainly, to establish freedom of trade.[67] But it also contained a number of provisions intended to protect the general public. Thus, pedlars had to obtain a licence, and a number of articles were excluded from their sphere of business.[68] The Act was repeatedly amended and, in particular, the range of excluded articles was considerably extended.[69] This was motivated by a desire to prevent the exploitation of purchasers who might be tempted to buy objects the value of which could not easily be assessed. In the course of the debate leading up to the amendments, the term 'consumer' came to be used, increasingly, in the place of 'general public'.[70] Once again, the relevant provisions were not

[62] Gottlieb Planck, 'Zur Kritik des Entwurfes eines bürgerlichen Gesetzbuches für das deutsche Reich', (1889) 75 *Archiv für die civilistische Praxis* 406 ff.   [63] See, for example, *infra*, n. 108.

[64] Council Directive 85/577/EEC of 20 December 1985, OJ L 372/85, 31.

[65] For a detailed discussion, see Geyer (n. 47) 9 ff.

[66] *Gewerbeordnung für den Norddeutschen Bund, Bundesgesetzblatt des Norddeutschen Bundes* (1869), 245; applicable in the German Empire as from 1873.

[67] For general background, see Hans-Peter Benöhr, 'Wirtschaftsliberalismus und Gesetzgebung am Ende des 19. Jahrhunderts', (1977) 8 *Zeitschrift für Arbeitsrecht* 187 ff.

[68] §§ 61, 56 *Gewerbeordnung*.   [69] For details, see Geyer (n. 47) 15 ff.

[70] Geyer (n. 47) 21 ff.

incorporated into the BGB. Special problems should be left to special legislation which could easily be amended and adapted to the changing needs of time.[71] In addition, the Act concerning Trade and Industry was still wedded to the traditional idea of preventing abuses of contractual freedom by way of public law regulation rather than by granting potential or disappointed purchasers rights and remedies against the other party. The policing of lawful trade was a matter for the State rather than the private parties to an individual transaction.[72] It was in the same spirit that innkeepers and bakers were required to inform the general public about the prices for their goods and services by displaying notices.[73] Pawnbrokers were only allowed to carry out their business after having obtained a licence.[74] The Trademark Acts of 1874 and 1894 can also be mentioned in this context; they were designed, in the first place, to protect businessmen from unfair competition but also, of course, had the effect of enabling purchasers to make better informed choices.[75]

6. Industrial workers, domestic servants, railway engines

The 'social question': in the late nineteenth century that was, above all, the question of how to regulate the position of industrial workers. It was hardly touched upon in the deliberations leading up to the BGB and the main reason for what appears to be, from a modern point of view, a surprising lack of concern was the conviction that what needed to be done had been done, or was about to be done, by way of special legislation.[76] Once again, many of the matters to be dealt with were not regarded as falling within the domain of private law. This applied to the emerging rules concerning industrial relations as much as to the social security legislation that has been mentioned.[77] But it also applied to most of the rules contained in the Act concerning Trade and Industry. The Act was amended in 1891, in response to an initiative of the Emperor.[78] The most important innovations were: the prohibition on work on Sundays, the protection of women and children from work during the night and below ground, the duty to issue work regulations, and permission to establish workers' committees. The legal relations of domestic servants and farmhands were also, incidentally, excluded from regulation within the BGB; the matter was left to legislation by the individual state within the German *Reich*.[79]

---

[71] Benöhr, (1977) 8 *Zeitschrift für Arbeitsrecht* 187, 216.
[72] For historical background see *HKK*/Duve (n. 12) §§ 1–14, nn. 67 ff.
[73] §§ 73 ff. *Gewerbeordnung*; for discussion, see Geyer (n. 47) 79 ff.
[74] § 34 *Gewerbeordnung* (as amended in 1879).   [75] For discussion, see Geyer (n. 47) 92 ff.
[76] For a detailed discussion, see Repgen (n. 22) 215 ff.   [77] *Supra* n. 38.
[78] See Repgen (n. 22) 220, 228.
[79] For details, see Thomas Vormbaum, *Politik und Gesinderecht im 19. Jahrhundert* (1980).

The various *Gesindeordnungen* were only repealed after the First World War. The same pattern of development, based on the idea of a division of tasks between the general private law codification and special legislation can, incidentally, be observed in other fields, most prominently that of liability law. From the 1830s onwards monstrous machines called railway engines had been steaming through the German territories, pulling carriages for the transportation of goods and persons but also, occasionally, wreaking death and destruction around them. As early as 1838 Prussia had set a precedent by imposing a strict liability law regime on railway owners.[80] It was a limited, and policy-based, deviation from the general principle of fault-based liability that was firmly entrenched in nineteenth-century pandectist scholarship.[81] This pioneering piece of legislation was followed by similar statutes in other German states;[82] and when in 1871 the Empire was founded, the *Reichstag* followed suit almost immediately. The Imperial Liability Act[83] which, albeit under another name and in a substantially expanded form, is still in force today,[84] provided for strict liability for harm to persons arising 'through the operation' of a railway. In a way, of course, this statute can be regarded, like the Act concerning Instalment Sales, as an early piece of consumer legislation; for specific protection was granted to those who travelled on the railway and who thus availed themselves (not of the goods but) of the services offered by the railway entrepreneur.[85]

7. Usury

There was one issue, however, that eventually prompted the *Reichstag* to amend the draft BGB. It had been a major policy concern since time immemorial:[86] the protection of borrowers against excessive interest rates. Until well into the nineteenth century, legislation imposing maximum rates had been in force, but in 1867 all restrictions on contractual interest rates were lifted.[87] But in the economic crisis following 1873,[88] when small-scale traders, artisans, and farmers

---

[80] § 25 *Gesetz über die Eisenbahn-Unternehmungen*. The Act was introduced under the aegis of Friedrich Carl von Savigny; see Theodor Baums, 'Die Einführung der Gefährdungshaftung durch F.C. von Savigny', (1987) 104 *Zeitschrift der Savigny-Stiftung für Rechtsgeschichte (Germanistische Abteilung)* 277 ff.   [81] *Law of Obligations* (n. 13) 1033 ff.

[82] See Justus Wilhelm Hedemann, *Die Fortschritte des Zivilrechts im XIX. Jahrhundert*, vol. I (1910), 88 ff.; Regina Ogorek, *Untersuchungen zur Entwicklung der Gefährdungshaftung im 19. Jahrhundert* (1975), 61 ff.

[83] *Reichs-Haftpflichtgesetz* of 7 June 1871; on the origins of which see Ogorek (n. 82) 98 ff.

[84] *Haftpflichtgesetz* (as re-promulgated on 4 January 1978).

[85] Strict liability eventually came to be conceptualized as a second 'track' of extra-contractual liability, apart from fault-based delictual liability; see *Law of Obligations* (n. 13) 1130 ff.; Nils Jansen, *Die Struktur des Haftungsrechts* (2003), 14 ff. and *passim*.   [86] See *supra* n. 13 and related text.

[87] *Bundesgesetzblatt des Norddeutschen Bundes* 1867, 159; for background information, see Landau (n. 47) 388 ff.   [88] On which see Nipperdey (n. 26) 284, 336.

increasingly required credit in order to be able to carry on their farms and businesses, it had become obvious that the lack of any restriction lent itself to abuse. Potential borrowers tend to be in urgent need of money and are not, therefore, normally in a position to negotiate the terms of the loan at arm's length. Characteriztically, the *Reichstag* reacted by criminalizing the objectionable conduct of moneylenders. The Act concerning Usury of 1880[89] amended the Criminal Code by introducing §§ 302 a–d; in addition, however, it also determined that usurious contracts were to be invalid. In 1893 the policy adopted by the Act concerning Usury was extended to other types of contracts apart from monetary loans;[90] also, those engaged in the business of credit transactions became subject to a duty to render an annual account vis-à-vis their contractual partners.[91] A Commission of the *Reichstag* established in early 1896 in order to vet the draft BGB eventually decided to adopt what was to become § 138 II BGB.[92] Following the pattern of the provisions contained in the Criminal Code, this rule renders void any legal transaction that satisfies two requirements: there has to be a striking disproportion in value between the performances promised or exchanged between the two parties; and the transaction has to have been brought about by way of exploitation of the distress, gullibility, or inexperience of the disadvantaged party. It was regarded as inappropriate to leave a rule so deeply affecting private law in a special statute outside the BGB.[93]

The rule of § 138 II BGB has to be read in the context of the time-honoured prohibition on contracts *contra bonos mores*,[94] as codified in its immediate vicinity: it merely specifies for one particular type of situation (disproportion in value between performance and counter-performance) what would otherwise have had to be deduced from the general standard contained in § 138 I BGB. Both §§ 138 II and 138 I are designed to keep commercial life, and legal relations in general, 'clean':[95] a legal system cannot countenance transactions which offend a just and fair-thinking person's sense of decency.[96] Compared to

---

[89]   *Wuchergesetz* of 24 May 1880, *Reichsgesetzblatt* 1880, 109.

[90]   § 302 e Criminal Code (*Strafgesetzbuch*), as introduced in 1893.

[91]   Art. 4 *Wuchergesetz*, as introduced in 1893.

[92]   See Geyer (n. 47) 46 ff.; generally on the history of usury legislation in the nineteenth century, see Klaus Luig, 'Vertragsfreiheit und Äquivalenzprinzip im gemeinen Recht und im BGB', in *Aspekte europäischer Rechtsgeschichte: Festgabe für Helmut Coing, Ius Commune* (Sonderheft 17) (1982), 171 ff.; Reinhard Zimmermann, *Richterliches Moderationsrecht oder Totalnichtigkeit?* (1979), 145 ff.; cf. also Hans-Peter Haferkamp, in Mathias Schmoeckel, Joachim Rückert and Reinhard Zimmermann (eds.), *Historisch-kritischer Kommentar zum BGB*, vol. I (2003), § 138, n. 12.

[93]   See Geyer (n. 47) 46; Zimmermann (n. 92) 148 ff.

[94]   On which see *Law of Obligations* (n. 13) 706 ff.

[95]   See, for § 138 II BGB, Hedemann (n. 82) 132.

[96]   This is the prevailing formula used in Germany to describe the intention of § 138 I BGB: RGZ 48, 114, 124; RGZ 55, 367, 373; RGZ 79, 415, 418; see, today, Theo Mayer-Maly and Christian Armbrüster, in *Münchener Kommentar zum Bürgerlichen Gesetzbuch*, vol. I, 4th edn. (2001), § 138, nn. 14 ff.

the clearly structured and restrictively worded § 138 II BGB, however, § 138 I BGB is notoriously uncertain and open to the dangers, and opportunities, of 'unlimited interpretation'.[97] It is hardly surprising, therefore, that the courts have fallen back on the latter provision when embarking on the process of 'materializing' German contract law that has been a characteristic feature of twentieth-century legal development.[98] In particular, they have used this rule in order to protect what they regarded as the structurally disadvantaged party to the bargain.[99] This could be a main debtor's impecunious spouse or child who was asked to sign a suretyship contract.[100] Or it could be a consumer who was charged an excessive interest rate by an instalment credit institution for a loan repayable by instalments.[101] Instalment credit transactions have provided German courts with an opportunity to establish what effectively amounts to a judicial price control. It was introduced for the protection of consumers, via § 138 I BGB, by side-stepping the restrictive requirements of § 138 II BGB. The relevant line of cases dates back to the late 1970s.

III. The Rise of Modern Consumer Legislation

1. The first period: until the end of the 1970s

a) Origins

By that time the issue of consumer protection had become the subject of a broadly based academic, political, and sometimes ideological debate. That debate was one of the many manifestations of an atmosphere of departure generated by the student protests in 1968 and the change of government in 1969. But it had also been stimulated by international developments sparked off, most prominently, by President Kennedy's Special Message to Congress on

---

[97] See the famous title of Bernd Rüthers' book: *Die unbegrenzte Auslegung: Zum Wandel der Privatrechtsordnung im Nationalsozialismus*, 6th edn. (2005).

[98] Claus-Wilhelm Canaris, 'Wandlungen des Schuldvertragsrechts—Tendenzen zu seiner "Materialisierung"', (2000) 200 *Archiv für die civilistische Praxis* 273 ff.; Hans Christoph Grigoleit, *Vorvertragliche Informationshaftung* (1997), 64 ff.; Heiderhoff (n. 9) 295 ff.; Rösler (n. 6) 61 ff.; cf. also Riesenhuber (n. 9) 553 ff. (from a European perspective). For a general historical analysis of the interpretation of § 138 BGB over the last century, see *HKK*/Haferkamp (n. 92) § 138, nn. 1 ff., 12 ff. (usury); for the use of this provision today, from a comparative and European point of view, Remien (n. 9) 345 ff. [99] See, in particular, BVerfGE 89, 214, 232 ff.

[100] Mathias Habersack and Reinhard Zimmermann, 'Legal Change in a Codified System: Recent Developments in German Suretyship Law', (1999) 3 *Edinburgh Law Review* 272, 275 ff.; *HKK*/Haferkamp (n. 92) § 138, nn. 5 ff.; and see *infra* pp. 207 ff.

[101] Volker Emmerich, 'Rechtsfragen des Ratenkredits', [1998] *Juristische Schulung* 925 ff.; *Münchener Kommentar*/Mayer-Maly/Armbrüster (n. 96) § 138, nn. 117 ff.; and see *infra* pp. 209 f.

Protecting the Consumer Interest.[102] 'Consumers, by definition, include us all', Kennedy had stated and had recognized a special obligation of the Federal Government 'to be alert to the consumer's needs and to advance the consumer's interests'. Moreover, he had specified four basic rights of all consumers: the right to safety, the right to be informed, the right to choose, and the right to be heard. In Germany, the Government published two reports on consumer policy, in 1971 and 1975, in which it undertook to improve the legal position of consumers.[103] That programme was implemented by a number of enactments starting with the Brokers Act of 1972:[104] brokers had to obtain a licence to carry on their trade, and such licence had to be refused to those who were unreliable or in financial difficulties. In 1973, a duty was established for businesses to mark their goods with a price. In loan transactions the effective interest rate had to be stated.[105] In 1974 the law relating to food production and distribution was fundamentally reformed in order to protect consumers from health risks and deception.[106] The Production and Distribution of Pharmaceutical Products Act followed suit in 1976.[107]

b) *Instalment sales, distance teaching, package travel*

In addition, the 1970s saw four important reforms affecting contract law. In the first place, the Act concerning Instalment Sales was amended so as to grant purchasers a right to revoke the contract within one week after having received a notice informing them about their right of revocation.[108] Secondly, distance teaching contracts were subjected to a comprehensive regulation.[109] Again, the customer was granted a right to revoke the contract, this time within a period of two weeks after having received his first batch of teaching materials.[110] A number of provisions often contained in distance teaching contracts were declared illegal, and advance payments were restricted to three months.[111] The Distance Teaching Act was necessitated by an increased desire of many Germans to improve their standard of education.

---

[102] Easily accessible in von Hippel (n. 54) 281 ff. For an introduction to the historical development of consumer protection, see *HKK*/Duve (n. 12) §§ 1–14, nn. 67 ff.; Heiderhoff (n. 9) 241 ff.; Mathias Schmoeckel, in Mathias Schmoeckel, Joachim Rückert and Reinhard Zimmermann (eds.), *Historischer Kommentar zum BGB*, vol. II (in preparation).

[103] The second of these reports is reproduced in von Hippel (n. 54) 295 ff.

[104] *Maklergesetz, Bundesgesetzblatt* 1972 I, 1465.

[105] *Verordnung über Preisangaben, Bundesgesetzblatt* 1973 I, 461.

[106] *Gesetz zur Gesamtreform des Lebensmittelrechts, Bundesgesetzblatt* 1974 I, 1945.

[107] *Arzneimittelgesetz, Bundesgesetzblatt* 1976 I, 2445.

[108] § 1 b *Abzahlungsgesetz* (introduced by the *Zweites Gesetz zur Änderung des Abzahlungsgesetzes, Bundesgesetzblatt* 1974 I, 1169).

[109] *Gesetz zum Schutz der Teilnehmer am Fernunterricht (Fernunterrichtsschutzgesetz), Bundesgesetzblatt* 1976 I, 2525; for discussion, see von Hippel (n. 54) 248 ff.

[110] § 4 *Fernunterrichtsschutzgesetz.*   [111] §§ 2 II, III, IV, V, 10 *Fernunterrichtsschutzgesetz.*

Germans of the 1970s did not, however, only want to be better educated; they were also very keen on travelling. In 1978, 56.8 per cent of the German population above the age of fourteen undertook one or several holiday trips, predominantly abroad.[112] The rapid expansion of tourism was facilitated, particularly, by the availability of inexpensive 'package tours'. As in the case of distance learning contracts, the way in which package holiday contracts were drafted usually put customers, often ill-informed about their destination, at a disadvantage. Again, therefore, the Government intervened by introducing a set of unilaterally mandatory rules strengthening the position of customers vis-à-vis the organizers of package holiday tours.[113] The organizers were no longer allowed to claim that they had merely acted as agents for those who were to supply the individual services if they had created the impression of being something more than mere brokers.[114] Moreover, and particularly, their liability in case of non-conformity was considerably tightened; thus, for instance, the customer was granted a claim for financial compensation for the immaterial detriment of having spoilt his holidays.[115] As for instalment sales and distance learning it was, at first, envisaged dealing with package tours by way of special legislation; eventually, however, the relevant rules were incorporated into the BGB[116] where they constitute an appendix to the law relating to contracts for work to be done (*locatio conductio operis*).

c) Standard terms of business

aa) A 'Page of glory' in the history of private law adjudication

The most important set of rules drafted, and enacted, in the field of contract law during the 1970s is that concerning unfair standard contract terms. This is true in spite of the fact that the Standard Terms of Business Act of 1976[117] did not substantially change the law; nor was it, strictly speaking, a statute aiming at the protection of consumers. The use of standard contract terms has a long tradition. It dates back, at least, to Roman sales and lease, and banking

---

[112] See von Hippel (n. 54) 255.

[113] §§ 651 a–651 k BGB, introduced by the *Reisevertragsgesetz, Bundesgesetzblatt* 1979 I, 505. By that time, however, the Federal Supreme Court had already mapped out the future direction of the law relating to package holidays in a number of leading cases; cf., in particular, BGHZ 61, 267; BGHZ 60, 14; BGHZ 63, 98; and see Klaus Tonner, 'Die Entwicklung des Reisevertragsrechts durch Rechtsprechung, Gesetzgebung und Verbandsverhandlungen', (1989) 189 *Archiv für die civilistische Praxis* 122 ff. That the regime set out in §§ 651 a ff. BGB is unilaterally mandatory follows from § 651 k BGB (old version; now: § 651 m BGB).   [114] § 651 a II BGB.

[115] § 651 f II BGB.

[116] For background information, see Klaus Tonner, in *Münchener Kommentar zum Bürgerlichen Gesetzbuch*, vol. IV, 3rd edn. (1997), Vorbem. § 651 a, nn. 20 ff.

[117] *Gesetz zur Regelung des Rechts der Allgemeinen Geschäftsbedingungen (AGB-Gesetz), Bundesgesetzblatt* 1976 I, 3317. In this instance, again, the Government decided not to amend the BGB, but tackled the problem of unfair standard terms of business by way of special legislation.

practice.[118] But it was only in the age of mass production following the Industrial Revolution that they started to present serious problems.[119] These problems resulted from the sheer frequency with which they were employed in legal practice and also from the fact that they were no longer drafted by an independent third party but by one of the contractual partners. Many of those who drafted standard terms of business could not resist the obvious temptation to tilt them in their favour and to displace the *ius dispositivum* contained in the BGB by a set of rules particularly favourable to their own interests. The courts reacted in a variety of ways. Thus, for instance, they availed themselves of the *contra proferentem* rule in order to resolve uncertainties in standard contract terms: the interpretation has to be adopted which is against the interests of the party who has drafted the terms and introduced them into the contract.[120] This was based, essentially, on a reasoning advanced by the Roman lawyers for their rule of *ambiguitas contra stipulatorem*: any ambiguity was attributable to the stipulator (i.e. the party who formulated the question which determined the content of the contract), for he could just as well have made it clear what he wanted the other party to promise to him.[121] In other cases the courts had argued that terms contained in a standard contract form could not be taken to have become part of the contract if they were 'surprising' to the other party.[122] To a considerable extent, of course, these rules of interpretation constituted covert tools for policing the substantive justice of standard terms of business.[123]

But in the course of time, the courts also arrogated to themselves a much more direct power to strike down unfair standard terms. Ludwig Raiser, the man who had written the first great monograph devoted to the topic,[124] referred to a 'page of glory' in the history of private law adjudication in Germany.[125] At first, from 1906 onwards, the Imperial Court had only objected to unfair standard terms of business if one party had been able to impose them on the other as a result of abusing the position of a monopolist. The doctrinal peg was the *contra bonos mores* provision of § 138 I BGB.[126]

---

[118] For references, see Sibylle Hofer, in Mathias Schmoeckel, Joachim Rückert and Reinhard Zimmermann (eds.), *Historisch-kritischer Kommentar zum BGB*, vol. II (in preparation) §§ 305–310 (Teil I), n. 2.

[119] Robert Pohlhausen, *Zum Recht der allgemeinen Geschäftsbedingungen im 19. Jahrhundert* (1978); *HKK*/Hofer (n. 118) §§ 305–310 (Teil I), nn. 2 ff.

[120] See, for example, RGZ 116, 198, 207; and see the analysis by Stefan Vogenauer, in Mathias Schmoeckel, Joachim Rückert and Reinhard Zimmermann (eds.), *Historisch-kritischer Kommentar zum BGB*, vol. II (in preparation), §§ 305–310 (Teil III).   [121] *Law of Obligations* (n. 13) 639 ff.

[122] BGHZ 60, 353, 360; BGHZ 54, 106, 109.

[123] For the dangers inherent in such approach, see Robert Fischer, Book Review (1963) 125 *Zeitschrift für das gesamte Handelsrecht und Wirtschaftsrecht* 202, 205 ff.; and, more generally, Karl Llewellyn, Book Review (1939) 52 *Harvard Law Review* 700, 703 ('Covert tools are never reliable tools').   [124] *Das Recht der Allgemeinen Geschäftsbedingungen* (1935).

[125] Ludwig Raiser, 'Vertragsfreiheit heute', [1958] *Juristenzeitung* 1, 7.

[126] RGZ 62, 264, 266.

Subsequently, the Court regarded it as sufficient that the party using the standard terms was carrying on an 'indispensable' trade and therefore, 'in a manner of speaking', had a monopoly.[127] The Federal Supreme Court in the first few years of its existence followed the same approach but then, from 1956 onwards, significantly extended its range of control by switching from § 138 I BGB to the good faith provision of § 242 BGB.[128] A standard business term was now regarded as invalid if, contrary to the precepts of good faith, it placed the other party at an unreasonable disadvantage. An unreasonable disadvantage was taken to exist, if the relevant term could not be reconciled with essential notions of justice and fairness, as expressed in the non-mandatory provisions of the German Civil Code from which the term proposed to deviate, or if the term restricted essential rights or duties arising from the nature of the contract. Very largely, the Standard Terms of Business Act of 1976 merely cast these, and a number of other rules developed by the Federal Supreme Court, in statutory form.[129] The power granted to the courts in § 9 openly to police the fairness of standard terms of business constituted its core component; it was specified by two long lists of individual contractual provisions that were to be regarded as objectionable.[130]

bb) Consumer protection?

In the years leading up to the Standard Terms of Business Act the pertinent political and academic discussions had been dominated by the notion of consumer protection. This specific perspective was due, largely, to the first report on consumer policy of 1971 where the Federal Government had committed itself to provide 'effective protection of consumers against unreasonable contract terms which improperly serve to pursue unilateral interests'.[131] Protection of the weaker party was now taken to be the aim legitimating the policing of standard business terms. It is a view that has proved to be surprisingly long-lived. It is still widely held today. For it is often said that the consumer 'submits' to the terms presented to him in view of the entrepreneur's psychological, intellectual, and, above all, economic superiority.[132] His unequal

---

[127] RGZ 103, 82, 83; cf. also, for example, RGZ 104, 308; RGZ 106, 386, 388; *Reichsgericht*, [1925] *Juristische Wochenschrift* 1395; RGZ 132, 305.

[128] *Bundesgerichtshof,* [1956] *Neue Juristische Wochenschrift* 908; *Bundesgerichtshof,* [1957] *Neue Juristische Wochenschrift* 1065; BGHZ 41, 151, 154; BGHZ 54, 106, 109 ff. For a comprehensive historical analysis and references to the pertinent case law and literature, see *HKK*/Hofer (n. 118) §§ 305–310 (Teil I), nn. 9 ff.

[129] See von Hippel (n. 54) 121 ff.; Jürgen Basedow, in *Münchener Kommentar zum Bürgerlichen Gesetzbuch*, vol. I, 4th edn. (2001), Einl. AGBG, nn. 10 ff.; *HKK*/Hofer (n. 118) §§ 305–310 (Teil I), nn. 20 ff.

[130] §§ 10 ff. AGBG. For comment in English, see Otto Sandrock, 'The Standard Terms Act 1976 of West Germany', (1978) 26 *American Journal of Comparative Law* 551 ff.; 562 ff.

[131] *Bericht zur Verbraucherpolitik, Bundestags-Drucksache* 6/2724, 8.

[132] Karl Larenz and Manfred Wolf, *Allgemeiner Teil des Bürgerlichen Rechts*, 9th edn. (2004), § 43, nn. 1, 7; Helmut Köhler, *BGB Allgemeiner Teil*, 26th edn. (2002), 259.

bargaining power is seen as the essential reason forcing the consumer to accept the contract on the basis of the other party's standard terms of business. It is a view, however, which is inconsistent with the fact that in exercising its power openly to control standard terms, the Federal Supreme Court had usually dealt with contracts concluded between two entrepreneurs.[133] Consumer protection had not, therefore, been the real reason supporting the courts' interventionist attitude. Consumers as well as businessmen tend to accept the proffered standard terms because they regard it as futile to invest time and money in studying a complex set of rules relating to rights and contingencies which do not usually materialize, in drafting alternative provisions, and in conducting long drawn-out negotiations; or in seeking out other firms whose terms may be more favourable to their own interests. If customers do not normally avail themselves of the opportunity to influence the standardized contents of the contract this is not because of the superiority of the entrepreneur, but because of the prohibitively high transaction costs involved in utilizing any such opportunity. We are dealing, therefore, with a partial failure of the market which may legitimately be corrected by means of judicial intervention.[134] This is confirmed by the observation that no effective competition exists concerning standard contract terms. Competition, in other words, is not likely to lead, and has not led in the past, to the emergence of fairly balanced sets of standard contract terms.[135] Significantly, therefore, and contrary to the original proposals,[136] the German Standard Terms of Business Act was not confined to contracts concluded by consumers; it was also, at least in principle, made to apply to businessmen.[137] The case law concerning the open fairness control under § 9 AGBG continued to be dominated by standard contract terms involving commercial transactions;[138] and if, according to § 24 I AGBG, the two lists of objectionable terms contained in §§ 10 and 11 AGBG were not to be applied to standard terms of business proffered by one businessman to another, this was not intended to mean that such terms could not be struck down under the general provision of § 9 AGBG. Subsequent court practice demonstrates that the indirect application of §§ 10 and 11 AGBG, via § 9 AGBG, also to standard terms accepted by businessmen has become the rule rather than the exception.[139]

---

[133] The point is emphasized in *HKK*/Hofer (n. 118) §§ 305–310 (Teil I), n. 20 (fn. 139).

[134] Jürgen Basedow, in *Münchener Kommentar zum Bürgerlichen Gesetzbuch*, vol. IIa, 4th edn. (2003), Vorbem. § 305, nn. 1 ff.; Hein Kötz, 'Der Schutzzweck der AGB-Kontrolle—Eine rechtsökonomische Skizze', [2003] *Juristische Schulung* 209 ff.; Remien (n. 9) 485 ff.

[135] *Münchener Kommentar*/Basedow (n. 134) Vorbem. § 305, n. 6.

[136] *Münchener Kommentar*/Basedow (n. 129) § 24 ABGB, n. 2.   [137] § 24 ABGB.

[138] See *HKK*/Hofer (n. 118) §§ 305–310 (Teil I), n. 28 (fn. 171).

[139] See Hans Erich Brandner, in Peter Ulmer, Hans Erich Brandner, Horst-Diether Hensen and Harry Schmidt, *AGB-Gesetz*, 9th edn. (2001), § 24, nn. 19, 22 ff.

d) Which 'model of society'?

Thus, by the end of the 1970s, consumer protection had made some advances. But the approach adopted was sector-specific. In the pertinent legislation, as far as it affected private law, the term 'consumer' was not used. Protection was granted not to consumers as such, but to purchasers who had entered into an instalment contract, to customers of distance teaching enterprises, to travellers who had booked a package holiday, and to those who had accepted the other party's standard terms of business. With one exception,[140] these concerns were dealt with by way of special legislation, i.e. outside the BGB. The protective mechanisms that had begun to crystallize were intended, partly, to enable the customer to make a better informed choice. But they also included a right of revocation and an open fairness control. In addition, many of the new rules were of a unilaterally mandatory character, i.e. the parties were not allowed to change them to the disadvantage of the purchaser/customer/traveller/contractual partner of the person who had drafted the standard terms of business. Academic discussions had generated a considerable amount of literature. One of the key issues hotly debated was whether, for the protection of consumers, a special branch of private law with its own distinctive evaluations had to be developed which was based on a different 'model of society' (*Sozialmodell*) than the general private law. This view, forcefully propounded by some,[141] was equally forcefully rejected by others who regarded it as an assault on the legal foundations of a liberal market economy that was ultimately inspired by socialist ideals. Proponents of the latter school of thought attempted to preserve the integrity of classical contract law as far as possible and to vindicate the model conception of the fathers of the BGB even within the modern consumer society: the law merely had to ensure that consumers were properly informed to make rational choices. This, in a nutshell, was the 'liberal information model'.[142] Predominantly, however, it was realized that the supply of information alone would be unable to resolve all problems. Other devices of a genuinely

---

[140] *Supra* n. 116.

[141] Norbert Reich, 'Zivilrechtstheorie, Sozialwissenschaften und Verbraucherschutz', [1974] *Zeitschrift für Rechtspolitik* 187 ff.; *idem, Markt und Recht* (1977), 49 ff., 193 ff.; Udo Reifner, *Alternatives Wirtschaftsrecht am Beispiel der Verbraucherverschuldung* (1979).

[142] See, in particular, Barbara Dauner-Lieb, *Verbraucherschutz durch Ausbildung eines Sonderprivatrechts für Verbraucher: Systemkonforme Weiterentwicklung oder Schrittmacher der Systemveränderung?* (1983); cf. also Manfred Lieb, 'Sonderprivatrecht für Ungleichgewichtslagen? Überlegungen zum Anwendungsbereich der sogenannten Inhaltskontrolle privatrechtlicher Verträge', (1978) 178 *Archiv für die civilistische Praxis* 196 ff.; *idem*, 'Grundfragen einer Schuldrechtsreform', (1983) 183 *Archiv für die civilistische Praxis* 348 ff. and, more recently, Wolfgang Zöllner, 'Zivilrechtswissenschaft und Zivilrecht im ausgehenden 20. Jahrhundert', (1988) 188 *Archiv für die civilistische Praxis* 91 ff.; *idem, Die Privatrechtsgesellschaft im Gesetzes- und Richterstaat* (1996); Peter Hommelhoff, *Verbraucherschutz im System des deutschen und europäischen Privatrechts* (1996).

protective character were required. However, they had to supplement rather than replace the mechanisms of the market.[143] But it remained unclear whether the relevant rules were of an exceptional character or whether, or to what extent, they could be reconciled with the basic principles underlying German private law. Thus, it remained equally unclear whether they should ideally be integrated into the BGB, or whether it was wiser to leave them where they were, i.e. predominantly outside the general code of private law.[144] What was clear was that the new rules did not, in themselves, constitute a coherent body of law. At the same time, they were not always as well drafted as rules of private law had traditionally been drafted in Germany. §§ 651 a–k, in particular, were widely regarded as an unfortunate stain on the BGB;[145] in the course of time, they have given rise to a host of difficult doctrinal problems.[146] The Standard Terms of Business Act, on the other hand, is generally considered to be a considerable achievement,[147] and the way in which it came to be accepted as an essential component of modern German private law can be told as a success story.[148] It has become the piece of legislation to which more commentaries have been devoted than to any other (including the BGB itself).

With the enactment of the new rules on package holidays in 1979, the German Government appeared to have lost its élan in the field of consumer legislation. The social-liberal régime was soon to collapse anyway, and the new conservative-liberal cabinet had different policy priorities. Thus, the field was left to the Commission of the European Union.

2. The European Community takes over

a) A promising field of activity

At about the same time as the Governments of the Member States of the European Union, the European Union itself had discovered consumer protection as a

---

[143] See, for example, the discussion in Harm Peter Westermann, 'Verbraucherschutz', in Bundesminister der Justiz (ed.), *Gutachten und Vorschläge zur Überarbeitung des Schuldrechts*, vol. II (1983), 1 ff.; Franz Bydlinski, *System und Prinzipien des Privatrechts* (1996), 708 ff., 718 ff.; Dieter Henrich, 'Verbraucherschutz: Vertragsrecht im Wandel', in *Festschrift für Dieter Medicus* (1999), 199 ff.; Josef Drexl, 'Verbraucherrecht—Allgemeines Privatrecht—Handelsrecht', in Peter Schlechtriem (ed.), *Wandlungen des Schuldrechts* (2002), 97 ff.; Heiderhoff (n. 9) 233 ff.; Wiedenmann (n. 9) 49 ff.

[144] For a summary of the arguments *pro* and *contra* these two options, see Pfeiffer (n. 7) 481 ff.; Wulf-Henning Roth, 'Europäischer Verbraucherschutz und BGB', [2001] *Juristenzeitung* 475, 484 ff.

[145] See, for example, Hans Hermann Seiler, in *Erman, Bürgerliches Gesetzbuch*, 10th edn. (2000), Vorbem. § 651 a, nn. 7 ff.

[146] For an overview of the system of remedies in case of liability for defects (§§ 651 c–g BGB) and its relationship to the general rules on breach of contract under the old law, before the modernization of the German law of obligations, see *Erman/*Seiler (n. 145) Vorbem. §§ 651 c–651 g, nn. 1 ff.

[147] Pfeiffer (n. 7) 500 ff.; Peter Ulmer, 'Das ABG-Gesetz: ein eigenständiges Kodifikationswerk', [2001] *Juristenzeitung* 491 ff.

[148] Manfred Wolf, 'Vertragsfreiheit und Vertragsrecht im Lichte der AGB-Rechtsprechung des Bundesgerichtshofs', in *50 Jahre Bundesgerichtshof: Festgabe aus der Wissenschaft*, vol. I (2000), 111 ff.

promising field of activity.[149] In 1973 the Commission established an office for the environment and consumer protection which was turned into an office for consumer protection in 1989 and raised to the level of an independent directorate general (for health and consumer protection) in 1995. The significance of consumer protection within the common market was stressed by the European Court of Justice in 1979 in the case of *Cassis de Dijon*.[150] 'Compelling reasons of public interest', it was held, could justify an infringement of the freedom to trade (as well as the other market freedoms), and consumer protection was specifically mentioned as an example of such compelling reason. In the meantime, it has become a 'community policy' to which an individual title within the third part of the EC Treaty is devoted. According to Article 153, the Community 'contributes' to the protection of the health, safety, and economic interests of consumers and to the promotion of their right of adequate information in order to safeguard 'a high level of consumer protection'. Some thirty directives have been issued since 1979 in the area of consumer protection,[151] about half of them affecting contract law, some of them tangentially, others profoundly. Unfair terms in consumer contracts, contracts negotiated away from business premises, consumer credit, distance contracts, contracts of sale relating to consumer goods, package travel; time share agreements: the respective rules of German law are all based on European Community legislation. This entails, *inter alia*, that they have to be interpreted in conformity with the European directives[152] and that the European Court of Justice has attained, at least potentially, an important role in private law adjudication.[153]

b) The beginning: doorstep selling, product liability, consumer credit

The German Government, at first, followed the pattern established by the Act concerning Instalment Sales to keep the new rules locked in special statutory

[149] For an overview, see von Hippel (n. 54) 17 ff.; Hans-W. Micklitz, in *Münchener Kommentar zum Bürgerlichen Gesetzbuch*, vol. I, 4th edn. (2001), Vor §§ 13, 14, nn. 23 ff.; Werner Berg, in Jürgen Schwarze (ed.), *EU-Kommentar* (2000), Art. 153, nn. 1 ff.; Brigitta Lurger, in Rudolf Streinz (ed.), *EUV/EGV* (2003), Art. 153, nn. 3 ff.; Remien (n. 9) 121 ff.; Heiderhoff (n. 9) 23 ff. For comprehensive discussion of the individual directives, see Stefan Grundmann, *Europäisches Schuldvertragsrecht* (1999); Norbert Reich and Hans-W. Micklitz, *Europäisches Verbraucherrecht*, 4th edn. (2003), parts II, III, and IV. [150] C-120/78 [1979] ECR 649.

[151] See the list compiled by *Streinz*/Lurger (n. 149) Art. 153, n. 40.

[152] Stefan Grundmann, 'Richtlinienkonforme Auslegung im Bereich des Privatrechts—insbesondere: der Kanon der nationalen Auslegungsmethoden als Grenze?', (1996) 4 *Zeitschrift für Europäisches Privatrecht* 399 ff.; Claus-Wilhelm Canaris, 'Die richtlinienkonforme Auslegung und Rechtsfortbildung im System der juristischen Methodenlehre', in *Im Dienste der Gerechtigkeit—Festschrift für Franz Bydlinski* (2002), 47 ff.; Heiderhoff (n. 9) 87 ff.

[153] A number of important decisions concerning the consumer contract directives (i.a. *Dillenkofer, Dietzinger, Oceano Groupo, Heininger*) are listed in *Streinz*/Lurger (n. 149) Art. 153, n. 41. For forceful criticism that problems of interpretation are not sufficiently frequently referred to the European Court of Justice by national courts of law, see Jürgen Basedow, 'Die Klauselrichtlinie und der Europäische Gerichtshof—eine Geschichte der verpassten Gelegenheiten', in Schulte-Nölke and Schulze (n. 9) 277 ff.

compartments. Thus, in January 1986 a Revocation of Doorstep Contracts Act came into effect which introduced a right for customers to revoke contracts concluded away from the business premises of the trader within one week. In view of the surprise element inherent in such transactions, it was regarded as appropriate to grant the customer some time in order to assess the obligations incurred by him. Even though the term consumer was not used, the Act essentially aimed at his protection,[154] for customers who had concluded the 'doorstep' contract as part of their professional activity were excluded from the range of application of the Act.[155] The Act, therefore, attempted to establish a new, substantive criterion in order to distinguish those who deserved to be protected from those who did not deserve such protection.[156] Earlier enactments had focused on more formal criteria, particularly on whether the customer had been entered as a merchant in the commercial register.[157] The scene was thus set for a considerable amount of debate surrounding the concept of 'consumer' underlying German consumer protection law; lack of conceptual clarity and uniformity became the subject of repeated criticism.[158] The Revocation of Doorstep Contracts Act had been preceded by more than ten years of discussion,[159] and it was passed a few weeks before the European Community issued its 'Directive to protect the consumer in respect of contracts negotiated away from business premises'.[160] The Directive, too, had been in the offing for many years,[161] and the discussions surrounding it had, of course, influenced the German debate. In fact, the German Act was regarded as an anticipated implementation of the Directive.[162] Certain differences in detail had to be taken account of by the way in which the provisions of the German Act were interpreted.[163]

Another important piece of European consumer legislation from about the same time—though not one affecting contract law—was the Directive 'on the approximation of the laws, regulations and administrative provisions of

---

[154] Peter Ulmer, in *Münchener Kommentar zum Bürgerlichen Gesetzbuch*, vol. III, 3rd edn. (1995), Vorbem. § 1 HausTWG, n. 1.   [155] § 6 no. 1 HausTWG.

[156] *Münchener Kommentar*/Ulmer (n. 154) § 6 HausTWG, n. 2.

[157] See Westermann (n. 143) 66 ff.

[158] See the contributions by Dieter Medicus and Meinrad Dreher, quoted *supra* n. 9; and see the evaluation by *HKK*/Duve (n. 12) §§ 1–14, nn. 78 ff.

[159] For references, see *Münchener Kommentar*/Ulmer (n. 154) Vorbem. § 1 HausTWG, n. 5.

[160] Council Directive 85/577/EEC of 20 December 1985, easily accessible in Oliver Radley-Gardner, Hugh Beale, Reinhard Zimmermann and Reiner Schulze, *Fundamental Texts on European Private Law* (2003), 69 ff.

[161] See *Münchener Kommentar*/Ulmer (n. 154) Vorbem. § 1 HausTWG, n. 6.

[162] See *Münchener Kommentar*/Ulmer (n. 154) Vorbem. § 1 HausTWG, n. 6.

[163] *Münchener Kommentar*/Ulmer (n. 154) Vorbem. § 1 HausTWG, nn. 8, 21.

the Member States concerning liability for defective products'.[164] It was implemented in Germany, one and a half years after it was supposed to have been implemented, by means of the Product Liability Act of 15 December 1989.[165] Since the Act did not go beyond the level of protection afforded by the German Federal Supreme Court under the general law of delict to those who had been injured by defective products, it has not made a significant impact on German law.[166] The third significant initiative completed in the period before the Member States of the European Community changed gear by committing themselves to the establishment of the internal market (Single European Act of 1987)[167] was the Directive 'for the approximation of the laws, regulations and administrative provisions of the Member States concerning consumer credit' of December 1986,[168] implemented in Germany by the Consumer Credit Act of December 1990. This enactment replaced the old Act concerning Instalment Sales.[169] It applied, beyond instalment sales, to all consumer credit transactions and was designed, at a time when the indebtedness of consumers had risen to a record level,[170] to provide consumers with adequate information on the conditions and cost of credit, on the content of the obligation they were about to incur,[171] and to protect them from disadvantageous conditions being imposed upon them concerning the discharge of their obligations and the consequences of their failure to discharge these obligations.[172] In addition, the consumer's right to revoke the contract within a period of one week, introduced into the Instalment Sales Act in 1974,[173] was not only preserved but extended to cover all consumer credit transactions.[174] This right of revocation, as well as a number of other details in the Act,[175] were not required by the Directive. The range of persons protected was defined in similar (though not identical) terms to the Doorstep Selling Act: it covered natural persons who did not receive the credit in the course, and for the purpose, of their professional activity. This time, the term 'consumer' was expressly used.[176]

---

[164] Council Directive 85/374/EEC of 25 July 1985, easily accessible in Radley-Gardner, Beale, Zimmermann and Schulze (n. 160) 187 ff.

[165] *Bundesgesetzblatt* 1989 I, 2198.

[166] See, for instance, Dieter Medicus, *Bürgerliches Recht*, 20th edn. (2004), nn. 650 ff.

[167] See *Streinz*/Lurger (n. 149) Art. 153, nn. 5 ff.

[168] Council Directive 87/102/EEC of 22 December 1986, easily accessible in Radley-Gardner, Beale, Zimmermann and Schulze (n. 160) 75 ff.   [169] On which see *supra* pp. 165 ff., 172.

[170] For details, see *Münchener Kommentar*/Ulmer (n. 154) Vorbem. § 1 VerbrKrG, nn. 7 ff.

[171] § 4 VerbKrG.   [172] §§ 11–13 VerbKrG.

[173] *Zweites Gesetz zur Änderung des Abzahlungsgesetzes* of 15 May 1974, *Bundesgesetzblatt* 1974 I, 1169.   [174] § 7 VerbKrG.

[175] See *Münchener Kommentar*/Ulmer (n. 154) Vorbem. § 1 VerbKrG, n. 14.

[176] § 1 VerbKrG. The term 'consumer' had entered German statutory language in the Act on the Reform of Private International Law of 25 July 1986: see Art. 29 EGBGB; Medicus (n. 9) 478 ff.

c) Changing gear: developments up to the Consumer Sales Directive
aa) Package travel and unfair terms in consumer contracts

The Single European Act invested the Council of the European Union with a comprehensive power to adopt measures for the approximation of the laws of the Member States 'which have as their object the establishment and functioning of the common market' (Article 100 a of the EC Treaty, now Article 95). All subsequent consumer protection statutes were to be based on this new provision.[177] First came the Directive on package travel, package holidays, and package tours (1990).[178] It required a number of amendments to §§ 651 a ff. BGB. The most important one provided protection to the customer in cases of insolvency of the organizer of the package deal.[179] Apart from that, the legal position of the traveller was strengthened by the imposition of a comprehensive network of duties of information on the tour organizer, the details of which were not incorporated into the BGB but enacted by way of subordinate legislation.[180] The Directive on Unfair Terms in Consumer Contracts of April 1993[181] constituted a milestone in the history of EC contract law regulation. For even though it did not significantly change the face of German law, it brought home the clear message that the European Union was prepared to interfere with core areas of contract law. For some time, the introduction of a fairness control concerning all provisions contained in consumer contracts had even been considered, no matter whether they were standardized or not.[182] Vociferous protests, particularly from Germany, had forced the European Commission to back down in that respect.[183] If the German Standard Terms of Business Act could be left largely unchanged, this was due to the introduction of § 24 a ABGB providing for an increased level of protection, in certain respects, for consumers faced with terms not individually negotiated contained in a contract concluded with an entrepreneur. Consumer protection had thus become a

---

[177] The standard formula at the beginning of the pertinent directives is: 'Having regard to the Treaty etablishing the European Community, and in particular article 100a (now: Art. 95) thereof . . .'.

[178] Council Directive 90/314/EEC of 13 June, easily accessible in Radley-Gardner, Beale, Zimmermann and Schulze (n. 160) 149 ff.

[179] § 651 k BGB; for comment, see *Erman*/Seiler (n. 145) § 651 k, n. 1 ff.

[180] §§ 651 a III–V BGB and *Verordnung über die Informationspflichten von Reiseveranstaltern* of 14 November 1994 (*Bundesgesetzblatt* 1994 I, 3436); the text is printed in *Erman*/Seiler (n. 145) § 651 a, n. 38.

[181] Council Directive 93/13/EEC of 5 April; easily accessible in Radley-Gardner, Beale, Zimmermann and Schulze (n. 160) 49 ff.

[182] Proposal for a Council Directive on Unfair Terms in Consumer Contracts, OJ C 243/2.

[183] Peter Hommelhoff, 'Zivilrecht unter dem Einfluss europäischer Rechtsangleichung', (1992) 192 *Archiv für die civilistische Praxis* 90 ff.; Claus-Wilhelm Canaris, 'Verfassungs- und europarechtliche Aspekte der Vertragsfreiheit in der Privatrechtsgesellschaft', in *Wege und Verfahren des Verfassungslebens: Festschrift für Peter Lerche* (1993), 873 ff., 887 ff.

second important policy objective underlying the German Standard Terms of Business Act.[184] At the same time, three different levels of protection were now envisaged by the Act: a lower level, as far as standard terms of business used vis-à-vis a business person were concerned; a higher level for consumer contracts; and the standard level for the remaining, but practically much less significant situations, such as the one of standard terms used in transactions between two consumers.[185]

bb) Timeshare agreements and cross-border credit transfers

Next came the Timeshare Agreements Act of December 1996[186] which was based on the Directive on the protection of purchasers in respect of certain aspects of contracts relating to the purchase of the right to use immovable properties on a timeshare basis.[187] Following a trend established in the United States, timeshare agreements had, in the course of the 1980s, become an increasingly popular proposition on the expanding holiday market, particularly in cross-border situations involving Southern European holiday resorts.[188] Aggressive sales methods and misleading advertising had induced holidaymakers, impressed by southern sun and sand, to enter grossly disadvantageous contracts. The principal devices employed by the Directive (and, consequently, the German Act) in order to protect purchasers in this situation were: an insistence on the supply of adequate information prior to the conclusion of the contract; the granting of a right of revocation within ten days after conclusion of the contract, and a prohibition on advance payments.[189] Both the Directive and the German Act used a neutral term ('purchaser', *Erwerber*) which, however, they defined in such a way that it approximated the concept of consumer. The Directive on cross-border credit transfers of January 1997[190] was not confined to consumers in whatever sense of the word. It was intended to improve cross-border credit transfer services and thus to promote the efficiency of cross-border

---

[184] *Münchener Kommentar*/Basedow (n. 129) § 24 a AGBG, nn. 5 ff.; Helmut Heinrichs, in *Palandt, Bürgerliches Gesetzbuch*, 61th edn. (2002), Einführung, n. 6; Remien (n. 9) 491.

[185] Dagmar Coester-Waltjen, 'Änderungen im Recht der Allgemeinen Geschäftsbedingungen', [1997] *Juristische Ausbildung* 272 ff.

[186] *Gesetz über die Veräußerung von Teilzeitnutzungsrechten an Wohngebäuden, Bundesgesetzblatt* 1996 I, 2154.

[187] Directive 94/47/EC of the European Parliament and the Council of 26 October 1994, easily accessible in Radley-Gardner, Beale, Zimmermann and Schulze (n. 160) 197 ff.

[188] Michael Martinek, 'Das Teilzeiteigentum an Immobilien in der Europäischen Union', (1994) 2 *Zeitschrift für Europäisches Privatrecht* 473 ff.

[189] For trenchant criticism of the German Act, see Michael Martinek, 'Das neue Teilzeit-Wohnrechtsgesetz—missratener Verbraucherschutz bei Time-Sharing-Verträgen', [1997] *Neue Juristische Wochenschrift* 1393 ff.

[190] Directive 97/5/EC of the European Parliament and of the Council of 27 January 1997, easily accessible in Radley-Gardner, Beale, Zimmermann and Schulze (n. 160) 159 ff.

payments. Significantly, this Directive was not implemented by way of special legislation, but by amending the BGB. At the same time, the new §§ 676 a–k BGB went far beyond what was required by the Directive, in that their range of application was not confined to cross-border credit transfers within the EC; these provisions were made to cover all cross-border credit transfers as well as all domestic credit transfers.[191] This may have been a reason prompting the German Government to include the respective provisions into the BGB. Also, we are dealing here with a special type of transaction which can be added, relatively easily, to the other types of transactions regulated by the BGB. The same approach had, previously, been adopted with regard to package tours.[192]

cc) Distance contracts

The implementation of the Directive on Cross-border Credit Transfers, though not geared towards consumer contracts, was to establish a pattern affecting the development of German consumer contract law. This became apparent when the Directive on the Protection of Consumers in Respect of Distance Contracts of May 1997[193] was implemented in June 2000. For even though a special piece of legislation relating to distance contracts was enacted,[194] the German Government also decided to change the BGB in certain respects. This was done in an attempt to provide a nucleus of general rules concerning consumer contracts and to establish consumer contract law as part of general contract law.[195] Thus, in particular, the lengthy new provision of § 361a BGB dealt with the details of the right of revocation granted to consumers not only by the Distance Contract Act but also by the Distance Teaching, Doorstep Selling, Consumer Credit and Timeshare Agreements Acts. It attempted to provide uniformity, as far as that was possible in view of the requirements established by the pertinent EC Directives in each specific context. Thus, the period within which the right of revocation may be exercised was standardized (two weeks). Where a contract is concluded on the basis of a sales prospectus, the right of revocation is usually replaced by a right of return. § 361 b BGB regulated circumstances in which this is permissible and how the right of return may be exercised.[196] Another provision (§ 241 a BGB) was introduced in order to deal with the delivery of

---

[191] For a critical evaluation of the new regime, see Dorothee Einsele, 'Das neue Recht der Banküberweisung', [2000] *Juristenzeitung* 9 ff.   [192] *Supra* n. 116.

[193] Directive 97/7/EC of the European Parliament and of the Council of 20 May 1997, easily accessible in Radley-Gardner, Beale, Zimmermann and Schulze (n. 160) 91 ff.

[194] *Fernabsatzgesetz* of 27 June 2000, *Bundesgesetzblatt* 2000 I, 897; for comment, see Herbert Roth, 'Das Fernabsatzgesetz', [2000] *Juristenzeitung* 1013 ff.; Christiane Wendehorst, in *Münchener Kommentar zum Bürgerlichen Gesetzbuch*, vol. II, 4th edn. (2001), 2117 ff.

[195] Peter Ulmer, in *Münchener Kommentar zum Bürgerlichen Gesetzbuch*, vol. II, 4th edn. (2001), § 361 a n. 7; *Münchener Kommentar*/Wendehorst (n. 194) Vorbem. § 1 FernAbsG, n. 15.

[196] The differences between a right of revocation and a right of return are explained in *Münchener Kommentar*/Ulmer (n. 195) § 361 b, nn. 11 ff.

unsolicited goods or the supply of unsolicited services by a business person to a consumer. Most importantly, however, the BGB was now amended by a definition of the key terms of 'consumer' (*Verbraucher*) and 'entrepreneur' (*Unternehmer*). Consumers are all natural persons effecting a legal act the purpose of which cannot be attributed to their trade or independent professional activity;[197] entrepreneurs are natural persons, or legal entities, or partnerships possessing legal personality, who in effecting a transaction, act in pursuit of their trade or independent professional activity.[198] As a result of the reform of June 2000, the BGB thus, in a way, contained several 'anchors'[199] to which the special rules outside the BGB could intellectually be tied. Core features of the Distance Contract Act itself were the provisions requiring suppliers to give adequate information prior to the conclusion of the contract and granting the consumer a right of revocation. While, therefore, the consumer was to be placed in as good a position as possible to make an informed choice, this did not change the fact that a consumer engaging in a distance transaction does not actually see the product or ascertain the nature of the service before concluding the contract. This was the reason advanced by the draftsmen of the Directive in support of the right of revocation.[200]

dd) Late payments, electronic signatures, e-commerce

In June 2000, a Directive on combating late payment in commercial transactions was enacted.[201] It was intended to improve the position of businesspeople faced with increasingly slack payment habits on the part of their debtors and had nothing to do with consumer protection. None the less, it affected a core component of the traditional rules relating to breach of contract: the concept of *mora debitoris*. Barely two months before the enactment of the Directive an Acceleration of Due Payments Act[202] had come into force in Germany pursuing exactly the same aim and amending § 284 BGB.[203] This Act was heralded as an anticipated implementation of the Directive. A comparison between the new § 284 III BGB and the requirements of the Directive, however, immediately revealed that both regulations were incompatible.[204] A reform of the reform

---

[197] § 13 BGB.   [198] § 14 BGB.

[199] Heinrich Dörner, 'Die Integration des Verbraucherrechts in das BGB', in Schulze and Schulte-Nölke (n. 9) 181 ff.   [200] See recital 14 of the Distance Contracts Directive.

[201] Directive 2000/35/EC of the European Parliament and of the Council of 29 June 2000, easily accessible in Radley-Gardner, Beale, Zimmermann and Schulze (n. 160) 59 ff.

[202] *Bundesgesetzblatt* 2000 I, 330.

[203] For detailed comment on the new § 284 III BGB, see Ulrich Huber, 'Das neue Recht des Zahlungsverzugs und das Prinzip der Privatautonomie', [2000] *Juristenzeitung* 743 ff.; cf. also Wolfgang Ernst, 'Deutsche Gesetzgebung in Europa—am Beispiel des Verzugsrechts', (2000) 8 *Zeitschrift für Europäisches Privatrecht* 767 ff.

[204] Ulrich Huber, 'Das Gesetz zur Beschleunigung fälliger Zahlungen und die europäische Richtlinie zur Bekämpfung von Zahlungsverzug im Geschäftsverkehr', [2000] *Juristenzeitung* 957 ff.

was, therefore, necessary and it was implemented on 1 January 2002, in the course of the modernization of the German law of obligations.[205] The Directive on a Community framework for electronic signatures of December 1999[206] had no specific consumer orientation; its implementation in Germany, however, necessitated both a special act (the Signature Act of May 2001)[207] and the introduction of two new provisions into the BGB.[208] The same approach was adopted with regard to the Directive on certain aspects of information society services, in particular electronic commerce, in the Internal Market of June 2000.[209] It was implemented, partly, by the Legal Framework for Electronic Commerce Act of December 2001,[210] and partly by the introduction of § 312 e into the BGB;[211] the latter step was taken as part of the modernization of the German law of obligations. § 312 e BGB aims to protect both entrepreneurs and consumers from the risks inherent in using 'information society services' in order to buy goods or obtain the supply of services, but consumers enjoy a higher level of protection. Consumer protection can, therefore, be regarded as one of the purposes pursued by the new provision.[212] The risks from which customers engaging in e-commerce are to be protected are (i) to enter into the contract without having been supplied with adequate information, and (ii) to place another order than the one intended by them, or to place the same order several times as a result of the way in which the 'information society service' has been programmed.

ee) Consumer sales

Finally, then, the Directive on certain aspects of the sale of consumer goods and associated guarantees of May 1999[213] which brought about the culmination of the new approach. For not only was the Directive used as the political trigger to implement a far-ranging modernization of the German law of obligations

---

[205] See the new § 286 BGB.

[206] Directive 1999/93/EC of the European Parliament and of the Council of 13 December 1999; easily accessible in Radley-Gardner, Beale, Zimmermann and Schulze (n. 160) 33 ff.

[207] *Gesetz über Rahmenbedingungen für elektronische Signaturen* of 16 May 2001, *Bundesgesetzblatt* 2001 I, 876.   [208] §§ 126 a and b BGB; cf. also § 126 III BGB.

[209] Directive 2000/31/EC of the European Parliament and of the Council of 8 June 2000; easily accessible in Radley-Gardner, Beale, Zimmermann and Schulze (n. 160) 3 ff.

[210] *Gesetz über rechtliche Rahmenbedingungen für den elektronischen Geschäftsverkehr* of 14 December 2001, *Bundesgesetzblatt* 2001 I, 3721.

[211] As far as the duties of information contained in Arts. 10 and 11 of the Directive are concerned, see § 3 *Verordnung über Informationspflichten nach Bürgerlichem Recht* of 5 August 2002, *Bundesgesetzblatt* 2002 I, 3002.

[212] Christiane Wendehorst, in *Münchener Kommentar zum Bürgerlichen Gesetzbuch*, vol. IIa, 4th edn. (2003), Vorbem. § 312 b, n. 5 and § 312 e, n. 3.

[213] Directive 1999/44/EC of the European Parliament and of the Council of 25 May 1999, easily accessible in Radley-Gardner, Beale, Zimmermann and Schulze (n. 160) 107 ff.

including, particularly, a reform of the law of prescription, breach of contract, and liability for non-conformity.[214] It was also taken to provide the appropriate opportunity for integrating a range of special statutes into the BGB. Since all of these statutes concern the protection of consumers, this step (which was not necessitated by the Consumer Sales Directive) must be seen as an expression of the German Government's desire to integrate consumer law and general law, as far as possible.[215] The statutes affected are the Standard Terms of Business, Doorstep Selling, Consumer Credit, Distance Contracts and Timeshare Agreements Acts. They have all been replaced by provisions contained in the BGB. Somewhat surprisingly, two other important consumer protection statutes, i.e. the ones on Distance Teaching and Product Liability, have remained untouched.

IV. Incorporation: The Law as it Stands Today

1. Definitions, unsolicited performances, standard terms of business

The new consumer protection provisions have been spread over the first two books of the BGB in an attempt to find appropriate niches within the system of the BGB. That system, as is well known, proceeds from the general to the specific: general part for the BGB as a whole (Book I), general part of the law of obligations (Book II, sections 1–6) and particular kinds of obligations (Book II, section 7; this is a section split into twenty-five titles, ranging from sale to delict). The general part of the BGB has been amended by the two definitions of the terms 'consumer' and 'entrepreneur' (§§ 13 and 14 BGB) mentioned above.[216] These definitions do indeed belong together in view of the fact that consumer contracts are defined as contracts between an entrepreneur and a consumer.[217] So, for example, protection is not granted to a consumer who has concluded a contract with another consumer. This has, incidentally, led some commentators to suggest that the entire subject matter should be regarded as a special branch of business law.[218] All the other consumer

---

[214] *Supra* pp. 1 f.

[215] See 'Diskussionsentwurf eines Schuldrechtsmodernisierungsgesetzes', in Claus-Wilhelm Canaris, *Schuldrechtsmodernisierung 2002* (2002), 66, 95; 'Begründung der Bundesregierung zum Entwurf eines Gesetzes zur Modernisierung des Schuldrechts', in Canaris (as above) 601 ff.; 'Bericht des Rechtsausschusses', in Canaris (as above) 1067 ff.   [216] *Supra* p. 185.

[217] § 310 III BGB.

[218] Stefan Grundmann, *Europäisches Schuldvertragsrecht* (1999), *passim*; *idem*, 'Europäisches Handelsrecht—vom Handelsrecht des laissez faire im Kodex des 19. Jahrhunderts zum Handelsrecht der sozialen Verantwortung', (1999) 163 *Zeitschrift für das gesamte Handelsrecht und Wirtschaftsrecht* 635, 665 ff., 669 ff.

protection provisions have become part of the law of obligations. The new § 241 a BGB on unsolicited performances has been mentioned;[219] it has obtained a prominent position within the provisions dealing with the 'subject matter of obligations'. The substantive provisions of the Standard Terms of Business Act have been slotted in, en bloc, by way of a new section 2 on 'the shaping of contractual obligations by means of standard terms of business' (§§ 305–310 BGB). The text of the new rules does not differ much from those contained in the old statute. There has been some rearrangement, and the number of provisions has been reduced from fourteen to ten. § 307 I 2 BGB now provides that an unreasonable advantage (as a result of which a provision in standard terms of business may be regarded as invalid) may also result from the fact that that provision is not clear and comprehensible. This is, however, nothing new since it is merely a statutory restatement of the transparency requirement developed by the courts under the old law.[220] The fairness control has been extended to employment contracts governed by the rules of labour law (§ 310 IV 2 BGB; but 'appropriate regard must be had to the special features of labour law').[221] The most important change, however, is not reflected in the text of the new rules. It results from the fact that the Modernization of the Law of Obligations Act has reformed, *inter alia*, the law relating to prescription, non-conformity in contracts of sale, and breach of contract in general,[222] and these reforms are bound to affect the standard for evaluating whether a provision contained in standard terms of business places the contractual partner at an unreasonable disadvantage.[223] For, according to § 307 II no. 2 BGB an unreasonable disadvantage is to be presumed to exist, if a provision 'cannot be reconciled with essential notions of justice underlying the statutory provision from which it deviates'. In particular, it remains to be seen whether, or to what extent, the new rules of German sales law which relate to the sale of consumer goods or which, even if they apply to contracts of sale in general, originate from the *Consumer* Sales Directive,[224] will be taken to embody such essential notions of justice.

---

[219] *Supra* pp. 184 f.

[220] BGHZ 104, 82, 92; BGHZ 106, 42, 49; BGHZ 106, 259, 264; BGHZ 108, 52, 57; BGHZ 115, 177, 185; *Palandt*/Heinrichs (n. 184) § 9 AGBG, nn. 15 ff.; *Münchener Kommentar*/Basedow (n. 129) § 9 AGBG, nn. 28 ff.; Ulmer, Brandner, Hensen and Schmidt (n. 139) § 9, nn. 87 ff.; and see Art. 5 of the Directive on unfair terms in consumer contracts.

[221] For details, see *Münchener Kommentar*/Basedow (n. 134) § 310, nn. 87 ff.

[222] *Supra* pp. 39 ff., 79 ff., 122 ff.

[223] See Joachim Hennrichs, in *Anwaltkommentar, Schuldrecht* (2002), § 307, n. 13; Helmut Heinrichs, in *Palandt, Bürgerliches Gesetzbuch*, 64th edn. (2005), § 307, n. 26; Astrid Stadler, in Othmar Jauernig (ed.), *Bürgerliches Gesetzbuch*, 11th edn. (2004), § 307, n. 10; W.-H. Roth, [2001] *Juristenzeitung* 475, 486 ff., 489; Harm Peter Westermann, 'Das neue Kaufrecht einschliesslich des Verbrauchsgüterkaufs', [2001] *Juristenzeitung* 530, 535 ff.   [224] *Supra* p. 97.

2. Particular forms of marketing

Section 3 ('Contractual obligations'), title 1 ('Creation, subject matter and termination') now contains a new subtitle on 'particular forms of marketing'. Here we find a regulation of the specificities concerning doorstep transactions, distance contracts, and e-commerce, particularly the granting of a right of revocation in the case of doorstep transactions (§ 312 BGB) and distance contracts (§ 312 d BGB), the right of return as an alternative to the right of revocation in distance contracts (§ 312 d BGB), a general provision concerning information to be given to consumers in the case of distance contracts (§ 312 c BGB), and another concerning the duties (including the duties of information) of an entrepreneur using a television or media service for the purpose of concluding a contract for the delivery of goods or the supply of services (§ 312 e BGB). All the rules contained in this subtitle (i.e. also the right of revocation concerning doorstep transactions)[225] now apply to consumer contracts, except for § 312 e BGB, where the two parties are referred to as 'entrepreneur' and 'customer'. All of these rules (including § 312 e BGB) are unilaterally mandatory, i.e. they may not be derogated from to the detriment of the consumer/customer. The common denominator of the three types of transactions covered in this subtitle is that they constitute forms of direct marketing.[226] Thus, it is not their content which puts them apart from other transactions but the manner in which they are concluded.

3. Right of revocation (general rules)

Another new subtitle introduced into the general part of the law of obligations provides general rules on the right of revocation in consumer contracts.[227] It covers the rights of revocation granted in the case of doorstep transactions (§ 312 I 1 BGB), distance contracts (§ 312 d I 1 BGB), timeshare agreements (§ 485 I BGB), consumer loan contracts (§ 495 I BGB), instalment supply contracts (§ 505 I 1 BGB), and distance teaching contracts (§ 4 I Distance Teaching Act), and it is based on §§ 361 a and b BGB which had been introduced one and a half years before the enactment of the Modernization of the Law of Obligations Act[228] in order to replace the previously prevailing chaotic coexistence of different rules and approaches[229] with as uniform a regime as

---

[225] See *supra* p. 180.

[226] Peter Ulmer, in *Münchener Kommentar zum Bürgerlichen Gesetzbuch*, vol. IIa, 4th edn. (2003), Vorbem. §§ 312, 312 a, n. 8.

[227] §§ 355 ff. BGB. This subtitle also covers the right of return, insofar as it is available to a consumer; cf. *infra* pp. 190 f.   [228] See *supra* pp. 184 f.

[229] *Palandt*/Heinrichs (n. 184) § 361 a, n. 3.

possible.[230] Thus, for example, the right of revocation is now regarded as a special instance of a statutory right to terminate the contract.[231] This means that, until the consumer exercises his right of revocation, the contract is valid.[232] Revocation, like termination, has the effect of transforming the contract into a winding-up relationship.[233] Save where otherwise provided, the provisions on statutory termination apply *mutatis mutandis*.[234] Notice of revocation has to be given to the entrepreneur within two weeks after the consumer has been informed clearly, and by way of a text supplied to him, about the details of his right of revocation. No reason has to be given for exercising the right of revocation.[235]

The new law also provides for a standardized period of six months from conclusion of the contract, after which the right of revocation ceases to exist.[236] As regards doorstep transactions, this rule is not in conformity with the respective European Community Directive.[237] This is why only a few months after the enactment of the new § 355 BGB its third paragraph was amended[238] by a sentence stating that, irrespective of § 355 III 1 BGB, the right of revocation does not cease to exist, if the consumer has not been duly informed about his right of revocation.[239] This very largely deprives the six-month period of its practical effect, and that not only for doorstep transactions but also for all other rights of revocation where such a step would not have been required under EC law. Thus, in many situations there will be no temporal limitation at all for the right to revoke, and the existence of the contract can be in jeopardy for a long time. This is hardly desirable.[240] Where a contract has been concluded on the basis of a sales prospectus, the right of revocation can sometimes be replaced by an unrestricted right of return.[241] Details concerning this right of return are

---

[230]   For comment, see *Münchener Kommentar*/ Ulmer (n. 195) § 361 a, nn. 1 ff.

[231]   *Münchener Kommentar*/Ulmer (n. 226) § 355, n. 9; *Jauernig*/Stadler (n. 223) § 355, n. 3.

[232]   For an extensive discussion of this approach, in comparison with the legal position prevailing before June 2000, see Peter Mankowski, *Beseitigungsrechte* (2003), 33 ff.

[233]   *Münchener Kommentar*/Ulmer (n. 226) § 355, n. 33.   [234]   § 357 I 1 BGB.

[235]   § 355 I 2, II 1 BGB.   [236]   § 355 III 1 BGB.

[237]   See Art. 4 (3) of Directive 85/577/EEC; ECJ Decision of 13 December 2001 (C-481/99) *Heininger v. Bayerische Hypo- und Vereinsbank AG* [2001] ECR I-9945.

[238]   This happened as part of a statute reforming the right of appearance of lawyers before Regional Supreme Courts: *Gesetz zur Änderung des Rechts der Vertretung durch Rechtsanwälte vor den Oberlandesgerichten* of 23 July 2002, *Bundesgesetzblatt* 2002 I, 2850.   [239]   § 355 III 3 BGB.

[240]   See *Münchener Kommentar*/Ulmer (n. 226) § 355, nn. 56 ff.; *Palandt*/Heinrichs (n. 223) § 355, n. 22; Sven Timmerbeil, 'Der neue § 355 III BGB—ein Schnellschuss des Gesetzgebers?', [2003] *Neue Juristische Wochenschrift* 569 ff.

[241]   See §§ 312 I 2, 312 d I 2, 503 I BGB. That the right of revocation can only be replaced by a right of return if the contract has been concluded on the basis of a sales prospectus, is not apparent from these rules themselves but follows from the reference in these rules to § 356 BGB: cf., for example, *Münchener Kommentar*/Ulmer (n. 226) § 312, n. 8; *Münchener Kommentar*/Wendehorst (n. 212) § 312 d, n. 112. On the significance of the term 'unrestricted' (right of return), see *Münchener Kommentar*/Ulmer (n. 226) § 356, n. 15.

specified in §§ 356 ff. BGB. It is a formalized type of revocation which follows very similar rules.[242] In particular, as for the right of revocation, the provisions on statutory termination apply *mutatis mutandis*.[243] Often a consumer will only be able to finance the goods to be delivered, or the services to be performed, by way of concluding a consumer loan contract with the entrepreneur offering the goods or services, or with a third party, i.e. typically a bank. As a result, he will be exposed to two creditors. §§ 358 and 359 BGB are designed to provide protection in cases where the loan serves to finance the other contract and where both contracts constitute an economic unit.[244] If the consumer has a right of revocation against the businessperson, and has exercised this right of revocation, he also ceases to be bound by the contract of loan.[245] The same also applies the other way round: if the consumer has revoked the loan transaction (this is possible under § 495 BGB), he also ceases to be bound by the contract for the supply of goods or services. The legal consequences of revocation of the one contract, in other words, are extended to the other contract. Details concerning the winding-up relationship now also existing with regard to the 'linked' contract are provided in § 358 IV BGB. § 359 BGB also deals with linked contracts, though not with rights of revocation: the consumer may also raise defences available to him under the contract financed by the consumer loan transaction against the party with whom he has concluded that consumer loan transaction. All the provisions contained in the subtitle on rights of revocation and return in consumer contracts, with two small exceptions,[246] are unilaterally mandatory. This has not been specifically stated but may be gathered by way of interpretation.[247]

4. Sale of consumer goods

The regulation of 'Particular types of obligations' commences with the contracts of sale and exchange (section 8, title 1). Here we find a new subtitle on the 'sale of consumer goods' (§§ 474–479). The label (in German, *Verbrauchsgüterkauf*) is misleading in view of the fact that the provisions in this subtitle do not deal with the sale of a specific type of goods but with the sale of movables from an entrepreneur to a consumer in general.[248] Obviously, §§ 474 ff. BGB constitute a set of special rules implementing the Consumer Sales

---

[242] Formalized, in so far as it can only be exercised 'by return of the thing or, if it cannot be dispatched as a parcel, by a demand for collection': § 356 II BGB.   [243] § 357 I BGB

[244] For background information, see *Münchener Kommentar*/Ulmer (n. 226) § 358, nn. 1 ff.

[245] § 358 I BGB.   [246] §§ 356 I 1, 357 II 3 BGB.

[247] *Münchener Kommentar*/Ulmer (n. 226) § 355, n. 4; *Jauernig*/Stadler (n. 223) § 355, n. 2.

[248] Florian Faust, in Heinz Georg Bamberger and Herbert Roth (eds.), *Kommentar zum Bürgerlichen Gesetzbuch*, vol. I (2003), § 474, n. 3.

Directive. Since, however, the regulatory model contained in that Directive has largely found its way into the new *general* law of sale,[249] only a few additional rules were necessary for 'consumer sales'. Most importantly, § 475 BGB declares the provisions of general sales law on the seller's liability for non-conformity, as well as the provisions relating to consumer sales themselves, to be unilaterally mandatory in favour of the purchaser/consumer.[250] In addition, there is a presumption that an object, which turns out to be defective within six months after it has been handed over to the purchaser, was already defective at the time when it was handed over, unless such presumption is incompatible with the nature of the object or of the defect.[251] There are special provisions for warranties, for the seller's right of recourse against the entrepreneur from whom he himself had previously bought the object, and on the prescription of these rights of recourse.[252] Title 1 ('Sale, exchange') is now followed by a new title 2 devoted to timeshare agreements (§§ 481–487 BGB). It serves the purpose of incorporating the provisions of the Timeshare Agreements Act into the BGB. A definition of the concept of 'timeshare agreements' is followed by provisions imposing the duty on an entrepreneur who offers a timeshare agreement to issue a prospectus containing detailed information, specifying the language of the contract and of the prospectus, imposing a form requirement for timeshare agreements, granting the consumer a right of revocation, and establishing a prohibition on advance payments. All provisions of this title are unilaterally mandatory.[253]

5. Credit transactions

The Consumer Credit Act used to be one of the most important consumer protection statutes. Its incorporation into the BGB provided the Government with a welcome opportunity to revise the entire law relating to credit transactions, particularly contracts of loan. The old rules, contained in §§ 607 ff. BGB, were regarded as outdated,[254] particularly since they still appeared to perpetuate, conceptually, the Roman notion of a 'real' contract:[255] a contract which comes into existence with the handing over of an

---

[249] *Supra* p. 97.   [250] For details, see Faust (n. 248) § 475, nn. 3 ff.

[251] § 476 BGB. Nature of the object: objects the durability of which does not come close to six months (food); see 'Motivation to the Discussion Draft of the Law of Obligations Modernization Act', in Canaris (n. 215) 296; nature of the defect: diseases in animals that have been sold; see Faust (n. 248) § 476, n. 4.   [252] §§ 477–479 BGB.

[253] § 487 BGB.

[254] See the 'Motivation to the Government Draft of the Law of Obligations Modernization Act', in Canaris (n. 215) 884.

[255] Dieter Medicus, *Schuldrecht II*, 12th edn. (2004), n. 287; Johannes Köndgen, 'Modernisierung des Darlehensrechts: eine Fehlanzeige', in Ernst and Zimmermann (n. 7) 457 ff.

object (or, in this case, a sum of money).[256] The history of the reform was brief but turbulent. The so-called Discussion Draft had contained a set of rules which were widely regarded as entirely unsatisfactory,[257] for example, it had failed to provide for contracts for the loan of a thing.[258] As a result of the criticism, a number of changes were made which have led to the following pattern of regulation. What used to be the contract of loan is now split between contracts for the loan of a thing (§§ 607–609 BGB) and contracts of loan (meaning contracts for the loan of a sum of money; §§ 488–498 BGB). The latter have become part of a new title 3 on 'Contracts of loan; financing aids and instalment supply contracts between an entrepreneur and a consumer'. Loan brokerage contracts between an entrepreneur and a consumer have found their new place in §§ 655 a–655 e BGB, as part of title 10 on brokerage contracts. The new rules on contracts for the loan of a sum of money constitute a modernized version of the old rules on contracts of loan in general (§§ 488–490 BGB). They are supplemented by a number of provisions specifically dealing with consumer loan contracts (i.e. loan contracts for remuneration between an entrepreneur and a consumer). Here we find, *inter alia*, a form requirement,[259] detailed duties of information on the part of the businessperson vis-à-vis the consumer,[260] a regulation of the legal consequences of non-compliance with the form requirement,[261] the consumer's right of revocation,[262] and provisions on the treatment of default interest, the attribution of part performance, and repayment of the entire loan in the case of loans payable in instalments.[263]

A new subtitle is devoted to financing aids (extension of time for payment and other financing aids).[264] Most of the rules concerning consumer loan contracts apply *mutatis mutandis*.[265] For instalment payment transactions (i.e. the most important form of 'extension of time for payment') and finance leasing contracts (i.e. the most important form of 'another financing aid') special rules have been enacted.[266] Instalment supply contracts between an entrepreneur and a consumer are covered by § 505 BGB. In the tradition of § 1 c of the Instalment Sales Act and, subsequently, § 2 Consumer Credit Act, the consumer is granted a right of revocation even though we are not dealing with a credit transaction. All the provisions just mentioned, with the exception of those on contracts for loan of a thing and on contracts of loan in general, are

---

[256] See *Law of Obligations* (n. 13) 153 ff., 163 ff.

[257] See Köndgen (n. 255) 457 ff.; Peter Bülow, 'Kreditvertrag und Verbraucherkreditrecht im BGB', in Schulze and Schulte-Nölke (n. 9) 153 ff.

[258] See the criticism raised by Teichmann, Huber and Koller at the Regensburg meeting of German professors of private law: Ernst and Zimmermann (n. 7), 479.   [259] § 492 I 1–3 BGB.

[260] § 492 I 5 BGB.   [261] § 494 BGB.   [262] § 495 BGB.   [263] §§ 497, 498 BGB.

[264] §§ 499–504 BGB.   [265] § 499 I BGB.

[266] § 499 II in connection with §§ 500–504 BGB.

unilaterally mandatory.[267] The provisions of §§ 491–506 BGB not just apply to consumers in the sense of § 13 BGB, but also to those to whom a loan, extension of time for payment, or other financing aid is granted for the taking up of a trade or self-employed professional activity, or who conclude an instalment supply contract for that purpose, unless the net amount of the loan, or the cash price, exceeds €50,000.[268] This extension of the protection granted to consumers is based on a provision of the Consumer Credit Act; it was not required by the Consumer Credit Directive.[269]

6. Package travel

Finally, of course, there is the codification of the package travel contract in §§ 651 a ff. BGB. The respective subtitle was incorporated into the BGB in 1979[270] and amended, as a result of the package travel Directive, in 1990.[271] Further amendments were made in July 2001 (Second Package Travel Provisions Amendment Act) and yet again, in November 2002 (Modernization of the Law of Obligations Act).[272] All provisions concerning package travel (with one exception)[273] are unilaterally mandatory.[274] Even today the person to whom protection is granted is referred to as the 'traveller', i.e. §§ 651 a ff. BGB have not been tied to the consumer concept of § 13 BGB.

V. General Comments

1. Consumer contract law and the EC

This, in brief outline, is the law as it stands today. A few comments may be apposite.

In the first place it is open to doubt to what extent the European Union, which has dominated the development of consumer contract law over the past twenty-five years, is competent to regulate this area of the law. All of the Directives mentioned above have been based on Article 95 EC Treaty (i.e. Article 100 a, according to the old numbering); or, more precisely, and in the words of

---

[267] §§ 506, 655 e BGB.   [268] § 507 BGB.
[269] Cosima Möller and Christiane Wendehorst, in Heinz Georg Bamberger and Herbert Roth (eds.), *Kommentar zum Bürgerlichen Gesetzbuch*, vol. I (2003), § 507, nn. 1, 3.
[270] *Supra* p. 173.   [271] *Supra* p. 182.
[272] For details of the rules that were amended on both occasions, see Hartwig Sprau, in *Palandt, Bürgerliches Gesetzbuch*, 64th edn. (2005) Einf. v. § 651 a, n. 2.
[273] §§ 651 g II BGB (extinctive prescription).   [274] § 651 m BGB.

the Directives themselves, 'in particular' Article 95.[275] In its decision on the Tobacco Advertising Directive, the European Court of Justice has, however, emphasized that the European Community may only adopt measures for the approximation of the laws prevailing in the Member States if they aim at improving the functioning of the internal market.[276] This can only be the case if the divergence of the respective national rules constitutes an impediment to free trade or leads to noticeable distortions of competition.[277] In view of these strict standards, many provisions of the consumer protection Directives rest on fragile foundations. For it is less than obvious, to mention one example, that the introduction of a right of revocation in doorstep sales—i.e. the introduction of a legal device *hampering* direct marketing—should be able to remove trade barriers between the Member States of the EU.[278] Moreover, the Member States are not usually prevented from adopting or maintaining more favourable provisions for the protection of consumers.[279] This is an indication that the real aim pursued by the EC is the promotion of a certain minimum level of consumer protection across all Member States rather than the removal of supposed trade barriers resulting from a diversity of levels of protection in the Member States. Noticeable distortions of competition are also often more pretended than real; in doorstep selling situations, for example, they can hardly arise given the fact that all traders compete, on equal terms, under the conditions prevailing on the respective sales markets. For, according to Article 5 of the Rome Convention on the law applicable to contractual obligations, the mandatory rules of the law of the country in which the consumer has his habitual residence are applicable to these types of consumer contracts.[280] The Consumer Sales Directive, apart from stating, but not making plausible, that 'competition between sellers may be distorted' as a result of the fact that the laws of the Member States concerning consumer sales 'are somewhat disparate',[281] also evokes the notion of the confident consumer when it states that 'the creation of a common set of minimum rules of consumer law, valid no matter where goods are purchased within the Community, will strengthen consumer confidence and enable consumers to make the most of the internal market'.[282]

[275] *Supra* n. 177; cf. also Heiderhoff (n. 9) 223 ff. On the phenomenon of 'competence creep' in the present context, Stephen Weatherill, 'Why Object to the Harmonization of Private Law by the EC?', (2004) 12 *European Review of Private Law* 634 ff.

[276] ECJ Decision of 5 October 2000, *Germany v. European Parliament* (C-481/99) [2000] ECR I-8419; generally on the role of the European Court of Justice see, most recently, Heiderhoff (n. 9) 94 ff.

[277] ECJ Decision of 5 October 2000, *Germany v. European Parliament* (C-481/99) [2000] ECR I-8419.   [278] Wulf-Henning Roth, [2001] *Juristenzeitung* 475, 477.

[279] The problem of harmonization on the basis of a minimum standard is discussed, in the present context, by Helmut Heiss, 'Verbraucherschutz im Binnenmarkt: Art. 129 a EGV und die wirtschaftlichen Verbraucherinteressen', (1996) 4 *Zeitschrift für Europäisches Privatrecht* 637 ff.; Heiderhoff (n. 9) 38 ff.   [280] Wulf-Henning Roth, [2001] *Juristenzeitung* 475, 477 ff.

[281] Directive 1999/44/EC, third recital.   [282] Directive 1999/44/EC, fifth recital.

Consumers, in other words, can be prevented from entering into cross-border purchases because they may be faced with different and unfamiliar legal rules. If this consideration were taken to constitute a valid basis for legal harmonization, it would provide the EC with the competence to harmonize the entire law of contract (as well as adjacent areas of the law, like the rules on unjustified enrichment):[283] a conclusion which is usually not accepted today.[284] Whether, and to what extent, future Directives in the field of consumer contract law may be based on Article 153 rather than Article 95 EC Treaty remains to be seen. It depends, essentially, on whether such Directives can be understood as 'measures which support, supplement and monitor the policy pursued by the Member States' in the field of consumer protection; for Article 153 (3) (b) specifically empowers the Community to adopt such measures in order to 'contribute' to the attainment of 'a high level of consumer protection'.[285]

2. Being caught by surprise

If, in the course of the 1980s and 1990s, German lawyers had become used to the idea that the development of German consumer contract law was ultimately determined in Brussels, that one Directive after another had to be transformed into national law, and that, as a result, a patchwork of special statutes had been added to the tapestry of private law, they were caught off-guard by the decision of the *German* Government to incorporate these statutes into the BGB.[286] In hindsight, of course, they might have been alerted by the way in which the Government had started to place 'anchors' for consumer protection statutes into the BGB in the course of implementing the Distance Contracts Directive.[287] But that had been in June 2000, a mere fifteen months before the Discussion Draft for a Modernization of the Law of Obligations Act was published. The *one* surprise contained in the Discussion Draft was the decision

---

[283] See W.-H. Roth, [2001] *Juristenzeitung* 475, 478 ff.

[284] For the interpretation of Art. 95, in the light of the decision of the ECJ on the Tobacco Advertising Directive, see, along these lines, Wulf-Henning Roth, 'Die Schuldrechtsmodernisierung im Kontext des Europarechts', in Ernst and Zimmermann (eds.) (n. 7) 231 ff.; Riesenhuber (n. 9) 135 ff.; Rösler (n. 6) 284 ff.; but see Reich and Micklitz (n. 149) 1.21 ff.; Heiderhoff (n. 9) 29 f., 220 ff.

[285] *Streinz*/Lurger (n. 149) Art. 153, nn. 34 ff.; Heiderhoff (n. 9) 28 ff.; Wiedenmann (n. 9) 48. Art. 153 (3) a EU Treaty does not provide the EU with a competency to regulate consumer affairs; see Werner Berg, in Jürgen Schwartze (ed.), *EU-Kommentar* (2000), Art. 153, n. 14; but cf. also *Streinz*/Lurger (n. 149) Art. 153, nn. 32 ff.

[286] Barbara Dauner-Lieb, 'Die geplante Schuldrechtsmodernisierung—Durchbruch oder Schnellschuss', [2001] *Juristenzeitung* 8 ff.; Heinrich Honsell, 'Einige Bemerkungen zum Diskussionsentwurf eines Schuldrechtsmodernisierungsgesetzes', [2001] *Juristenzeitung* 18 ff.; Reinhard Zimmermann, 'Schuldrechtsmodernisierung?', [2001] *Juristenzeitung* 171 ff.

[287] *Supra* n. 199. *Münchener Kommentar*/Micklitz (n. 149) Vorbem. §§ 13, 14, n. 1 refer to 'a kind of revolution' in this respect.

to use the Consumer Sales Directive, and the necessity of implementing it, as a vehicle for fundamentally reforming the German law of obligations; for the Directive could have been implemented by a few, relatively marginal, changes to the then existing German law of sale.[288]

Of course, it was well known that a blueprint existed for a reform of the German law of obligations; it was contained in the final report of the Commission charged with the revision of the law of obligations.[289] That report had been published in 1992. But the scope of the reform envisaged by the Commission was confined to the law of breach of contract, liability for non-conformity in contracts of sale and contracts for work, and extinctive prescription. This, then, was the *second* surprise hidden in the pages of the Discussion Draft: the Government had decided to revive an issue that had initially been on the reform agenda but had, in the meantime, been dropped:[290] the incorporation of consumer protective legislation into the BGB. The report of the Reform Commission was thus amended accordingly. The main problem associated with this way of proceeding was, however, that the matter had hardly been discussed. And since barely one and a half years were left before the reform was to enter into effect, not many of the issues could now be subjected to close scrutiny.[291] It is obvious that the quality of reform has suffered from this lack of time for reflection.

3. A newly gained transparency?

The incorporation of the consumer protection legislation into the BGB has not been comprehensive. The Distance Teaching and Product Liability Acts continue to exist (as does the Product Safety Act of April 1997).[292] There is a Duties of Information in Private Law Regulation[293] which specifies the duties of information in the case of distance contracts (§ 1), timeshare agreements (§ 2), e-commerce (§ 3), and package travel contracts (§§ 4–11); in addition it details the duties of information of credit institutions vis-à-vis their clients concerning the transfer of payments (§§ 12 ff.). Procedural aspects of consumer protection are dealt with by an Injunctions Act, as promulgated in August 2002.[294] Certain

---

[288] *Supra* p. 33, n. 186.   [289] *Supra* p. 32.   [290] *Supra* pp. 30, 32.

[291] For the main contributions to the debate, see Roth (n. 284) 225 ff.; Pfeiffer (n. 7) 481 ff.; Jürgen Schmidt-Räntsch, Heinrich Dörner, Hans-W. Micklitz and Peter Ulmer, all in Schulze and Schulte-Nölke (n. 9) 169 ff.; W.-H. Roth, [2001] *Juristenzeitung* 475 ff.; Ulmer, [2001] *Juristenzeitung* 491 ff.

[292] *Produktsicherheitsgesetz, Bundesgesetzblatt* I 1997, 934.

[293] *Verordnung über Informations- und Nachweispflichten nach bürgerlichem Recht, Bundesgesetzblatt* I 2002, 3002.

[294] *Gesetz über Unterlassungsklagen bei Verbraucherrechts- und anderen Verstößen, Bundesgesetzblatt* 2002 I, 3422.

associations are given the right to sue those who use, or recommend for use, standard terms of business infringing the provisions of §§ 307–309 BGB, or who contravene in any other manner provisions which serve to protect consumers. The Act contains a list of statutes which are to be treated as serving the protection of consumers,[295] and it specifies the range of associations which may bring an action.[296] The action aims at putting to an end objectionable practices as effectively as possible. Consumers, therefore, cannot gauge how far, and in what respect, they enjoy legal protection by glancing through the BGB; they have to refer to a number of other statutory instruments.

The transparency of consumer protection under the BGB also leaves much to be desired. Thus, for example, §§ 355 ff. BGB are designed to provide uniform rules concerning rights of revocation and return in consumer contracts. Yet, a number of modifications concerning the legal consequence of revocation and return are contained in special rules, such as § 495 II 1 BGB, § 485 V BGB and § 4 III Distance Teaching Act. The reader is alerted to these modifications by the phrase 'save where otherwise provided' contained in § 357 BGB. But there are also special provisions establishing additional, or different, requirements for the right of revocation under § 355 BGB, even though that rule does not contain a similar proviso. § 4 I 2 Distance Teaching Act and §§ 312 d, 312 e III 2 and 485 IV BGB have to be mentioned in this context. Contrary to the somewhat simplistic expectations of the draftsmen of the reform legislation, the assessment of a consumer's legal position still requires a considerable amount of legal skill. § 13 BGB has also, so far, failed to achieve conceptual uniformity, for both the Distance Teaching Act and §§ 651 a ff. BGB are consumer protection statutes[297] but continue to use their own terminology in order to define the range of those to be protected. Persons taking up a trade or self-employed professional activity are treated as consumers in the context of the transactions described in § 507 BGB.

4. The new provisions and the system of the BGB

One of the characteristic features of a codification is its systematic nature.[298] It is based on the belief that the legal material does not constitute an indigestible and arbitrary mass of individual rules and cases but that it can be reduced to a rational system. Codification thus promotes the internal coherence of the law and facilitates its comprehensibility. The German Civil Code used to be a showpiece for the truth of this assertion. The draftsmen of the reform legislation have

---

[295] § 2 UKlaG.   [296] § 4 UKlaG.   [297] See § 2 II nos. 1 and 3 UKlaG.

[298] Reinhard Zimmermann, 'Codification: History and Present Significance of an Idea', (1995) 3 *European Review of Private Law* 95 ff.; Jürgen Basedow, 'Das BGB im künftigen europäischen Privatrecht: Der hybride Kodex', (2000) 200 *Archiv für die civilistische Praxis* 465 ff.

attempted to preserve the system of the BGB and to find appropriate systematic niches for the new consumer contract provisions. But they have been only partly successful.[299] The provisions that used to be contained in §§ 1–11 Standard Terms of Business Act can now be found in §§ 305–310 BGB. They deal with a number of different issues. They concern themselves with the question how standard terms of business can become part of a contract,[300] they include rules of interpretation,[301] they regulate the consequences of non-incorporation and invalidity (and, in the process, deviate from the general rule on partial invalidity in § 139 BGB),[302] and they set standards for the policing of unfair standard contract terms.[303] Systematically, these issues need to be related to §§ 145 ff. (formation of contract), §§ 133, 157 BGB (interpretation), § 139 (partial invalidity), and either § 138 (contracts *contra bonos mores*), or § 242 (good faith), or possibly even §§ 315 ff. BGB (unilateral determination of performance). The German Government, however, decided to preserve the integrity of what used to be the Standard Terms of Business Act without preserving the Act itself. The provisions were thus shoved, lock, stock, and barrel, into one place, and the place chosen for this purpose was the one immediately following the rules on *mora creditoris* (and immediately preceding a section of the code entitled 'contractual obligations': as if standard terms of business were part of non-contractual obligations). There is no good reason at all to deal with standard terms of business at this specific place; and the only reason that can possibly be advanced is that a convenient space could relatively easily be created by dropping, removing, or compressing the rules previously located here. As a result, the new §§ 305–310 seem like a piece of pop music tossed into the second movement of a classical symphony: a *corpus alienum* without intellectual connection to its surroundings. The incorporation of the Standard Terms of Business Act into the BGB, in other words, has been a purely formal exercise; it has not led to anything that could be called an integration into the fabric of the BGB.[304]

Another example of an unhappy form of integration is provided by § 241 a BGB, i.e. the rule on unsolicited performances.[305] It sits awkwardly between two of the most fundamental rules within the German law of obligations,[306]

---

[299] See, for example, the criticism in Wiedenmann (n. 9) 34 ff.

[300] §§ 305, 305 a, 305 c I BGB.   [301] §§ 305 b, 305 c II BGB; cf. also § 306 a BGB.

[302] § 306 BGB.   [303] §§ 307, 308, 309 BGB.

[304] As has been mentioned (*supra* p. 188), §§ 305 ff. BGB contain a statutory restatement of the transparency requirement developed by the courts under the old law. The new § 307 I 2 BGB has, however, been placed in the wrong position, given the internal system of what used to be the Standard Terms of Business Act: see *Münchener Kommentar/*Basedow (n. 134) § 307, n. 51.

[305] *Supra* pp. 184 f., 188.

[306] § 241 BGB (i.e. the rule with which book II of the BGB on the law of obligations is introduced) defines the duties arising under an obligation whereas § 242 BGB is the famous general good faith provision.

and there is no apparent reason for this choice of place, not even, in this case, a lacuna in the numbering of the BGB provisions. Werner Flume regards this as 'monstrous',[307] and one of the standard commentaries refers to an 'unparalleled legislative blunder'.[308]

Occasionally, the draftsmen of the new law attempted to patch up a systematic awkwardness. The first section of Book I (General Part) of the BGB deals with persons. It is subdivided into two titles, one dealing with natural persons, the other with legal persons. The definitions of the terms 'consumer' and 'entrepreneur' have been added to the first title as if it contained a random collection of definitions. An 'entrepreneur', as § 14 BGB itself makes clear, can be a natural or legal person. Hence the change of the heading over title one; it now reads 'Natural person, consumer, entrepreneur'. Still, however, this is an uneasy compromise given the fact that title 2, now as previously, deals with 'legal persons'.[309] Also, the definitions contained in §§ 13 ff. BGB are relevant only for the law of obligations; they should, therefore, have been placed into the general part of the law of obligations rather than into the general part of the BGB. That loan contracts in general (including consumer loans) and contracts for the loan of a thing have been dealt with in two different corners within section 8 of the BGB's book on obligations ('Particular kinds of obligations')[310] can also only be attributed to the vagaries of the new law's drafting history.

5. 'Throw-away' legislation

The new provisions amending the BGB are easily recognizable in view of the fact that they tend to be long-winded, badly drafted, and also, not rarely, illconsidered. The quality of modern legislation has often been deplored. Dieter Medicus has remarked, with characteristic understatement, that those responsible for legislation have 'not rarely been infelicitous' in their efforts.[311] Others have used stronger language. The piece of legislation relating to credit transfers has been characterized as *monstrum horribile*,[312] the act on distance contracts has prompted a respected practitioner (the former Vice-President of the Supreme Court of Appeal for the State of Hamburg) to remark that 'one might

[307] Werner Flume, 'Vom Beruf unserer Zeit für Gesetzgebung', [2000] *Zeitschrift für Wirtschaftsrecht* 1428.

[308] Heinz-Peter Mansel, in Othmar Jauernig (ed.), *Bürgerliches Gesetzbuch*, 11th edn. (2004), § 241 a, n. 1.

[309] See, for example, Flume, [2000] *Zeitschrift für Wirtschaftsrecht* 1427 ff.; *HKK*/Duve (n. 12) §§ 1–14, n. 89.   [310] *Supra* pp. 192 ff.

[311] Dieter Medicus, 'Entscheidungen des BGH als Marksteine für die Entwicklung des allgemeinen Zivilrechts', [2000] *Neue Juristische Wochenschrift* 2927.

[312] Flume, [2000] *Zeitschrift für Wirtschaftsrecht* 1430; cf. also Einsele, [2000] *Juristenzeitung* 9 ff.; Horst Heinrich Jakobs, 'Gesetzgebung im Banküberweisungsrecht', [2000] *Juristenzeitung* 641 ff.

want to cry',[313] and the change effected, in anticipation of the Directive on combating late payment in commercial transactions, has been described as 'infinitely ill-conceived and inappropriate'; the consequences for commercial life were predicted to be 'disastrous'.[314] Rolf Knütel has devoted a thirty-page article to the Consumer Credit Act as the paradigmatic example of a 'statutory failure',[315] while Christiane Wendehorst has characterized the quality of the German rules concerning e-commerce as 'extremely bad' and as having descended to the level of the respective EC Directive.[316] Hans Hermann Seiler generally speaks of the phenomenon of 'throw-away' legislation.[317] In summary, I think, it is safe to say that the incorporation of the *ius novum* into the BGB has not enhanced its technical quality. It is a fitting testimony to the fast food approach to legislation that some areas of the law have been the subject of repeated change over the past few years[318] and that even a number of rules that had been put in place by the Modernization of the Law of Obligations Act at the beginning of 2002 had to be amended shortly afterwards. These amendments have sometimes been necessary as the result of the fact that the European Court of Justice held the respective rules to be incompatible with EC legislation. One example has been mentioned above; it concerns the question when the right of revocation of doorstep transactions ceases to exist (§ 355 III BGB).[319] The same decision of the ECJ also prompted a fundamental revision of § 312 a BGB concerning the relationship of a right of revocation or return under § 312 BGB (doorstep transactions) with other rights of revocation or return which might be applicable in the same situation.[320] At the time of preparation of the Modernization of the Law of Obligations Act, the case was pending before the ECJ; the decision was handed down on 9 December 2001, a mere thirteen days after the Act had been promulgated and about three weeks before it came into force.[321] The problem of whether § 5 II of the Doorstep

---

[313] Horst-Diether Hensen, 'Das Fernabsatzgesetz oder: Man könnte heulen', [2000] *Zeitschrift für Wirtschaftsrecht* 1151 ff.

[314] Wolfgang Ernst, 'Deutsche Gesetzgebung in Europa—am Beispiel des Verzugsrechts', (2000) 8 *Zeitschrift für Europäisches Privatrecht* 767, 769; cf. also Ulrich Huber, 'Das neue Recht des Zahlungsverzugs und das Prinzip der Privatautonomie', [2000] *Juristenzeitung* 743 ff.

[315] Rolf Knütel, 'Das Verbraucherkreditgesetz als misslungenes Gesetz', in Uwe Diederichsen and Ralf Dreier (eds.), *Das missglückte Gesetz* (1997), 62 ff.

[316] *Münchener Kommentar*/Wendehorst (n. 212) § 312 e, n. 5.

[317] Hans Hermann Seiler, 'Bewahrung von Kodifikationen in der Gegenwart am Beispiel des BGB', in Okko Behrends and Wolfgang Sellert (eds.), *Der Kodifikationsgedanke und das Modell des Bürgerlichen Gesetzbuches (BGB)* (2000), 110.

[318] For examples, see *supra* pp. 185 f., 194.   [319] *Supra* p. 190.

[320] See *Münchener Kommentar*/Ulmer (n. 226) § 312 a, nn. 2 ff.; *Jauernig*/Stadler (n. 223) § 312 a, n. 1.

[321] ECJ Decision of 13 December 2001 (C-481/99) *Heininger v. Bayerische Hypo- und Vereinsbank AG* [2001] ECR I-9945.

Selling Act (= § 312 a BGB old version) was compatible with EC law had been the subject of academic discussion[322] but the draftsmen of the Modernization of the Law of Obligations Act did not take the opportunity to examine the matter: time was too short for subtleties of this kind.[323]

Many details of the new rules immediately became the subject of dispute: because the respective rules are conceptually unclear, because they are ill-adjusted to each other or to other areas of the law, because they are the result of an obvious mistake,[324] or because they do not correctly implement the provisions of a European Directive. § 241 a I BGB does not say what it intends to say.[325] Moreover, it is one of those rules that have created more problems than they have solved, for the issue tackled by it has not constituted a problem under the old law.[326] Even the key definition of 'consumer' in § 13 BGB is defective in that it wrongly insinuates that only someone who normally engages in an independent professional activity or trade, but does not do so in the present context, can be regarded as a consumer;[327] and in that it is confined to natural persons 'concluding a legal act' which cannot be attributed to their independent professional activity or trade.[328] Whether the concept of 'consumer' can be taken to relate

---

[322] See the references in *Jauernig*/Stadler (n. 223) § 312 a, n. 1.

[323] *Münchener Kommentar*/Ulmer (n. 226) § 312 a, n. 2.

[324] For an example, see *Münchener Kommentar*/Wendehorst (n. 212) § 312 c, n. 6.

[325] The rule states that the delivery of unsolicited things—or the supply of other unsolicited services—does not give rise to a (contractual) claim (for the purchase price, or remuneration) against the consumer. This is self-evident. What § 241 a BGB wants to prevent is that a consumer who does not return the thing supplied to him can be taken to have accepted a contractual obligation; see Ernst A. Kramer, in *Münchener Kommentar zum Bürgerlichen Gesetzbuch*, 4th edn., vol. IIa (2003), § 241 a, n. 11.

[326] *Palandt*/Heinrichs (n. 223) § 241 a, n. 1. § 241 a BGB excludes all claims against the consumer, even those based not on contract but on unjustified enrichment or ownership: *Münchener Kommentar*/Kramer (n. 325) § 241 a, n. 13; *Palandt*/Heinrichs (n. 223) § 241 a, n. 4; *Jauernig*/Mansel (n. 308) § 241 a, n. 5. This is intended to be a sanction for what essentially constitutes an objectionable marketing practice. *Contra*: Reiner Schulze, in Reiner Schulze and Heinrich Dörner, *Bürgerliches Gesetzbuch, Handkommentar*, 3rd edn. (2003), § 241 a, n. 7. According to Flume, [2000] *Zeitschrift für Wirtschaftsrecht* 1429, § 241 a BGB is to be treated as *pro non scripto*. Cf. also the criticism by Christian Berger, 'Der Ausschluss gesetzlicher Rückgewähransprüche bei der Erbringung unbestellter Leistungen nach § 241 a BGB', [2001] *Juristische Schulung* 649 ff.; Peter Krebs, in Barbara Dauner-Lieb, Thomas Heidel, Manfred Lepa and Gerhard Ring (eds.), *Anwaltkommentar, Schuldrecht* (2002), § 241 a, n. 5; Heiderhoff (n. 9) 385 ff.

[327] Flume, [2000] *Zeitschrift für Wirtschaftsrecht* 1427 ff.; Repgen (n. 9) 30 ff.; see also Medicus (n. 11) 216; Wiedenmann (n. 9) 137 ff. For comparative comment as to the distinction between private and professional activities, see Remien (n. 9) 248 ff.

[328] It is generally agreed that, contrary to the wording of § 13 BGB, a consumer need not be a (natural) person who concludes a contract but can also be someone to whom unsolicited services are supplied (§ 241 a BGB), or to whom legally relevant information has to be given (§§ 312 c, 482 BGB), etc.: Othmar Jauernig, in Othmar Jauernig (ed.), *Bürgerliches Gesetzbuch*, 11th edn. (2004), § 13, n. 5; *Palandt*/Heinrichs (n. 223) § 13, n. 5; *HKK*/Duve (n. 12) §§ 1–14, n. 82. See also Medicus (n. 11) 214 ff. who points out that the combination of the words 'to conclude' and 'legal act' is inappropriate in view of the fact that, while contracts are 'concluded', legal acts (which include unilateral acts, such

to associations which do not constitute a juristic person (i.e. private law partnerships) is disputed.[329] The exclusion of all legal persons (i.e. also those that do not constitute a business enterprise, such as non-profit organizations) is widely criticized.[330] The definition of a 'consumer' contained in Article 29 EGBGB is slightly different from that in § 13 BGB; also, the official heading of Article 29 EGBGB ('Consumer contracts') does not correspond to the definition of consumer contracts provided in § 310 III BGB. Whether, or to what extent, a transaction can be regarded as a consumer contract which can only partly be attributed to the independent professional activity, or trade, of the consumer, is controversial.[331]

6. Excessive implementation

Where the German Government has had to implement European Directives, it has often decided to go beyond what was required by the Directive. Thus, most importantly, the system of remedies provided in the Consumer Sales Directive has become the model for sales contracts in general;[332] and, as a result, the subtitle dealing specifically with consumer sales only contains a few additional rules.[333] Even here, the draftsmen of the new German law, however, did more than would have been necessary under EC law. If a consumer, on account of a defect in the object sold, successfully sues the seller, the seller, in turn, will want to seek recourse against his supplier. According to § 478 IV 1 BGB, the seller's rights against the supplier are, effectively, mandatory.[334] This constitutes an unprecedented interference with the private autonomy of one entrepreneur vis-à-vis another.[335] The German rules on standard terms of

---

as the giving of notice or the declaration of set-off) are 'effected' rather than concluded. For an unconvincing attempt to justify the choice of terminology see Jürgen Schmidt-Räntsch, in Heinz Georg Bamberger and Herbert Roth (eds.), *Kommentar zum Bürgerlichen Gesetzbuch*, vol. I (2003), § 13, n. 11.

[329] See the references in *Jauernig/*Jauernig (n. 328) § 13, n. 2; *Palandt/*Heinrichs (n. 223) § 13, n. 2; *Münchener Kommentar/*Micklitz (n. 149) § 13, n. 16; Medicus (n. 11) 214. According to BGHZ 149, 80, 84 ff. private law partnerships can be 'consumers'. But see ECJ Decision of 22 November 2001, [2002] *Neue Juristische Wochenschrift* 205.

[330] Wolfgang Faber, 'Elemente verschiedener Verbraucherbegriffe in EG-Richtlinien, zwischenstaatlichen Übereinkommen und nationalem Zivil- und Kollisionsrecht', (1998) 6 *Zeitschrift für Europäisches Privatrecht* 854, 864; Flume, [2000] *Zeitschrift für Wirtschaftsrecht* 1428; Pfeiffer (n. 9) 138; *HKK/*Duve (n. 12) §§ 1–14, n. 82; cf. also *Münchener Kommentar/*Micklitz (n. 149) § 13, nn. 12 ff.; Remien (n. 9) 247 ff. But see Wiedenmann (n. 9) 171 ff.

[331] Othmar Jauernig, 'Verbraucherschutz in "Mischfällen"', in *Festschrift für Peter Schlechtriem* (2003), 569 ff.; Medicus (n. 11) 216 ff.; Wiedenmann (n. 9) 190 ff.   [332] *Supra* p. 97.

[333] *Supra* pp. 191 f.

[334] This includes the prescription of these rights (§ 479 BGB). It does not, however, apply to the claim for damages: § 478 IV 2 BGB.

[335] For criticism, see Stephan Lorenz, ' "Unternehmer—Unternehmerlein—Verbraucher": Ein neues Leitbild?', [2004] *Recht der internationalen Wirtschaft* Issue 10, 'Die erste Seite'. On the complex problems arising under § 478 BGB, see Matthias Jacobs, 'Der Rückgriff des Unternehmers nach § 478 BGB', [2004] *Juristenzeitung* 225.

business also have a scope of application extending far beyond consumer contracts. This was the approach adopted in the Standard Terms of Business Act of 1976 and it was retained at the time when the Directive on Unfair Terms in Consumer Contracts had to be implemented.[336] The implementation was effected by appending a provision to the Act (§ 24 a Standard Terms of Business Act; now § 310 III BGB) modifying some of its provisions for consumer contracts.[337]

Outside the area of consumer law, the Directive on cross-border credit transfers has become the model for the regulation of credit transfers in general (i.e. including, in particular, domestic credit transfers).[338] A right of revocation has been introduced into German law for consumer credit transactions[339] even though this was not required by the Consumer Credit Directive. Consumers are also granted a right of revocation in the case of instalment supply contracts;[340] again, this was not necessitated by EC legislation. § 241 a BGB on the delivery of unsolicited things and the supply of unsolicited services is based on Article 9 of the Distance Contracts Directive; it exceeds the requirements of the Directive in that it does not only protect the recipient/consumer from any obligation to pay for the unsolicited things or services, but even excludes any duty to return the object.[341] The right of revocation in consumer contracts does not cease to exist, at the latest, six months after the conclusion of the contract if the consumer has not been duly informed about that right of revocation.[342] Under EC law this kind of rule was required only for rights of revocation in the case of doorstep transactions.[343] None the less, the German Government decided to generalize it so as to apply to the other rights of revocation covered by § 355 BGB.[344] Other individual instances of an implementation exceeding the requirements of EC law could be mentioned.[345] In many of these situations the question will arise whether the provisions of German law need to be interpreted in conformity with the relevant Directive only as far as they are required by that Directive or also as far as they constitute instances of an excessive implementation. From the point of view of EC law, national courts are under no duty to follow the second alternative.[346] Considerations concerning the systematic coherence of the national legal system, however, should normally prompt the courts to avoid a split interpretation so far as that is

---

[336] *Supra* pp. 175 f., 182 f.

[337] For all details, see *Münchener Kommentar*/Basedow (n. 134) § 310, nn. 18 ff.

[338] *Supra* p. 184.   [339] § 495 BGB.   [340] § 505 BGB.

[341] See, for example, *Anwaltkommentar*/Krebs (n. 326) § 241 a, n. 3; Heiderhoff (n. 9) 385 ff.

[342] § 355 III 3 BGB.   [343] See Art. 4 of the Doorstep Selling Directive 85/577/EEC.

[344] *Supra* p. 190.

[345] See, for example, *Münchener Kommentar*/Wendehorst (n. 212) § 312 c, n. 4.

[346] Ulrich Büdenbender, 'Die Bedeutung der Verbrauchsgüterkaufrichtlinie für das deutsche Kaufrecht nach der Schuldrechtsreform', (2004) 12 *Zeitschrift für Europäisches Privatrecht* 36 ff.

possible.³⁴⁷ As a result, considerable parts of German contract law will have to be interpreted in conformity with some or other EC Directive, most notably a range of provisions of the general law of sale and the rules on standard terms of business. Many individual questions are disputed, as is the associated question to what extent German courts may (or perhaps even have to) refer the relevant cases to the European Court of Justice.³⁴⁸

VI. The Decision to Incorporate: An Evaluation

1. General background

a) Freedom of contract and self-determination

Has the decision to incorporate the consumer statutes into the BGB been right? An answer to this question has to take account of the fact that the development of consumer contract law reflects changes of perception affecting German contract law more generally. Of course, contract law is, and remains, based on freedom of contract.³⁴⁹ But it has long been recognized that freedom of contract is not an end in itself. Rather, it must be regarded as a means of promoting the self-determination of those who wish to conclude a contract. More than a hundred years ago Rudolf von Jhering emphasized that he could not think of a more fatal mistake than to imagine that any contract could justly claim the protection of the law, as long as its content was not illegal or immoral.³⁵⁰ But his statement was of a prescriptive rather than descriptive character, for it did not correspond to the approach adopted by contemporary courts and writers towards general contract law. This approach, in turn, was rooted in a desire to prevent the State from tampering with the freedom to establish and carry on trade or industry—a freedom which had only just been secured with the enactment of the Trade Act of 1869.³⁵¹ Judicial control is a

---

³⁴⁷ See, apart from Büdenbender, (2004) 12 *Zeitschrift für Europäisches Privatrecht* 36 ff., Mathias Habersack, 'Die überschiessende Umsetzung von Richtlinien', [1999] *Juristenzeitung* 913 ff.; Peter Hommelhoff, 'Die Rolle der nationalen Gerichte bei der Europäisierung des Privatrechts', in *50 Jahre Bundesgerichtshof* (n. 148) vol. II (2000), 914 ff.; York Schnorbus, 'Autonome Harmonisierung in den Mitgliedstaaten durch die Inkorporation von Gemeinschaftsrecht', (2001) 65 *Rabels Zeitschrift für ausländisches und internationales Privatrecht* 654 ff.; Christian Mayer and Jan Schürnbrand, 'Einheitlich oder gespalten?—Zur Auslegung nationalen Rechts bei überschiessender Umsetzung von Richtlinien', [2004] *Juristenzeitung* 545 ff.
³⁴⁸ As far as the provisions on standard terms of business are concerned, see *Münchener Kommentar*/Basedow (n. 134) Vorbem. § 305, nn. 45, 50.
³⁴⁹ Canaris (n. 183) 873 ff.; Hein Kötz, 'Freiheit und Zwang im Vertragsrecht', in *Festschrift für Ernst-Joachim Mestmäcker* (1996), 1037 ff.; Drexl (n. 9) 218 ff.; Heiderhoff (n. 9) 295 ff.
³⁵⁰ Rudolf von Jhering, *Der Zweck im Recht*, vol. I (1877–1883), 107 ff.   ³⁵¹ *Supra* p. 167.

type of State control, and thus it was bound to appear as an undue interference with the private sphere of the individual citizen. The core of contract law, as it was to be embodied in the Civil Code, was to be kept free from such interference; it was to be based on the principles of freedom and equality.[352]

This view began to be challenged, towards the middle of the last century, by a theory focusing upon the conditions for the proper functioning of the market.[353] Contracts are supposed to bring about, without any interference on the part of the State, a 'just' result in a specific situation. This expectation is based upon the way in which a contract is concluded. The selfish will of one party alone does not ensure any correspondence between what that party wants and the precepts of substantive fairness. A proper balance is achieved only as a result of the other party having to agree: a requirement which allows that other party to bring his own interests to bear upon the content of the contract.[354] If the parties manage to reconcile their antagonistic interests, the balance established by them may be accepted as being just for them under the prevailing circumstances. If, on the other hand, the parties fail in their endeavour, a contract does not come into existence. This entails that no 'unjust' contract is concluded, i.e. a contract which fails to take account of the interests of both parties concerned. This model, however, is based upon certain preconditions. A contract cannot be the means of bringing about a just regulation in situations where one of the parties is typically deprived of his freedom of choice: for example, where he cannot make do without what is offered by the other party, or where he is in some other way dependent upon the goods or services to be supplied by the latter. Nor can the contract fulfil its normal function where, for any other reason, a proper evaluation and balancing of the consequences of the transaction does not normally occur on the side of one of the parties concerned.[355] If, therefore, the legal community accepts a contract as the product of the self-determination of two parties, it has to exercise some kind of control as to whether a contract can in fact be regarded as the proper expression of the self-determination of both of these parties.[356]

---

[352] See generally Rückert (n. 8) Vorbem. § 1, nn. 39 ff. and *passim*.

[353] Walter Schmidt-Rimpler, 'Grundfragen einer Erneuerung des Vertragsrechts', (1941) 147 *Archiv für die civilistische Praxis* 130 ff. Today see, among many others, Mathias Habersack, 'Richtigkeitsgewähr notariell beurkundeter Verträge', (1989) 189 *Archiv für die civilistische Praxis* 403 ff.; Heiderhoff (n. 9) 300 ff.; Lorenz Fastrich, *Richterliche Inhaltskontrolle im Privatrecht* (1992), 29 ff., 51 ff.;

[354] Schmidt-Rimpler, (1941) 147 *Archiv für die civilistische Praxis* 130, 151 ff.; cf. also Jhering (n. 350) 103.

[355] Schmidt-Rimpler, (1941) 147 *Archiv für die civilistische Praxis* 130, 133 ff., 157 ff., 179 ff.; cf. also *idem*, 'Zum Problem der Geschäftsgrundlage', in *Festschrift für Hans Carl Nipperdey zum 70. Geburtstag* (1965), 16 ff.; *idem*, 'Zum Vertragsproblem', in *Funktionswandel der Privatrechtsinstitutionen: Festschrift für Ludwig Raiser zum 70. Geburtstag* (1974), 12 ff.

[356] A modern theory of consumer protection legislation along these lines has been developed by Josef Drexl, *Die wirtschaftliche Selbstbestimmung des Verbrauchers* (1998).

b) A combination of criteria

This is the intellectual background for the Federal Supreme Court's use of § 242 BGB as a means of policing the substantive fairness of standard terms of business. These standard terms have been formulated in advance by one of the parties and, therefore, typically only reflect that party' interests. The other party, in turn, even if he is a businessman, does not usually regard it as worth his time and trouble to enter into negotiations about the content of these terms.[357] This is why judicial control is not limited to consumer contracts. The Federal Supreme Court's approach towards standard contract terms clearly illustrates one very important point: it is not the substantive unfairness of the contract term *per se* that justifies judicial interference, but the substantive unfairness in combination with another consideration explaining why the normal mechanisms of the market fail to bring about a just result. This specific combination of criteria, incidentally, merely develops the evaluations embodied in a key provision of the original BGB: § 138 II, i.e. the rule on 'usury'.[358] For it is not the excessive interest rate, or the exorbitant purchase price, as such, that justifies the verdict of invalidity, but only the striking disproportion in value between a performance and the pecuniary advantages paid, or promised to be paid, for it, plus an exploitation of the distress, gullibility, or inexperience of the other party.[359] It is clear that, under these circumstances, the contract cannot be regarded as an expression of the self-determination of *both* parties concerned and as having led, typically, to a fairly balanced result.

c) Close family members of the main debtor as sureties

Similar considerations have, more recently, induced German courts to tighten the control of contracts of suretyship concluded by close family members of the main debtor.[360] This development was initiated by a spectacular decision of the Federal Constitutional Court[361] enjoining the Federal Supreme Court, when applying open-ended provisions such as §§ 138 I and § 242 BGB, to pay due attention to the guarantee of the autonomy of private individuals, as enshrined in Article 2 I of the Basic Law (*Grundgesetz*, 66).[362] Such autonomy, the Court held,

---

[357] *Supra* p. 176.   [358] See *supra* pp. 169 ff.

[359] The point is emphasized, particularly clearly, by Bydlinski (n. 143) 753 ff. and Canaris, (2000) 200 *Archiv für die civilistische Praxis* 273, 280 ff.

[360] Habersack and Zimmermann, (1999) 3 *Edinburgh Law Review* 272 ff.; Bydlinski (n. 143) 760 ff.; Drexl (n. 9) 263 ff., 505 ff.; Remien (n. 9) 356 ff.; for an overview of the more recent developments, see *Palandt*/Heinrichs (n. 223) § 138, nn. 37 ff.; *Jauernig*/Stadler (n. 223) § 765, n. 4.

[361] BVerfGE 89, 214 ff.; cf. also BVerfG [1994] *Neue Juristische Wochenschrift* 2749 ff.; BVerfG [1996] *Zeitschrift für Wirtschaftsrecht* 956 ff.

[362] Art. 2 I GG, in spite of its more restrictive wording, has been consistently interpreted as establishing 'a general right of freedom of action'. Of fundamental importance, in this respect, is the

is not properly safeguarded by a regime of unrestricted freedom of contract. On the contrary, the civil courts are bound to control the content of contracts which are unusually burdensome for one of the parties and which result from a structural inequality of bargaining power. In this context, the Federal Constitutional Court pointed out that the parties engaging in private transactions are fundamentally equal, as regards the protection of their fundamental rights enshrined in the first part of the Basic Law. This fundamental equality would be disregarded if only the right of the more powerful party were to prevail. Where one of the parties dominates to such an extent that he can, for all practical purposes, unilaterally determine the content of the contract, the autonomy of the other party is replaced by a state of heteronomy. Of course, the maintenance of legal certainty makes it impossible for each and every contract to be scrutinized as to whether it is based on an inequality of bargaining power. In typical situations, however, where one party is in a structurally inferior position, the legal system has to come to his rescue in order to maintain private autonomy and to comply with the requirements of social responsibility.[363]

This decision of the Federal Constitutional Court has led to a far-reaching reappraisal of the German law of suretyship on the part of the Federal Supreme Court.[364] The doctrinal peg chosen for policing suretyship transactions was § 138 I BGB: invalidity of contracts *contra bonos mores*. Significantly, the contract of suretyship concluded by a close relative of the main debtor is not to be regarded as void merely in view of the extent of the obligation incurred and the resulting condition of over-indebtedness. For the Federal Supreme Court regards a striking discrepancy between the obligation incurred and the financial potential of the surety as only *one* of two elements sustaining the verdict of invalidity; there have to be additional circumstances indicating that the surety's ability to reach a free and responsible decision was impaired, thereby creating an intolerable imbalance between the contracting parties.[365] This is the case, for instance, if a spouse or descendant of the main debtor complies with the latter's wish in a situation of psychological distress, or as a result of lack of business experience. Essentially, in these cases, German courts have to have recourse to the general *contra bonos mores* provision for lack of a modern civilian notion of undue influence (or, as the lawyers of the earlier *ius commune* used to put it, *metus reverentialis*).[366]

Elfes decision of the Federal Constitutional Court: BVerfGE 6, 32 ff.; more recently, see BVerfGE 80, 137, 154 ff. ('Reiten im Walde' = horse riding in the forest).

[363] BVerfGE 89, 214, 233 ff.; and see previously BVerfGE 81, 242, 255. On the principle of Germany as being a state with social responsibility (*Sozialstaatsprinzip*), see David P. Currie, *The Constitution of the Federal Republic of Germany* (1994), 20 ff.

[364] See, for example, BGH [2002] *Neue Juristische Wochenschrift* 747.

[365] Habersack and Zimmermann, (1990) 3 *Edinburgh Law Review* 272, 281 ff.

[366] Jacques du Plessis and Reinhard Zimmermann, 'The Relevance of Reverence: Undue Influence Civilian Style', (2003) 10 *Maastricht Journal of European and Comparative Law* 345 ff.

d) Excessive interest rates

These decisions concerning suretyship contracts can be contrasted to another line of cases dating back to the late 1970s and involving loans repayable by instalments and granted by instalment credit institutions to consumers.[367] Such loans may be *contra bonos mores*, according to the Federal Supreme Court,[368] if there is an obvious disproportion between the obligations of the bank and of the borrower, and if the bank displayed a reprehensible attitude, either by deliberately exploiting the weaker economic position of the consumer, or by grossly negligently failing to realize that the latter entered into the contract only because of his precarious situation. This 'subjective' component, however, is of an almost fictitious character, since the courts are prepared to draw inferences from the objective circumstances of the contract (especially the disproportion in values) without requiring specific evidence as to whether the conduct in question was wilful or grossly negligent. Of central importance, therefore, is the interest rate charged by the bank, and here the rule has been established that the effective rate of interest must not exceed the current interest rate by more than 100 per cent (relatively) or 12 to 13 per cent (absolutely). The Federal Supreme Court has based these pronouncements on the *contra bonos mores* provision of § 138 I BGB, thereby sidestepping, the additional, restrictive requirements contained in § 138 II BGB. It has effectively established a thinly veiled interest control for consumer loans. This is incompatible with the basic evaluations of German contract law and the existing economic order, and it cannot be justified by merely pointing out that the borrower is a consumer and, as such, finds himself always and necessarily in a weaker position.[369] More plausible, as a point of departure for interfering with excessive interest rates in consumer credit situations, would have been the impairment of the consumer's ability to reach a free and responsible decision resulting from the lack of transparency that used to be associated with instalment credit transactions: for the way in which these contracts were drafted tended to make it difficult for inexperienced customers of instalment credit banks to gauge the effective annual rate of interest charged to them. The problem has subsequently been taken care of by § 492 BGB (previously § 4 VerbrKrG) in that the document containing the consumer loan contract (which has to be signed by the borrower) must indicate, *inter alia*, the effective interest rate, including all

[367] Volker Emmerich, 'Rechtsfragen des Ratenkredits', [1988] *Juristische Schulung* 925 ff.; *Münchener Kommentar*/Mayer-Maly/Armbrüster (n. 96) § 138, nn. 117 ff.; *Palandt*/Heinrichs (n. 223) § 138, nn. 25 ff.; *Jauernig*/Jauernig (n. 328) § 138, n. 16.
[368] BGH [1979] *Neue Juristische Wochenschrift* 805; BGH [1979] *Neue Juristische Wochenschrift* 2089; BGHZ 80, 153, 160.
[369] Helmut Koziol, 'Sonderprivatrecht für Konsumentenkredite?', (1988) 188 *Archiv für die civilistische Praxis* 197 ff.; Canaris, (2000) 200 *Archiv für die civilistische Praxis* 273, 300 ff.

charges applicable to the loan, and also the costs of insuring the outstanding balance of the loan. Thus, the notorious transparency problems can no longer be used as an explanation for the judicial control of an interest rate agreed upon between a credit institution and its fully informed customer. Apart from that, the borrower's right of termination according to § 489 (previously § 609 a) BGB provides the consumer with an opportunity to extricate himself from charges which he subsequently considers to be too burdensome.

e) Consumer protection

The legitimacy of specific rules concerning consumer contracts has to be assessed in the light of these developments. Such rules should not, from the outset, be denounced as constituting inappropriate infringements of the freedom of the parties to make their own contractual arrangements. Rather, they may be seen as legitimate attempts to sustain private autonomy by providing mechanisms which aim at preventing contracts from coming into existence, or from being enforced, which cannot be regarded as the result of acts of self-determination of *both* parties concerned.[370] These rules can therefore make an essential contribution towards the proper functioning of a market economy based on freedom of contract. However, they can only be accepted as legitimate to the extent that they are indeed suitable to remedy the impairment of a contractual party's self-determination. In the interests of legal certainty, of course, the law has to typify; it cannot intervene in each individual case where such impairment has occurred or is impending. Nor should the law use indeterminable criteria such as whether one party is in an economically weaker, or inferior, position compared to the other. And, in particular, it may not object to contract terms merely because they are unduly burdensome to one of the parties concerned. Of central importance is the inquiry whether, for some reason or other, that party has not been able to influence the content of the contract in a way which can lead the legal community typically to accept it as representing a just balance of both parties' interests.

2. The main devices for protecting consumers

The main devices used by German law, in this context, are the imposition of duties of information on the entrepreneur, the granting of a right of revocation to the consumer, the establishment of mandatory rules of law, or even contractual regimes, and, of course, the notion of 'consumer'.[371]

---

[370] See recently, above all, Drexl (n. 9) *passim*; *idem*, in Schlechtriem (n. 143) 109 ff.

[371] There are, of course, other devices such as the establishment form requirements (see §§ 484, 492, 655 b BGB, the former two being based on EC Directives; generally on form requirements

a) Duties of information

The imposition of duties of information is the mildest form of legal intervention.[372] It does not constitute an interference with the principle of *pacta sunt servanda* but attempts to ensure that both parties' decision to contract rests on firm foundations. Duties of information, therefore, can be regarded as a means of strengthening adherence to *pacta sunt servanda*. Over the years, a host of very specific duties of information has been laid down, first in various consumer protection statutes, now in the BGB and the Duties of Information in Private Law Regulation.[373] They relate to transactions typically involving an informational deficit on the part of the consumer vis-à-vis the entrepreneur: because they are of considerable complexity (e.g. timeshare agreements), entail the use of new technologies and the specific risks associated with it (e-commerce), do not provide the consumer with an opportunity to see the product or ascertain the nature of the service before concluding the contract (distance contracts, package holidays), are notoriously non-transparent (consumer credit), etc. The information provided by the entrepreneur is designed to place consumers, who are about to embark on these types of transactions, in a position to make a free and responsible choice.[374] This is, in principle, an excellent idea. At the same time, however, it is vaguely reminiscent of some of the utopian ideals of the Age of Enlightenment. In the first place, many people

contained in EC Directives, see Peter Bydlinski, 'Formgebote für Rechtsgeschäfte und die Folgen ihrer Verletzung', in Reiner Schulze, Martin Ebers and Hans Christoph Grigoleit (eds.), *Informationspflichten und Vertragsschluss im Acquis communautaire* (2003), 141 ff.; Rösler (n. 6) 148 ff.); or the reversal of the onus of proof (see, for example, § 476 BGB); or the right, granted to consumers who have taken up a loan in order to finance another contract, to raise defences available to them under the contract financed by the consumer loan transaction against the party with whom they have concluded the consumer loan transaction, provided both contracts can be regarded as 'linked contracts' (*verbundene Geschäfte*): § 359 BGB. The former two devices are well known also outside the area of consumer contract law; see, for example, the form requirements introduced by the draftsmen of the original BGB in §§ 313 (old version), 518 and 766 for contracts of sale of land, donation, and suretyship (for comment, see *Law of Obligations* (n. 13) 85 ff.)), and the reversal of the onus of proof effected by the courts in order to cope with the problem of product liability (see, for example, Medicus (n. 166) nn. 650 ff.). The rule in § 359 BGB, deviating from the well-established principle governing *exceptiones ex iure tertii*, essentially constitutes a codification of the rules developed by the German courts on the basis of § 6 AbzG (prohibition to evade the provisions of the Act concerning Instalment Sales); on which see Harm Peter Westermann, in *Münchener Kommentar zum Bürgerlichen Gesetzbuch*, vol. III/I, 2nd edn. (1988), § 6 AbzG, nn. 23 ff.

[372] See, for example, Bydlinski (n. 143) 741 ff.   [373] *Supra* p. 197.

[374] See, for example, Dauner-Lieb (n. 142) 62 ff.; Rainer Kemper, *Verbraucherschutzinstrumente* (1994), 33 ff., 186 ff.; Lurger, *Vertragliche Solidarität* (1998), 14 ff.; Repgen (n. 9) 90 ff.; Riesenhuber (n. 9) 292 ff.; Remien (n. 9) 270 ff.; Heiderhoff (n. 9) 366 ff.; Rösler (n. 6) 142 ff. For an analysis of the concept of the informed consumer and its implementation in primary and secondary EC law, see Holger Fleischer, 'Vertragsschlussbezogene Informationspflichten im Gemeinschaftsprivatrecht', (2000) 8 *Zeitschrift für Europäisches Privatrecht* 781 ff.; Stefan Grundmann, 'Privatautonomie im Binnenmarkt: Informationsregeln als Instrument', [2000] *Juristenzeitung* 1133 ff.; Repgen (n. 9) 31 ff.

are resistant to any form of forced instruction: they simply do not read lengthy standard business documents presented to them. Secondly, and more importantly, the amount of obligatory information descending upon the consumer does not always lead to an exemplary state of transparency: a consumer faced with an information overload can be equally unable to take a well-informed decision as one who has not been informed at all.[375] The imposition of duties of information on the entrepreneur, in other words, does not always remedy the existing informational deficit of the consumer.[376]

Consumer contracts are transactions between an entrepreneur (i.e. a person who acts in his professional capacity) and a consumer (i.e. a person who is not professionally involved in transactions of this kind). Thus, they can reasonably be taken to constitute typical situations of imbalance in the level of information available to the contracting parties. But they are not the only situations. The rules on the avoidance of contracts for mistake and fraudulent non-disclosure[377] as well as the rules on non-conformity[378] can be seen as attempts to cope with informational imbalances on a more general level. Moreover, the past decades have seen a significant expansion of differentiated duties of information under the label of *culpa in contrahendo*[379] inspired, ultimately, by an increased sensitivity for the requirements of good faith.[380] One of the great challenges posed by these developments consists in an intellectual coordination of the general and the specifically consumer-oriented duties of information on the level both of evaluation and legal doctrine. This, presumably, will be a two-way process. For just as it should be possible to domesticate the jungle of informational requirements concerning individual consumer contracts, so these requirements can act as pointers as to what is owed, more generally, in situations of an informational imbalance.[381] At the same time, it is clear that the issues raised pertain to the core of contract law and should be discussed in that context.

---

[375] Cf. also Martinek, [1997] *Neue Juristische Wochenschrift* 1393, 1395 ff., 1399, concerning the Timeshare Agreement Act: 'Crushing masses of information which threaten to choke the consumer...'; generally Herbert Roth, 'EG-Richtlinien und Bürgerliches Recht', [1999] *Juristenzeitung* 533 ('inflationary use' of duties of information); Bydlinski (n. 143) 758 ff.

[376] For further discussion, see Rösler (n. 6) 151 ff.

[377] For all details, see Holger Fleischer, *Informationsasymmetrie im Vertragsrecht* (2001), 244 ff., 336 ff.   [378] Fleischer (n. 377) 469 ff.

[379] See the detailed analysis by Fleischer (n. 377) 416 ff.; Grigoleit (n. 98) 50 ff. The doctrine of *culpa in contrahendo* as a tool for 'materializing' contract law is also discussed by Canaris, (2000) 200 *Archiv für die civilistische Praxis* 273, 304 ff.

[380] For a succinct overview, see *Jauernig/*Mansel (n. 308) § 242, nn. 19 ff. Fleischer describes the existence of duties of information at the pre-contractual stage as a core element of (modern) European private law: 'Vertragsschlußbezogene Informationspflichten im Gemeinschaftsprivatrecht' (2000) 8 *Zeitschrift für Europäisches Privatrecht* 772; cf. also Hein Kötz, *European Contract Law* (1997) (transl. Tony Weir), 198 ff.   [381] See, along the same lines, Fleischer (n. 377) 207 ff., 570 ff.

b) Right of revocation

aa) 'Being caught off-guard'

An informational asymmetry is not the only potential source of objectionable imbalances in contracts concluded between consumers and entrepreneurs. Another situation where consumers may be tempted to enter into contracts which are detrimental to their own interests and which therefore, upon sober reflection, they subsequently regret, is the one where they are caught 'off their guard'. This typically happens where the contract is negotiated away from the business premises of the entrepreneur: particularly where the entrepreneur visits the consumer at his house, or place of work, without having been asked to do so, but also where the entrepreneur uses the opportunity of a chance encounter on the street, or in a bus or subway, in order to talk the consumer into the contract, or where the parties have met in the course of a leisure-time event.[382] In all these situations the consumer is unprepared for the negotiations, and also usually is unable to compare the quality and price of the offer with other offers. Thus, it is the surprise element which puts the consumer at a specific disadvantage.[383] Here it appears to be reasonable to allow for a 'cooling-off period', in the form of a right subsequently to revoke the contract.[384] The period within which this right may be exercised has been increased, in the course of the modernization of the German law of obligations, from one week to two.[385] An informational component has been incorporated by providing that the period only begins when the consumer has been informed by a clearly formulated notice of his right of revocation.[386]

Obviously, the granting of a right of revocation is a more serious interference with the freedom of the parties to regulate their own affairs than the imposition of specific duties of information.[387] After all, it entails a qualification of the principle of *pacta sunt servanda*. Compared to other qualifications of that principle (right of termination in case of breach of contract, right of rescission on account of fraud or threats, *clausula rebus sic stantibus*) it is entirely novel, in that the consumer does not have to adduce any reason for revoking the

---

[382] For the range of situations covered by the German term 'doorstep transaction' (*Haustürgeschäft*), see § 312 I nos. 1–3; and see *Münchener Kommentar*/Ulmer (n. 226) § 312, nn. 33 ff.

[383] Canaris, (2000) 200 *Archiv für die civilistische Praxis* 273, 346 ff.; *Münchener Kommentar*/Ulmer (n. 226) Vorbem. §§ 312, 312 a, n. 1; Wiedenmann (n. 9) 242 ff.; Mankowski (n. 232) 224 ff. [384] § 312 BGB.

[385] See § 355 I 2 BGB, as opposed to § 1 I HaustürWG; for criticism, see Drexl (n. 143) 124 ff.
[386] § 355 II BGB.

[387] See Henrich (n. 143) 204 ff. ('. . . the most serious interference with the prevailing principles of contract law'); Remien (n. 9) 334. Remien (n. 19, 328 ff.) draws attention to the fact that the granting of a right of revocation can be regarded as an alternative to the establishment of a form requirement; he even refers to the right of revocation as the 'form requirement of the ordinary man' (328). Kemper (n. 374) 220 ff. also deals with form requirements and rights of revocation under the same heading.

contract. He may exercise his right of revocation simply because he regrets the transaction. On the other hand, however, we are still dealing here with a procedural device for coping with a potential source of contractual imbalance.[388] The contract, in a way, has to be treated as if it had been placed under a resolutive condition. There is, at first, a state of pendency at the end of which the contract either remains effective exactly as it has been concluded, or it fails altogether. In particular, therefore, the granting of a right of revocation avoids any necessity for judicial interference with the substance of the contract. Also, it can be argued that it constitutes a more efficient means of protecting the consumer than having recourse to general devices such as invalidity under § 138 I BGB, or restitution in terms of *culpa in contrahendo*, since, while the consumer will usually be unaware of his legal position in general, he has to be informed about his right to revoke which he must then exercise within a relatively short period of time.[389]

Even if the right of revocation is a novel addition to the remedial armoury available, in certain situations to certain types of disappointed customers, the substantive concern motivating the introduction of this right is not novel at all. If someone uses a situation where another person is unable, for some reason or other, properly to collect his thoughts and to evaluate his legal position, in order to secure a contract which is disadvantageous to that other person, the contract can be regarded as *contra bonos mores* and, therefore, void.[390] Alternatively, a person who has been caught off-guard can be granted protection against an unwelcome contract concluded in this situation by means of a claim based on *culpa in contrahendo*.[391] Once again, therefore, the problem is of a more general nature and does not lend itself to an isolated regulation in a consumer contract code. Characteristically, in his report on a possible codification of the law relating to *culpa in contrahendo*, Dieter Medicus included the problem of protection against unwelcome contracts and proposed a general rule granting a right of revocation to every person who has been 'caught off-guard' in the conclusion of a contract.[392] This was to be followed by a number of provisions containing details of the right of

---

[388] Canaris, (2000) 200 *Archiv für die civilistische Praxis* 273, 344 ff.; Rösler (n. 6) 172 ff.

[389] Canaris, (2000) 200 *Archiv für die civilistische Praxis* 273, 345; cf. also Remien (n. 9) 330.

[390] See, for example, Dieter Medicus, 'Verschulden bei Vertragsverhandlungen', in Bundesminister der Justiz (ed.), *Gutachten und Vorschläge zur Überarbeitung des Schuldrechts*, vol. I (1981), 520; BGH [1997] *Neue Juristische Wochenschrift* 1980.

[391] See, for example, Stephan Lorenz, *Der Schutz vor dem unerwünschten Vertrag* (1997), 445 ff.; *idem*, 'Vertragsaufhebung wegen unzulässiger Einflussnahme auf die Entscheidungsfreiheit: Der BGH auf dem Weg zur reinen Abschlusskontrolle?', [1997] *Neue Juristische Wochenschrift* 2578 ff.; *Jauernig*/Stadler (n. 223) § 311, n. 62; Volker Emmerich, in *Münchener Kommentar zum Bürgerlichen Gesetzbuch*, 4th edn., vol. IIa (2003), § 311, n. 116.

[392] Medicus (n. 390) 519 ff., 531, 548; cf. also Kemper (n. 374) 255.

revocation and granting a claim for compensation in other situations of *culpa in contrahendo*.[393]

bb) Other policy considerations

German law, following European Community law in that respect, not only provides for a right of revocation in doorstep selling (and similar)[394] situations, but also with regard to timeshare agreements and distance contracts.[395] In addition, there are rights of revocation concerning consumer credit transactions,[396] instalment supply contracts,[397] and distance teaching contracts,[398] none of them based on EC law. What is the justification for jeopardizing the principle of *pacta sunt servanda* in such a variety of individual instances? The right of revocation with regard to doorstep contracts, as we have seen, is 'situation-specific':[399] it is granted because the consumer has been caught off-guard and needs an extra period for cool reflection. The same argument cannot be advanced to justify the right of revocation in the case of consumer credit transactions. Here it is maintained that the consumer requires the extra period in view of the great economic significance as well as the considerable complexity of this type of transaction.[400] A careful examination of the obligations incurred by him will often lead the borrower to have second thoughts and to reconsider his decision to take up the loan; moreover, he may be able to find credit institutions offering more favourable terms. These arguments, however, are hardly convincing. The consumer has been under no pressure to rush into the contract; he could easily have assessed the obligations to be incurred by him before concluding the contract. This is so even if the relevant information only has to be provided in the contract form which must be signed by the borrower/consumer:[401] he is entirely free to take that document home for close scrutiny before signing it. It is not clear why the consumer should need another two weeks after conclusion of the contract. Also, an extra period of two weeks does not appear to be a suitable means for achieving the aim for which it has been granted. It is usually much later that the borrower begins to feel how onerous the obligations undertaken by him actually are and that he may have overestimated his ability to meet

---

[393] Medicus (n. 390) 548 ff. It must be borne in mind, in this respect, that compensation has to be made, in the first place, 'in kind'; i.e. the aggrieved party has to be restored to his former position: § 249 BGB.   [394] See *supra* n 382.

[395] §§ 312 d I 1, 485 I BGB.   [396] § 495 I BGB.   [397] § 505 I 1 BGB.

[398] § 4 I FernUSG.

[399] For the distinction between 'situation-specific' and 'type-of-transaction specific' rights of revocation, see Mankowski (n. 232) 222 ff.; Canaris, (2000) 200 *Archiv für die civilistische Praxis* 273, 346 ff.; a similar, though more refined, typology has been proposed by Lurger (n. 374) 33 ff.; Susanne Kalss and Brigitta Lurger, 'Zu einer Systematik der Rücktrittsrechte insbesondere im Verbraucherrecht', [1998] *Juristische Blätter* 153 ff.

[400] Peter Ulmer, in *Münchener Kommentar zum Bürgerlichen Gesetzbuch*, vol. III, 4th edn. (2004), § 495, n. 2; Mankowski (n. 232) 239 ff.   [401] § 492 I 5 BGB.

them.[402] A right of termination such as the one granted in § 489 I no. 2 BGB is both more suitable and quite sufficient to meet these concerns.

cc) Timeshare agreements

The right of revocation in consumer credit transactions can be regarded as 'type-of-transaction-specific' as opposed to 'situation-specific'; the policy considerations supporting it, however, are unconvincing. The right of revocation concerning timeshare agreements is often brought home under both heads.[403] For, on the one hand, the complexity of these transactions, and the associated lack of transparency, are often advanced as arguments supporting the granting of an extra period for sober deliberation:[404] the consumer has to be protected against the danger of precipitately rushing into the contract. On the other hand, attention is drawn to the aggressive marketing methods often pursued by timeshare salesmen and aimed at customers charmed by the attractions of southern holiday resorts.[405] The former consideration focuses on the type of transaction, whereas the latter aspect is a situative one. Once again, however, the former consideration is unconvincing, both in itself and in the way in which it is implemented. The advantages deriving from a timeshare agreement, and the burdens associated with it, often become apparent only after a considerable period[406] and not within two weeks after the consumer has received notice of his right of revocation (which normally happens when the contract is concluded). Even if such two-week period were meaningful, account would have to be taken of the fact that the consumer cannot realistically be expected to unravel the details of the transactions, to ponder its financial consequences, and possibly to exercise his right of revocation, until after his return home.[407] The second, situative, aspect is much more plausible but does not require the introduction of a right of revocation for timeshare agreements: it is quite adequately taken care of by the provisions concerning contracts negotiated away from business premises.[408]

---

[402] See Medicus (n. 390) 524; Lorenz (n. 391) 191. And see Kemper (n. 374) 255 ff.; Remien (n. 9) 335 for further critical comment.

[403] Martin Franzen, in *Münchener Kommentar zum Bürgerlichen Gesetzbuch*, 4th edn., vol. III (2004), § 485, n. 1; cf. also Riesenhuber (n. 9) 329 ff.; but see Mankowski (n. 232) 241 ff.

[404] See, for example, *Palandt*/Heinrichs (n. 223) § 485, n. 1; Mankowski (n. 232) 241 ff.

[405] *Münchener Kommentar*/Franzen (n. 403) Vorbem. § 481, n. 12, and § 485, n. 1; cf. also Martinek, [1997] *Neue Juristische Wochenschrift* 1393.   [406] This is conceded also by Mankowski (n. 232) 241.

[407] Martinek, [1997] *Neue Juristische Wochenschrift* 1393, 1397; the same point is made, in a different context, by Drexl (n. 143) 124. Martinek also argues that the establishment of a form requirement (the execution of a notarial instrument) would have been more in tune with the German legal system and would, moreover, have offered better protection to the purchaser: [1997] *Neue Juristische Wochenschrift* 1393, 1396, cf. also Remien (n. 9) 329.

[408] The sales methods of timeshare salesmen are often covered by § 312 BGB; see *Münchener Kommentar*/Franzen (n. 403) § 485, n. 6; Riesenhuber (n. 9) 331. According to § 312 a BGB, however, if a doorstep transaction also falls within the scope of application of the provisions on timeshare contracts, only the latter provisions prevail.

dd) Instalment supply contracts, distance contracts, distance teaching contracts

Instalment supply contract are another type of transaction with regard to which consumers have been granted a right of revocation.[409] The specific temptation arising from the fact that the consumer is immediately able to use an object which he only has to pay for at a later stage, which has been noted for a long time,[410] does not change the fact that a right of revocation which has to be exercised (normally) within two weeks after conclusion of the contract is hardly a suitable means for protecting consumers from yielding to this temptation.[411]

The right of revocation in § 312 d BGB (distance contracts) is supposed to take account of the fact that the consumer, prior to concluding the contract, does not have an opportunity to see the goods to be purchased and to assess their quality.[412] Here it may be argued that the consumer, when using one of the means of distance communication, and particularly those provided by the new technologies, must be quite aware of these disadvantages. Thus, it can hardly be maintained that his right of self-determination is impaired in any way. On the other hand, however, the right of revocation may be seen as a legitimate incentive for entrepreneurs to enhance the quality of their goods so as to minimize the return of these goods as a result of the contract being revoked.[413] The right of revocation, in other words, counteracts the temptation inherent in distance contracts to land customers with products which are unfit for their intended use, in that it places the customer, as far as possible, in the same situation as if he had bought the object in a shop. It is in tune with this rationale that the two-week period does not start to run until the goods reach the recipient.[414] At the same time, it must be said that the right of revocation will usually fail to serve a meaningful function when it comes to the supply of services by way of distance contracts.[415] For, under § 312 d III BGB, the right of revocation expires if the entrepreneur has begun to provide the service with the consent of the consumer before the end of the revocation period.

The right of revocation granted by § 4 Distance Teaching Act can be justified with the same arguments as for distance sales, particularly in view of the fact

---

[409] It dates back to § 1 b AbzG; see *supra* n. 108.

[410] See, as early as 1890, Philipp Heck, *Verhandlungen des Einundzwanzigsten Deutschen Juristentags* (1891), vol. II, 148. Today, see Canaris, (2000) 200 *Archiv für die civilistische Praxis* 273, 348 ff.; Wiedenmann (n. 9) 243 ff.   [411] Medicus (n. 390) 524 ff.

[412] *Münchener Kommentar*/Wendehorst (n. 212) § 312 d, n. 1; Mankowski (n. 232) 235 ff.; Wiedenmann (n. 9) 238 ff.; cf. also Riesenhuber (n. 9) 326 ff.; Kalss and Lurger, [1998] *Juristische Blätter* 155 f.; Rösler (n. 6) 173 ff.   [413] Mankowski (n. 232) 236 ff.

[414] § 312 d II BGB.   [415] See *Münchener Kommentar*/Wendehorst (n. 212) § 312 d, n. 2.

that the two-week period does not commence before the first instalment of the distance teaching material has been received by the customer.[416]

Every right of revocation has to be based on a convincing policy consideration,[417] otherwise the path will inevitably lead to a generalized right of revocation in consumer/entrepreneur relationships, as it has indeed been proposed.[418] This, in turn, would tend to set consumer law apart from the concerns of general contract law. Recognition of the 'complexity' or 'economic significance' of a transaction as bases for a right of revocation[419] are unfortunate steps in that direction.

c) Unilaterally mandatory rules of law

aa) Specific protective rules

Another hallmark of modern consumer protection legislation is the establishment of mandatory, or rather unilaterally mandatory, rules of law.[420] These are rules which may not be departed from to the detriment of the consumer, though the parties remain free to agree upon a legal regime more favourable to the consumer.[421] This is no longer a merely procedural device but one that substantially impinges upon the freedom of the parties to regulate the content of their contract. At the same time, it is a very familiar device. The BGB in its original form contained a number of mandatory rules that were designed to ensure a minimum level of decency in business life,[422] that were intended to guard against the dangers associated with specific types of transactions,[423] or that were aimed to protect a weaker party from being taken advantage of.[424]

---

[416] Mankowski (n. 232) 238 ff.; but see the criticism advanced by Medicus (n. 390) 523 ff.

[417] The point is emphasized also by Canaris, (2000) 200 *Archiv für die civilistische Praxis* 273, 345 and Remien (n. 9) 341 (who calls on the EC to re-examine the existing rights of revocation and to develop a convincing general scheme).

[418] Hans-W. Micklitz, 'Perspektiven eines Europäischen Privatrechts', (1998) 6 *Zeitschrift für Europäisches Privatrecht* 265.   [419] The same point is made by Kemper (n. 374) 256.

[420] See, most recently, Josef Drexl, 'Zwingendes Recht als Strukturprinzip des Europäischen Verbrauchervertragsrecht?', in *Privatrecht in Europa: Vielfalt, Kollision, Kooperation—Festschrift für Hans Jürgen Sonnenberger* (2004), 771 ff. Generally on the role of mandatory rules of contract law, see Remien (n. 9) 461 ff. and *passim*.

[421] See § 312 f BGB (concerning §§ 312 ff. BGB on doorstep transactions, distance contracts and e-commerce); § 475 BGB (covering consumer sales); § 487 BGB (concerning §§ 481 ff. on timeshare agreements); § 506 BGB (concerning §§ 491 ff. on consumer loans, financing aids, and instalment supply contracts); § 651 m BGB (concerning §§ 651 a ff. on package travel contracts); § 655 e (concerning §§ 655 a ff. on loan brokerage contracts). In other cases the unilaterally mandatory character has to be established by way of interpretation; see *Münchener Kommentar*/Ulmer (n. 226) § 355, n. 4 (concerning §§ 355 ff. on the right of revocation).

[422] See, for example, §§ 138, 276 II, 443, 476, 540, 637 BGB.

[423] See, in particular, the form requirements in §§ 313, 518, 766 BGB (sale of land, donation, suretyship).

[424] See, for example, §§ 247 I, 248 I, 343, 559 3, 617–619, 624 BGB. In earlier nineteenth-century legislation we also find mandatory rules; see Repgen (n. 9) 14, 80 ff.

Even the establishment of legal regimes that were unilaterally mandatory was not unknown: § 225 BGB which used to allow the parties to facilitate prescription, especially by providing for a period that is shorter than the statutory one, while it refused to recognize agreements rendering prescription more difficult, particularly by extending the statutory period, provides an example.[425]

In modern consumer legislation, of course, the protective purpose of mandatory rules of law prevails; this also explains why we are dealing with unilaterally mandatory rules. The rules elevated to this status are, in the first place, the ones already discussed in the preceding sections: those imposing duties of information on the entrepreneur and granting rights of revocation to the consumer. If they are considered necessary in order to ensure that a contract concluded between consumer and entrepreneur can typically be regarded as the proper product of the self-determination of both parties, it appears reasonable to prevent the parties from sidestepping the protection by way of private agreement (though this may be questionable in cases where that agreement itself can be regarded as the proper product of the self-determination not only of the entrepreneur but also of the consumer). Secondly, there are other rules specifically aiming at the protection of the consumer which are of a unilaterally mandatory character: the form requirements concerning timeshare agreements or consumer credit contracts,[426] the provision dealing with the remuneration of the contractor under a loan brokerage contract,[427] etc.

bb) Policing types of contract

But German law, following (or anticipating) the respective European Community Directives, has gone much further: it has converted either the entire regime governing the details of specific types of contract, or large parts of it, to a (unilaterally) mandatory status. In some ways, this comes close to the comprehensive control established for standard terms of business in §§ 307 ff. BGB (and the respective provisions of the Unfair Terms in Consumer Contracts Directive).[428] The BGB contains two types of contract of this kind.

---

[425] A large number of unilaterally mandatory rules can also be found in the Insurance Contract Act of 1908; see Roth (n. 49) 79, 503.   [426] §§ 484, 492 BGB.

[427] § 655 c BGB.

[428] W.-H. Roth, therefore, deals with all three sets of rules under the heading 'control of the contractual content': [2001] *Juristenzeitung* 475, 481; cf. also Drexl (n. 143) 125 ff. On the relationship between the control of unfair standard terms and mandatory law (*ius cogens*), see Remien (n. 9) 469 ff.; cf. also Fastrich (n. 353) 5 ff., who draws a distinction between control of the contractual content in a wide and narrow sense. There is, of course, one crucial difference in that mandatory rules of law cannot even be derogated from by individually negotiated agreements; they thus constitute an even more serious interference with the freedom of the parties, formally conceived, to conclude their own contract than the control of unfair standard terms. German law, therefore, today distinguishes between *ius dispositivum* (which is, of course, still the rule in contract law), rules of law which are

One is the consumer sale, the other the package travel contract.[429] In the one case, large areas of general contract law as well as the specific rules on consumer sales cannot be departed from,[430] in the other case the entire statutory regime governing package travel contracts has become unilaterally mandatory.[431] Again, however, we are dealing here with an issue that cannot be separated from the development of contract law in general. §§ 307 ff. BGB provide the best confirmation for this assertion, for the policing of unfair standard terms of business is not confined to consumer contracts but covers, in principle, all types of transactions.[432] And before the introduction of the Standard Terms of Business Act in 1976, the courts had arrogated to themselves the power to strike down unfair standard terms under the general provision of § 242 BGB.[433] Also, the key decisions subsequently enshrined, in statutory form, in §§ 651 a ff. BGB, were arrived at by the Federal Supreme Court under general contract law.[434] In the meantime, there are other instances where the courts have started to control the content of specific types of transactions: be it on the basis of § 138 I BGB (as in the case of matrimonial property agreements)[435] or even of § 242 BGB (as in the case of contracts concluded on the basis of standard provisions preformulated by a notary).[436] At the same time, incorporation of the provisions on consumer sales and package travel contracts into the BGB serves as a reminder that it always has to be checked very carefully whether, or to what extent, the new rules are justifiable within a general body of law characterized by the notion of freedom of contract.

It has been argued, above, that duties of information and the introduction of rights of revocation can serve as legitimate tools to strengthen the

mandatory vis-à-vis standard terms of business, and rules of law which are mandatory vis-à-vis individually negotiated agreements: Remien (n. 9) 471 ff. and, generally, Dieter Medicus, *Schuldrecht I, Allgemeiner Teil*, 15th edn. (2004), nn. 86 ff.

[429] A third type of contract with regard to which German law has, very largely, established a mandatory regime is the lease of residential accommodation; for the justification of which, see Fastrich (n. 353) 109 ff. The respective body of law which has developed around the cornerstones of notice protection and rent control has been built up, after the Second World War, by way of special legislation, i.e. outside of the BGB. In the summer of 2001 it had largely been incorporated into the BGB (*Mietrechtsreformgesetz, Bundesgesetzblatt* I, 1149; see, today, §§ 549 ff. BGB). Distance teaching contracts and loan transactions are two other areas of the law dominated by mandatory rules; cf. § 9 FernUSG and §§ 491 ff. BGB.   [430] § 475 I BGB

[431] § 651 m BGB.   [432] *Supra* pp. 175 f., 182 f.   [433] *Supra* pp. 174 f.

[434] *Supra* n. 113.

[435] See, for example, Gerd Brudermüller, in *Palandt, Bürgerliches Gesetzbuch*, 63rd edn. (2004), § 1408, nn. 7 ff.; cf. also Ingeborg Schwenzer, 'Vertragsfreiheit im Ehevermögens- und Scheidungsfolgenrecht', (1996) 196 *Archiv für die civilistische Praxis* 111 ff. (arguing for the application of § 242 BGB).

[436] See BGHZ 101, 350, 353 and Günter H. Roth, in *Münchener Kommentar zum Bürgerlichen Gesetzbuch*, 4th edn., vol. IIa (2003), § 242, n. 436. For criticism, see Dieter Medicus, *Zur gerichtlichen Inhaltskontrolle notarieller Verträge* (1989); Fastrich (n. 353) 94 ff. Today § 310 III BGB will largely prevail in these cases; see Heiderhoff (n. 9) 428 ff.

self-determination of both parties and thus effectively to fortify the notion of freedom of contract.[437] The same can be said about the judicial control of unfair contract terms[438] as well as for a variety of mandatory rules of law.[439] Whether the unilaterally mandatory regime for consumer sales and package travel contracts also meets this standard is much more doubtful.[440] So, for example, there does not appear to be any good reason why a consumer should not be able, by way of individually negotiated agreement (!), to buy a second-hand car on the basis of a complete exemption of the entrepreneur/ seller from his liability for latent defects, provided he only has to pay a reduced purchase price.[441] In fact, it has been argued that under the new regime some people may no longer be able to afford the purchase of a car.[442] The imposition of mandatory rules of law can also be prejudicial to private autonomy in view of the schematic approach necessarily adopted by them. It is not easy to see why a pastor or sports club, organizing a day trip, should be subject to the doctrinal corset tailored by §§ 651 a ff. BGB. Again, however, it must be said that many mandatory rules of law not specifically motivated by consumer concerns meet with a similar objection. It hardly appears to be appropriate, for example, for a widow letting a flat within her house to a solicitor to have to draw his attention, in her letter giving notice of termination, to the possibility of filing an objection against such notice, and to the form in which, and period within which, the objection has to be raised.[443] Moreover, it should also be borne in mind that individually negotiated agreements are hardly of great importance with regard to package travel contracts, distance teaching contracts, and probably also consumer sales; and that the necessity of so strictly regulating these types of transactions

---

[437] *Supra* pp. 211 ff.

[438] *Supra* p. 176. For a general theory of the phenomenon of judicial control of individually and non-individually negotiated contract terms, see Fastrich (n. 353) 29 ff., 215 ff.

[439] The point is made by Kötz (n. 349) 1037 ff.; Repgen (n. 9) 9 ff. and *passim*; Drexl (n. 420) 780 ff.

[440] For particularly forceful criticism, concerning consumer sales, see Canaris, (2000) 200 *Archiv für die civilistische Praxis* 273, 362 ff.; cf. also Drexl (n. 420) 786 ff. *Contra*: Repgen (n. 9) 98 ff. Generally, see Fastrich (n. 353) 117 ff.; Riesenhuber (n. 9) 490 ff. The Consumer Sales Directive attempts to justify the far-reaching restriction of private autonomy by pointing out that 'the legal protection afforded to consumers would be thwarted', if they were able to restrict or waive the rights granted to consumers (recital 22). This, however, is no more than a restatement of the assertion for which a good reason would have had to be advanced; see Canaris, (2000) 200 *Archiv für die civilistische Praxis* 273, 362 ff.; Drexl (n. 143) 126. Heiderhoff (n. 9) 326 even quite generally asserts that freedom of contract is neither the basis nor the aim of European community legislation.

[441] Stephan Lorenz, in *Münchener Kommentar zum Bürgerlichen Gesetzbuch*, 4th edn., vol. III (2004), § 475, n. 9; Klaus Adomeit, 'Das Günstigkeitsprinzip—jetzt auch beim Kaufvertrag', [2003] *Juristenzeitung* 1053 ff.; Drexl (n. 420) 778.

[442] Canaris, (2000) 200 *Archiv für die civilistische Praxis* 273, 363.

[443] § 568 II BGB (previously § 564 a II BGB old version). The rule, in spite of its wording, is of a mandatory character: Walter Weidenkaff, in *Palandt, Bürgerliches Gesetzbuch*, 63rd edn. (2004), § 568, n. 3.

can be seriously questioned in view of the control devices contained in the Standard Terms of Business Act.

d) The concept of 'consumer'

Who is to benefit from the various protective devices so liberally spread across the new German law of obligations? Essentially, the legal system has two options. It can either attempt to establish a flexible system which would allow for a supple levelling-out of structural, or situative, imbalances (concerning information, freedom of choice, etc.) between two parties to a contract.[444] While such an approach would have the advantages of being based, directly, on the substantive concern motivating the introduction of rules of law of a protective character, and of targeting only those who actually deserve to be protected, the disadvantage necessarily associated with it is equally obvious: a considerable lack of legal certainty. Both European law and German law have, therefore, understandably pursued the second option: by focusing on the concept of 'consumer' they have endeavoured to tie the application of the relevant body of law to specific criteria which can be easily applied in practice. They have, in other words, adopted a typological approach.[445] At the same time they have had to accept the inevitable drawback of occasionally offering protection to parties who do not deserve to be protected—the professor of law who buys a book, the car mechanic who acquires an exhaust pipe for his private vehicle, the bank director who takes up a loan in order to buy a family home[446]—and of occasionally not offering protection to parties who deserve to be protected.

These examples also demonstrate that German law does not attempt to conceptualize the term consumer as a kind of legal status:[447] a certain range of persons deserves to be protected because specific attributes (or perhaps, rather, lack of specific attributes) can typically be ascribed to them.[448] Such an approach

---

[444] See, along these lines, Bydlinski (n. 143) 766 ff. who wishes to recognize a 'control principle'. Cf. also Medicus (n. 9) 485 ff.; Dreher, [1997] *Juristenzeitung* 170; Helmut Koziol, 'Verbraucherschutz als Selbstzweck oder als Mittel sachgerechter Interessenwahrung?', in *Verbraucherschutz in Europa: Festgabe für Heinrich Mayrhofer* (2002), 201 ff.; idem, 'Bankrecht und Verbraucherschutz', in Wolfgang Wiegand (ed.), *Banken und Bankrecht im Wandel* (2004), 129 ff.

[445] *Supra* p. 161.

[446] See Canaris, (2000) 200 *Archiv für die civilistische Praxis* 273, 348; Mohr, (2004) 204 *Archiv für die civilistische Praxis* 675 ff.

[447] This is a criticism sometimes levelled at modern consumer protection; see, very pointedly, Hans Hattenhauer, *Grundbegriffe des Bürgerlichen Rechts*, 2nd edn. (2000), 23; Horst Ehmann and Ulrich Rust, 'Die Verbrauchsgüterkaufrichtlinie', [1999] *Juristenzeitung* 864 (who refer to 'the danger of a new, deep class division').

[448] For critical discussion, see Bydlinski (n. 143) 718 ff.; *Münchener Kommentar*/Micklitz (n. 149) Vorbem. §§ 13, 14, nn. 62 ff.; *HKK*/Duve (n. 12) §§ 1–14, n. 79. On the distinction between 'role' and '(personal) attribute' as the starting point for legal consequences see, in the present context, Medicus (n. 11) 211 ff.

would have more than a faintly discriminatory flavour in that it appears to insinuate that consumers, unguarded and unguided, lack the ability to engage in legal transactions. It would place consumers in close proximity of infirm persons who are in need of being taken care of.[449] The BGB, in turn, commendably, I think, subscribes to what may be called both a functional and a 'situative' approach to consumer protection.[450] In the first place, it definees as consumer all natural persons effecting a legal act the purpose of which cannot be attributed to their trade or independent professional activity (§ 13 BGB). The infelicities surrounding the definition as it is today enshrined in the BGB have been pointed out above.[451] But, in principle, this approach appears to be both plausible and practicable, for it can realistically be assumed that a person will typically be more alert, more inclined to look at his own advantage, and better informed, in his professional than in his private sphere.[452] Secondly, consumers, so defined, are not protected at random. They are protected only vis-à-vis an entrepreneur, i.e. a (natural or legal) person who in concluding a transaction *does* act in pursuit of his trade or independent professional activity. Hence, the key term for the application of the rules of consumer protection is not so much that of the 'consumer', but of the 'consumer contract', i.e. a contract between a consumer and an entrepreneur.[453] Undoubtedly, the mere fact that one party acts in his professional capacity whereas the other does not, creates an imbalance between them. But it is not, *per se*, an imbalance which the legal system needs to redress. The crucial factor justifying legal interference is the impairment of the consumer's freedom to take a free and rational decision.[454] Such impairment, of course, only exists in specific situations, and not merely because a person acts in the role of consumer. This is why the law attempts to identify the situations (complexity of the transaction, being caught off-guard, etc.) where a consumer faces the real danger of concluding a contract which reflects the interests of the entrepreneur rather than those of both parties. At the same time, this is the touchstone for determining whether the legal system may not occasionally have gone too far in the execution of a policy

[449] §§ 1896 ff. BGB.

[450] See Pfeiffer (n. 9) 27 ff.; *idem* (n. 7) 495 ff.; *Münchener Kommentar*/Micklitz (n. 149) Vorbem. §§ 13, 14, nn. 65 ff.; *HKK*/Duve (n. 12) §§ 1–14, n. 80; Drexl (n. 143) 120 ff., 128 ff.; Riesenhuber (n. 9) 250 ff., 260 ff.; Heiderhoff (n. 9) 261 ff.; Wiedenmann (n. 9) 152 ff.; Rösler (n. 6) 46 ff.

[451] *Supra* pp. 202 f.

[452] Canaris, (2000) 200 *Archiv für die civilistische Praxis* 273, 360; and see Klaus J. Hopt, 'Nichtvertragliche Haftung außerhalb von Schadens- und Bereicherungsausgleich', (1983) 183 *Archiv für die civilistische Praxis* 645 ff.; Riesenhuber (n. 9) 256 ff.; Wiedenmann (n. 9) 115 ff. *Contra*: Remien (n. 9) 259 ff.

[453] See the definition now provided in § 310 III BGB. The point is also emphasized by Pfeiffer (n. 9) 139 ff.; Drexl (n. 143) 113; Michael Becker, 'Verbrauchervertrag und allgemeines Privatrecht', in *Aufbruch nach Europa: 75 Jahre Max-Planck-Institut für Privatrecht* (2001), 85 ff.

[454] *Supra* pp. 206, 210.

which is, in principle, entirely in tune with a market economy based on freedom of contract.

Again, incidentally, there is nothing special in the legal system's endeavour to protect persons who act in a specific role vis-à-vis other persons acting in a different role.[455] German law also protects employees vis-à-vis their employers,[456] tenants of residential space against their lessors,[457] and those who are faced with standard terms of business vis-à-vis those who have introduced these terms into the contract.[458] In all these cases the question may legitimately be asked whether, and to what extent, the protective devices are both necessary and appropriate to remedy a situative, or perhaps even structural, imbalance. That, however, is a general question,[459] since it has to be addressed in terms of every person's right of self-determination which the legal system has to safeguard.[460]

3. Possible objections

This, then, is the most important reason why, of the three imaginable solutions to dealing with the question of consumer contracts—piecemeal legislation, the drafting of a separate code of consumer contract law, or incorporation into the general Civil Code—the third one is to be preferred:[461] both general contract law and consumer contract law are designed to serve the same aim. It would be fatal for the integrity of the legal system if general contract law were seen to be

---

[455] See Dieter Medicus, 'Schutzbedürfnisse (insbesondere der Verbraucherschutz) und das Privatrecht', [1996] *Juristische Schulung* 761 ff.; *idem* (n. 11) 219 ff.

[456] Particularly by granting them protection against termination of the contract; see, for an overview, *Jauernig/*Mansel (n. 308) § 622, nn. 7 ff.

[457] For an overview, see Medicus (n. 255) nn. 237 ff.

[458] §§ 305 ff. BGB; on which see *supra* pp. 175 f., 188.

[459] Consequently, German law has now re-integrated the rules on standard terms of business as well as the 'social lease law' into the framework of the BGB.

[460] See the references to Drexl, *supra* n. 370; cf. also Repgen (n. 9) 70 ff. (with many references); Rösler (n. 6) 71 ff.

[461] This view is shared by Bydlinski (n. 143) 718 ff.; Pfeiffer (n. 7) 494 ff.; W.-H. Roth, [2001] *Juristenzeitung* 475, 484 ff.; Drexl (n. 143) 117 ff.; *HKK/*Duve (n. 12) §§ 1–14, nn. 84 ff.; Rösler (n. 6) 269 ff. *Contra*, most recently, Wiedenmann (n. 9) 267 ff. and *passim* (who argues in favour of a consumer contract code); *HKK/*Schmoeckel (n. 102) vor §§ 312 ff., nn. 55 ff. A consumer code (comprising not only contract law) has existed in France since 1993; it is sharply criticized by Claude Witz and Gerhard Wolter, 'Das neue französische Verbrauchergesetzbuch', (1995) 3 *Zeitschrift für Europäisches Privatrecht* 35 ff.; for a somewhat more positive evaluation, see Dennis Heuer, *Der Code de la consommation: Eine Studie zur Kodifizierung des französischen Verbrauchsrechts* (2002). Austria also has a Consumer Protection Act; it dates from 1979 and is neither comprehensive nor systematic; see Helmut Koziol and Rudolf Welser, *Grundriss des bürgerlichen Rechts*, vol. II, 12th edn. (2001), 372 ff. On the Greek Consumer Act of 1994, see Elisa Alexandridou, 'The Greek Consumer Protection Act of 1994', [1996] *Gewerblicher Rechtschutz und Urheberrecht International* 400 ff. Incorporation into the general Civil Code has been the path pursued in the Netherlands; see Ewoud Hondius,

the domain of a very formal conception of freedom of contract while consumer contract law were to be taken to be informed by loosely defined social concerns. The notion of freedom of contract has to be the lodestar for the entire law of contract; but at the same time, a contract may only be accepted by the legal community if it can typically be regarded as reflecting both parties' right of self-determination. The latter consideration cannot simply be relegated to a separate part of contract law but has to (and in fact does) permeate contract law as a whole. The process of 'materializing' German contract law,[462] over the past hundred years, has gone too far, and has been too pervasive, for what then used to be called the accomplishment of the 'social task of private law'[463] to be left to special legislation. It has become a concern of central significance.

In comparison with this central line of reasoning, most of the arguments advanced in favour of a separate Consumer Contract Code pale into insignificance. Thus, it has been argued that, since German consumer contract law is based on European Community law, the European dimension of this body of law (including, particularly, the need to interpret German law in conformity with the respective Directives) would become more apparent; at the same time, the conceptual devices of European Community law could be transformed into German law in an undistorted form, i.e. without the necessity of an adjustment to the conceptual world of the BGB. Also, the detailed style of legal drafting prevailing in the institutionalized Europe could be preserved without conflicting with the more elegant and economical approach traditionally preferred in German law.[464] But then it has to be taken into consideration that the European Community has also enacted a number of Directives pertaining to contract law, though not specifically to consumer contract law: on combating late payment in commercial transactions, cross-border credit transfers, a Community framework for electronic signatures and, partly at least, electronic commerce. These Directives have been transformed into German law by amending the BGB.[465] The same is true of the Directives on the implementation of the principle of equal treatment for men and women as regards access to

'Niederländisches Verbraucherrecht—vom Sonderrecht zum integrierten Zivilrecht', [1996] *Verbraucher und Recht* 295 ff.; *idem*, 'European Contract Law: The Contribution of the Dutch', in Hans-Leo Weyers (ed.), *Europäisches Vertragsrecht* (1996), 62 ff.; for Italy, integration has recently been advocated by Pietro Sirena, 'L'integrazione del diritto dei consumatori nella disciplina generale del Contratto', (2004) 50 *Rivista di Diritto Civile* 787 ff. For comparative discussion, see Ewoud Hondius, 'Consumer Law and Private Law: Where the Twain Shall Meet', in *Law and Diffuse Interests in the European Legal Order—Festschrift für Norbert Reich* (1997), 311 ff.; Mario Tenreiro, 'Un code de la consommation ou un code autour du consommateur? Quelques reflexions critiques sur la codification et la notion du consommateur', in *Festschrift Reich* (as above) 339 ff.; Rösler (n. 6) 275 ff.; and the contributions to the volume Filali Osman (ed.), *Vers un Code Européen de la Consommation* (1998).

[462] *Supra* pp. 205 ff.   [463] *Supra* n. 20.
[464] See the discussion by W.-H. Roth, [2001] *Juristenzeitung* 475, 485.
[465] *Supra* pp. 183 f., 185 f., 186.

employment, vocational training and promotion, and working conditions,[466] and on the safeguarding of employees' rights in the event of transfers of undertakings, businesses or parts of undertakings and businesses.[467] The BGB, in other words, cannot remain, and has not in fact remained unaffected (or, some would say, untainted), by the development of European Community law, even if consumer contract law is not taken into consideration. Some form of adjustment is inevitable, anyway. And as far as the prolix nature of European Community legislation is concerned, it will sometimes be possible to place a doctrinal anchor within the BGB and to leave the details to subordinate legislation; this has in fact happened with regard to the duties of information imposed on the entrepreneur in a number of contexts.[468] At the same time, it must be said that the BGB has been sullied on many occasions and in many respects by the German legislature even without any prompting from Brussels.[469] The modern German style of legal drafting is no longer what it was one hundred years ago. Also, it should be remembered that a general code of contract law would be a pretty poor thing were it not to cover consumer contracts. It could hardly claim to be comprehensive. Nor could it achieve its task of promoting the internal coherence of the law, of facilitating its comprehensibility, and of providing the intellectual and doctrinal fulcrum for the further development of the law.[470] Such development would very largely occur outside its parameters. A Consumer Contract Code, on the other hand, would provide a mere collection of additional rules which have to be read against the background of the BGB. Then it would increase the complexity of the law and disappoint the expectations not rarely engendered by law reformers that such a code would provide an easily comprehensible statement of a consumer's rights and duties. Or it would aim to be comprehensive, in which case it would have to duplicate many of the provisions contained in the BGB, and that would be equally problematic.[471]

4. Building site or museum?

There is one argument against the incorporation of consumer contract law into the BGB the truth of which can hardly be disputed. Consumer contract law is not yet an area with stable doctrinal structures. It will remain unsettled

---

[466] Council Directive 76/207/EEC of 9 February 1976; easily accessible in Radley-Gardner, Beale, Zimmermann and Schulze (n. 160) 119 ff.

[467] Council Directive 2001/23/EC of 12 March 2001, easily accessible in Radley-Gardner, Beale, Zimmermann and Schulze (n. 160) 127 ff.   [468] *Supra* p. 197; and see Henrich (n. 143) 209.

[469] See the examples discussed by Seiler (n. 317) 105 ff.

[470] For these aims of codification, see the references *supra* n. 298.

[471] W.-H. Roth, [2001] *Juristenzeitung* 475, 485 ff.

and subject to further change and amendment. Recently, the Commission of the European Union has announced its intention to review the existing consumer *acquis* in order to assess whether it achieves 'the key goals . . . to enhance consumer and business confidence in the internal market through a high common level of consumer protection and the elimination of internal market barriers and regulatory simplification'.[472] At the same time, it intends to develop, first, a 'common frame of reference'[473] and, subsequently, possibly also an 'optional instrument' of European contract law.[474] The optional instrument will effectively constitute a model code (at least) of general contract law.[475] But even the common frame of reference will provide common fundamental principles of European contract law, definitions of key concepts, and model rules of contract law; thus, the 'possible structure of the common frame of reference' suggested in Annex I to the communication[476] closely follows that of the Principles of European Contract Law drafted by the Lando Commission.[477] As a result, the focus of European Community consumer contract legislation will have to move away from the establishment and functioning of the internal market. For while it is obvious that this goal has hitherto inspired the relevant Community Directives,[478] consideration of contract law at large is bound to reveal that it cannot sensibly be conceptualized as a mere instrument for the constitution of markets, but that it has to reflect fundamental concerns such as freedom and responsibility, good faith, and the protection of reasonable reliance.[479] In particular, freedom of contract will have to be perceived as a means of self-determination. A number of the regulatory excesses presently disfiguring German contract law[480] are symptomatic of the partial clash of orientation between national German contract law (of which consumer contract law forms only an integral part) and European Community consumer contract law.[481] As things stand, German lawyers may question the wisdom of much that has to be implemented; but they cannot change the necessity of implementing it as well as possible. The impending large-scale revision instigated by the European Commission offers

---

[472] Communication from Commission of the European Communities to the European Parliament and the Council: European Contract Law and the revision of the *acquis*: the way forward of 11 October 2004, COM (2004) 651 final, 3.   [473] Communication (n. 472) 2 ff.

[474] Communication (n. 472) 8 ff.

[475] For details, see Annex II to the Communication (n. 472) 17 ff.

[476] Communication (n. 472) 14 ff.   [477] *Supra* n. 5.

[478] See, most recently, the analysis by Heiderhoff (n. 9) 265 ff., 318 ff. As far as the Community's competence to regulate consumer contract law is concerned, see *supra* pp. 194 f.

[479] That point was made by the editors of *Zeitschrift für Europäisches Privatrecht* as early as 1993, in the founding editorial of that journal.   [480] See, for example, *supra* pp. 221 f.

[481] For a detailed substantiation of this statement, see Heiderhoff (n. 9) 238 ff.; cf. also *eadem*, 'Vertrauen versus Vertragsfreiheit im europäischen Verbrauchervertragsrecht', (2003) 11 *Zeitschrift für Europäisches Privatrecht* 769 ff.

the chance of a re-orientation and of a more coherent contract law[482] not only on the European but also on the national level.

What does this mean, as far as the German Civil Code is concerned? The decision to incorporate consumer contract law has effectively converted the BGB into a permanent building site.[483] But then, perhaps, a modern code of private law should rather resemble a building site, bristling with the cheery voices of craftsmen and artisans, than a museum, in which only the weary murmurs of the occasional tourist group can be heard.

---

[482] See the title of the Action Plan of 2003 (quoted *supra* p. 159) on which the new Communication is based.   [483] W.-H. Roth, [2001] *Juristenzeitung* 475, 488.

Index

This index was compiled by Kim Harris.

Lightning Source UK Ltd.
Milton Keynes UK
UKOW06n1402010817

306459UK00001B/94/P

9 780199 291373